Peter Oliver

The Scripture Lexicon

a dictionary of above four thousand proper names of persons and places,

mentioned in the Bible

Peter Oliver

The Scripture Lexicon
a dictionary of above four thousand proper names of persons and places, mentioned in the Bible

ISBN/EAN: 9783337095857

Printed in Europe, USA, Canada, Australia, Japan

Cover: Foto ©Andreas Hilbeck / pixelio.de

More available books at **www.hansebooks.com**

THE
SCRIPTURE LEXICON;

OR A

DICTIONARY

OF ABOVE

FOUR THOUSAND PROPER NAMES

OF

PERSONS AND PLACES,

MENTIONED IN THE BIBLE:

DIVIDED INTO SYLLABLES WITH THEIR PROPER ACCENTS;

WITH THE DESCRIPTION OF

THE GREATER PART OF THEM.

ALSO

THE EXPLANATION OF MANY

WORDS AND THINGS IN THE BIBLE,

WHICH ARE NOT GENERALLY UNDERSTOOD.

By PETER OLIVER, LL.D.

LATE HIS MAJESTY'S CHIEF JUSTICE OF MASSA-
CHUSETT'S BAY, NEW-ENGLAND.

THE FOURTH EDITION.

LONDON:

PRINTED FOR F. AND C. RIVINGTON,
NO. 62, ST. PAUL'S CHURCH YARD.

1797.

PREFACE.

AN uniformity of accentuation hath been much wished for, as it gives a grace, and attracts the attention of an audience, to a public or to a private speaker—for this purpose the following *Lexicon* was compiled.—It includes, chiefly, the proper names of *perfons*, *places*, and of *several objects* of importance in sacred writ— it was selected from a large work under compilation, on a more extensive scale; and it was judged that it might be of use, not only to young scholars, especially to those who may be designed for the sacred desk, but also to many who are more advanced in life, of all denominations.

The most distinct works on this plan, and which highly merit the applause of the publick, are the *pronouncing Dictionaries* of Mr. J. WALKER, and of Mr. SHERIDAN—had they made their plan more extensive, and included in it the proper names of perfons and places, the great trouble of this compilation had been saved, and the publick had been more benefited.

The *first* design of the compiler, was, to have presented a mere *vocabulary* only; but on a further consideration, it was judged that an explanation of the names would be more satisfactory,

as

as it would more enlarge the mind, and give
fubftance to what, by fome, might be thought to
be fhadow only—and on further thought, it was
determined to give the meaning of the names,
which would, at leaft, give play to curiofity ;
and, poffibly, be of real ufe—for this purpofe,
the meaning of moft of the words is inferted,
according to the *hebrew, chaldee, fyriac, greek,
latin,* and other *antient* languages ; which often
make a difference in the meaning of the fame
word—the names are divided into fyllables and
marked by this ftroke (') for the accent, fo that
they may be eafily read with a proper accentuation.

This *Lexicon*, as it is now offered, criticifm
will either juftify or cenfure ; but as it is offered
with a good intention, the compiler claims the
candour of criticifm. Had any thing of this kind
and on this plan been exhibited, or not have
been wanted, the compiler would have been
gladly excufed from fo laborious a tafk—if the
errors are fuch as may miflead, he will wifh that
he had faved his own time and trouble—but if
it fhall tend to public advantage, he will then
efteem the approbation of the publick an ample
compenfation for the pains he hath taken for its
benefit.

ADVER-

ADVERTISEMENT

FOURTH EDITION.

THE candour of the publick having encou-
raged the fale of a pretty large impreffion
of the SCRIPTURE LEXICON, a fourth edition is
now offered; in which there are many additions
which enlarge the work—the *greek* of moft of the
proper names are affixed to them, by which the
Literati may judge of the propriety or impropri-
ety of the accentuation.

Several alterations are made, in the divifion
of the fyllables of the proper names, and of the
accents alfo, which the compiler, upon the re-
vifal of them, thought proper to alter, and
which he fubmits to the judgment of others;
but he flatters himfelf, that this edition is not
quite fo incomplete as the former—on one account it is lefs fo; as the *Lexicon* and its *Appen-
dix* are now united in one alphabetical feries.

The method taken, in order, more accurately,
to afcertain the accentuation, was this—the compiler adverted to an obfervation of that learned
Hebraiſt as well as *ornament to human nature,*
Dr. LOWTH (the late Bifhop of LONDON) in
the preface to his *Iſaiah,* 2d edition A. D. 1779;

wherein

wherein he faith, " but the true pronunciation
" of Hebrew is loft—the hebrew language, like
" moft of the other oriental languages, expref-
" fing only the confonants, and being deftitute
" of its vowels, has lain now for two thoufand
" years in a manner mute and incapable of ut-
" terance—the number of fyllables is in a great
" many words uncertain, the quantity and ac-
" cent wholly unknown."—The compiler, therefore, chofe for his guides, the *Septuagint* verfion
of the *Old Teftament* and of the *Apocrypha*, and
the verfion of the *New Teftament* by *B. Arius
Montanus*—but as the former fometimes failed
him, he had recourfe to other authorities: but
even, in fome inftances, he was obliged to grope
out his way in the beft manner he could, having no clue at all.

It may be obferved, that over the three vowels
E, O, U; there are frequently, *hyphens*—the
defign of which, is to exprefs the length of the
found of thofe vowels—in fuch cafes they are
to be pronounced.

The Ē as in the word *feen.*
The Ō as in the word *tone.*
The Ū as in the word *tune.*

as alfo where they are accented; when there is
no hyphen over them—otherwife they are to be
pronounced, *generally*,

The E as in the word *men.*
The O as in the word *not.*
The U as in the word *run.*

It may be further obferved, that after feveral
of the greek letters, is added an L. as in the
word

'word *Sab'-a-oth*, L. *Sab'aoth*, which are references to that moft valuable work the *Catholici Indices* of the learned Father *Labbe*, printed in *London*, A. D. 1771: and they are inferted whether they conform or not to the compiler's accentuation.

Some of the proper names which are ufed in common converfation, as they are *accented* in *this Lexicon* may appear aukward in the pronunciation; but had they been ufually pronounced in this manner, they would have been as familiar as the prefent mode of accenting them.—No doubt every fpeaker will adopt that mode of accentuation which may be moft agreeable to him.

The compiler was in fome hopes to have prefented this edition with fewer errors than it is now foiled with: but the *Scripture Lexicon* is of fo complicated a texture, that it was morally impoffible to preferve every thread, either unbroken, or even—fome of the errors are corrected; but he hath not the vanity to think that he hath corrected all of them: an accurate eye will, doubtlefs, perceive more—but he flatters himfelf, that the candour which was exercifed in the reception of the former impreffions will be continued to this—fortunate he would have been, had he ftood in no need of the exercife of any candour; although there is fome degree of fatisfaction, to an author or to a compiler, in being indebted to the publick for the favourable fentiments which it indulges him with.

NOTES

A. D.		Anno Domini, or the year of Christ.
Æt.		In the year of a person's age.
A. M.		Anno Mundi, or the year of the world, or from the creation.
B. C.	stand for	Before the christian æra, which generally begins in the year of the world 4004.
i. e.		That is.

THE
SCRIPTURE
LEXICON.

A *before* A.

A'-A-LAR, ['Ααλάρ.] One who returned from the babyloniſh captivity.

A'-A-RŌN, ['Ααρὼν, i. e. *a teacher; an hill; a mountain; a ſtrong hill.*] It is moſt commonly pronounced *'A-ron*, but ſometimes *A-a'-ron.* The ſon of *Am-ram* and *Jochebed*, the elder brother of *Moſes*, and the brother of *Miriam.* He was the firſt high prieſt of the *Jews;* was three years older than *Moſes;* and was born, 1574 years B. C. and died, Æt. 123.

A *before* B.

AB. The *eleventh* month of the jewiſh *civil* year, and the *fifth* of the *ſacred* year, anſwering to part of our *July* and *Auguſt.*

AB-AD'-DON, ['Αβαδδὼν, i. e. *deſtroying.*] One of the names for the *devil*, in the *hebrew* tongue.

AB-AD-I'-AS, ['Αβαδίας.] One whoſe family returned from the babyloniſh captivity.

B

AB-AG- "

AB-AG'-THA, ['Αβαγαθὰ, i. e. *father of the wine-press.*] One of the seven chamberlains of king *Ahasuerus.*

A'-BAL. A son of *Asher* the patriarch.

AB'-A-NA, ['Αβανά, i. e. *stony; a building; father! I beseech now.*] A river of *Damascus* in *Syria.* Its source supposed to be at the foot of mount *Libanus* towards the east.

AB'-A-RIM, ['Αβαρίμ, i. e. *goings over; conceiving; all kinds of corn.*] Mountains to the east of the river *Jordan,* running into the tribe of *Reuben,* and land of the *Moabites,* on both sides of the river *Arnon;* the mountains *Nebo, Pisgah,* and *Peor* were parts of the *Abarim;* here was the *forty-first* encampment of the Israelites in the wilderness; and here *Moses* died.

AB'-A-RON, ['Αυαρὰν, i. e. *strength.*] The son of *Mattathias,* and grandson of *John,* in the book of the *Maccabees.* He is also called *Eleazar.* See *Avaran.*

A'B-BA, ['Αββᾶ.] It signifies, in the Syriac language, *father.*

AB'-DA, ['Αβδά, i. e. *a servant; this cloud.*] The father of *Adoniram,* who was over king *Solomon's* tribute which he exacted from other nations—also one of the *Levites.*

AB'-DI, ['Αβδὶ, i. e. *my servant.*] The father of *Kish* and the grandfather of king *Saul.*

AB'-DI-AS or OB-'A-DI'-AH, [Ο'βδιὰς, i. e. *servant of the Lord.*] The steward of king *Ahab's* houshold.

AB'-DI-ĒL, ['Αβδιὴλ, i. e. a *servant of God; a cloud of God's store.*] The father of *Ahi,* of the posterity of the patriarch *Gad.*

AB'-DON, ['Αβδὼν, i. e. *a servant; a cloud of justice.*] The fourteenth judge of *Israel,* who died A. M. 2849, after eight years' rule—also a city of *Palestine,* in the tribe of *Asher.*

AB-ED'-NE-GO, ['Αβδεναγώ, i. e. *servant of shining.*] The name given by the king of *Babylon's* officer to *Azariah* the companion of *Daniel:* He was saved from death in the fiery furnace.

A'-BEL,

A'-BEL, ['Αβελ, i. e. *mourning; vanity; vapour.*] The second son of *Adam*, who was slain by his brother *Cain;* supposed to be slain, A. M. 130 —also a city of *Syria*, to the north of *Damascus*, between *Libanus* and *Anti-Libanus*, called also *Abel-Beth-Maacah* and *Abel-Maim*, in the half tribe of *Manasseh*.

A'BEL, (*great stone*) ["Αβελ, i. e. *great mourning.*] A great stone in *Bethshemesh*, whereon the ark of GOD was placed. It is supposed to have been a boundary between the tribe of *Judah* and the *Philistines;* and it was here that there was a great slaughter of the *Bethshemites.*

A'-BEL BETH MA'-AC-AH, ["Αβελ οικη Μααχα, i. e. *mourning in the house of Maacar.*] The same place with *Abel*.

A'-BEL MA'-IM, ['Αβελμαιν, i. e. *mourning of waters.*] The same place as *Abel*.

A'-BEL ME-HO'-LATH or ME-A, ["Αβελμευλα, i. e. *sorrow of weakness.*] The country of the prophet *Elisha*, near to the river *Jordan*, about sixteen miles from *Scythopolis*, in the half tribe of *Manasseh*.

A'-BEL MIS'-RA-IM, [i. e. *the mourning of Egyptians.*] The floor of *Atad*, beyond the river *Jordan*, where *Joseph* buried *Jacob* his father.

A'-BEL SHIT'-TIM, ['Αβελσατιμ, i. e. *sorrow of thorns.*] A city in the plains of *Moab*, beyond the river *Jordan*, opposite *Jericho*.

AB-E'-SAN. See IBSAN. L. *A'besan*.

AB'-EZ, [Ρεβες, i. e. *an egg; dirty; of linnen.*] A city of *Palestine*, in the tribe of *Issachar*.

AB'-I, ['Αβι, i. e. *my father.*] The daughter of *Zechariah*, and mother of *Hezekiah*, king of *Judah*.

AB-I'-A or AB-I'-AH, ['Αβια, i. e. *the will of the Lord.*] The second son of the prophet *Samuel*— also a son of king *Rehoboam*, called also *Abijam*— also the wife of *Hezron*.

AB-I-AL'-BON, ['Αβι 'Αλβων, i. e. *the father of great understanding, or of much building; wrong.*] A native of *Arbath*, and one of king *David's* worthies.

AB-I′-A-SAPH, ['Αϐιασαφ, i. e. *a gathering; con-suming father.*] A fon of *Korah*, and a defcen-dant of the patriarch *Levi*.

AB-I′-A-THAR, ['Αϐιαθαϱ, i. e. *father of the remnant or of contemplation; excellent father.*] The fon of *Abimelech*; and the tenth high prieſt of the Jews in king *David's* reign; but having been an accom-plice in *Abfalom's* treafon, king *Solomon* diveſted him of the prieſthood, and baniſhed him, 1014 years B. C.

A′-BIB, [i. e. *green fruits; ears of corn.*] The name of the firſt Hebrew *facred* month before the de-parture from *Egypt*; afterwards called *Nifan*, an-fwering to part of our *March* and part of *April*.

AB-I′-DAH, ['Αϐειδαι, i. e. *father of knowledge.*] The fon of *Midian*, and grandfon of *Abraham* by *Ke-turah*.

AB′-I-DAN, ['Αϐιδαν, i. e. *father of judgment.*] The fon of *Gideoni* a prince of the tribe of *Benjamin*.

AB′-I-ĒL, ['Αϐιηλ, i. e. *my father is God.*] The grandfather of king *Saul*; he is alfo called *Abi-Albon*.

AB-I-EZ′-ER, ['Αϐιεξεϱ, *the father's help.*] One of king *David's* worthies.

AB-I-EZ′-RITE. *Ophrah* was a city of *Paleſtine* of the *Abiezrites*; probably defcendants from *Abiezer*.

AB-I-GA′-IL, ['Αϐιγαια, Αϐιγαιλ, i. e. *the father's joy.*] The wife of the churliſh *Nabal* of *Carmel*; afterwards married to king *David*, A. M. 2975, about 1060 years B. C.—Alfo the daughter of *Nahaſh* whom *Amafa* deflowered.

AB-I-HA′-IL, [Αϐιχαιλ, i. e. *the father of ſtrength, riches, or forrow.*] The father of *Zariel*, of the houfe of *Merari*—alfo king *Rehoboam's* wife, the grand-daughter of *Jeſſe*—alfo the wife of *Abiſhur*, of the poſterity of the patriarch *Judah*.

AB-I′-HŪ, ['Αϐιꙅ, i. e. *he is father; father himfelf.*] The fon of *Aaron* the high prieſt, by *Eliſheba*; who with his brother *Nadab*, was confumed by fire from Heaven, for offering incenfe with ſtrange fire, inſtead of taking it from the altar

of

of burnt offerings, A. M. 2445, and 1490 years B. C.

AB-I'-HŪD, ['Αϐιὰδ, i. e. *the father of praise*; *con-feſſion.*] The father of *Bela*, and grandſon of the patriarch *Benjamin*.

AB-I'-JAH, ['Αϐιὰ, i. e. *the will of the Lord.*] The wife of *Ahaz*; and the mother of *Hezekiah* king of *Judah*;—alſo the ſon of *Jeroboam*—alſo the ſon of *Rehoboam* king of *Judah*, who ſucceeded his father, and reigned three years.

AB-I'-JAM, ['Αϐιὰ, i. e. *the father of the ſea.*] The ſon of *Rehoboam*, and king of *Judah*, who died about 955 years B. C.

AB-I-LE'-NE, ['Αϐιληνὴ, i. e. *weeping*; *murmuring*; *the ſon of a manſion.*] A province of *Syria*, between *Libanus* and *Anti-Libanus*.

AB-IM'-A-EL, ['Αϐιμαὴλ, i. e. *a father from God*; *of God.*] One of the ſons of *Joktan*.

AB-IM'-EL-ECH, ['Αϐιμελεχ, i. e. *the king's father*; *my father the king*; *father of counſel.*] Two kings of *Gerar*, in *Philiſtia*, ſo named; it was the title of the *Philiſtine* kings, as *Cæſar* was of the Roman emperors, or *Pharaoh* of the Egyptian kings; —alſo the name of the *eighth* judge of Iſrael, and the ſon of *Gideon* the judge, of the tribe of *Manaſſeh*; he ſlew ſeventy of his father's ſons, and was killed by a piece of mill-ſtone let fall upon him by a woman, A. M. 2773, and about 1241 years B. C.

AB-IN'-A-DAB, ['Αμιναδαϐ, i. e. *the father of a vow*; *or of a free mind*; *prince.*] The ſon of *Jeſſe* and brother of king *David*, in whoſe houſe the ark of God was placed, and from thence carried to the houſe of *Obed-Edom*;—alſo a ſon of king *Saul*.

AB-IN'-O-AM, ['Αϐινεὲμ, i. e. *father of beauty*; *gladneſs.*] The father of *Barak*;—alſo one of king *David*'s wives.

AB-I'-RAM, ['Αϐειρων, i. e. *an high father*; *a father of election*; *deceit.*] The eldeſt ſon of *Hiel* the rebuilder of *Jericho*—alſo the ſon of *Eliah*, who

with

with *Corah* and *Dathan* were swallowed by the earth, for usurping the priesthood.

AB-I-SE'-I, [Ἀβισαί.] An ancestor of *Esdras*.

AB'-I-SHAG, [Ἀβισάγ, i. e. *the father's ignorance, or error; the multiplying father.*] A beautiful Shunamite virgin, who was sent to comfort king *David* in his old age.

AB-I-SHA'-I, [Ἀβεσαί, i. e. *the father's reward; the father of a reward.*] The son of *Zeruiah* king *David*'s sister, and one of his generals.

AB-I-SHA'-HAR, [Ἀχισάρ.] A descendant from the patriarch *Benjamin*.

AB-ISH'-A-LŌM, [Ἀβεσσαλώμ, i. e. *father of peace; the father's peace; reward or end.*] The father of *Maachah*, who was the mother of *Abijam* king of *Judah*.

AB-I-SHU'-A, [Ἀβισού, i. e. *the father of salvation.*] The son of *Phinehas*, and fourth high priest of the *Jews*—also a son of *Bela*, and grandson of the patriarch *Benjamin*.

AB'-I-SHŪR, [Ἀβισούρ, i. e. *the father of a song; a wall; of righteousness.*] The son of *Shammai*, of the posterity of *Judah*.

AB'-I-SŪM, [Ἀβισούμ.] An ancestor of *Ezra*.

AB'-I-TAL, [Ἀβιτάλ, i. e. *the father of the dew.*] The fifth wife of king *David*, and mother of *Shephatiah*.

AB'-I-TŪB, [Ἀβιτώβ, i. e. *the father of goodness.*] One of the posterity of the patriarch *Benjamin*.

AB'-I-ŪD, [Ἀβιούδ, i. e. *father of praise; glory of my father.*] The son of *Zerobabel* mentioned in St. *Matthew*'s genealogy.

AB'-NĒR, [Ἀβεννήρ, i. e. *the father's candle.*] The son of *Ner* the uncle of king *Saul*, and general of his armies.

AB'-RAM or AB'-RA-HAM, [Ἀβράμ or Ἀβραάμ, i. e. *an high father; a father of a great multitude.*] The son of *Terah*, born at *Ur* in *Chaldæa*, and father of *Isaac*, and husband to *Sarah*; he died A. M. 2183 and B. C. 1821 years. Æt. 175.

AB'-SA-

AB-SA-LŌM, ['Αβεσσαλώμ, i. e. *a father of peace; the father's peace; reward or end.*] The son of king *David*, by *Maachah:* he rebelled againſt his father, and was ſlain by *Joab* about 1020 years B. C.—alſo a ſon of *Solomon* called *Uriel.*

AB-U'-BUS, ['Αβꝍβꝍ.] An high prieſt; the father-in-law of *Ptolomeus,* who betrayed *Simon Maccabeus.*

A *before* C.

AC'-CAD, ['Αχὰδ, i. e. *a ſpark.*] A city of *Aſia,* built by *Nimrod;* ſince called *Niſibius.*

AC'-A-RŌN, ['Αχχαρὼν.] See EK-RON.

AC'-A-TAN, ['Αχαταν.] One who returned from the babyloniſh captivity.

AC'-CHŌ, ['Αχχὼ, i. e. *thruſt; preſſed together; rubbed.*] A city of *Paleſtine,* in the tribe of *Aſher,* north of *Mount Carmel,* with an harbour towards the ſea; afterwards called *Ptolemais.*

AC'-CŌS, ['Αχκὼς.] The grandfather of *Eupolemus.*

AC'-CŌZ, ['Ακϐὼς.] One whoſe ſons returned from the babyloniſh captivity.

A-CEL'-DA-MA or A-KEL'-DA-MA, ['Ακελδαμὰ, i. e. *the field of blood.*] The field purchaſed with the money that betrayed our *Saviour,* and aſſigned to be a burial place for ſtrangers.

A'CHAB, ['Αχαὰβ.] See AHAB.

A'CHAD, [Αϝχαδ.] See ACCAD.

A-CHA-I'-A, ['Αχαία, i. e. *grief; ſadneſs.*] A province of *Greece, Corinth* being its capital: here St. *Paul* preached, and St. *Andrew* ſuffered martyrdom by crucifixion.

A-CHA-I'-CUS, ['Αχαϊκυς, i. e. *ſorrowing or ſad.*] A diſciple of St. *Paul,* whom he mentions in his firſt epiſtle to the *Corinthians.*

A'CHAN, ['Αχαν, i. e. *troubling; gnaſhing.*] The ſon of *Carmi,* of the tribe of *Judah,* who had taken of the ſpoils of *Jericho* contrary to command, and was ſtoned for the ſame; he is alſo called *Achar:* alſo a ſon of *Ezer* or *Ezar,* a deſcendant of the patriarch *Eſau.*

                    A'-CHAR,

A'-CHAR, [Αχας.] See ACHAN.

A'-CHAZ, [Αχαξ.] See AHAZ.

ACH'-BOR, [Αχοϐωρ, i. e. *a moufe*; *bruifing*; *inclofing a well.*] The father of *Baal-hanan*, king of *Edom* —alfo an officer of king *Jofiah*, the fon of *Micaiah*, who was by him fent to *Huldah* the prophetefs, to inquire about the book of the law which was found by *Hilkiah* the high prieft.

A-CHI-ACH'-A-RUS, ['Αχιαχαρθ.] Cupbearer to *Sarchedonus* king of *Affyria*.

ACH'-IM, ['Αχειμ, i. e. *rifing again*; *confirming*; *revenging*; *their brother.*] A perfon mentioned in St. *Matthew's* genealogical lift.

A-CHIM'-EL-ECH, [Αϐιμελεχ, i. e. *a king's brother*; *of his counfel.*] A prieft of *Nob*, to whom king *David* went, and for which he was put to death by king *Saul:* he is called *Ahiah*. See *Abimelech*.

A'-CHI-OR, ['Αχιωρ, i. e. *the brother's light*; *brother of fire.*] A general of the *Ammonites*, who, at the fiege of *Bethulia*, about 750 years B. C. fpake freely to *Holofernes* the general of *Nebuchadnezzar*, in favour of the *Jews*; for which he was delivered bound to the *Jews*, but they received him kindly, and he became a profelyte to their religion.

ACH-I'-RAM, ['Ιαχιϱαν. 'Αχειραμ, i. e. *a brother of craft*; *protection.*] Called alfo *Ahiram*. He was the fon of the patriarch *Benjamin*.

ACH'-ISH, ['Αγχⲩs, i. e. *it is fo*; *fure it is.*] A king of *Gath* in *Philiftia*, to whom *David* repaired for fhelter; and who gave *Ziklag* to him.

ACH'-I-TOB or A'-HI-TUB, ['Αχιτωβ, i. e. *brother of goodnefs.*] The father of the high prieft *Zadok*.

A-CHIT'-OPH-EL, ['Αχιτοφελ, i. e. *brother of ruin*; *a brother which is forfaken.*] An eminent counfellor in the reign of king *David*; but joining *Abfalom's* party, and giving him advice which was not followed, he hanged himfelf about 1055 years B. C.

ACH'-ME-THA, ['Αμαθα.] See ECBATANA.

A'-CHOR,

A'-CHŌR, ['Αχὼϱ, i. e. *trouble.*] A valley of *Palestine* in the tribe of *Judah*, near to *Gilgal*, and north of *Jericho.*

ACH'-SA, ['Αχσά, i. e. *adorned*; *wantonness*; *dishonesty.*] The daughter of *Caleb*, and the wife of *Othniel.*

ACH'-SHAPH, ['Αζιφ. Κεὰφ, i. e. *a prisoner*; *a sorcerer*; *a witch.*] A city of *Palestine*, in the tribe of *Asher.*

ACH'-ZIB, ['Αχαζì. 'Εχαζοβ, i. e. *a liar.*] A city of *Palestine*, in the tribe of *Judah* in the valley.

AC'-I-PHA, ['Αχιϐà. 'Αχιφà.] One whose sons were servants of the temple.

AC'-I-THŌ, ['Αχιϑà.] An ancestor of *Judith*, in the Apocrypha.

ACTS, [ΠΡΑΞΕΙΣ.] The name of the fifth canonical book of the New Testament: being a relation of the acts of the apostles for about 30 years; supposed to have been written by St. *Luke.*

AC-U'-A, ['Αχὰδ. 'Αχùά.] One who returned from the babylonish captivity, and his sons servants of the temple.

AC'-ŪB, ['Αχùφ.] One who returned from the babylonish captivity.

A before D.

A'-DA, ['Αδà, i. e. *an assembly or congregation.*] The second wife of *Lamech*—also one of *Esau's* wives, called also *Adah.*

A'-DAD, ['Αδάδ.] The chief god of the *Assyrians*—also the fourth king of *Edom.*

A-DA'-DA or A-DA'-DAH, ['Αδαδà, i. e. *the witness of an assembly or congregation.*] A city of *Palestine* in the tribe of *Judah.*

A-DAD-EZ'-ER, ['Αδρααζὰϱ. 'Αδαδέζεϱ.] See HADADEZER.

A'DAD-RIM'-MŌN, ['Αδàδ Γίμμων.] See HADAD RIMMON.

A'-DAH, ['Αδà.] See ADA.

AD-AI'-AH,

AD-AI'-AH, ['Εδεῒα. 'Αδαία, i. e. *the witnefs of the Lord.*] The father of *Jedidah*, the mother of king *Jofiah*.

AD-A-LI'-A, ['Αδαλιά, i. e. *poverty; drawing water; a cloud; death.*] One of the fons of *Haman*, whom the Jews flew.

AD'-AM, ['Αδαμ, i. e. *man; earthy; red; bloody.*] The firft man who was created, who died Æt. 930—alfo a city near to *Zaretan*, not far from the river *Jordan*, in the tribe of *Reuben*.

AD'-A-MA or -MAH, ['Αδαμι, i. e. *earthy; red; bloody.*] It is alfo called AD-MAH. A city of *Pentapolis*, which was deftroyed by fire at the fame time *Sodom* was.

AD'-A-MI, [Αρμαι, i. e. *red; earthy; human.*] A city of *Paleftine*, which was the boundary of the lot of *Napthali*.

AD'-A-MI NEK'-EB, ['Αρμαι Ναχέβ, i. e. *human deception; a cloud of malediction.*] The fame with *ADAMI*.

A'-DAR, ['Αδίε. 'Αδάε, i. e. *power; greatnefs.*] The *twelfth* month of the ecclefiaftical jewifh year, and the *fixth* of their civil, anfwering to part of our *February* and *March*—alfo a city of *Paleftine*, a boundary of the tribe of *Judah*, called *Hazel-Addar.*

AD'-A-SA, ['Αδασα.] A city of *Paleftine*.

AD'-A-THA. A city of *Paleftine* in the tribe of *Judah*. See ADITHAIM.

AD'-BE-EL, [Ναβδεηλ, i. e. *a vapour or cloud of* GOD; *a vexer of* GOD.] One of the fons of *Ifhmael*.

AD'-DAN, ['Ηδαν, i. e. *Lord; foundation, or ground; an ear of the head.*] A city of the babylonifh empire.

AD'-DAR, ['Αδίε.] A fon of *Bela*, a defcendant from the patriarch *Benjamin*.

AD'-DI, ['Αδδι, i. e. *witnefs.*] The father of *Melchi*, in St. *Luke*'s genealogical lift.

AD'-DIN, ['Αδδιν, i. e. *delicious; voluptuous.*] See ADIN.

AD'-DO,

AD'-DO, ['Aδδώ.] A governor of *Syria*, in *Asia*— alfo the name of *Iddo*.

AD'-DŪS, ['Aδδὰς.] One whofe fons returned from the babylonifh captivity—alfo a fervant of *Solomon*.

AD'-ER, ['Eδεϱ.] A place near *Bethlehem* in *Judea*.

AD'-I-DA, ['Aδιδὰ.] A city of *Paleftine* in the tribe of *Judah*.

AD'-I-EL, ['Aδιήλ, i. e. *the witnefs of God*.] One of the pofterity of the patriarch *Simeon*.

AD'-IN, ['Aδδὶν, i. e. *delicious; voluptuous*.] One who returned from the babylonifh captivity.

A-DI'-NA, ['Aδινὰ, i. e. *the fame as* A-DIN.] The fon of *Shiza*, of the tribe of *Reuben*, and one of king *David*'s worthies.

A-DI'-NO, ['Aδινω.] One of king *David*'s worthies, fuppofed to be the fame with *Jafhobeam*.

A-DI'-NUS, ['Iaδινὸς.] A *Levite* who returned from the babylonifh captivity.

AD'-I-THA. See ADATHA.

AD-I-THA'-IM, ['Aδιαγεβθαϊ, i. e. *affembly; congregation; witnefs*.] A boundary city of *Paleftine*, in the tribe of *Judah*, in the valley.

AD'-LA-I, ['Aδλι. Aδλαϊ, i. e. *witnefs to me*.] A principal herdfman of king *David*; the father of *Shaphat*.

AD'-MAH, ['Aδαμὰ.] See ADAMA.

AD'-MA-THA, ['Paμαθὰ, i. e. *a cloud; vapour of death*.] One of the feven counfellors of king *Ahafuerus*, and a prince of *Perfia* and *Media*.

AD'-NA, ['Eδνὰ, i. e. *everlafting reft or pleafure*.] A fon of *Pa-hath-Mo-ab*, who returned from the babylonifh captivity.

AD'-NAH, ['Eδναά, i. e. *the fame as Adna*.] One of the tribe of *Manaffeh* who reforted to king *David* at *Ziklag*.

AD-O'-NI-AS, ['Aδωνία, i. e. *a ruling God; the Lord is the ruler; the foundation of the Lord*.] The fourth fon of king *David*, by *Haggith*; he was flain about 1400 years B. C.

AD-Ō-NI-BEZ'-EK, ['Αδωνιϐεζὲκ, i. e. *the Lord of Bezek, or thunder; the Lord's thunder.*] A king of the city of *Bezek* in *Palestine*, in the tribe of *Judah*, he was very cruel, was taken in battle by the Israelites, and died 1424 years B. C.

AD-Ō-NI'-JAH, ['Αδωνίας, i. e. *the same as Adonias.*] See Adonias.

AD-O'-NI-KAM, ['Αδωνικὰμ, i. e. *the Lord is risen.*] One who returned from the babylonish captivity.

AD-Ō-NI'-RAM, ['Αδωνιρὰμ, i. e. *the high Lord; the Lord of might.*] The receiver of the tributes of king *Solomon.*

A-DO'-NIS, ['Αδωνις.] An assyrian idol; the same as *Thammuz.*

AD-O'-NI-ZED'-EK, ['Αδωνιϐεζὲκ, i. e. *the righteousness of the Lord; the Lord's justice; or the Lord of justice.*] A king of *Salem* or *Jerusalem* before the Israelites conquered *Canaan.*

AD-O'-RA, ['Αδωρα.] A place in the land of *Palestine.*

AD-O'-RA-IM, ['Αδωραὶ. 'Αδυραίμ, i. e. *the strength of the sea.*] A city of *Palestine* in the tribe of *Judah*, built by king *Rehoboam.*

AD-O'-RAM, ['Αδωνιρὰμ, i. e. *their comeliness or praise; an high cry, or confession.*] The receiver of the tributes of king *David*, and king *Rehoboam.*

AD-RAM'-EL-ECH, ['Αδραμέλεχ, i. e. *the king's cloak; the greatness, power, or counsel of the king.*] The son of *Senacherib* king of *Assyria*, who, with his brother *Sharezer*, slew his father while he was worshipping in the temple of his God *Nisroch*— Also an idol of the inhabitants of *Sepharvaim*, a country of *Assyria.*

AD-RA-MYT'-TI-UM, [Αδραμύτιον, *the court or mansion of death; a neat commonalty.*] A city of *Mysia* in lesser *Asia* near to *Mitylene:* now *Endromit.*

A'-DRI-A, ['Αδρία.] A town of *Venice* on the adriatick sea: by St. *Paul's* being in *Adria*, is meant the adriatick sea, now the gulph of *Venice.*

AD'-RI-ĒL, ['Εσδριὰλ, i. e. *the flock of God.*] The
son of *Barzillai*, who married *Merab* the daughter of king *Saul*, who was first promised to
David.

AD-U'-ĒL, [Αδυηλ.] The great grand-father of
Tobit.

AD-UL'-LAM, ['Οδολλὰμ, i. e. *witness; an ornament
to them; a witness or ornament of their misery.*] A
city of *Palestine* in the tribe of *Judah.*

AD-UL'-LAM-ITES, [Οδολλαμίται.] The inhabitants of *Adullam.*

AD-UM'-MIM, ['Αδαμμὶν. 'Αδωμείμ, i. e. *earthy;
red; bloody things.*] A city of *Palestine* in the
tribe of *Benjamin.*

A before Æ and E.

A-E'-DI-AS, ['Αϊδίας.] A porter or guard of the temple who returned from the babylonish captivity.

Æ'-GYPT, ['Αιγυπℱ, i. e. *anguish; tribulation.*] In
hebrew it is *Mizraim:* a large country of *Africa*
to the south west of *Palestine.*

Æ-GYPT'-I-ANS, ['Αιγύπℓοι.] The inhabitants of
Ægypt.

Æ'-NE-AS, ['Αινέας, i. e. *praised.*] A man whom the
apostle *Peter* miraculously healed of the palsy.

Æ'-NŌN, ['Αινὼν, i. e. *a cloud; his well; an eye.*] A
village of *Palestine* by the river *Jordan* where
John baptized.

Æ'-NŌS, ['Ενὼς.] See ENOS.

Æ-THI-OP'-I-A, ['Αιθιοπία, i. e. *burning,* or *black.*]
An extensive country of *Africa*, to the south of
Ægypt; including *Abyssinia, Nubia, &c.*

Æ-THI-OP'-I-ANS, ['Αιθιοπες.] The inhabitants
of *Æthiopia.* Note, They are called *Morians* in
the *Psalms* annexed to the *Common Prayer Book* of
the *Church of England.*

A before F.

AF'-RI-CA, ['Αφρικὴ.] One of the four quarters
of this globe; above 4000 miles in length from
north

north to *south*; and above 4000 miles in breadth, from *east* to *west*: it is a *peninsula*, made by the *isthmus* of *Suez*, running from the *mediterranean sea* to the *red sea*.

A *before* G.

AG'-A-BA, ['Αγαβὰ, i. e. *a grashopper*.] One who returned from the babylonish captivity, and his sons servants of the temple.

AG'-A-BUS, ['Αγαβ☉, i. e. *a locust*; *grashopper*; *lobster*; *the joyfulness of the father*:] A prophet mentioned in the book of *Acts*, about A. C. 44.

A'-GAG, ['Αγὰγ, i. e. *a garret or upper room*.] A king of the *Amalekites* who was hewn in pieces by the order of *Samuel*.

A'-GAG-ITE, [Γωγαῖος.] One of the house of *Agag*.

A'-GAR, ["Αγαξ, i. e. *a stranger*; *chewing the cud*; *fearing*.] Mount *Sinai* is so called.

AG'-ATE, ['Αχάτης.] A precious stone of the lowest class; partly transparent, partly opake, variegated with veins and spots; it was the *second* stone in the *third* row of the high priest's breast plate.

AG'-EE, ['Αγοά, i. e. *valley*; *deepness*.] The father of *Shammah* who was one of king *David*'s warriors.

AG-GE'-US, ['Αγγαῖος.] See HAGGAI.

A-GRIP'-PA, ['Αγρίππ☉, i. e. *sick*; *sorrowful*; *wearied*.] A grand-son of *Herod* the great, sur-named *Herod*; he began to reign in *Judea* about A. C. 37 under *Caligula* the roman emperor, and reigned seven years—also the son of *Agrippa*, before whom and his sister *Bernice* St. Paul preached.

A'-GUR, [i. e. *a stranger*; *gathering*.] One who is mentioned in the book of *Proverbs*, supposed to be an inspired prophet.

A *before* H.

A'-HAB, ['Αχαὰβ, i. e. *the brother's father*.] A king of *Israel*, who reigned twenty two years, and
                                                        died

died 897 years B. C.—alſo one of the falſe prophets who ſeduced the Iſraelites at *Babylon*.

A-HAR'-AH, ['Aαρὰ, i. e. *a ſmelling brother; a ſweet
ſavouring meadow*.] A ſon of the patriarch
Benjamin.

A-HAR'-HAL, ['Pηχάλ, i. e. *another hoſt; the laſt
ſorrow; the ſheep of the brother*.] The ſon of
Harum, of the poſterity of the patriarch *Judah*.

A-HAS-A'-I. One who returned from the babyloniſh captivity.

A-HAS'-BAI, ['Aσ℟ιτας, i. e. *truſting in me; a brother
compoſing; a brother of age*.] The father of *Eliphalet*, who was one of king *David*'s worthies.

A-HAS-U-E'-RUS, ['Aσσυηρℴ, i. e. *a prince or head*.]
A king of *Perſia* who married *Eſther:* called alſo
Artaxerxes; he began to reign about A. M. 3540
or 464 years B. C. and reigned about 40 years,
when he died Æt. 44.

A-HA'-VA, ['Aυὲ, i. e. *an eſſence; being; generation*.]
A town of *Aſſyria* on the banks of the river *Euphrates*; and a river alſo.

A'-HAZ, ['Aχάζ, i. e. *taking; apprehending; poſſeſſing; ſeeing*.] A king of *Judah*, the ſon of *Jotham*; he is called *Eliezer*; he died 726 years B. C.
—alſo the ſon of *Meribbaal* or *Mephiboſheth* the ſon
of *Jonathan*, and great grandſon to king *Saul*.

A-HAZ-A'-I. See AHASAI.

A-HAZ-I'-AH, ['Oχοζιας, i. e. *an apprehenſion, poſſeſſion, or ſight of the Lord*.] A ſon and ſucceſſor
of *Ahab* king of *Iſrael*; he reigned but one year,
and died 894 years B. C.—alſo a king of *Judah*,
ſon and ſucceſſor of *Jehoram*, by *Athaliah*; he
reigned one year, and died A. M. 3120 and 814
years B. C.

AH'-BAN, ['Aℬὰν.] The ſon of *Abiſhur* of the poſterity of *Judah*.

A'-HER, ['Aό℟.] A deſcendant from the patriarch
Benjamin.

A'-HI, ['Aχίℰ. i. e. *my brother, or my brethren*.] The
ſon of *Shamer* of the tribe of *Aſher*—alſo the ſon
Abdiel, of the tribe of *Gad*.

A'-HI-

A'-HI-AH, ['Αχιὰ, i. e. *the brother of the Lord.*] A son of *Shisha*, and one of king *Solomon's* secretaries—also a priest in king *Saul's* reign, the son of *Ahitub.*

A'-HI-AM or -HAN, ['Αχιὰμ, i. e. *brother of the mother; brother of a nation.*] One of king *David's* worthies.

A-HI'-AN, ['Αϊμ. 'Αεὶν, i. e. *a brother of wine.*] The son of *Shemida*, of the tribe of *Manasseh.*

A-HI-EZ'-ER, ['Αχιέζερ, i. e. *brother of help; the brother's help.*] A prince of the tribe of *Dan*, the son of *Ammishaddai.*

A'-HI-HUD, ['Ιαχαχὸδ. 'Αχιὼβ, i. e. *brother of vanity; brother of darkness or joy.*] A descendant from the patriarch *Benjamin.*

A-HI'-JAH, ['Αχὶα, i. e. *the same as Ahiah.*] A prophet in the reign of *Jeroboam* king of *Israel*; he dwelt at *Shiloh*—also the son of *Baasha* king of *Israel*—also a *Pelonite* one of king *David's* worthies.

A'-HI-KAM, ['Αχικὰμ, i. e. *a brother arising or revenging.*] The son of *Shaphan* and father of *Gedaliah*; the protector of the prophet *Jeremiah.*

A'-HI-LUD, ['Αχιλὺδ, i. e. *a brother born or begotten.*] The father of *Jehosaphat* king *David's* recorder.

A-HI-MA'-AZ, ['Αχιμὰας, i. e. *brother of counsel.*] Father to *Abinoam* the wife of king *Saul*—also the son of *Zadok* the high priest.

A'-HI-MAN, ['Αχιμὰν, i. e. *a brother prepared; a brother of the right hand.*] One of the sons of *Anak* —also one of the porters or guards of the temple at *Jerusalem.*

A-HIM'-EL-ECH, ['Αβιμελέχ, i. e. *the king's brother, or of his counsel.*] A priest of *Nob*, to whom *David* went, and whom king *Saul* put to death, with other priests, for assisting *David*—also a priest in king *David's* reign, the son of *Abiathar*; he is also called *Abimelech.*

A'-HI-MOTH, ['Αχιμὼθ, i. e. *a brother of death or of days; a dead brother.*] A son of *Elkanah*, a descendant from *Levi.*

A-HIN-

A-HIN'-A-DAB, ['Αχιναδὰβ, i. e. *a willing brother; a brother of a vow.*] The fon of *Iddo*, a governor of the canton of *Mahanaim* beyond *Jordan*, in the reign of king *Solomon.*

A-HIN'-O-AM, ['Αχινοὸμ, i. e. *the brother's beauty.*] The daughter of *Ahimaaz*, and wife of king *Saul* —alfo a wife of king *David*, a native of *Jezreel* and mother of *Ammon.*

A-HI'-O, ['Αἰὸ, i. e. *his brother; his brethren.*] A fon of *Abinadab*, and mother of *Uzza*; who with *Uzza* drove off the cart which carried the ark of the covenant—alfo two of that name who were of the tribe of *Benjamin.*

A'-HI-RA, ['Αχιρὲ, i. e. *brother of iniquity; a fhepherd; a rough brother.*] The fon of *Enan*, a prince of the tribe of *Naphtali.*

A-HI'-RAM, ['Αχειράμ, i. e. *a brother of craft; protection.*] A fon of the patriarch *Benjamin*, father of the *Ahiramites.*

A-HI'-RAM-ITES. The defcendants from *Ahiram.*

A-HI'-SA-MACH, ['Αχισαμὰχ, i. e. *brother of fuftentation.*] The father of *Aholiab*, who was employed by *Mofes* in building the tabernacle in the wildernefs.

A-HI-SHA'-HUR, ['Αχισαὰρ, i. e. *the brother of the morning or dew; brother of blacknefs.*] A fon of *Bilhan*, a defcendant of the patriarch *Benjamin.*

A'-HI-SHAM, ['Αχισαὰρ, i. e. *brother of the prince; brother of direction of a fong; a fpying or waiting brother.*] The high fteward of king *Solomon's* houfhold.

A'-HI-SHAR. See AHISHAM.

A-HIT'-OPH-EL, ['Αχιτόφελ.] See ACHITO-PHEL.

A'-HI-TUB, ['Αχιτὼβ, i. e. *brother of goodnefs.*] The fon of *Phineas* and grandfon to *Eli*, and an high prieft—alfo the fon of *Amariah*, and father of the high prieft *Zadok.*

A'-HI-UD, ['Αχιὼρ, i. e. *brother of praife.*] A prince of the tribe of *Afhur*, the fon of *Shelomi.*

AH'-LAB, [Δαλὰφ, i. e. *which is of milk; which is fat; forrowing; brother of the heart.*] A city of *Paleftine* in the tribe of *Afher.*

C

AH'-LAI,

AH'-LAI, ['Λαδαὶ, i. e. *befeeching; expecting; beginning; forrowing.*] The daughter of *Shefhan,* of the tribe of *Judah.*

A-HO'-E or A-HO'-AH, ['Αὼδ, i. e. *a quick or living brother; a thiftle.*] The father of *Dodo,* from whom came the *Ahohites;* a defcendant from the patriarch *Benjamin.*

A-HO'-HITE, ['Αωίτη.] The defcendants from *Ahoe* or *Ahoah.*

A-HOL'-AH, ['Οολὰ, i. e. *a manfion; dwelling in herfelf.*] *Samaria* figuratively fo called.

A-HOL'-BA or A-HOL'-BAH, [Οολιϐα, i. e. *my manfion in her.*] *Jerufalem* is fo called in a figurative fenfe, by the prophet *Ezekiel.*

A-HOL'-I-AB, ['Ελιὰβ, i. e. *the tabernacle or tent of the father; the brightnefs of the father.*] A fon of *Ahifamach* of the tribe of *Dan,* who, with *Bezaleel,* undertook the building of the tabernacle.

A-HOL'-I-BAH. The fame with *Aholba.*

A-HOL-I-BA'M-AH, ['Ολιϐεμὰ, i. e. *my tent or famous manfion.*] One of the wives of the patriarch *Efau*—alfo a duke of *Edom.*

A-HU-MA'-I, ['Αχιμαὶ, i. e. *a meadow of waters; a brother of waters.*] A *Zorathite,* or inhabitant of *Zora* in *Paleftine,* a defcendant from the patriarch *Judah.*

A-HU'-ZAM, ['Ωχαία. 'Ωχαζάμ, i. e. *their taking, or poffeffion, or vifion.*] One of the defcendants from the patriarch *Judah.*

A-HUZ'-ZAH, ['Οχοζὰθ, i. e. *poffeffion; apprehenfion; collection; vifion.*] A friend of *Abimelech* king of *Gerar.*

A *before* I.

A'-I or AI, ['Αιὰ. 'Αι. Γαι. Γαι, i. e. *an heap; or laying on heaps.*] A city of ancient *Canaan* near to *Bethel.*

A-I'-AH, ['Αιὰ. Αιθ, i. e. *a vulture; raven; alas; where is it; an ifle.*] The father of *Rizpah,* one of king *Saul's* concubines.

A'-I-AIH,

A-I'-ATH, ['Aἰν. 'Aγ̌αὶ, i. e. *an hour; an eye; a fountain.*] A city of *Palestine* in the tribe of *Simeon.*

AI'-JA, [Γαϐαὰ, i. e. *the same as Ajalon.*] A city of *Palestine* in the tribe of *Judah.*

A-I'-JAH, ['Aἲἐ.] The son of *Zibeon,* a descendant from the patriarch *Esau.*

AI'-JA-LŌN, ['Aɩλὼν, i. e. *an oak; strength.*] Two cities of *Palestine,* one in the tribe of *Dan* where *Joshua* caused the moon to stand still: another in the tribe of *Judah.*

AI'-JE-LĒTH SHA'-HAR, [i. e. *the hind of the morning.*] A note of musick, but uncertain what.

A'-IN, ['Aἰν.] The same with *Aiath.*

A-I'-RUS, ["Γαἲρ☉.] One who returned from the babylonish captivity.

A before K.

AK'-KŪB, ['Aκὺβ, i. e. *the print of a foot; supplantation; lewdness; crookedness; reward.*] One whose sons were porters or guards of the temple of *Solomon.*

AK-RAB'-BIM, ['Aκραϐὶν, i. c. *Scorpions.*] A city of the *Amorites.*

A before L.

AL-AM'-EL-ECH, ['Eλιμελέχ, i. e. *the kingdom of God; the counsel of God.*] A city of *Palestine* in the tribe of *Asher.*

AL'-AM-ETH, ['Eλνεμέϑ.] The son of *Becher,* a descendant from the patriarch *Benjamin.*

A-LA'-MŌTH, ['Aλαιμώϑ. 'Aλνμώϑ.] A word in the title of some of the *Psalms;* but is uncertain whether it means an instrument of musick, or a tune; some think it a psaltery.

AL'-CI-MUS, ["Aλκιμ☉, i. e. *strong; of strength.*] An high priest of the *Jews,* about 1162 years B. C.

AL'-EM-A, ['Aλέμ☉, i. e. *strength.*] A city to the east of the river *Jordan* in the country of *Gilead.*

C 2

A-LE'-METH, ['Σαλαιμὰϑ, i. e. *an hiding; youth; worlds; upon the dead.*] The fon of *Jehohadah,* of the tribe of *Benjamin*—alfo a city of refuge in *Paleftine,* in the tribe of *Benjamin.*

AL-EX-AN'-DER, ['Αλεζανδρ⊙, i. e. *an helper of men; moft ftrong; virtuous.*] A king of *Macedonia,* called the great, was born November 14, 355 years B. C. and died May 22, 323 years B. C. Æt. 33—alfo *Alexander Balus,* fo called from *Balus* his mother; he was natural fon of *Antiochus Epiphanes,* who was flain by *Zabdiel* king of *Arabia,* about 151 years B. C.—alfo the fon of *Simon* the *Cyrenian* who bore our *Saviour's* crofs—alfo a kinfman of *Caiaphas* the high prieft—alfo a Jew who was in the tumult at *Ephefus* when St. *Paul* preached there—alfo a copperfmith, whom St. *Paul* complains of as inimical to him.

AL-EX-AN'-DRA. A queen of the Jews A. C. 78 —widow of Alexander a king of the Jews.

AL-EX-AN-DRI'-A, ['Αλεξάνδρεῖα, i. e. *raw; irritation; prohibition.*] Once a celebrated feaport city of *Egypt* in *Africa,* built by *Alexander* the great—alfo many other cities, built by him, of that name.

AL-EX-AN'-DRI-ON. The name of a fortrefs in the land of *Judea* or *Paleftine.*

AL-LE-LU'-JAH, ['Αλληλϐῖα.] See HALLELU-JAH.

AL-I'-AH, ['Αλϫα. Γωλά.] A duke of *Edom.*

AL-I'-AN, ['Αλὼν.] A fon of *Shobal,* a defcendant from the patriarch *Efau*—called alfo *Alvan.*

AL'-LOM, ['Αλλὼμ.] One who returned from the babylonifh captivity.

AL'-LON, ['Αλὼν, i. e. *oak; ftrong.*] A defcendant from the patriarch *Simeon*—alfo a city of *Paleftine,* in the tribe of *Naphtali.*

AL'-LON BAC'-HUTH, [i. e. *the oak of mourning.*] An oak near to *Bethel,* where *Deborah* the nurfe of *Rebekah* was buried.

AL-MO'-DAD, ['Ελμωδαδ, i. e. *the meafure of God; the entry or court of the beloved.*] The fon of *Joktan,* a defcendant from the patriarch *Shem.*

AL'-MON,

AL'-MŌN, [Γάμαλα, i. e. *hidden*.] A city of *Paleſtine*, in the tribe of *Benjamin*.

AL'-MŌN DIB-LA-THA'-IM,[Γελμὼν᾽Δεϐλαθαΐμ,
i. e. *hiding, or hidden in a heap of fig-trees*.] The
40th encampment of the Iſraelites, in the wilderneſs.

AL'-MUG TREE, [Σφόδρα.] Some ſuppoſe to be
the ſame with *Shittim wood*.

AL'-NA-THAN, ['Αλιαθάν.] A principal man a-
mong the Jews after the babyloniſh captivity.

AL'-ŌTH, [Βααλὼϑ.] A place in the land of *Paleſtine*.

AL'-PHA, [A.] The firſt letter of the *greek* alphabet; *Omega* is the laſt letter: *Alpha* and *Omega*
is an appellation which *Chriſt* appropriates to himſelf in the *Revelation* of *St. John*, as the beginning
and end of all things.

AL-PHE'-US, ['Αλφαῖος, i. e. *the thouſand; learned*.]
The father of St. *Matthew*—alſo the father of
James the leſs, whom ſome ſuppoſe to be the
Cleophas of *St. Luke*; *Alpheus* being his Greek
name, and *Cleophas* his Hebrew or Syriac name.

AL-TA-NE'-US, ['Αλϊαναῖος.] One who returned
from the babyloniſh captivity.

AL-TAS'-CHITH. A word in the title of ſeveral
of the *Pſalms*, but the meaning uncertain.

AL-TEK'-ŌN, [Θεκὖμ, i. e. *God's correction*.] A city
of *Paleſtine*, in the tribe of *Judah*, in the mountains.

AL'-VAH or AL'-VAN, ['Αλὼν. Γωλὰ, i. e. *his riſing
up-higher*.] A duke of *Edom*, the eldeſt ſon of
Shobal, a deſcendant from the patriarch *Eſau*.

A'-LŪSH, ['Αιλὰς, i. e. *a mingling together*.] The
place of the 10th encampment of the Iſraelites.

A *before* M.

AM'-AD, ['Αμὶηλ, i. e. *people of witneſs; a people
everlaſting; a prey*.] A city of *Paleſtine* in the
tribe of *Aſher*.

AM-AD'-A-THUS, ['Αμαδαϑός.] See HAMME-
DATHA.

A'-MAL,

A'-MAL, ['Αμὰλ, i. e. *labour; iniquity.*] A fon of *Helem*, a defcendant from the patriarch *Afher*.

A-MAL'-DA. The fame as AMAL.

AM'-A-LĒK, ['Αμαλὴκ, i. e. *a fmiting or ftriking people.*] The fon of *Eliphaz*, and grandfon of the patriarch *Efau*; the father of the Amalekites.

AM'-A-LĒK-ĪTES. The defcendants from *Amalek*; they dwelt in *Arabia Petreea*, and were avowed enemies to the *Hebrews*.

A'-MAN, ['Αμὰν, i. e. *mother; fear of them.*] A city of *Palefline*, in the tribe of *Judah*, towards *Edom* fouthward.

AM'-A-NA, ['Αμανά, i. e. *faith; truth; a nurfe.*] Suppofed to be a mountain in *Cilicia*; or one beyond *Jordan*, in the tribe of *Manaffeh*.

AM-A-RI'-AH, ['Αμαρία, i. e. *the Lord faid; the excellency of the Lord; the Lamb of the Lord.*] Great grandfather to *Zephaniah* the prophet, a defcendant from *Aaron*, and high prieft in the time of the Judges, the oldeft fon of *Meraioth*.

'AM'-A-SA, ['Αμεσσαῖ. 'Αμασία, i. e. *fparing the people.*] The fon of *Ithra* and *Abigail* the fifter of king *David*, and general of the army of *Abfalom*; he was treacheroufly murdered by *Joab*.

AM-A-SA'-I, ['Αμεσσὶ. Αμασαῖ, i. e. *ftrong.*] The fon of *Elkanah*, fuppofed to be the fame who went to *David* in the wildernefs, whither he was purfued by king *Saul*—alfo a Levite, the father of *Mahath*.

AM-A-SHA'-I, ['Αμασαῖ. 'Αμασία, i. e. *the gift or prefent of the people.*] One who returned from the babylonifh captivity.

AM-A-SHI'-AH, ['Αμασία, i. e. *the ftrength of the Lord.*] The father of *Jofhah*—alfo the fon of *Hilkiah*—alfo a prieft of *Bethel*.

AM-A-THE'-IS, ['Αμαθίας.] One who returned from the babylonifh captivity.

AM'-A-THIS, ['Αμαθῖτις.] A city of *Palefline*.

AM-A-ZI'-AH, ['Αμασία, i. e. *the ftrength of the Lord; the burden of the Lord.*] The tenth king of *Judah*, the fon of *Joafh*; he reigned 29 years, and was flain

flain 810 years B. C.—alfo the fon of *Joſbah* of the tribe of *Simeon*—alfo the fon of *Hilkiah* of the tribe of *Levi*—alfo a wicked prieſt of *Bethel*.

A-MĒN', ['Αμήν, i. e. *true*; *faithful*; *certain*.] It is a word of affirmation, as *amen, amen, verily I ſay unto you*; or it is a wiſh, as *amen, ſo be it*.

AM'-ETH-YST, ['Αμέθυςℙ.] A precious ſtone of a purple colour, the *ninth* in order, or the *third* ſtone in the *third* row upon the Jewiſh high prieſt's breaſt plate; it reprefented the tribe of *Iſſachar*.

A'-MI, ['Ημεί, i. e. *mother*; *fear*; *people*.] One whoſe children were king *Solomon*'s ſervants.

A-MIN'-A-DAB, ['Αμιναδαβ, i. e. *a free people*; *a vowing people*; *prince of people*.] See ABINADAB.

A-MIT'-TAI, ['Αμαθì, i. e. *true, fearing*.] The father of the prophet *Jonah*.

AM-I'-ZA-BAD, [Ζαβαδ. 'Αμειζαβαλ. i. e. *the dowry of the people*.] The fon of *Benaiah* one of king *David*'s generals, and an officer himſelf.

AM'-MAH, ['Αμμὰν, i. e. *his people*.] An hill where *Aſahel*, the brother of *Joab*, was ſlain by *Abner*.

AM-MAD'-A-THA, ['Αμαδαθℙ, i. e. *troubling the law*.] The father of *Haman*.

AM'-MI, [i. e. *my people*.] A word mentioned by *Hoſea*, in alluſion to the tribes of *Judah* and *Benjamin*, whom he ſpeaks of by the names of *Ammi* and *Ruhamah*.

AM-MI'-DI-OI, ['Αμμιδιοι.] A place mentioned in the *1ſt book of Eſdras*, ch. 5. ver. 20.

AM'-MI-ĒL, ['Αμιηλ, i. e. *the people of God*; *God with me*.] The fon of *Gemalli* of the tribe of *Dan*, who was deputed to view the land of *Canaan* —alfo the fixth fon of *Obed-Edom*—alfo the father of *Bathſheba* the mother of *Solomon*—alfo the father of *Machir* of *Lo-Debar*.

AM'-MI-HŪD, ['Σαμιηδ, i. e. *people of praiſe or confeſſion*; *praiſe or confeſſion*.] Father of *Eliſhama* a prince of the tribe of *Ephraim*—alfo the father of *Shemuel*—alfo the fon of *Omri*—alfo a king of *Geſhur*, the father of *Talmai*.

AM-I-SHAD'-DA-I, ['Αμισαδαι, i. e. *the people of the Almighty.*] The father of *Abiezer*, a prince of the tribe of *Dan*.

AM'-MŌN, ['Αμμων, i. e. *a people*; *the son of my people.*] A people, who defcended from *Ben-ammi* the fon of *Lot*, by his youngeft daughter; the father of the *Ammonites*—alfo the city *No*, called *No-Ammon*. See NO.

AM-MŌN'-AI, ['Αμμωνὰ, i. e. *our people.*] A city of *Palefine* in the tribe of *Benjamin* called *Chephar-ha-ammonai*.

AM-MŌN'-ITES, ['Αμμωνιτοι.] The defcendants from *Ammon*.

AM'-NŌN, ['Αμνων, i. e. *faithful*; *true*; *an artificer*; *a nourifher.*] The firft born fon of king *David* by *Ahinoam*; he ravifhed his fifter *Tamar*; for which, *Abfalom*, two years after, murdered him when difguifed with liquor.

A'-MOK, ['Αμὲκ, i. e. *a valley*; *a depth.*] The name of two priefts or levites who went up with *Zerubbabel* at the dedication of the new temple 'at *Jerufalem*.

A'-MŌN, ['Αμων, i. e. *faithful*; *true.*] The fixteenth king of *Judah*, the fon of *Manaffeh*, and father of king *Jofiah*; he was flain by his fervants after a reign of two years, 642 years B. C.

AM'-OR-ITES, ['Αμοββι. 'Αμοββαιοι, i. e. *bitter people*; *cruel rebels*; *talkative.*] A people defcended from *Emori* the fourth fon of *Canaan*; they inhabited the mountains to the weft of the *Dead-fea*, or lake of *Sodom*; as alfo on the eaft fide of it.

A'-MŌS or A'-MŌZ, ['Αμως, i. e. *a burden*; *burdened*; *burdening*; *ftrong*; *mighty.*] *Amoz* was the father of the prophet *Ifaiah*, and fuppofed to be the fon of king *Joafh*—alfo the third minor prophet after whom is named the canonical book of the Old Teftament *Amos*: he was an herdfman of *Tekoa*, a fmall town about four leagues from *Jerufalem*: he prophefied in the reign of *Uzziah* king of *Judah*, and *Jeroboam* king of *Ifrael*.

AM-PHIP'-

AM-PHIP'-OL-IS, ['Αμφίπολις, i. e. *a city compassed or walled.*] A city of *Macedonia* in *Asia.*

AM'-PLI-AS, ['Αμπλίας, i. e. *make more.*] One whom St. *Paul* mentions in his epistle to the *Romans,* and who, the Greeks say, was bishop of *Odyssopolis* in *Mæsia* in *Asia*; and that he was one of the seventy-two disciples, and suffered martyrdom.

AM'-RAM, ['Αμράμ, i. e. *an high people.*] Of the tribe of *Levi*; the father of *Miriam, Aaron* and *Moses*; he died 1504 years B. C. Æt. 137.

AM'-RAM-ITES. The family of *Kohath,* descendants from *Amram.*

AM'-RAN, ['Εμερών, i. e. *an ass; clay; wine.*] The son of *Dishon,* a descendant from *Esau* the patriarch.

AM-RA'-PHEL, ['Αμαρφάλ, i. e. *speaking, destruction or ruin, or a secret or judgment.*] A king of *Shinar,* who plundered *Pentapolis* and took *Lot* prisoner; *Abraham* pursued him and retook *Lot* and the spoil.

AM'-ZI, ['Αμασὶ, i. e. *strong; mighty.*] A *Levite,* the son of *Bani.*

A *before* N.

A'-NAB, ['Ανὼν. 'Ανὰβ, i. e. *a grape; a knot.*] A city of *Palestine* in the tribe of *Judah,* in the mountains.

AN'-A-ĒL, ['Αναὴλ.] Brother to *Tobit* in the *Apocrypha.*

A'-NAH, ['Ανὰ, i. e. *answering; singing; afflicting; poor.*] The mother of *Aholibamah* one of *Esau's* wives—also the son of *Seir* the *Horite*—also the son of *Zibeon.*

AN-A-HA'-RATH, ['Ρευρὼθ, i. e. *dryness; burning; wrath; neighing; suffocation; hoarseness.*] A city of *Palestine* in the tribe of *Issachar.*

AN-A-I'-AH, ['Αναία.] One of the assistants of *Ezra* in reading the law.

AN'-AK,

'AN'-AK, [Εναχ, i. e. *a giant.*] From whom the *Anakims* defcended, who were of gigantic race and very fierce.

AN'-AK-IMS, ['Εναχίμ.] A pepple defcended from *Anak*, a people of ancient *Canaan*.

AN'-A-MIM, ['Αινομιείμ, i. e. *a fountain; an anfwer; affliction; a found of waters.*] The fon of *Mizraim*, and grandfon of the patriarch *Ham*.

AN-AM'-EL-ECH, ['Ανημελὲχ, i. e. *an anfwer; the king's fon; the affliction or poverty of the king; of his counfellor.*] The deity of *Sepharvaim* in *Affyria*.

A'-NAN, ['Αινὰν. 'Ηνὰμ, i. e. *a cloud; a prophecy; a divination.*] One of thofe who fealed the covenant with *Nehemiah* the governor.

A-NA'-NI, ['Ανὰν, 'Αναγὶ, i. e. *a cloud; a prophecy; a divination.*] The fon of *Eliænai*, of the royal race of *David*.

AN-A-NI'-AH, ['Αναγία. 'Αγία, i. e. *the cloud or deliverance of the Lord.*] A city of *Palefline*, where the *Benjamites* dwelt after the babylonifh captivity.

AN-A-NI'-AS, ['Αναγίας. L. *Ananias.* i. e. *the fame as Ananiah.*] The fon of *Nebedecus*, the high prieft of the *Jews*, whom St. *Paul* treated very unguardedly, A. D. 47.: he was afterwards murdered by a band of mutineers, his fon being at their head—alfo one who baptized St. *Paul* at *Damafcus*—alfo one, who, with his wife *Sapphira*, was ftruck with fudden death for lying to the *Holy Ghoft*—alfo the name of the father of *Elcia* in the *Apocrypha*.

AN-A-NI'-EL, ['Αναγιὴλ, i. e. *grace from God; grace of God.*] The grandfather of *Tobit* in the *Apocrypha*.

A'-NATH, ['Αινὰχ. Αναϑ, i. e. *an anfwer; a fong; affliction; poverty.*] The father of *Shamgar* the fourth judge of *Ifrael*.

AN-ATH'-EM-A, ['Ανάθεμα.] A curfe denoting the cutting off one from the communion of the faith, from the living, or from the privileges
of

of society; or devoting a city, an animal or other thing to destruction †.

AN-ATH'-EM-A MAR-AN-A'-THA, ['Ανάθεμα Μαράναθά.] A form of cursing among the *Jews*; the word *Maran-atha* being *Syriack* for, *the Lord comes, or is come.*

A-NATH'-ŌTH, ['Αναθώθ, i. e. *answers*; *songs.*] A city of *Palestine* in the tribe of *Benjamin*, where the prophet *Jeremiah* was born—also the son of *Becher*, a descendant from the patriarch *Ephraim.*

AN'-DREW, ['Ανδρέας, i. e. *very strong*; *manly.*] One of the twelve apostles of *our Saviour*; a native of *Bethsaida*, a fisher-man, and the brother of *Simon Peter*: he was crucified at *Patræ* in *Achaia.*

AN-DRON-I'-CUS, [Ανδρονικ©, i. e. *a victorious man.*] A worthy man whom St. *Paul* salutes in his epistle to the *Romans*; he was the apostle's fellow prisoner—also one who slew *Onias* the high-priest; in the second book of the *Maccabees.*

A'-NEM or A'-NEN, ['Αινάν, i. e. *an answer*; *song of them*; *their affliction or poverty.*] A city of *Palestine*, in the tribe of *Issachar*, given to the sons of *Gershom* as *Levites.*

A'-NER, ['Αυνάν. 'Αυνὲρ, i. e. *an answer; song of the light*; *afflicting the light.*] The brother of *Mamre*, a confederate with the patriarch *Abraham*—also a city of *Palestine* in the half tribe of *Manasseh.*

A'-NES, [Τάυης.] See *Hanes.*

A'-NETH. A city of *Idumea* or *Edom* in *Asia.*

A-NATH'-ŌTH-ITE. An inhabitant of *Anathoth.*

AN'-GEL, ['Αγγελ©.] The word angel signifies a messenger, or a spy: the men of God, and prophets are called angels in scripture: and by attending to the different meanings of the word *angel*, several texts may be elucidated: the spies sent out by *Joshua*, are called *angeloi*, (ἀγγέλοι) i. e. angels or spies.

---

† AN-A-THE'-MA, ['Αναθήμα.] Is an offering or present to some deity.

AN'-I-AM, ['Aνιάν, i. e. *a people*; *the ship of people*; *the strength or sorrow of the people*.] The son of *Shemida*, of the tribe of *Manasseh*.

AN'-IM, ['Aνών, i. e. *answerings*; *singings*; *afflicted*; *poor*.] A city of *Palestine*, in the tribe of *Judah*, in the mountains.

AN'-NA, ['Aννα, i. e. *merciful*; *taking rest*; *gracious*.] A prophetess mentioned by St. *Luke*, a widow of eighty four years of age, the daughter of *Phanuel* of the tribe of *Asher*—also the wife of *Tobit* in the Apocrypha.

AN'-NA-AS, [Σαναας.] One who returned from the babylonish captivity, with his family.

AN'-NAS, ['Aννας, i. e. *answering*; *singing*; *afflicting*; *poor*.] Father in law to *Caiaphas*; he had been high priest before *Caiaphas*, and is supposed to have resigned the office the same year in which our *Saviour* was condemned to die.

AN-NU'-US, ['Aννυ©.] One who returned from the babylonish captivity.

A'-NUS, [Aνας.] A *Levite* who returned from the babylonish captivity.

AN-TI-CHRIST', ['Aντιχριστ©, i. e. *against Christ*.] He is called the man of sin; but who he was or is, is undetermined; some say that he was *Mahomet*; some, *Caligula* the Roman emperor; others, the *pope*; others *Simon Magus*; and others refer it to the destruction of the Jews.

AN-TI-LIB'-A-NUS, ['Aντιλιβαν©, i. e. *against Libanus*.] An high hill to the north of *Judæa* opposite mount *Libanus*.

AN'-TI-OCH, ['Aντιοχεια, i. e. *a thing instead of*; *for, or against a chariot or waggon*.] A city in the province of *Pisidia* in *Asia*, where St. *Paul* and *Barnabas* preached—also *Antioch* the capital of *Syria* which was built by *Seleucus Nicanor* 301 years B. C. and called *Antioch* in memory of his father *Antiochus*.

AN-TI'-OCH-IS, ['Aντιοχις, i. e. *the same as Antioch*.] The daughter of *Antiochus* the great, married to *Ariarathes* king of *Cappadocia*.

AN-TI'-

AN-TI'-OCH-US, ['Αντιοχ@-, i. e. the same as Antioch.] The common names of the kings of Syria, particularly Antiochus Epiphanes, or, the illustrious, who was a great persecutor of the Jews, and died 164 years B. C.

AN'-TI-PAS, ['Αντιπας, i. e. for all; against all.] A martyr mentioned in the book of Revelation, said to have been bishop of Pergamos—also Herod Antipas, the son of Herod the great; he was tetrarch of Galilee and Petræa, and married the daughter of Aretas king of Arabia, and divorced her to obtain Herodias his brother Philip's wife.

AN-TIP'-A-TER, ['Αντιπαιρ@-, i. e. for or against the father.] The son of Jason, who was sent by Judas Maccabæus to renew the alliance with the Lacedæmonians.

AN-TIP'-A-TRIS, ['Αντιπατρις, i. e. the same meaning as Antipater.] A town of Palestine in the half tribe of Manasseh, named so by Herod the great, in honour to his father Antipater; about seventeen miles from Joppa.

AN-TIPH'-A, ['Ατεφα.] One who returned from the babylonish captivity.

AN-TO'-NI-A. A tower or fortress in Jerusalem, built by Herod the great, in honour of Mark Antony his friend.

AN-TO-THI'-JAH, ['Αναθωθια, i. e. answers or songs of the Lord; afflictions.] One of the descendants of the patriarch Benjamin.

AN-TO'-THITE, ['Αναθωθιτης, i. e. an answer; a song; affliction; poverty.] An inhabitant of Anathoth.

AN'-UB, ['Ενωβ, i. e. a grape; a knot.] The son of Coz, of the posterity of Judah the patriarch.

A before P.

AP-A-ME'-A, ['Απαμη, i. e. expelling; driving; chasing away.] The concubine of Darius king of Persia.

A-PEL'-LES, ['Απελλης, i. e. the same etymon as Apamea.] One whom St. Paul commendeth as approved

proved in *Chrift*: the Greeks fuppofe him to be one of the feventy-two difciples and bifhop of *Heraclea*.

APH-AR'-A-IM, [Αφεραειμ, i. e. *digging*; *fearching*; *confounding the fea.*] See *Hapharaim*.

A-PHAR-SATH'-CHITES or A-PHAR-SACH'-ITES, ['Αφαρσαθαχαῖοι, i. e. *dividing*; *tearing in pieces.*]   A people of *Samaria*, who petitioned *Artaxerxes* againft the rebuilding of *Jerufalem*.

A-PHAR'-SITES, ['Αφαρσαῖοι, i. e. *the fame etymon as Apharfathchites.*]   A people of *Samaria*, who petitioned *Artaxerxes* againft the rebuilding of *Jerufalem*.

APH'-EK, ['Οφὲκ. 'Αφὲκ, i. e. *ftrength*; *vigor*; *going forth.*]   A city of ancient *Canaan*, which fell to the lot of the tribe of *Afher*.

A-PHEK'-AH, [φαχυὰ, i. e. *the fame etymon as Aphek.*]   A city of *Palefine* in the tribe of *Judah*, in the mountains.

APH-Æ'-REM-A, ['Αφαίρεμα.]   A government of *Samaria*.

APH-ER'-RA, ['Αφερρὰ.]   One who returned from the babylonifh captivity.

APH'-I-AH, ['Αφὲκ, i. e. *fpeaking*; *blowing.*]   An anceftor of king *Saul*; the great grandfather of *Kifh*, a *Benjamite*.

APH'-RAH, [i. e. *duft.*]   A city of *Palefine*, called *Beth-Aphrah*.

APH'-SĒS, ['Αφεσὴ.]   Head of the eighteenth family of the priefts, one of the *twenty-four* which king *David* appointed for the fervice of the temple.

A-POC'-A-LYPSE, ['Αποκάλυψις, i. e. *revelation.*]   The canonical book of the New Teftament, called the *Revelation*, is fo termed.

A-POC'RY-PHA, ['Αποκρυφὴ, i. e. *to hide or conceal.*]   A term given to thofe books often inferted in the Bible, which are not admitted into the canon of fcripture; as *Ecclefiafticus*, *Wifdom*, *Maccabees*, &c.

A-POL-LO'-NI-A, ['Απολλωνία, i. e. *perdition*; *deftruction.*]   A city of *Macedonia*.

A-POL-

A-POL-LO'-NI-US, 'Απολλώνιος, i. e. *leafing*; *deftroy-ing.*] An officer belonging to *Antiochus Epiphanes.*

A-POL-LOPH'-A-NĒS, ['Απολλοφάνης.] A physi-cian, who was killed in the fortrefs of *Gazana* by the foldiers of *Judas Maccabæus.*

A-POL'-LŌS, ['Απολλὼς, i. e. *deftroyer*; *deftroying.*] A Jew of *Alexandria*, who went to *Ephefus* in the abfence of St. *Paul*, and was inftructed in the chriftian faith by *Aquila* and his wife *Prifcilla*; he was eloquent, and well verfed in the Scrip-tures, and it is faid, that he became bifhop of *Corinth.*

A-POL'-LY-ŌN, ['Απολύων, i. e. *deftroying*; *deftroyer.*] The name of the angel of the bottomlefs pit, or the *Devil*, in the *Greek* tongue.

A-POST'-LE, [Απoςoλ⊕-, i. e. *a meffenger.*] In the chriftian fenfe, is one commiffioned by *Jefus Chrift* to preach his gofpel, and propagate his religion.

AP'-PA-IM, ['Απφαίν, i. e. *a countenance or face*; *the noftrils*; *bakers.*] A fon of *Nadab*, of the pofte-rity of *Judah.*

AP'-PHI-A, ['Απφία, i. e. *bringing forth*; *increafing.*] One whom St. *Paul* addreffes in his epiftle to *Philemon.*

AP'-PHŪS, ['Απφᾶς.] The furname of *Jonathan* the fon of *Mattathias*, in the *Apocrypha.*

AP'-PI-I FO'-RUM, ['Αππίu Φόρον.] A town of an-tient *Italy*, not far from *Rome*: fome fay *fifty-one* miles from *Rome*, others *eighteen* miles.

A *before* Q.

AQU'-I-LA, ['Αxuλᾶs, i. e. *an eagle.*] The name of St. *Paul*'s hoft; he was a native of *Pontus* in *Afia Minor*; and was, together with his wife *Prifcilla*, converted to Chriftianity by that apoftle.

A *before* R.

AR, ['Hρ. 'Αρονὴ, i. e. *a rearing up*; *watches.*] It was the capital city of the *Moabites*, which was given to the children of *Lot.*

A'-RA,

A'-RA, ['Apá, i. e. *cursing; seeing.*] A son of *Je-ther*, a descendant from the patriarch *Asher*.

A'-RAB, ['Aιρὲμ, i. e. *multiplying; sowing sedition; a window; a locust.*] A city of *Palestine*, in the tribe of *Judah*, in the mountains.

AR'-A-BAH, [Βαιθάραβα.] A city of *Palestine* in the tribe of *Benjamin*.

AR-A-BAT'-TI-NE, ['Ακραβατλίνη.] A city of *A-rabia* in *Asia*.

A-RA'-BI-A, ['Αραβία, i. e. *even; evening; sweetness; a crow; a desart.*] An extensive country of *Asia*, divided into *Arabia deserta,* or the *desert*; *Arabia Petræa,* or the *stony*; and *Arabia Felix*, or the *happy*; where dwelt the *Moabites, Ammonites,* with many others: in *happy Arabia* dwelt the *Sabeans:* here St. *Paul* preached, and they were the first gentiles he preached to.

A-RA'-BI-ANS, ['Αραβες.] The people of *Arabia* in *Asia*.

A'RAD, ['Αράδ, i. e. *a wild ass; a dragon.*] A city of the *Amorites* in *Arabia Petreea*, lying to the south of *Judæa*—also a man who was a descendant from the patriarch *Benjamin*.

A'-RAD-ITE. The inhabitants of *Arad*.

A'R-A-DUS, [Αραδ☉.] An inland city of the *Phœ-nicians*.

AR'AH, ['Ορὲχ. 'Αρεέ, i. e. *the way; a traveller.*] One who returned from the babylonish cap-tivity.

A'-RAM, ['Αράμ, i. e. *highness; deceiving; their curse.*] The fifth son of the patriarch *Shem*; the father of the *Syrians*, who were called *Aramites*.

A'-RAM NA-HA-RA'-IM. Syria is called *Aram*, and *Naharaim* was a part of it lying between the rivers *Tigris* and *Euphrates*.

A'-RAN, ['Αράν, i. e. *an ark; their malediction.*] A son of *Dishon*, a descendant from the patriarch *Esau*.

AR'-A-RAT, ['Αραράτ, i. e. *a curse of trembling; a curse; light of a runner.*] A mountain of *Armenia*, famous for *Noah's* ark having rested upon it after the deluge.

AR-AU'-

AR-AU'-NAH, ['Ορνὰ, i. e. *an ark; a song; rejoicing; our light; a curse now.*] A *Jebusite* who fold to king *David* his threshing-floor on mount *Moriah*, to build an altar upon.

AR'-BA or AR'BAH, ['Αρβὸκ, i. e. *four.*] The name of a great man among the *Anakims*, who built *Kirjath-arba*, afterwards called *Hebron*; the father of *Anak*.

AR'-BAL. The name of a king of *Arad*.

AR-BAT'-TIS, ['Αρβάτℑⓞ.] A term for cultivated places.

AR-BE'-LA, ['Αρβήλα.] A city of *Affyria* in *Afia*; the country was called *Arbelis*, or *Arbelitis*.

AR-BEL'-LA, ['Αρβήλλⓞ.] The limits of *Judæa* beyond *Jordan*.

AR'-BITE. An inhabitant of *Kirjath-Arba*.

AR-BO'-NAI, ['Αβρωνᾶ.] A river mentioned in the Apocrypha.

ARCH-ANG'-EL, ['Αρχαγℑελⓞ, i. e. *principal or excellent among the angels.*] A prince of the angelic order, as *Michael* is called, who the *Jews* fay was the protector of the people of *Ifrael*.

AR-CHEL-A'-US, ['Αρχέλαⓞ, i. e. *a prince of the people.*] The fon of *Herod* the great, who fucceeded his father, but only to one half of his territories in *Judæa*.

AR-CHES'-TRA TUS. A poet of *Greece*.

AR-CHE-VITES, ['Αρχυαῖοι.] A people who petitioned *Artaxerxes* againft the rebuilding the city of *Jerufalem*.

AR'-CHI. A city of *Palefine* in the tribe of *Mannaffeh*.

AR'-CHI-AT-A'-ROTH, ['Αρχιεταῖρⓞ, i. e. *the longitude of crowns or circles.*] See *ATAROTH*, it being the fame city.

AR-CHIP'-PUS, [Αρχιππⓞ, i. e. *a prince or governor of horfes.*] One whom St. *Paul* mentions in the book of *Coloffians*.

ARCH'-ITES, ['Αραχοί.] Inhabitants of *Archi* a city of *Palefine* in the tribe of *Benjamin*.

ARC-TU'-RUS, ['Αρχτῦρⓞ, i. e. *a gathering together.*] A ftar of the firft magnitude in the nor-

 thern

thern hemifphere, in the fkirt of *Bootes*, near to the *Bears-tail*: it rifes the firft of *September*, and fets the fecond of *May*.

ARD, ['Αρὰδ, i. e. *ruling*; *defcending*.] A fon of the patriarch *Benjamin*.

AR'-DATH. A field mentioned in the Apocrypha.

ARD'-ITES. The defcendants from *Ard*.

AR'-DŌN, ['Αρδών, i. e. *ruling*; *the judgment of malediction*.] A fon of *Caleb* the fon of *Hezron*, of the pofterity of *Judah*.

A-RE'-LI, ['Αριήλεις, i. e. *the altar*, or *the light of God*, or *the fight of God*.] A fon of the patriarch *Gad*.

A-RE'-LITES, ['Αριηλι.] The defcendants from *Areli*.

A-RE-OP'-A-GITE, ['Αρεοπαγίτης.] The title given to a member of the council of *Areopagus*.

A-RE-OP'-A-GUS, ['Αρειόπαγ©.] An hill at *Athens*, called *Mars-hill*; where was a court or tribunal called the *Areopagus*: St. *Paul* made a fpeech in this court and converted *Dionyfius* who was one of the judges of it.

A'-RES, ['Αρès.] One who returned from the babylonifh captivity.

AR'-ET-AS, ['Αρέτας, i. e. *virtuous*.] A king of *Arabia*, whofe daughter *Herod-Antipas* married and afterwards divorced.

A-RE'-US, ['Ονειάρης.] A king of the *Lacedæmonians*, called *Oniares*.

AR'-GOB, ['Αργὸϐ, i. e. *turf of earth*; *fat land*; *curfe of the well*.] A region of antient *Canaan*, of which *Og* was king.

AR'-GOL. The capital city of the country of *Argol*, to the eaft of the river *Jordan*, in the half tribe of *Manaffeh*.

A-RID'-A-I, ['Αριδαὶ.] The ninth fon of *Haman*, who was hanged with his nine brethren.

A-RID'-A-THA, ['Αριδαθά.] The fixth fon of *Haman* who was hanged with his nine brethren.

AR'-I-EH, ['Αρία.] An officer of *Pekahiah* king of *Ifrael*.

A'-RI-ĒL, ['Αριήλ, i. e. *the altar*, or *lion*, or *light of God*.] The capital city of *Moab*.

AR-I-

AR-I-MA-THE'-A, ['Αριμαθαία, i. e. *a lion dead unto God; or the light of the Lord's death.*] A city of *Paleftine*, in the tribe of *Ephraim*, where *Jofeph*, the councellor, who begged the body of our Savior lived; it is alfo called *Dumiah*, *Arumah*; and alfo *Ramath* where the prophet *Samuel* lived.

A'-RI-ŌCH, ['Αριώχ, i. e. *long; tall; thy drunkennefs; the lion.*] The king of *Ellafar*, who was in league with *Chederlaomer* againft the kings of *Sodom* and *Gomorrah*—alfo the general of king *Nebuchadnezzar's* army.

A-RIS'-A-I, ['Αρισαι.] The feventh fon of *Haman*, who was hanged with his nine brethren.

AR-I-STAR'-CHUS, ['Αρίςαρχ⊚-, i. e. *a right good prince; the beft prince.*] A companion and fellow prifoner with St. *Paul*; he was a Macedonian and native of *Theffalonica*; and was beheaded with St. *Paul* at *Rome* in the reign of *Nero*, A. D. 67.

AR-I-STIP'-PUS, ['Αρέςιππ⊚-.] A celebrated philofopher of *Cyrene*.

A-RI-STOB-U'-LUS, ['Αριςοβ⊚λ⊚-, i. e. *a very good, or the beft councellor.*] One whom St. *Paul* mentions in his epiftle to the *Romans*, who, the Greeks fay, was brother to St. *Barnabas*—alfo the mafter of *Ptolomy*, in the fecond book of Maccabees.

ARK, ['Κεβωτὸς, i. e. *to dwell or inhabit.*] The ark of *Noah* was 547 feet in length, about 91 feet wide and above 55 feet in height; it was capacious to hold as much as forty fhips, of a thoufand tons each—alfo the ark of the covenant, which was a fmall cheft or coffer, three feet and nine inches long, two feet and three inches high, and two feet and three inches broad, which contained the golden pot of *Manna*, *Aaron's Rod*, and the *two Tables* of the covenant.

ARK'-ITES, ['Αρκαιοι.] A people of antient *Canaan*.

AR-MA-GED'-DŌN, ['Αρμαγεδων, i. e. *the hill of the Gofpel; the hill of Apples or of fruit or of meeting.*] A

place

place mentioned in the book of *Revelation*, which literally signifies the mountain of *Megiddo*, a city at the foot of mount *Carmel*.

AR-MEN'-I-A, ['Αρμενία.] A province of *Asia*, suppofed to be fettled by *Aram*, and where it is fuppofed that *Paradife* was fituated: now *Turcomania*.

AR'-MON, ["Ερμωνοί.] A fon of king *Saul* by *Rizpah*, flain by the *Gibeonites*—alfo a city of *Paleftine* in the tribe of *Gad*.

AR'-NA. An anceftor of *Efdras*, in the *Apocrypha*.

AR'-NAN, ['Ορνὰ, i. e. *rejoicing*; *their ark*.] One of the pofterity of the patriarch *Judah*.

AR'-NE-PHER, [Αρναφὰρ.] See *Harnephar*.

AR'-NON, ['Αρνῶν, i. e. *rejoicing*; *their ark*; *the light of the fun*; *the light eternal*.] A river or brook rifing in the mountains of *Gilead*, and running into the *dead fea*; the border of *Moab*.

A'-ROD, ['Αροαδὸς, i. e. *ruling*; *defcending*.] A fon of the patriarch *Gad*, from whom defcended the *Arodites*.

A-RO'-DI, ['Αροηδεὶς, i. e. *ruling*; *domineering lion*.] One of the fons of the patriarch *Gad*.

A'-RO-ER, ['Αροὴρ, i. e. *the watch of watches*; *raifing up of watches*.] A city of *Paleftine*, in the tribe of *Gad*, whofe citizens are called *Aroerites*.

A'-ROM, ['Αρὸμ.] One whofe family returned from the babylonifh captivity.

AR'-PAD or AR'-PHAD, ['Αρφὰδ, i. e. *the light of redemption*.] A city in the land of *Hamath* in *Syria*, called *Epiphania* by the Greeks.

AR-PHAX'-AD, ['Αρφαξὰδ, i. e. *healing*.] A fon of the patriarch *Shem*, from whom the Chaldeans proceeded; he died A. M. 2096 Æt. 438—alfo a king whom *Nebuchadnezzar* vanquifhed.

AR'-SA-CES, ['Αρσάκης, i. e. *lifting up the fhield*.] A king of the *Parthians* who died 245 years B. C.

AR'-TAX-ER'-XES, ['Αρταξέρξης, i. e. *light*; *malediction*; *fervent to fpoil*.] Several kings of *Perfia* of that name; but *Artaxerxes Longimanus* reigned from A. M. 3540 to A. M. 3581, or 41 years:
he

he permitted the Jews, with *Ezra*, to return to *Judæa*, and alfo gave leave to *Nehemiah* to re-build the walls of *Jerufalem*, and made him go-vernor of *Judæa* A. M. 3560; he died 423 years B. C.

AR'-TEM-AS, ['Αρτεμὰς, i. e. *whole*; *found*; *fightly*, *without fault*.] A difciple of St. *Paul*, whom he fent to *Crete* in the room of *Titus*.

AR'-VAD, ['Αραδιον.] A country mentioned by the prophet *Ezekiel*; but uncertain where.

AR'-VAD-ITES, ['Αραδιοι.] A people of antient *Canaan*.

AR'-U-BŌTH, ['Αραϐὼϑ.] A city of *Paleftine* in the tribe of *Judah*.

A-RU'-MAH, ['Αρημὰ, i. e. *high*; *exalted*; *caft away*.] A city of *Paleftine* in the tribe of *Ephraim*, near to *Sichem*.

AR'-ZA. A fteward to king *Afia*.

A *before* S.

A'-SA, ['Ασὰ, i. e. *a phyfician*.] A king of *Judah*, who fucceeded his father *Abijam* 954 years B. C. he reigned about 41 years, and died 914 years B. C.

AS-A'-DI-AS, ['Ασαδιος.] Great, great grandfather to *Baruch*.

A'-SA-ĒL, ['Ασιηλ, i. e. *God hath wrought*.] An anceftor of *Tobit*.

A-SA'-HĒL, ['Ασαηλ, i. e. *God hath wrought*.] The fon of *Zeruiah*, and brother of *Joab*, remarkable for his fwiftnefs in running; he was flain by *Abner* in the battle of *Gibeon*—alfo the father of *Jonathan* the prieft in the book of *Ezra*.

A-SA-I'-AH, [Ασαϊα, i. e. *the Lord hath wrought*.] A prince of the tribe of *Simeon*—alfo one of the tribe of *Levi*—alfo one who was fent by king *Jofiah* to confult the prophetefs *Huldah* concerning the book of the law; he is alfo called *Afahiah*.

AS'-A-NA, ['Ασσανὰ.] One whofe family returned from the babylonifh captivity.

A'-SAPH, ['Ασὰφ, i. e. *gathering*.] A recorder in king *Hezekiah*'s reign—alfo a celebrated finger of

D 3

the

the temple, the fon of *Berachiah* of the tribe of
Levi: he fang in concert with the cymbals.

AS'-A-PHAR, [Ασφαϱ.] See *Afphar.*

AS'-A-RA, ['Ασαρὰ.] One who returned from the
babylonifh captivity.

AS-AR-E'-EL, ['Εσεϱεὴλ, i. e. *the beatitude of God.*] A
fon of *Jehalaleel,* of the tribe of *Judah.*

AS-A-RE'-LAH, ['Ασειρηλά. 'Εϱαὴλ, i. e. *the bleffednefs of God.*] A fon of *Afaph,* a finger of the
jewifh temple.

AS-BAZ'-A-RETH, ['Ασϐαχαφὰs.] A king of the
Affyrians.

AS'-CA-LON, ['Ασχάλων, i. e. *the fire of infamy, a
balance.*] A famous city of the Philiftines, in
the tribe of *Judah,* and about 40 miles weft of
Jerufalem.

A-SE'-AS, ['Ασαίας.] One who returned from the
babylonifh captivity.

AS-EB-I'-A, ['Ασεϐία.] See *Hafhabiah.*

AS-EB-E'-BI-A, [Ασεϐηϐίαs.] One who returned
from the babylonifh captivity.

AS'-EN-ATH, ['Ασενὲϑ, i. e. *a peril; a thing unfortunate.*] The daughter of *Potipherah,* and wife
to the patriarch *Jofeph.*

A'-SER, ['Ασὴρ.] A place in *Paleftine,* not far from
Galilee.

A-SE'-RAR, ['Σεϱὰϱ. 'Ασηϱάϱ.] One who returned
from the babylonifh captivity.

ASH-AB-I'-AH, ['Ασαϐίαs.] See *Hafhabiah.*

A'-SHAN, ['Ασάν, i. e. *a fume or fmoke.*] A city of
Paleftine, in the tribe of *Judah,* in the valley.

ASH'-BE-A, ['Εσοϐὰ.] One of the pofterity of the
patriarch *Judah.*

ASH-BEL, ['Ασϐὴλ, i. e. *an old fire.*] A defcendant
from the patriarch *Benjamin,* called alfo *Jediael:*
from him came the *Afhbelites.*

ASH'-BEL-ITES. The defcendants from *Afhbel.*

ASH'-DOD, ['Ασηδὼθ. 'Αξώτϴ, i. e. *a robbing of a
country; the fire of the beloved; inclination; leaning.*]
A city of the *Philiftines,* famous for the temple of
their god *Dagon;* it afterwards belonged to the
tribe

tribe of *Judah*; it was ten miles north of *Gaza*, on the Mediterranean fea; here St. *Philip* preached.

ASH'-DŌTH-ITES, [Αξώτιοι.] Inhabitants of *Afh-dod*, a diftrict of the *Philiftines*.

ASH-DŌTH PIS'-GAH, ['Ασηδωθ Φασγὰ.] A city of *Paleftine* in the tribe of *Reuben*.

A'-SHE-AN, [Σομὰ.] A city of *Paleftine* in the tribe of *Judah* in the mountains.

ASH'-ĒR, ['Ασηρ, i. e. *bleffednefs or felicity*.] The fecond fon of the patriarch *Jacob*, by *Zilpah* the handmaid of *Leah*.

ASH'-I-MATH or MA, [Ασιμὰϑ, i. e. *the fire of the fea; the offence*.] An idol worfhipped by the people of *Hamath*.

ASH'-KE-NAZ, ['Αχανὰζ, i. e. *fire that diftils or fpreads*.] The eldeft fon of *Gomer*, and grand-fon to *Japhet*—alfo a country of *Afia*, under the dominion of the *Medes*; fuppofed to be *Bithynia*.

ASH'-NAH, ['Ασσα, i. e. *change; fire now*.] A city of *Paleftine* in the tribe of *Judah* in the valley.

A'-SHON, ['Ασὰν.] A city of *Paleftine*, in the tribe of *Simeon*.

ASH'-PE-NAZ, ['Ασφανὲζ.] The governor or officer over the eunuchs in *Nebuchadnezzar*'s court.

ASH'-RI-ĒL, ['Εσριὴλ, i. e. *the beatitude of God*.] A fon of the patriach *Manaffeh*, of whom came the *Afrielites*.

ASH'-TA-RŌTH, ['Αϛαρὼϑ, i. e. *flocks; riches; horns*.] A city of the *Moabites*, in the tribe of *Gad*—alfo another, in the half tribe of *Manaffeh*—alfo an idol of the Philiftines.

ASH'-TA-RŌTH CAR'-NA-IM, ['Αγαρὼϑ Καρναἰν, i. e. *flocks; riches; horns*.] A place of antient *Canaan*, mentioned in the book of *Genefis*.

ASH'-TEM-ŌTH, ["Εϛ. Εϑεμὼ, i. e. *the fire of divi-nation or of perfection; or fimplicity*.] A city of *Pa-leftine* in the tribe of *Judah*.

ASH'-TE-RATH-ITES, ['Ασαρώθι.] The people of *Afhtaroth* in *Moab*.

A-SHU'-ATH, ['Ασιθ. 'Ασυὰϑ, i. e. *doing or making veftments*.] A fon of *Japhet* of the tribe of *Afher*.

 ASH'-ŪR,

ASH'-ŪR, ['Ασσὲρ, i. e. *blessed*; *travelling*; *beholding*.] The son of *Shem*—also the country of *Assyria*, so called from *Asher* the son of *Shem* the patriarch.

ASH-U'-RIM, ['Ασσυρείμ, i. e. *layers in wait*; *slow goers*; *beholders*.] A son of *Dedan*, the grandson of the patriarch *Abraham* by *Keturah*.

ASH'-ŪR-ITES. The people of *Assyria*.

A'-SI-A, ["Ασία.] One of the four quarters or divisions of the *earth*: about 4800 miles in length from *east* to *west*, and about 4300 miles from *north* to *south*.

AS-IB-I'-AS, ['Ασεβίας.] One who returned from the babylonish captivity.

A'-SI-ĒL, ['Ασιὴλ, i. e. *the work of God*.] One of the posterity of the patriarch *Simeon*.

AS'-I-PHA, ['Ασιφὰ.] One who returned from the babylonish captivity.

AS'-KE-LŌN, ['Ασκάλων.] See *Asculon*.

AS'-MA-VĒTH, ['Ασμὼϑ, i. e. *a strong death*; *a buck goat*; *the strength of death*.] One of king *David*'s worthies.

AS-MOD-E'-US, ['Ασμοδαῖος, i. e. *a destroyer*; *abounding in sin*; *measuring the fire*.] An evil spirit mentioned in the book of *Tobit*, in the apocrypha.

AS-NO-NE'-ANS. A name given to the *Maccabees*, the descendants of *Mattathias*.

AS'-NAH, ["Ασενὰ.] One who returned from the babylonish captivity.

AS-NA'P-PER, ['Ασσεναφὰς, i. e. *unhappiness*; *misfortune of the calf*; *fruitfulness*; *increase of danger*.] A king of *Assyria* in the reign of *Manasseh* king of *Judah*: he is also called *Esarhaddon*.

A-SO'-CHIS. A city of *Galilee* in the land of *Palestine*.

A'-SOM, ['Ασὸμ.] One who returned from the babylonish captivity.

AS'-PA-THA, ['Ασφαθὰ.] The third son of *Haman*, who was hanged with his nine brethren.

AS'-PHAR,

AS'-PHAR, ['Ασφάρ.] A lake mentioned in the firſt book of *Maccabees*, ſuppoſed to be the lake of *Sodom* or *Dead-ſea*.

AS-PHAR'-A-SUS, ['Ασφάσ©.] One who returned from the babyloniſh captivity.

AS'-RI-ĒL, ['Εσριηλ, i. e. *the beatitude of God.*] A ſon of *Gilead*, the head of the *Aſrielites*—alſo a ſon of the patriarch *Manaſſeh*.

ASS, [*wild.*] This animal inhabits the deſarts of *Arabia*, as alſo *Africa* and *India*—it is now called *Zebra*—it is a beautiful creature, and more re-ſembles an horſe than an aſs; his ears are more like to thoſe of an horſe than of an aſs—he is well made, active and very ſwift— he has fine legs, a tufted tail, and ſmooth ſkin—the males are white and brown, and the females white and black—the colours are placed alternately in pa-rallel lines, diſtinct and narrow—he is ſtreaked in that admirable manner, as to appear, at a diſtance, as if covered with ribbons—he is larger than the common aſs, and is ſuppoſed to be un-tameable, being very vicious.

AS-SA-BI'-AS, ['Ασαβίας.] One of king *Joſiah*'s captains over thouſands.

AS-SAL'-I-MŌTH, ['Ασσαλιμώϑ.] One who re-turned from the babyloniſh captivity.

AS-SA-NI'-AS, ['Ασσαμίας.] A prieſt who returned from the babyloniſh captivity.

AS-SI-DE'-ANS, ['Ασιϑαῖοι, i. e. *pious*; *merciful.*] A numerous ſect among the Jews, who not only adhered ſtrictly to the law, but obliged them-ſelves to do more than the law required; as taking up arms to maintain the honour of the temple.

AS'-SIR, ['Ασειρ. Ασιρ,] *bound*; *impriſoned*; *prohibited.*] A ſon of *Jeconiah* king of *Judah*—alſo one of the ſons of *Korah*.

AS'-SOS, ['Ασσ©, i. e. *drawing near to.*] A ſea port town to the ſouth weſt of *Troas*, oppoſite the iſle of *Leſbos*.

AS'-SŪR,

AS'-SUR, ['Aσὰg. Aσσɴg.] The *Aſſyrians* are ſo called —alſo one whoſe ſons were ſervants of the temple.

AS-SYR'-I-A, ['Aσσυρίας, i. e. *happy.*] An antient country of *Aſia,* which derived its name from *Aſhur,* a ſon of *Shem:* now *Curdiſtan.*

AS-SYR'-I-ANS, ['Aσσύριοι.] The people of *Aſſyria.*

AS'-TA-ROTH ASH'-TA-ROTH, or AS-TAR'-TE, ['Aσταρὶὴ, i. e. *ſheep; ewes.*] A goddeſs of the *Aſſyrians* and *Phœnicians,* to whom *Solomon,* to pleaſe one of his concubines, raiſed an altar on the *Mount of Olives.*

AS'-TATH, ['Aςὰθ.] One who returned from the babyloniſh captivity.

AS-TY'-A-GES, ['Aςυάγης, i. e. *a leader; a governor of the city; a duke.*] The laſt king of the *Medes* in *Aſia,* about 559 years B. C.

AS-UP'-PIM, ['Eσεφίμ, i. e. *the counſel of God.*] The treaſury place of the temple at *Jeruſalem.*

A-SYN'-CRI-TUS, ['Aσύγκριτ☉, i. e. *incomparable.*] One who is mentioned by the apoſtle *Paul;* ſuppoſed to have been biſhop of *Hircania.*

A before T.

A'-TAD, ['Aτὰδ, i. e. *a thorn.*] The name of a man, at whoſe threſhing floor the ſons of *Jacob,* with ſome of the *Egyptians,* mourned for the death of the patriarch *Jacob:* it was afterwards called *Abel-Mizraim.*

AT'-A-RAH, ['Aτάρα, i. e. *a crown.*] One of the wives of *Jerahmeel,* of the poſterity of *Judah;* the mother of *Onam.*

A-TAR'-GA-TIS, ['Aταργατϡ☉.] A goddeſs of the *Syrians.*

AT'-A-ROTH, ['Aταρὼθ, i. e. *crowns; a quill to fill one with; the counſel of making one drunk.*] A city of *Paleſtine,* in the tribe of *Gad.*

AT'-A-ROTH AD'-DAR, ['Aτρὼθ 'Eδδὰρ, i. e. *the cloak; powers; greatneſs.*] A city of *Paleſtine,* in the tribe of *Ephraim.*

A'-TER,

A'-TĔR, ['Ατὴρ, i. e. *the left hand*; *ſhut.*] One who returned from the babyloniſh captivity.

AT.ER-EZ'-I-AS, ['Ατηρ 'Εζεκίм.] One whoſe family returned from the babyloniſh captivity.

A'-THACH, ['Aθáχ, i. e. *thy hour*; *thy time.*] A city of *Paleſtine*, to which king *David* ſent preſents from *Ziklag*.

ATH-A-I'-AH, ['Aθαïα, i. e. *the hour or time of the Lord.*] A ſon of *Uzziah* the ſon of *Zechariah*, of the tribe of *Judah*.

ATH-AL-I'-AH, [Γοθολία, i. e. *the hour or time for the Lord.*] The daughter of *Omri* king of *Iſrael*, and wife of *Jehoram* king of *Judah*: ſhe uſurped the kingdom, and was ſlain after a ſix years reign A. M. 3126 and 878 years B. C.

ATH-A-RI'-AS, ['Aθαρίας.] One whoſe family returned from the babyloniſh captivity.

ATH-EN-OB'-I-US, ['Aθανόβι☉, i. e. *the love of Minerva.*] An ambaſſador which *Antiochus* ſent to *Simon Maccabæus*.

ATH'-ĔNS, ['Aθήνη, i. e. *without increaſe*; *of Minerva.*] A famous city of *Achaia* in *Greece*: here St. *Paul* preached and converted *Dionyſius* a member of the *Areopagus*: now *Sentines* in european *Turky*.

ATH-E'-NI-ANS, ['Aθήναι.] The inhabitants of *Athens*.

ATH'-LAI, [Θαλί, i. e. *my hour*; *my time*; *time unto me.*] One who returned from the babyloniſh captivity.

AT'-ROTH. A city of *Canaan* built by the children of *Gad*. See *Ataroth*.

AT'-TAI, ['Eθì. 'Ιεθì, i. e. *the ſame etymon as Athlai.*] A grandſon of *Sheſhan*, of the tribe of *Judah*— alſo one who reſorted to king *David* at *Ziklag*, of the tribe of *Gad*—alſo the ſon of king *Rehoboam* by *Maachah* the daughter of *Abſalom*.

AT-TA-LI'-A, ['Aτ7αλεία, i. e. *increaſing*; *nouriſhing.*] A city of *Pamphylia* in *Aſia*, where St. *Paul* and St. *Barnabas* preached the goſpel A. D. 45.

AT'-TA-

AT'-TA-LUS, [Ατ7αλ☉, i. e. *increased*; *nourished*.] A king of *Pergamus*, mentioned in the first book of *Maccabees*.

AT-THAR'-A-TES, ['Αθαράτης.] One whose family returned from the babylonish captivity.

A *before* U *and* V.

A'-VA, ['Αἱα.] See *Ivah*.

AV'-A-RAN, ['Αυαρὰν.] One of the five fons of *Mattathias* the high priest. See ABARON.

A'-VEN, ["Ων, i. e. *iniquity*; *forrow*; *ftrength*; *riches*.] A city of *Ægypt* in *Africa*; afterwards *Heliopolis* and *On*.

AU'-GI-A, ['Αυγία.] One who returned from the babylonish captivity.

AŪ-GUST'-US, [Αυγυς☉, i. e. *lucky*; *royal*; *confecrated*; *of great magnificence*.] An emperor of *Rome*, in the twenty-fifth year of whose reign our *Saviour* was born.

A'-VIM, 'Αυιμ, i. e. *wicked*; *perverfe*.] A city of *Palestine*, built by the *Benjamites*.

A'-VIMS, ['Ευαῖοι, i. e. *wicked men*; *perverfe*.] Inhabitants of antient *Palestine*.

A'-VITES. See *Avims*.

A'-VITH, ['Ευιθ, i. e. *wicked*; *perverfe*.] A city of *Idumæa* or *Edom*, whose king was *Hadad*.

AU-RA-NI'-TIS. A city of *Palestine* in the tribe of *Manaffeh*.

AU-RAN'-US, ['Αυρὰν☉.] A leader of a mob in the fecond book of *Maccabees*.

AU-TE'-AS, ['Αυ7αίας.] One whose family returned from the babylonish captivity.

A *before* Z.

AZ-A-E'-LUS, ['Αζαῆλ☉.] One who returned from the babylonish captivity.

AZ'-AH or AZ'-ZES, ['Αζᾶζ, i. e. *a ftrong one*. The father of *Bela*, of the tribe of *Reuben*.

AZ'-AL, ['Αοαηλ. 'Ιαοὸδ.] A place near to *Jerufalem*.

AZ'-A-

AZ-A-LI'-AH, ['Εζελιας, i. e. *departure of God.*] The father of *Shaphan.*

AZ-A-NI'-AH, ['Αζανία, i. e. *hearkening the Lord; the weapons of the Lord.*] The father of *Joshua* a Levite.

AZ-A'-PHI-ŌN, ['Αοσαπφιαθ.] One who returned from the babylonish captivity.

AZ'-A-RA, ['Ασαρά.] One whose sons were servants of the temple.

AZ'-A-REEL, ['Οζειλ, i. e. *the help of God.*] One of king *David's* worthies who resorted to him at *Ziklag*—also one who returned from the babylonish captivity—also a son of *Jeroboam* and a prince of the tribe of *Dan.*

AZ-A-RI'-AH, ['Αζαρίας, L. *Azariah,* i. e. *help of the Lord.*] The name of several of the Jewish high priests—also a prophet the son of *Oded,* in the reign of *Asa* king of *Judah*—also a king of *Judah* 810 years B. C. he is also called *Uzziah*—also the son of *Nathan* the prophet.

AZ-A-RI'-AS, ['Αζαρίος.] A name which the angel *Gabriel* assumed in the book of *Tobit.*

AZ'-AZ, ['Αζάζ.] See *Azzah.*

AZ-A-ZI'-AH, ['Οζιάς, i. e. *the strength of the Lord.*] One who was appointed in king *David's* reign, to sing in the temple of *Jerusalem,* to the *Sheminith* or harp with eight strings.

AZ-BAZ'-A-RETH, ['Ασβασαρεθ.] A king of *Assyria.*

AZ'-BŪK, ['Αζαβήχ.] The father of *Nehemiah.*

AZ-E'-KAH, ['Αζηκά. Γαζηκά, i. e. *strength of walls.*] A city of *Palestine,* in the tribe of *Judah,* in the valley.

AZ'-EL, ['Εσήλ, i. e. *he departed.*] A descendant from king *Saul.*

AZ'-EM, ['Ασου.] A city of *Palestine,* in the tribe of *Simeon.*

AZ-E-PHU'-RITH, ['Αρσιφηριθ.] One who returned from the babylonish captivity.

AZ-E'-TAS, ['Αζητάς.] One who returned from the babylonish captivity.

AZ'-GAD,

AZ'-GAD, ['Ασγὰδ, i. e. *a ſtrong army; ſtrength of felicity; a gang of robbers; a troop of ſoldiers.*] One who returned from the babyloniſh captivity.

AZ'-I-A, ['Οζία.] One who returned from the babyloniſh captivity; and his ſons ſervants of the temple.

AZ-I-E'-I. An anceſtor of *Eſdras.*

AZ'-I-ĒL, ['Οζιήλ, i. e. *ſtrength of the Lord.*] A muſician who played upon the *Pſaltery.*

AZ-I'-ZA, ['Οζιζά, i. e. *ſtrength; of ſtrength.*] One who returned from the babyloniſh captivity.

AZ'-MA-VĒTH, ['Αζμὼθ.] See *Aſmaveth.*

AZ'-MŌN, ['Ασεμὼν, i. e. *bone of a bone; our ſtrength.*] A city which was on the ſouthern border of the land of *Canaan.*

AZ'-NŌTH TA'-BŌR, ['Αϑϑαβὼρ, i. e. *the ears of election or of purity, or of contrition or breaking.*] A city of *Paleſtine,* in the tribe of *Naphtali.*

AZ'-ŌR, ['Αζὼρ, i. e. *an helper; entry; a court; converted.*] The ſon of *Eliakim* in St. *Matthew's* genealogical liſt — alſo a place mentioned in the firſt book of *Maccabees.*

AZ-O'-TUS, ['Αζὼτ☉.] See *Aſhdod.*

AZ'-RI-ĒL, ['Ιεζριήλ, i. e. *the help of GOD.*] One of king *David's* worthies, of the tribe of *Manaſſeh.*

AZ'-RI-KAM, ['Εζριχὰμ, i. e. *help; riſing up; revenging; void ſtrength.*] One of *Ezra's* aſſiſtants in reading the law.

AZ-U'-BAH, ['Αζηϛὰ, i. e. *forſaken.*] The daughter of *Shilhi,* and the mother of *Jehoſhaphat* king of *Judah*—alſo the wife of *Caleb* the ſon of *Hezron.*

AZ'-ŪR, ['Αζὼρ, i. e. *holpen; helper.*] A prophet in the time of *Zedekiah* king of *Judah.*

AZ'-U-RAN, [Αζαϱος. 'Αζαϱάν.] One who returned from the babyloniſh captivity.

AZ'-ZAH, [Γάζης, i. e. *ſtrong.*] A country of the *Avims.*

AZ'-ZAN, ['Οζᾶ, i. e. *their ſtrength.*] The father of *Paltiel,* a prince of the tribe of *Iſſachar.*

AZ'-ZŪR, ['Αζὺρ, i. e. *holpen or helper.*] One who ſealed the covenant with *Nehemiah* the governor.

B.

B.

B *before* A.

BA'-AL or BEL, [Βάαλ, i. e. *master, lord, or hus-band.*] A Deity worshipped by the *Moabites* and *Phœnicians*—also a city of *Palestine*—also a son of *Joel.*

BA'-AL-AH, [Βάαλ. Βαλὰ, i. e. *her idol, or a spouse.*] A mountain and city of *Palestine*, in the tribe of *Judah*; called also *Kirjath-jearim.*

BA'-AL-ATH, ['Γεβεελὰν, i. e. *proud Lord.*] A city of *Palestine*, in the tribe of *Dan.*

BA'-A-LATH BE'-ER, [Βααλὰθ Βηῤῥαθμὰθ, i. e. *sub-jected pit.*] A city of *Palestine*, in the tribe of *Simeon.*

BA'-AL BE'-RITH, [Βααλβεὲρ, i. e. *idol of the cove-nant.*] A Deity worshipped, sometimes, by the *Israelites.*

BA'-AL-E. The same place with *Baalath*, which see.

BA'-AL GAD, [Βαλαγὰδ, i. e. *idol of the troop.*] A city in the valley of *Lebanon*, one of the bounds of *Joshua's* conquests.

BA'AL HAM'-ON, [Βεελαμὰν, i. e. *one who rules a multitude.*] A place which was near to the city of *Jerusalem.*

BA'-AL HAN'-AN, [Βαλλενὼν.] A king of the *Horites*, under whom the patriarch *Esau* settled.

BA'-AL HA'-ZOR, [Βελασώρ, i. e. *possessor of grace.*] One of the cities of *Palestine.*

BA'-AL HER'-MON, [Αεῥμὰν, i. e. *the possessor of destruction.*] A mountain of the land of *Palestine.*

BA'-AL-I, [Βααλὶμ, i. e. *my idol or lord.*] A general title of the heathen Deities which the *Israelites* sometimes worshipped.

BA'-AL-

BA'-AL-IM. See *Baali*.

BA'-AL-IS, [Βελεισσὰ, i. e. *a proud lord.*] One who was a king of the *Ammonites*.

BA-AL'-ME-ŌN, [Βεελμεὼν, i. e. *the idol.*] A city which was built by the children of *Gad*.

BA'-AL PE'-ŌR, [Βεελφεγὼρ, i. e. *mafter of the opening.*] A *Moabitifh* Deity: the fame with *Priapus* and *Adonis*.

BA'-AL PER'-A-ZIM, [Βαὰλ φαρασὶν, i. e. *mafter or God of divifions.*] A city of the Philiftines.

BA'-AL SHA-LI'-SHA, [Βαιθαρίσα, i. e. *the third idol.*] A place mentioned in the fecond book of *Kings*, but uncertain where.

BA'AL TA'-MAR, [Βάαλ θαμάρ, i. e. *mafter of the Palm tree.*] A place mentioned in the book of *Judges*.

BA-AL'-ZEB-ŪB, [Βεελζεβὴλ, i. e. *the mafter of flies.*] A Deity of the Philiftines, worfhipped as the God of *Flies*, becaufe it was fuppofed he defended his votaries from Flies which infefted thofe hot countries.

BA'-AL ZEPH'-ŌN, [Βεελσεπφῶν, i. e. *the idol.*] A city of *Egypt* in *Africa*, near to the *Red-Sea*—alfo an Egyptian Deity.

BA'-A-NA, [Βαανᾶ, i. e. *in afflidtion; anfwering.*] One who returned from the babylonifh captivity.

BA'-A-NAH, [Βαανὰ, i. e. *in afflidtion.*] One of king *Solomon*'s purveyors of provifions—alfo one of king *Saul*'s captains.

BA'-A-NAN, [Βαανὰ.] One who murdered *Ifhbofheth* the fon of king *Saul*.

BA'-A-NATH. See *Baanan*.

BA-AN-I'-AS, [Βαναίας.] One who returned from the babylonifh captivity.

BA'-A-RA, [Βααρὰ, i. e. *a flame or purging.*] A wife of *Shaharaim*, one of the patriarch *Benjamin*'s pofterity.

BA'-A SHA, [Βαασα, i. e. *in the work, or he who lays wafte.*] One of the kings of *Ifrael*, the fon of *Ahijah*.

BA-A-

BA-A-SI'-AH, [Βαασία, i. e. *in making, or pressing together.*] One of the anceſtors of *Aſaph*, a ſinger
in the temple of *Jeruſalem.*

BA'-BEL, [Βαϐυλων, i. e. *confuſion, or mixture.*] A
city of *Nimrod*, where the tower of *Babel* was
built.

BA'-BI, [Βαϐὶ.] One who returned from the babyloniſh captivity.

BAB'-Y-LŌN, [Βαϐυλῶν, i. e. *confuſion, or mixture.*]
A celebrated city on the river *Euphrates* in *Aſia*,
the capital of *Chaldæa*, built by *Nimrod.*

BAB-Y-LŌN-I-ANS, [Βαϐυλὼνιοι.] The inhabitants
of the kingdom of *Babylon.*

BA'-CA, [i. e. *mulberry-tree.*] A little village on the
edge of *Galilee.*

BAC'-CHI-DĒS, [Βακχιδης, i. e. *a drunkard.*] One
who was a governor of *Meſopotamia.*

BACH'-RITES. Deſcendants from *Becher*, one of
Ephraim's poſterity.

BAC-CHU'-RUS, [Βακχȣρ◌.] A ſinger at the
temple who returned from the babyloniſh captivity.

BAC'-CHUS, [Βάκχ◌.] The God of wine among
the heathens; the ſon of *Jupiter* and *Semele:* he
lived A. M. 1900—alſo the name of a martyr
who ſuffered in the reign of the emperor *Dio-
cleſian.*

BAC'-HUTH AL'-LŌN, [Βαλάν◌ Πένθȣς.] The
oak of weeping, under which the nurſe of *Rebeckah* was buried.

BA-GO'-AS, [Βαγώας, i. e. *the inwards; moſt ſecret;
advanced; lifted up; bodily.*] An eunuch of *Holofernes* mentioned in the *Apocrypha.*

BA'-GO-I, [Βαγοὶ.] One whoſe family returned
from the babyloniſh captivity.

BA-HU'-RUM-ITE. An inhabitant of *Bahurim.*

BA-HU'-RIM, [Βαȣρίμ, i. e. *warlike or valiant.*] A
city of *Paleſtine*, in the tribe of *Benjamin.*

BA'-JITH, [i. e. *an houſe.*] The name of an heathen
temple.

BAK-BAK'-KER, [Βακ6αχᾶρ.] One of the priefts of the Jews.

BAK'-BŪK, [Βακ6ὺκ, i. e. *a narrow mouthed bottle.*] One whofe children were of the loweft order in the fervice of the temple.

BAK-BŪK-I'-AH, [Βακθανίας. Βοκχείας.] One who officiated in the worfhip of the temple at *Jeru-falem.*

BA'-LA-AM, [Βαλαὰμ, i. e. *the antient of the people, or their deſtruɛtion.*] A foothfayer or magician among the heathen, of the city of *Pethor*, on the river *Euphrates.*

BA'-LA-DAN, [Βαλαδὰν, i. e. *without rule or judg-ment.*] One who was king of *Babylon.*

BA'-LAH, [Βωλὰ, i. e. *old; worn.*] A city of *Pa-leſtine*, in the tribe of *Simeon.*

BA'-LAK, [Βαλὰκ, i. e. *who lays waſte or deſtroys.*] A king of the *Moabites.*

BA'-LA-MO, [Βαλαμώ.] A city of *Paleſtine.*

BA'-LA-NUS. One who returned from the baby-lonifh captivity.

BA-LAS'-A-MUS, [Βααλσαμ℗.] One whofe fa-mily returned from the babylonifh captivity.

BAL-NU'-US, [Βαλνή℗.] One whofe fons returned from the babylonifh captivity.

BAL-THAS'-AR, [Βαλτασαρ.] A king of *Babylon.* See *Belſhazzer.*

BA'-MAH, ['Α6αμὰ, i. e. *an eminence or high place.*] One of the altars of the heathen, fo called.

BA'-MŌTH, [Βαμὼθ, i. e. *the high places.*] The name of a valley in the country of *Moab.*

BA'-MŌTH BA'-AL, [Βαιμὼν Βαὰλ, i. e. *high places of Baal.*] A city of *Paleſtine*, in the tribe of *Reuben.*

BAN, [Βάν.] One whofe fons returned from the babylonifh captivity.

BAN'-I, [Βανὶ. Βανϋι, i. e. *fons.*] One of king *David*'s worthies, of the tribe of *Gad* — alfo others.

BAN'-ID, [Βανίας.] One who returned from the babylonifh captivity.

BAN-AI'-AS, [Σαβαννᾶιος. Βαννάια.] One who returned from the babylonish captivity.

BAN'-NUS, [Βαννὸς.] One who returned from the babylonish captivity.

BAN'-U-AS, [Βαννῶ.] A *Levite* whose family returned from the babylonish captivity.

BAR-AB'-BAS, [Βαραββᾶς, i. e. *the son of confusion or shame.*] The robber who was released instead of *Jesus Christ*.

BAR'-ACH-EL, [Βαραχιὴλ, i. e. *who blesses God.*] The father of *Elihu*, mentioned in the book of *Job*.

BAR-A-CHI'-AH, [Βαραχίας, i. e. *who blesses God.*] Father of the prophet *Zechariah*.

BA'-RAK, [Βαρὰκ, i. e. *thunder, or in vain.*] One whom *Deborah* the prophetess induced to fight against *Sisera* who commanded the army of *Jabin* king of *Canaan*.

BAR-BA'-RI-AN, [Βαρβαρῶ.] A name formerly signifying a *foreigner*.

BAR-CE'-NOR, [Βακχήνορῶ, i. e. *a drunkard or wine bibber.*] An officer mentioned in the *second* book of *Maccabees*.

BAR'-GO, [Βαγὼ.] One who returned from the babylonish captivity.

BAR-HUM'-ITES, [Βαρχμῖται.] The inhabitants of *Bahurim*, so called.

BAR-I'-AH, [Βεῤῥί. Βερία.] One of the posterity of king *David*.

BAR JE'-SUS, [Βαρ Ιησὺς, i. e. *son of Jesus.*] A Jewish sorcerer of the isle of *Crete*—he is also called *Elymas*.

BAR-JO'-NA, [Βὰρ Ιωνᾶ, i. e. *the son of a dove or of Jonas.*] The term used for the son of *Jona*; *Bar* signifying *son*.

BAR'-KOS, [Βαρκὸς.] One whose children were *Nethinims*, or of the lowest order in the service of the temple.

BAR'-NA-BAS, [Βαρναβας, i. e. *the son of consolation.*] A companion of the apostle *Paul* in the propagation of Christianity.

BAR-O'-DIS, [Βαρωδὶς.] One whofe family returned
from the babyloniſh captivity.

BAR'-SA-BAS, [Βαρσαβᾶς, i. e. *ſon of return or of reſt.*]
Surnamed *Juſtus:* a perſon mentioned in the
Acts of the Apoſtles: he was probably one of the
feventy diſciples—alfo another *Barſabas* mentioned in the book of the *Acts.*

BAR'-TA-CUS, [Βαρτάκ☉.] The father of *Apame,*
Darius's concubine.

BART-HOL'-OM-EW, [Βαρθολομαῖος, i. e. *a ſon that*
ſuſpends the waters.] One of the twelve diſciples
or apoſtles of *Jeſus Chriſt.*

BAR-TI-ME'-US, [Βαρτιμαῖος, i. e. *blind ſon; or, ſon*
of blindneſs.] The name of a blind man mentioned by St. *Matthew,* the fon of *Timeus: Bar* being
the word for a *ſon.*

BA'-RŪCH, [Βαρὺχ, i. e. *who is bleſſed.*] One who
affiſted in repairing the walls of *Jeruſalem,* after
the babyloniſh captivity—alfo the name of one
of the books of the *Apocrypha.*

BAR-ZIL'-LA-I, [Βερζελλαί, i. e. *the ſon of contempt.*]
An old man of eighty years of age, who entertained king *David* when he was quelling the rebellion of *Abſalom* his fon.

BAS'-CA-MA, [Βασκαμᾶ.] A city of the land of
Gilead.

BA'-SHAN or BA'-SAN, [Βασάν, i. e. *in the chance*
or in the ſleep.] A famous fertile country and
mountain of the *Amorites: Og* was one of their
kings.

BA'-SHAN HA'-VOTH FA'-IR, [Βασὰν Θαυώθ
'Ιαὶρ.] The country of *Argob,* fettled by *Jair,*
fo called.

BA'-SHEM-ATH, [Βασέμαθ, i. e. *perfumed, or con-*
fuſion of death.] One of the daughters of *Iſhmael,*
and wife to *Eſau.*

BAS'-LITH, [Βασαλώθ.] One whofe children were
Nethinims, or the loweſt order in the temple
fervice.

BAS'-MATH, [Βασεμμὰθ, i. e. *things aromatical, or*
in defolation.] One of king *Solomon*'s officers—
alfo

alſo the wife of *Eſau*—alſo a daughter of king *Solomon*.

BAS'-SA, [Βασσαὶ.]   One who returned from the babyloniſh captivity, with his family.

BAS'-TA-I, [Βαθαὶ.]   One who returned from the babyloniſh captivity.

BAT'-A-NE, [Βετάνη.]   See *Ecbatana*.

BATH.   A jewiſh meaſure, containing ſeven gallons and an half.

BATH'-AL-ŌTH, [Βασαλώθ.]   One whoſe family returned from the babyloniſh captivity.

BATH-RAB'-BIM.   The name of a tower mentioned in the *ſong of Solomon*.

BATH'-SHE-BA, [Βηροαβεὲ, i. e. *ſeventh daughter, or the daughter of an oath*.]   The wife of *Uriah*, one of king *David*'s generals, whom *David* afterwards married.

BATH'-SHU-A.   See *Bathſheba*.

BATH ZECH-AR-I'-AS, [Βαθζαχαρίας.]   A place where *Judas Maccabæus* encamped againſt *Antiochus Eupator*; not far from *Jeruſalem*.

BA'-VAI, [Βεvεί.]   One of the repairers of *Jeruſalem* after the babyloniſh captivity.

B *before* D.

BDEL'-LI-UM, ['Ανθραξ.]   A reſinous gum, reſembling *myrrh*, brought from the *Levant*.

B *before* E.

BE-AL-I'-AH, ['Βααλιὰ, i. e. *the god of an idol, or in an aſſembly*.]   One who repaired to king *David* at *Ziklag*.

BE'-AL-ŌTH, [Βαλώθ, i. e. *caſt under*.]   A city of *Paleſtine* in the tribe of *Judah*.

BĒ'-AN, [Βαιὰv.]   A people of *Arabia*.

BE'-BA-I, [Βαβαὶ. Βηβαὶ, i. e. *void or empty*.]   One who returned from the babyloniſh captivity.

BECH'-ER, [Βοχὸρ. Βαχὶρ, i. e. *the firſt begotten, or firſt fruits*.]   One of the poſterity of the patriarch *Ephraim*.

BECH-O'-RATH, [Βεχωράθ, i. e. *first fruits.*] The great grandfather of *Kish* the father of king *Saul.*

BEC'-TIL-ETH, [Βαικτιλάιθ.] A place of *Assyria* three days journey from *Nineveh.*

BE'-DAD, [Βαρὰδ, i. e. *alone or solitary.*] The father of *Hadad* a king of *Moab.*

BE-DAI'-AH, [Βαδαία, i. e. *the only Lord.*] One who returned from the babylonish captivity, and had married an heathen wife.

BE'-DAN, [Βαδὰμ, i. e. *door; bar; or alone.*] A conqueror among the *Israelites.*

BE-DEI'-AH. See *Bedaiah.*

BE-EL-I'-A-DA, [Βεελιαδά, i. e. *an open idol.*] One of king *David's* sons. See *Eliada.*

BE-EL'-SA-RUS, [Βεελσάρ⊙.] One who returned from the babylonish captivity.

BE-EL-TETH'-MUS, [Βεελτεθμ⊙.] One of king *Artaxerxes's* court.

BE-EL'-ZEB-UB, [Βεελζεϐὺλ.] See *Baalzebub.*

BE'-ER, [Βαὴρ, i. e. *a well.*] A place in the wilderness through which the Israelites marched—also a city four miles from *Jerusalem.*

BE-E'-RA, [Βεηρά, i. e. *a well; declaring.*] The son of *Zophah,* a descendant from the patriarch *Asher.*

BE-E'-RAH or BE'-RAH, [Βεηρα.] A head of the tribe of *Reuben,* who was carried into captivity by *Tiglath Pileser.*

BE'-ER-E'-LIM, [Αἰλείμ, i. e. *the well of Elim.*] A place mentioned by the prophet *Isaiah.*

BEE'-RI, [Βηρεὶ, i. e. *a well.*] An *Hittite,* father in law to *Esau*—also the father of the prophet *Hosea.*

BE'-ER LA-HAI'-ROI, [Φρέαρ, i. e. *the well of him who lives and sees me.*] A well between *Kadesh* and *Shur,* where *Hagar* the maid of *Sarah* refreshed herself in her flight; when she gave it that name.

BE-E'-ROTH, [Βεηρωθὰ, Βηρὼθ, i. e. *wells or explaining.*] A city of the *Gibeonites,* afterwards in the tribe of *Benjamin* in *Palestine.*

BE-E'-ROTH-ITES, [Βηρωθαῖοι.] The inhabitants of *Beeroth.*

BEER'·

BEER'-SHE-BA, [Βηρσαϐεὲ, i. e. *the well of an oath.*] A city at the fouth extremity of *Paleſtine.*

BE-ESH'-TER-AH, [Βοσοϱὰν.] A city in one of the half tribes of *Manaſſeh*; given to the *Levites.*

BE-HEM'-OTH, [Θηϱία, i. e. *the multitude of earthly beaſts.*] It is much difputed, whether the *Hippopotamus* or *river horſe*, or the *elephant*, is meant by *Behemoth*—the name, in *Hebrew*, fignifies *the* beaſt or *greateſt among beaſts:* if fo, the *river-horſe* will not fupport that title; for it is faid, that in the rivers *Nile* and *Niger*, in *Africa*, they are not bigger than an afs; although *Thevenet* fays, that he faw one at *Cairo* in *Ægypt* as tall as a *camel*, and twice as large as an *ox:* but this was an uncommon phænomenon—but even this doth not equal the fize of a full grown *elephant*; for the common height of an *elephant* is ten feet and an half, and fome of them are twelve feet high, and more—the mountains fupply *him* with food; whereas the *river-horſe* feeds chiefly on fiſh, and never goes far from the river—the *elephant* alfo retires to fhady fenny places to cool himfelf—fome of the *elephants* are called mountaineers; and they are called, the *fen-animal,* by fome of the antients.

BE'-KAH. A jewiſh coin of half a fhekel, about thirteen-pence fterling.

BEL or BA'-AL, [Βὴλ.] See BAAL. *Bel fignifies ancient or vain.* *Bel and the Dragon* is the title of one of the Apocryphal books.

BE'-LA, [Βαλε. Βαλὰκ, i. e. *deſtroying.*] A king of *Edom.*

BE'-LAH, [Βαλὰ, i. e. *deſtroying.*] A fon of the patriarch *Benjamin.*

BE'-LA-ITES. Defcendants from *Belah.*

BE'-LEM-US, [Βήλεμ℈.] One of *Artaxerxes*'s court.

BEL'-GA-I, [Βελγαΐ.] One of the prieſts' family who returned from the babyloniſh captivity.

BEL'-I-AL, [Βελίαλ, i. e. *wicked or worthlefs.*] A term ufed for the devil.

BEL'-MA-IM, [Βελμαὶμ.] A place of *Palestine*, not far from *Bethulia*.

BEL'-MEN, [Βελμεν.] A place in the land of *Palestine*.

BEL-SHAZ'-ZER, [Βαλτάσαρ, i. e. *a searcher of treasure.*] The last king of *Babylon*, grandson to *Nebuchadnezzar*; about A. M. 3466.

BEL-TE-SHAZ'-ZAR, [Βαλτασαρ, i. e. *one who lays up treasures in secret.*] The name given to the prophet *Daniel* at the court of *Nebuchadnezzar*.

BEN, [i. e. *son.*] One of the porters of the temple of *Jerusalem*.

BEN-AI'-AH, [Βαναία, i. e. *the son of the Lord.*] The son of *Jehoiada*, one of king *David*'s worthies, and captain of his guard.

BEN AM'-MI, ['Αμμὰν, i. e. *son of my people.*] The father of the *Ammonites* and grandson to *Lot*.

BEN-E'-BE-RAK, [Βαναιβαχὰτ, i. e. *sons of lightning.*] A place of *Palestine*, situated in the tribe of *Dan*.

BEN-E-JA'-A-KAM, [Βαναία, i. e. *the sons of sorrow.*] A place in the wilderness through which the *Israelites* passed: their *twenty-eighth* encampment.

BEN'-HA-DAD, [Αχαὰβ, i. e. *the son of noise or clamour.*] Two kings of *Syria* of that name; the son was killed by *Hazael*—also a son of *Hazael*.

BEN-HA'-IL, [i. e. *the son of strength.*] One who was sent by king *Jehosaphat* to instruct the people of *Judah*, and to reclaim them from idolatry.

BEN-HA'-NAN, [Φάνα. Αναν, i. e. *the son of grace.*] One of the posterity of the patriarch *Judah*.

BEN'-JA-MIN, [Βενιαμιν, i. e. *son of the right hand.*] The youngest son of the patriarch *Jacob* or *Israel*, by *Rachel*.

BEN-JA-MITES. The descendants from the patriarch *Benjamin*.

BEN-I'-NU, [Βαναία, i. e. *our sons.*] One who joined in covenant with *Nehemiah* to renounce idolatry.

BEN-NU'-I, [Βαννι.] One who had married an heathen wife in the babylonish captivity.

BEN'-O,

BEN'-O, [Βοννὶ, i. e. *his son.*] One of the posterity of the patriarch *Levi.*

BEN-O'-NI, [Βενιαμὶν, i. e. *son of my grief.*] The name given to the patriarch *Benjamin,* by *Rachel* with her last breath, after her delivery of him.

BEN-ZO'-HETH, [Ζωὰν. Ζωχὰϑ, i. e. *the son of separation.*] One of the posterity of the patriarch *Judah.*

BE'-ON, [Βαιὰν, i. e. *in affliction.*] A place in the land of *Palestine.*

BE'-ŌR, [Βεὼϱ, i. e. *burning or mad.*] The father of *Balaam* the soothsayer or prophet—also the father of *Bela.*

BER'-A, [Βαλλα, i. e. *a well or declaring.*] A king of *Sodom,* who lived in the time of the patriarch *Abraham.*

BER'-A-CHAH, [Βεϱχια. Βαϱαχία, i. e. *blessing or bending of the knee.*] One who repaired to king *David* at *Ziklag*—also a valley in the tribe of *Judah.*

BER-A-CHI'-AH, [Βαϱαχία, i. e. *speaking well of the Lord.*] One of the posterity of *Levi*; he was the father of *Asaph.*

BER-A-I'-AH, [Βαϱαϊα, i. e. *the chusing of the Lord.*] One of the posterity of the patriarch *Benjamin.*

BER-E'-A, [Βέϱϱωα. Βεϱέα, i. e. *heavy or weighty.*] A city of *Macedon* in *Greece,* where St. *Paul* preached with success: now *Aleppo.*

BE'-RED, [Βαϱὰδ, i. e. *hail.*] A place mentioned in the book of *Genesis;* in the tribe of *Judah.*

BE'-RI, [Βαϱὶν. Βαϱὶ, i. e. *my son or my corn.*] A descendant from the patriarch *Asher.*

BE-RI'-AH, [Βαϱιὰ, i. e. *in fellowship or envy.*] The son of *Asher* the patriarch, and father of *Heber* and *Malchiel*—also a descendant from *Benjamin.*

BE'-RITES, [i. e. *chosen men.*] A people of *Berim* in *Palestine.*

BER'-ITH, [Βαιϑηλϭεϱὶϑ, i. e. *covenant.*] A deity worshipped by the *Canaanites:*—also an ancestor of *Ezra.*

BER-NI'-

BER-NI'-CE, [Βερνίκη, i. e. *the weight of victory.*] Sister to young *Agrippa* king of the Jews—also others of that name—also cities of that name.

BE-RŌ'-DACH BA'-LA-DAN, [Μαρωδὰχ. Βαλαδάν, i. e. *the son of death.*] A king of *Babylon,* the son of *Baladan,* in king *Hezekiah's* reign.

BE'-RŌTH, [Βηρὼγ.] See *Berothai.*

BE-RO'-THAI, [Βηρωθὶ, i. e. *wells, or a cypress tree.*] A city of *Hadadezer* king of Zobah in *Syria.*

BE-RO'-THATH, [Μααξθηρὰς. Βηρωθαμ, i. e. *of a well.*] One of the cities of *Syria,* which bounded the twelve tribes of *Israel:* supposed to be *Beroth.*

BER'-YL, [Βηρύλλιον.] A pellucid gem of a blueish green colour; it was the *tenth* stone, or the *first* stone in the *fourth* row, in the jewish high priest's breast plate.

BER-ZE'-LUS, [Βερζελλαιός.] One who returned from the babylonish captivity.

BE'-SAI, [Βησὶ. Βασὶ, i. e. *a despising or dirty.*] One of the *Nethinims* or lower order who served at the temple.

BE-SO-DEI'-AH, [Βασωδία, i. e. *the counsel of the Lord.*] The father of *Meshullam.*

BES'-OR, [Βοσὸρ, i. e. *glad news.*] A brook in *Philistia.*

BET'-AH. [Μετεξὰκ, i. e. *confidence.*] A city of *Hadadezer* king of Zobah in *Syria.*

BE'-TEN, [Βαιθὸκ, i. e. *the belly.*] A city of *Canaan,* one of the borders of the tribe of *Asher.*

BĒTH-AB'-A-RA or BĒTH-AB'-A-RAH, [Βηθαβαρᾶ, i. e. *the house of passage.*] A place beyond the river *Jordan* in the tribe of *Reuben,* where *John the baptist* baptized; supposed to be the common ford of the river. *Beth* signifies *house.*

BĒTH'-A-NATH, [Βαιφθαμὶ, i. e. *the house of affliction.*] A city which was one of the borders of the tribe of *Naphtali,* in *Palestine.*

BĒTH'-A-NŌTH, [Βαιθανὰμ.] A city of *Palestine* in the tribe of *Judah* in the mountains.

BĒTH-

BĒTH'-AN-Y, [Βηθανία, i. e. *the house of song or of affliction.*] A city of *Judæa,* at the foot of the mount of *Olives,* about two miles from *Jerusalem:* in the tribe of *Benjamin.*

BĒTH-AR'-A-BAH, [Βαιθάραβα, i. e. *the house of sweet smell.*] A city belonging to the tribe of *Benjamin* in *Palestine*—also a city of *Judah.*

BĒTH-A'-RAM, [Βηθαράμ, i. e. *the house of heighth.*] A city of *Palestine* in the tribe of *Gad.*

BĒTH-AR'-BEL, ['Ιεροβαάλ, i. e. *strong house of ambushment.*] A place of *Armenia* in *Asia.*

BĒTH-A'-VEN, [Βηθαυὲν, i. e. *the house of vanity or of iniquity.*] A city not far from *Ai,* the same with *Bethel,* where *Jeroboam* set up his golden calves. The patriarch *Jacob* called it *Beth-El,* or the house of GOD: but the prophet *Hosea* called it *Beth-Aven.*

BĒTH-AZ'-MA-VĒTH, [Βηθασμώθ, i. e. *the house of death's strength.*] A place mentioned in the book of *Nehemiah.*

BĒTH-BA-AL'-ME-ŌN, [Βεελμών, i. e. *an idol of the dwelling place.*] A city of *Palestine* in the tribe of *Reuben.*

BĒTH-BA'-RA or BĒTH-BA'-RAH, [Βαιθβηρὰ, i. e. *the chosen house.*] A place beyond the river *Jordan,* supposed to be *Bethabara.*

BĒTH-BA'-SI, [Βαιθβασὶ.] A city of *Palestine* in the tribe of *Judah.*

BĒTH-BI'-RE-I, [Βηθβαρεῖ, i. e. *the house or temple of my Creator.*] A city of *Palestine,* in the tribe of *Simeon.*

BĒTH'-CAR, [Βαιθχός, i. e. *the house of the lamb, or of knowledge.*] A city of the *Philistines,* in the tribe of *Dan.*

BĒTH DA'-GŌN, [Βηθδαγὼν, i. e. *the house of corn or of fish, or of Dagon.*] A city of *Palestine* in the tribe of *Judah* in the valley—another in *Dan.*

BĒTH DIB-LA-THA'-IM, [Δαιθλαθαίμ, i. e. *the house of dry figs.*] A city in the land of *Canaan.*

BĒTH-ĒL, [Βαιθήλ, i. e. *the house of God.*] A city of the land of *Canaan* in the tribe of *Benjamin,* so named by the patriarch *Jacob*: it was formerly called *Luz*.

BĒTH'-ĒL-ITE. An inhabitant of *Bethel*.

BĒTH'-E-MEK, [Σαρϑαιϐαιϑμὲ, i. e. *the houſe of deep-neſs.*] A city of *Paleſtine* in the tribe of *Aſher*.

BĒTH'-ĒR, [Βάθηρ, i. e. *diviſion*.] A mountainous country mentioned in *Solomon's* ſong.

BĒTH-ES'-DA, [Βηθεσδὰ, i. e. *the houſe of effuſion, or of pity, or of mercy*.] The name of a medicinal pool, ſituate near the ſheep market in *Jeruſalem*.

BĒTH-E'-ZEL, [i. e. *the houſe of ſeparation in the Hebrew idiom*.] The ſame place with *Bethel*.

BĒTH GAD'-ĒR, [Βεθγεδὼρ, i. e. *a houſe for a mouſe*.] One of the poſterity of *Caleb*.

BĒTH GA'-MŪL, [Γαιμὼλ, i. e. *the houſe of a camel*.] A city of the *Moabites* in the tribe of *Reuben*.

BĒTH HAC'-CE-REM, [Βηϑαχχαρὶμ, i. e. *the houſe the vineyard*.] Part of the city of *Jeruſalem* ſo called.

BĒTH HA'-RAN, [Βαιθαϱὰν, i. e. *the houſe of a hill*.] A fenced city of *Gilead* in the tribe of *Gad*.

BĒTH HOG'-LAH, [Βαιϑαῖλαάμ.] A city of *Paleſ-tine*, in the tribe of *Benjamin*.

BĒTH HO'-RŌN, [Ὡρωνὶν. Βαιϑωρὼν, i. e. *the houſe of wrath or of liberty*.] The name of two cities in the tribe of *Ephraim*.

BĒTH JES-I'-MŌTH, [Βαιτϑασϵινὼϑ, i. e. *the houſe of deſolation*.] A city of *Paleſtine*, in the tribe of *Reuben*: afterwards poſſeſſed by the *Moabites*.

BĒTH-LEB'-A-ŌTH, [Βαϑαρὼθ, i. e. *the houſe of lion-eſſes*.] A city of *Paleſtine* in the tribe of *Simeon*: ſometimes called *Lebaoth*.

BĒTH'-LE-HEM, [Βηθλεέμ, i. e. *the houſe of bread or of war*.] A city of *Paleſtine* in the tribe of *Judah*, where our *Saviour* was born; about ſix miles from *Jeruſalem*. It is ſometimes called *Ephrath* or *Ephratah*—alſo a city of the ſame name in the tribe of *Zebulun*.

BĒTH'-LE-HEM EPH'-RA-TAH, [Βηϑλεέμ Ἐϕραϑὰ.] The city of *Bethlehem*.

BĒTH.

BĒTH'-LE-HEM JU'-DAH, [Βηϑλεὶμ 'Ιϐδα.] The
same city with *Bethlehem Ephratah.*

BĒTH'-LE-HEM-ITE, [Βηϑλεεμίτης.] An inhabitant of *Bethlehem.*

BĒTH-LO'-MŌN, [Βαιϐλωμῶν.] One whofe family
returned from the babylonifh captivity.

BĒTH-MA'-AC-AH, [Βεϑμαχὰ, i. e. *houfe of bruifing.*]
A city of *Palefline.*

BĒTH-MAR'-CA-BŌTH, [Βαιϐμαρχαϐὰθ, i. e. *the
houfe of bitternefs wiped out.*] A city of *Palefline* in
the tribe of *Simeon.*

BĒTH-ME'-ŌN, [Μαὼν, i. e. *the houfe of the dwelling
place.*] A city of the *Moabites,* in the tribe of
Reuben.

BĒTH-NIM'-RAH, [Βαινϑαναϐρὰ. Ναμρὰμ, i. e. *the
houfe of rebellion.*] A fenced city of the tribe of
Gad, in the land of *Gilead.*

BĒTH-O'-RŌN, [Βαιθωρὼν, i. e. *the houfe of anger or of
liberty.*] A city of the Levites in *Palefline.*

BĒTH'-PA-LET, [Βαιφαλάθ, i. e. *the houfe of expul-
fion.*] A city of *Palefline,* in the moft fouthern
part of the tribe of *Judah.*

BĒTH-PAZ'-ZĒZ, [Βηϑφασῆς, i. e. *the houfe of dividing afunder.*] A city of *Palefline,* one of the
borders of the tribe of *Naphtali.*

BĒTH PE'-ŌR, [Φογὰρ, i. e. *the houfe of gaping or
opening.*] A city of *Moab,* given to the tribe of
Reuben: it is called *Rehob.*

BĒTH'-PHA-GE, [Βηϑφαγῆ, i. c. *the houfe of early
figs.*] A village of the priefts in *Palefline,* on
mount *Olivet,* about one mile from *Jerufalem.*

BĒTH'-PHE-LET, [Βαιφαλάθ.] See *Bethpalet.*

BĒTH'-RA-BAH. See *Betbarabah.*

BĒTH'-RAPH-A, [Βαιθρεφα, i. e. *the houfe of health.*]
One of the pofterity of *Judah,* fon of the patriarch *Jacob.*

BĒTH RE'-HOB, [Βαιθραὰμ Βεθρααβ, i. e. *houfe of
liberty.*] A city of *Syria,* poffeffed by the *Danites.*

BĒTH-SA'-I-DA, [Βηϑσαῖδα, i. e. *the houfe of fruits,
or of hunters, or of fnares.*] A village of *Galilee*
in *Palefline,* on the lake of *Gennefareth,* in the
tribe

tribe of *Naphtali*: *Philip* the tetrarch named it *Julia*, in honour to *Julia* the daughter of *Julius Cæsar*.

BĒTH'-SA-MŌS, [Βαιθασμὼν.] A place in the land of *Paleſtine*. See *Bethſhemeſh*.

BĒTH'-SHAN or BĒTH-SHĒ'-AN, [Βαιθσὰν, i. e. *the houſe of ivory, or of change, or of ſleep*.] A city of the *Philiſtines*, in the half tribe of *Manaſſeh*, about twenty miles from *Jeruſalem*.

BĒTH'-SHE-MĒSH, [Βαιθσαμὼς, i. e. *the houſe of the ſun, or of ſervice*.] Three cities of *Paleſtine*, one in the tribe of *Aſher*; another in the tribe of *Naphtali*; another in the tribe of *Dan*.

BĒTH SHIT'-TAH, [Βηθσεὲδ, i. e. *houſe of thorns*.] A place belonging to the *Midianites*.

BĒTH'-SI-MŌS. See *Bethſhemeſh*.

BĒTH TAP-PU'-A, [Βαιθαχὺ, i. e. *houſe of an apple tree*.] A city and mountain of *Paleſtine* in the inheritance of *Judah*.

BĒTH-SU'-RA, [Βηθσὰρ, Βεθσὴρα.] See *Bethzur*.

BĒTH-U'-ĒL, [Βαθυὴλ, i. e. *filiation of God*.] The ſon of *Nahor* and *Milcah*; *Abraham*'s nephew, and father to *Laban*, and to *Rebecca*, *Iſaac*'s wife.

BĒTH'-ŪL or BĒTH-Ū-LI'-A, [Βυλὰ. Βεῖυλὰα, i. e. *the virgin of the Lord*.] A city of *Paleſtine*, in the tribe of *Simeon*.

BĒTH'-ZŌR, [Βηθσὰρ. Βεθσὴρα.] See *Bethzur*.

BĒTH-ZŪR, [Βηθσὰρ. Βεθσὴρα, i. e. *the houſe of a rock*.] A mountain or fortreſs of *Paleſtine*, in the tribe of *Judah*, about twenty miles ſouth from *Jeruſalem* —alſo a man's name.

BET-OL-I'-US, [Βετολιῶ.] A place in the land of *Paleſtine*.

BET-OM-EST'-HAM, [Βετομεθαὶμ.] A city of *Paleſtine*, in the tribe of *Judah*.

BET'-O-NIM, [Βοῖανὶμ, i. e. *bellies*.] A city of *Paleſtine*, in the tribe of *Gad*.

BE-U'-LAH, [i. e. *inhabited*.] An Hebrew word ſignifying married.

BE'-ZAI, [Βηοὶ. Βασὸς, i. e. *eggs*.] The name of one who returned from the babyloniſh captivity.

BEZ-AL'-

BEZ-AL'-E-ĒL, [Βεσελεήλ, i. e. *in the shadow of God.*] The principal artificer of the tabernacle.

BEZ'-EK, [Βεζὲκ, i. e. *lightening, or in the chains or fetters.*] A city of the *Canaanites*, in the tribe of *Judah.*

BEZ'-ER or BOZ'-RA, [Βοσὸξ. Βασὴν, i. e. *munition, or vine branches.*] One of the posterity of *Asher* the son of *Jacob*—also a city of refuge beyond *Jordan* in the tribe of *Reuben.*

BE'-ZETH, [Βηζὲθ.] A city of *Palestine* on the west side of the river *Jordan.*

B *before* I.

BI'-A-TAS, [Βιάτας.] A *Levite* who returned from the babylonish captivity.

BICH'-RI, [Βοχορι, i. e. *first born, or first fruits.*] A *Benjamite*, the father of *Sheba.*

BID'-KAR, [Βαδεκὰρ, i. e. *in compunction, or sharp pain.*] One of *Jehu's* captains.

BIG'-THA or BIG'-THAN or BIG'-THA-NA, [Βαγαθὰ, i. e. *giving meat.*] One of the seven chamberlains to king *Ahasuerus.*

BIG-VA'-I, [Βαγυὰ. Βογυὶα, i. e. *in my body.*] The name of two men who returned from the babylonish captivity.

BIL'-DAD, [Βαλδαδ, i. e. *old friendship or old love.*] One of *Job's* three friends, a *Shuhite*, supposed to be an *Arabian.*

BI'-LE-AM, ['Ιεμβλάαν, i. e. *the antient of the people; the devourer.*] A city of the *Moabites* on the other side of *Jordan;* then, a city of the *Levites* in the half tribe of *Manasseh.*

BIL'-GAH, [Βελγὰς, i. e. *antient countenance.*] The name of one of the *Levites.*

BIL-GA'-I, [Βελγαὶ.] One of the princes who returned from the babylonish captivity.

BIL'-HA or BIL'-HAH, [Βαλλὰ, i. e. *who is old, troubled, or confused.*] One of the handmaids of *Rachel*; and *Jacob's* wife—also a place.

BIL'-HAN,

BIL'-HAN, [Βαλααν, i. e. *old; troubled.*] A fon of *Ezar*, a defcendant from the patriarch *Efau*—alfo a fon of *Jediael* a defcendant from the patriarch *Benjamin*.

BIL'-SHAN, [Βαλσαν, i. e. *in the tongue.*] One who returned from the babylonifh captivity.

BIM'-HAL, [Βαμαηλ.] One of the pofterity of the patriarch *Afher*.

BI'-NE-A, [Βαανα, i. e. *the fon of the Lord.*] One of the pofterity of king *Saul*.

BIN-NU'-I, [Βανυῖ, i. e. *building.*] A *Levite* who returned from the babylonifh captivity, and who had married an heathen wife.

BIR'-SHA, [Βαρσα, i. e. *in evil.*] One of the kings of *Gomorrah*.

BIR'-ZA-VITH, [Βερθαιθ.] One of the pofterity of the patriarch *Afher*.

BISH'-LAM. One of the Jews who wrote to *Artaxerxes* king of *Perfia*, about building the temple of *Jerufalem*.

BITH-I'-AH, [Βεθθια. Βεθια, i. e. *daughter of the Lord.*] An *Ifraelitifh* woman, of the tribe of *Judah*.

BITH'-RON, [i. e. *divifion, or daughter of the fong.*] A place of *Palefline*, on the eaft fide of the river *Jordan*.

BI-THYN'-I-A, [Βιθυνια, i. e. *violent precipitation.*] A large country of *Afia Minor*, bounded north by the *Euxine Sea*.

BI-ZI-JOTH-I'-AH or BIZ-JOTH-I'-JAH, [i. e. *defpite.*] A place in *Palefline*, in the tribe of *Judah*.

BIZ'-THA, [Βαθαζ. Βαζαν, i. e. *defpite.*] One of king *Ahafuerus*'s feven chamberlains.

B *before* L.

BLAS'-TUS, [Βλαστ⊕·, i. e. *one who fprouts and brings forth.*] Chamberlain to *Herod*, king of *Judæa*.

B *before* O.

BO-A-NER'-GES, [Βοανεργὲς, i: e. *fons of thunder.*] The name given to *James* and *John* the fons of *Zebedee*, on account of their requeſt to our *Saviour* to call down fire from Heaven on certain villages of the *Samaritans* which refuſed to entertain him.

BO'-AZ or BO'-OZ, [Βοὸζ, i. e. *in ſtrength.*] The ſon of *Salmon* and *Rahab* and the huſband of *Ruth* —alſo the left pillar of the porch of the temple of *Jeruſalem*, called *Boaz*.

BOC'-CAS, [Βοκχὰ.] An anceſtor of *Eſdras*.

BO'-CHE-RU, [Βωχρῦ, i. e. *firſt born.*] One of king *Saul's* poſterity.

BO'-CHIM, [i. e. *the place of weeping, or of mourning, or of mulberry-trees.*] A place near to *Jeruſalem*.

BO'-HAN, [Βαιὰν, i. e. *in them.*] One of the ſons of the patriarch *Reuben*.

BOS'-CATH, [Βασυκὼθ, i. e. *in poverty.*] A place of *Paleſtine*, in the tribe of *Judah*, in the valley.

BOS'-OR, [Βοσόρ, i. e. *taking away.*] The father of *Balaam* the ſoothſayer—alſo a city of *Gilead*.

BOS'-OR-A, [Βόσσορα.] A river and city of *Paleſtine*.

BOS'-RAH, [Βοσρὰ. Βοσὸρ, i. e. *in tribulation or diſtreſs.*] The metropolis of *Idumæa* in *Aſia*, in the half tribe of *Manaſſeh*.

BOZ'-EZ, [Βαοες. Βοζής, i. e. *dirt.*] The name of a rock in the land of *Paleſtine*.

BOZ'-RAH, [Βοσρὰ. Βοσὸρ. Βοσόῤῥας.] See *Beſrah*.

B *before* R.

BRIG-AN-DINE'. A coat of mail.

B *before* U.

BUK'-KI, [Βαχὶ. Βοκχὶ, i. e. *void.*] An high prieſt of the Jews, the ſon of *Abiſhua* and father of *Uzzi*.

BUK-KI'-AH [Βαχὶε. Βουκίας, i. e. *the diffipation of the Lord.*] One of the muficians of the temple of *Jerufalem*.

BUL, [Βαὰλ, i. e. *changeable or perifhing.*] The eighth month of the jewifh *ecclefiaftical* or fecond month of their *civil year*, now called *Mar-fchevan*, anfwering to part of our *October* and *November*.

BU'-NAH, [Βααvà. Βuvà, i. e. *building or underftanding.*] One of the pofterity of the patriarch *Judah*.

BUN'-NI, [Βοvvᾶ, i. e. *building me.*] A Levite who returned from the babylonifh captivity.

BŪZ, [Βuζ, i. e. *defpifed or plundered.*] A nephew to the patriarch *Abraham*.

BU'-ZI, [Βuζεὶ, i. e. *my contempt.*] A jewifh prieft, the father of the prophet *Ezekiel*.

BŪZ'-ITE. A defcendant of *Buz*.

C.

C before A.

CAB. An *hebrew* meafure of capacity, containing about two Englifh pints.

CAB'-BON, [Χαββὰv. Χαβρà, i. e. *as though under-ftanding.*] A city of *Palefline* in the tribe of *Judah* in the valley.

CAB'-HAM. A palace of *Palefline* in the tribe of *Judah*.

CA'-BUL, [Χωβαμασομèλ, i. e. *difpleafing or dirty.*] The name which *Hiram*, king of *Tyre*, gave to the twenty cities given him by king *Solomon*; *Hiram* not liking them, called them *Cabul*.

                    CAD'-DIS,

CAD'-DIS, [Καδδὶς.] A name of *Joannes* the fon of *Mattathias* in the hiſtory of the *Maccabees*.

CA'-DĒS, [Καδὴς, i. e. *holineſs*.] A place in *Galilee* in *Judæa*, in the tribe of *Iſſachar*.

CA'-DĒSH. See *Kadeſh*.

CÆ'-SAR, [Καισαρ, i. e. *a cut or gaſh*.] The general title of the *Roman* emperors.

CÆ-SAR-Æ'-A, [Καισαρεία, i. e. *a buſh of hair*.] A place near the borders of *Philippi*, in *Macedonia* in *Aſia*: now *Caiſar*.

CÆ-SAR-Æ'-A PHI-LIP'-PI, [Καισαρεία Φιλίππȣ.] A city of *Paleſtine*, ſo named by *Philip* the tetrarch after the Roman emperor and himſelf: it was called *Leſhem* and *Laiſh* by the *Canaanites*, but when the children of *Dan* took it, it was called *Dan*; it was alſo called *Paneas*, from the mountain beneath which it ſtood.

CA-I'-A-PHAS, [Καϊαφας, i. e. *a ſearcher*.] The high prieſt of the Jews at the time of our *Saviour's* death.

CA'-IN, [Καὶν, i. e. *poſſeſſion*.] The ſon of *Adam* who ſlew his brother *Abel*—alſo the name of a city of *Paleſtine*, in the tribe of *Judah* in the mountains.

CA-I'-NAN, [Καὶνᾶν, i. e. *poſſeſſor, or purchaſer, or one who laments*.] The ſon of *Enos* the patriarch, died A. M. 1235, Æt. 910.

CAI'-RITES. A ſect of Jews who adhered ſolely to the Scriptures.

CA'-LAH, [Χαλὰχ, i. e. *favourable, or as green fruit*.] A city of *Paleſtine*, in the tribe of *Aſher*.

CAL'-A-MUS, [Καλάμ☉, i. e. *ſweet*.] It is called *ſweet cane* by the prophet *Jeremiah*—it is a ſpicy root, belonging to a ruſh or flag.

CAL'-COL, [Καλχὰλ, i. e. *nouriſhing; or as conſuming all things*.] A ſon of *Zerah* a deſcendant from the patriarch *Judah*. See *Chalcol*.

CAL'-DEES, [Καλδαὶοι, i. e. *mingling, or as devils*.] Subjects of *Nebuchadnezzar* king of *Babylon*.

CA'-LEB, [Χάλεβ, i. e. *a dog, crow, baſket, or the heart*.] A famous *jewiſh* warrior, of the tribe of

Judah, in *Palestine*—also a place in *Palestine*, in the tribe of *Judah*.

CA'-LEB EPH'-RA-TAH, [Χαλὲβ 'Εφραθά.] A place of *Palestine*, in the tribe of *Ephraim*; so called from *Caleb* and his wife *Ephrata*.

CAL-IS'-THEN-ĒS, [Καλλισθένης.] One of the king of *Syria's* officers in the time of the *Maccabees*.

CAL'-I-TAS, [Καλιτὰς.] A *Levite* who returned from the babylonish captivity.

CAL-A-MO'-LA-LUS, [Καλαμωλάλ⊚.] One whose family returned from the babylonish captivity.

CAL'-NĒH, [Χαλάννη, i. e. *our consummation, or as murmuring.*] A city in the land of *Shinar*, built by *Nimrod*.

CAL'-NO, [Χαλάννη, i. e. *our consummation, or altogether himself.*] A place by the river *Euphrates* in *Asia*.

CAL'-PHI, [Χαλφὸς.] The father of *Judas* in the *Apocrypha*.

CAL'-VA-RY, [i. e. *the place of a skull.*] An hill to the north mount of *Zion*, and without the walls of *Jerusalem*, where criminals were executed: in *hebrew* it is called *Golgotha*, from its likeness to a skull or a man's head, as is supposed.

CAM-BY'-SĒS, [Καμβύσης.] The son and successor of *Cyrus* king of *Persia*, who is the *Ahasuerus* mentioned by *Ezra*.

CAM'-ĒL, [Κάμηλ⊚.] A large quadruped, of several species — the *Camel*, which is the largest size, chews the cud, but divides not the hoof—he has a stomach to hold water, which, by a contraction of its muscles, he can throw into his stomach which contains its dry food; and by means of the first mentioned stomach he is able to travel through the sandy deserts of *Africa* and *Asia*, for a long time, without a fresh supply of water—he is covered with a fine fur, shorter and softer than that of the ox-kind—he hath two bunches on his back; and about the bunches there grow hairs near a foot long—it is an excellent beast of burden, and some of them will carry *twelve* or *thirteen hundred pounds'* weight on their backs; for which load he kneels, being *seven* or *eight* feet high, or more—they travel flowly; though there is a fpecies of them very fwift.

The *Dromedary* is of the camel-kind, but hath only one bunch on his back.

CAM'-ŌN, [Ραμνών. Κάμων, i. e. *his refurrection*.] A place in the land of *Gilead*.

CAMP or EN-CAMP'-MENT of the *Ifraelites*.

The encampments of the *Ifraelites* muft have been a grand piece of fcenery. The whole body of the people, confifting of *fix hundred thoufand* fighting men, befides women and children, was difpofed under *four* battalions, fo placed as to enclofe the *tabernacle*, in the form of a fquare, and each under one general ftandard. Military men, well verfed in tacticks, admire their method of encampment, which was firft imitated by the *Greeks* and afterwards by the *Romans*.

There were *forty-one* encampments from their *firft* (in the month of *March*) at *Ramefes* in the land of *Gofhen* in *Ægypt*, and in the *wildernefs*, until they reached the land of *Canaan:* they are thus enumerated in the *thirty-third* chapter of *Numbers*.

1. At *Ramefes*.	14. *Hazeroth*.
2. *Succoth*.	15. *Rithmah*.
3. *Etham* on the edge of the wildernefs.	16. *Rimmon-parez*.
	17. *Libnah*.
4. *Pihahiroth*.	18. *Riffah*.
5. *Marah*.	19. *Kehelathah*.
6. *Elim*.	20. *Shapher*.
7. By the *Red Sea*.	21. *Haradah*.
8. *Wildernefs* of *Sin*,	22. *Makheloth*.
9. *Dophkah*.	23. *Tahath*.
10. *Alufh*.	24. *Tarah*.
11. *Rephidim*.	25. *Mithcah*.
12. *Wildernefs* of *Sinai*.	26. *Hafhmonah*.
13. *Kibroth-hattaavah*.	27. *Moferoth*.

28. *Bene-*

28. *Bene-jaakan.*	35. *Zalmonah.*
29. *Hor-hagidgad.*	36. *Punon.*
30. *Jotbathah.*	37. *Oboth.*
31. *Ebronah.*	38. *Ije-abarim.*
32. *Ezion-gaber.*	39. *Dibon-gad.*
33. *Kadeſh* or the wilder-	40. *Almon-diblathaim.*
neſs of *Sin.*	41. Mountains of *Abarim.*
34. Mount *Hor.*	

In the ſecond year after their *Exodus* from
Ægypt, they were numbered; and, upon an exact
poll, the number of their males amounted to
ſix hundred and three thouſand, five hundred, and
fifty, from *twenty* years old and upwards.

CA'-NA, [Κανᾶ, i.e. *zeal or emulation.*] A ſmall
town of *Galilee* in *Paleſtine,* in the tribe of *Zebulun,* where our *Saviour* performed his firſt miracle:
it is called *Cana* of *Galilee,* to diſtinguiſh it from
Cana in the tribe of *Aſher.*

CA'-NA-AN, [Χαναάν, i.e. *a merchant or trader.*] The
ſon of *Ham, Noah's ſon*—alſo a country, called
alſo *Paleſtine,* bounded on the eaſt by the river
Jordan, on the weſt by the Mediterranean ſea, on
the ſouth by the deſarts of *Arabia,* and on the north
by mount *Libanus,* about 180 miles in length, and
about 130 miles in breadth.

CA'-NA-AN-ITES, [Χαναναῖοι.] The antient inhabitants of the land of *Canaan.*

CAN'-DA-CĒ, [Κανδάκη, i.e. *who poſſeſſes contrition,
or pure poſſeſſion.*] A queen of *Æthiopia,* whoſe
eunuch was converted by *Philip* the deacon.

CAN'-NEH, [Χανναὰ, i.e. *a wall.*] A city in the
land of *Shinar,* and is ſuppoſed to be the ſame
with *Calno.*

CAN'-TI-CLES, [Ἄσμα, i.e. *a ſong.*] A canonical
book of the Old Teſtament, called the *ſong of
ſongs,* or *Solomon's ſong,* as allowed to be com-
poſed by king *Solomon.*

CAN'-VEH, [Χανναὰ.] See *Canneh.*

CA-PER'-NA-ŪM, [Καπέρναμμ, i.e. *the field of repen-
tance, or city of comfort.*] A place of *Paleſtine,* on
the

the borders of the tribes of *Zebulun* and *Naphtali*; the place where our *Saviour* ufually refided during his miniftry.

CA*-*PHAR-SAL*'*-A-MA, [Χαφαρσαλαμά.] A place near to *Jerufalem*.

CA-PHEN*'*-A-THA, [Χαφεναθά.] A part of the city of *Jerufalem*, fo called.

CAPH-I*'*-RA, [Κεφιρὰ. Καφειρας.] See *Chephirah*.

CAPH*'*-TOR, [Καππαδοκές, i. e. *a fphere, hand, doves, or thofe who inquire.*] An ifland from whence came the *Caphtorims*, or *Cherithims*, or *Cherithites*, or *Philiftines*: fuppofed to be the ifle of *Crete*.

CAPH*'*-TOR-IM, [Καφθοριεῖμ.] A fon of *Mifraim*.

CAPH*'*-TOR-IMS, [Καππαδοκες.] *Philiftines* who fettled in *Caphtor*.

CAP-PA-DOC*'*-I-A, [Καππαδοκία, i. e. *an apple; a violet.*] A large country of *Afia Minor*.

CAP-TIV*'*-ITY. There were *fix* captivities of the *Hebrews* during the government of the *Judges*: the firft under *Cufhanrifhathaim* king of *Mefopotamia*, for about eight years. The fecond, under *Eglon* king of *Moab*, from which *Ehud* delivered them. The third, under the *Philiftines*, from which *Shamgar* refcued them. The fourth, under *Jabin* king of *Hazor*, when *Deborah* and *Barak* delivered them. The fifth, under the *Midianites* from which they were freed by *Gideon*. The fixth, under the *Ammonites* and *Philiftines* during the judicatures of *Jephthah*, *Ibzan*, *Elon*, *Abdon*, *Eli*, *Samfon*, and *Samuel*.

The moft remarkable captivities were, firft, when *Tiglath-pilefer*, king of *Affyria*, A. M. 3264 or 740 years B. C. took feveral cities of *Ifrael* and made many captives, chiefly from the tribes of *Reuben*, *Gad* and the half tribe of *Manaffeh*. The fecond, when *Shalmanezer*, king of *Affyria*, A. M. 3283 and about 720 years B. C. who tranfplanted the tribes which *Tiglath-pilefer* had fpared, to the provinces beyond the *Euphrates*; and it is

fuppofed

ſuppoſed that the ten tribes never returned from their diſperſion.

As to the captivity of *Judah*; *Shiſhak*, king of *Egypt* about 960 years B. C. ſacked *Jeruſalem*.

Jeruſalem was taken and plundered three ſeveral times, by *Nebuchadnezzar* king of *Babylon*; firſt, in the reign of *Jehoiakim*, about 606 years B. C. Secondly, in the reign of his ſon *Jehoia=chin* or *Jeconias*, about 598 years B. C. Thirdly, in the reign of *Zedekiah*, about 587 years B. C. when *Nebuchadnezzar* carried them to *Babylon*, where they remained ſeventy years, when they returned from their captivity, and continued to be a people (though part of the time under the Roman government) until *Veſpaſian*, the Roman emperor, under his ſon *Titus*, entirely deſtroyed *Jeruſalem*, about 40 years after the crucifixion of our *Saviour*; ſince when they have not, as yet, recovered from their diſperſion.

CAR-A-BA'-SI-ŌN, [Καραβασιων.] One who returned from the babyloniſh captivity.

CAR'-BUNC-LE, [Σμαραγδ .] A gem of a deep red colour with a mixture of ſcarlet: it was the *third* ſtone, in the *firſt* row in the jewiſh high prieſt's breaſt plate.

CAR'-CHA-MIS, [Χαρχαμὸς.] See CARCHEMISH.

CAR'-CHE-MISH, [Χαρμεῖς, i. e. *a lamb carried off.*] A town of *Meſopotamia*, by the river *Euphrates* in *Aſia*.

CA-RE'-AH, [Καρήθ. Καρηὲ, i. e. *bald*; *ice.*] The father of *Johanan* who joined with *Gedaliah*, and was made a governor in *Judah* by *Nebuchadnezzar* king of *Babylon*.

CA'-RI-A, [Καρια.] A province of *leſſer Aſia*, which ſubmitted to the *Romans* under *Antiochus*, about 198 years B. C.—now *Palatſchia.*

CAR'-KAS, ['Αχαρβὰς, i. e. *the covering of the lamb, or the lamb of the throne.*] The name of one of the ſeven chamberlains to king *Ahaſuerus.*

CAR-MA'-

CAR-MA'-NI-ANS. A people of *Carmania*, a province of *Persia*.

CAR'-ME, [Χαρμὴ.] A prieſt who returned from the babyloniſh captivity with his family.

CAR'-MEL, [Χέρμελ, i. e. *knowledge of circumciſion, harveſt, or excellent vineyard.*] A city and mountain in the ſouth of *Paleſtine*, in the tribe of *Judah*, in *Galilee*, near the Mediterranean ſea: the mountain about thirty miles in circuit.

CAR'-MEL-ITE, [Καρμέλι®.] The inhabitants of *Carmel*.

CAR'-MEL-I-TESS. A woman of *Carmel: Abigail* the wife of *Nabal* was a *Carmeliteſs*.

CAR'-MI, [Χάρμι, i. e. *my vineyard, or the lamb of the waters.*] A ſon of the patriarch *Reuben*.

CAR'-MITES. A people who deſcended from *Carmi*, a ſon of the patriarch *Reuben*.

CAR'-NA-IM, [Καρναῖν, i. e. *horns.*] A city of *Gilead* conquered by *Judas Maccabæus*.

CAR'-PUS, [Κάρπ®, i. e. *fruit, or fruitful.*] A convert of the apoſtle *Paul*, who dwelt at *Troas*.

CAR-SHE'-NA, [Αρχεσαἰ®, i. e. *a lamb ſleeping.*] A principal officer in the palace of king *Ahaſuerus*.

CA-SIPH'-I-A, [Κασφιέ, i. e. *money, or covetouſneſs.*] Suppoſed to be *Caſpi* or *Caſpius* in *Parthia*, near the *Caſpian* ſea.

CAS'-LEU. See *Chiſleu*.

CAS-LU'-BIM, [Κασλωνιὲμ, i. e. *hopes of life, or as pardoned.*] A deſcendant from *Ham* the ſon of *Noah*.

CAS-PHOR, [Χασφώρ.] A city of *Gilead*.

CAS'-PIS or CAS'-PHIN, [Κάσπις.] A ſtrong city of *Syria*, on the eaſt ſide of the river *Jordan*.

CAS'-SIA. An aromatic bark, ſaid to be like the bark of cinnamon.

CAS'-TOR and POL'-LUX. Sons of *Jupiter* and *Leda*, in the heathen mythology; to whom ſeamen paid their particular devotions, as governors of the ſea.

CATH-U'-A, [Καθυὰ.] One whoſe family returned from the babyloniſh captivity, and his ſons ſervants of the temple.

C *before* E.

CED'-RŌN, [Κέδρων, i. e. *black or sad.*] A brook between *Jerusalem* and mount *Olivet*.

CEI'-LAN, [Κιλὰν, i. e. *dissolving that.*] One whose family returned from the babylonish captivity.

CEL-E-MI'-A. A scribe mentioned in the *second* book of *Esdras*.

CEN'-CHRE-A, [Κεγχρεαί, i. e. *millet, small pulse.*] A sea port town of *Corinth*, in the Archipelago of *Greece*.

CEN-DEB-E'-US, [Κενδεϭαῖος, i. e. *possession of grief.*] A general of the troops of *Antiochus Sidetes* king of *Syria*.

CEN-TU'-RI-ON, [Εκατονϊαρχ῀.] A *Roman* officer commanding an hundred soldiers.

CE'-PHAS, [Κηφᾶς, i. e. *a rock or stone.*] The name given by our *Saviour* to St. *Peter*.

CE'-RAS, [Κηρὰς.] One whose sons were servants to the temple.

CE'-TEB, [Κητάϭ.] One whose sons were servants to the temple.

C *before* H.

CHAB'-RIS, [Χάϭρις.] One who was a governor of *Bethulia*.

CHA'-DI-AS, [Χαδίας.] A place mentioned in the *first book of Esdras*, chap. v. ver. 20.

CHÆ'-RE-AS, [Χαιρεας.] A governor of *Gazara*, in the *Apocrypha*.

CHAL-CE-DO'-NY, [Χαλκηδών.] A precious stone of a flame colour.

CHAL'-COL, [Χαλκάλ, i. e. *who nourishes, consumes, and sustains the whole.*] A grand-son of the patriarch *Judah*.

CHAL-DE'-A, [Χαλδαία, i. e. *as dæmons, robbers, breasts, or fields.*] A country of *Asia*, known antiently by the name of *Shinar* or *Shinaar*; its metropolis was *Babylon*: now *Irac-Arabi*.

CHAL-

CHAL-DÆ'-ANS, [Χαλδαίοι.] The inhabitants of *Chaldæa.*

CHA-MOIS'. Suppofed to be the *Arabian goat,* called the *mountain goat.*

CHA'-NĒS. See *Hanes.*

CHAN-NU-NE'-US, [Χαννναῖ©.] One whofe family returned from the babylonifh captivity.

CHA-RA-ATH'-A-LAR, [Χάρααθαλὰϱ.] One whofe family returned from the babylonifh captivity.

CHA'-RA-CA, [Χάραϰα.] A city of *Paleftine* in the tribe of *Gad.*

CHA'-RA-SIM, [Χαραοιμ, i. e. *craftfman.*] A valley in the land of *Judæa.*

CHAR'-CŪS, [Χαϱϰύς.] One whofe fons returned from the babylonifh captivity, and were fervants of the temple.

CHA'-RE-A, [Χαρὲα, i. e. *bald or cold.*] One whofe family returned from the babylonifh captivity.

CHARM'-ER. Suppofed to be one who is an aftrologer or confulter of the ftars, in order to divination or foretelling future events.

CHAR'-MIS, [Χαρμις.] One who was a governor of *Bethulia.*

CHAR'-RAN, [Χαῤῥάν, i. e. *a finging or calling out, or the heat of wrath.*] The country of *Mefopotamia* in *Afia.*

CHA-SEB'-A, [Χασεϐὰ.] One whofe family returned from the babylonifh captivity, and his fons fervants of the temple.

CHEB'-AR, [Χοϐὰϱ, i. e. *ftrength or power.*] A river of *Chaldæa.*

CHED-ER-LA'-OM-ER, [Χοδολογομὸϱ, i. e. *a generation of fervitude, or the roundnefs of the fheaf.*] A king of the *Elamites* bordering upon *Perfia* in *Afia.*

CHEL'-AL, [Χαλὴλ, i. e. *as night.*] A fon of *Pahath-Moab.*

CHEL'-CI-AS, [Χελϰίος, i. e. *the portion, or gentlenefs of the Lord.*] The father of *Sufanna,* in the Apocrypha.

CHEL'-

CHEL'-LŪB, [Χαλώβ, i. e. *all.*] One who returned from the babylonifh captivity.

CHEL'-ŌD, [Χελεϐλ.] One mentioned in the book of *Judith.*

CHEL'-ŪB, [Χελϐβ, i. e. *a bafket.*] A defcendant from the patriarch *Afher.*

CHEL'-LI-ANS, [Χελλαίοι.] A people of *Chellus,* mentioned in the book of *Judith.*

CHEL'-LŪS, [Χελλϐs.] A place mentioned in the 1ft chapter of *Judith.*

CHEL-U'-BAI, [Χαλωϐι, i. e. *he altogether againft me.*] A fon of *Hezron.*

CHEL-U'-BAR. See *Chelubai.*

CHEM'-A-RIMS, ['Ιερέοι, i. e. *black or blacknefs.*] The names of the idolatrous priefts of *Judæa;* or the idols themfelves.

CHE'-MŌSH, [Χαμώs, i. e. *handling or taking away.*] An idol of the *Moabites:* fuppofed to be the *Sun,* or the god *Priapus.*

CHEN-A'-ANAH, [Χαναvà, i. e. *broken in pieces.*] The name of an artificer of king *Ahab.*

CHE-NAN'-I, [Χωνεvί, i. e. *my pillar.*] The name of one of the *Levites.*

CHE-NAN-I'-AH, [Χωνεvία, i. e. *preparation or ftrength.*] A chief of the Levites, and mafter of the temple mufick.

CHEPH'-AR HA-AM-MO'-NAI, [Καραφàμμωvà,] A city of the *Gibeonites* given to the tribe of *Benjamin.*

CHEPH'-I-RAH, [Καφαρà, i. e. *a little lionefs.*] The fame as *Chephar ha Ammonai.*

CHER'-AN, [Χαρράν, i. e. *anger.*] One of the defcendants from the patriarch *Efau.*

CHE'-RE-AS, [Χαιρέ⊙.] A governor of *Gazara.*

CHER'-ETH-IMS or CHER'-ETH-ITES, [Χερε-θεὶμ, i. e. *who cuts, tears away, or exterminates.*] The denominations for *Philiftines.*

CHER'-ITH or ISH, [Χαρρàθ, i. e. *cutting, piercing, flaying.*] A brook near to the river *Jordan.*

CHER'-ŪB, [Χερϐβ, i. c. *as a mafter; as a child; as fighting.*] A city of the babylonifh empire.

CHER'-ŪB

CHER'-ŪB or CHER-U'-BIMS, † [Χερυβίμ. Χερὺ6,
i. e. *as a mafter, or as a child.*] An order of angels
next to the *Seraphims.*

CHES'-A-LŌN, [Χασαλών, i. e. *truft.*] Mount *Jearim*
fo called—alfo a city of *Paleftine* in the tribe of
Judah.

CHE'-SED, [Χαζάδ, i. e. *a devil, a deftroyer, or a
breaft.*] A fon of *Nahor, Abraham's* brother,
and father of the *Chaldæans,* who in *Hebrew* are
called *Cafedim* or *Cafdim.*

CHE'-SIL, [Βαιθὴλ, i. e. *foolifhnefs.*] A city of *Paleftine* in the tribe of *Judah.*

CHE'-SUD. The fame as *Chefed.*

CHES'-UL-LŌTH, [Χασαλὼθ, i. e. *fearfulnefs.*] A
city of *Paleftine* near to mount *Tabor,* in the tribe
of *Iffachar.*

CHET'-TIM, [Χετθειμ.] *Macedonia* was fo called.
See *Chittim.*

CHET-TI'-IM, [Χετθειμ.] See CHITTIM.

CHEZ'-IB, [Χαζ6ί.] The fame place with *Achzib.*

CHI'-DŌN, [Χειδών, i. e. *a dart.*] One who lived in
the tribe of *Judah* in *Paleftine.*

CHI-LE'-AB. [Δαλυία, i. e. *perfection of the father.*]
The fon of king *David* and *Abigail:* he is alfo
called *Daniel.*

CHIL-I'-ŌN, [Χελαιών, i. e. *finifhed, compleat, wafted
or perfect.*] The fon of *Elimelech* and *Naomi.*

CHIL'-MAD, [Χαλμαβ, i. e. *teaching or learning.*] A
city of *Arabia.*

CHIM'-HAM, [Χαμαὰμ, i. e. *as they, or like to them.*]
The fon of *Barzillai;* one of king *David's* at-
tendants.

CHI'-OS, [Χίος, i. e. *open or opening.*] An ifland of
the *Archipelago,* next to *Lefbos* Ifle: called by the
Turks, *Sakifaduci.*

---

† This word ought to have been tranflated, either *cherubim*
or *cherubin,* without the final letter *s.*

CHIS'-LEU

CHIS'-LEU or CAS'-LEU or CIS'-LEU, [Κασελεῦ, i. e. *rashness, confidence.*] The *third* jewish month, answering to *November* and *December*.

CHIS'-LON, [Χασλών, i. e. *hope or trust.*] The father of *Elidad*, of the tribe of *Benjamin*.

CHIS'-LOTH TA'-BOR, [Χασελωθαὶϑ, i. e. *fears or purity.*] A city of *Palestine* in the tribe of *Zebulun*.

CHIT'-TIM, [Κητιεὶμ, i. e. *those that bruise; or gold.*] A descendant from *Japhet* the son of *Noah*—also, as some suppose, *Macedonia*—also an island in the Mediterranean sea, as others conjecture, which *Kittim, Noah*'s grandson, peopled.

CHI'-UN. An *Ægyptian* god, whom some suppose to be *Saturn*.

CHLO'-E, [Χλόη.] See *Cloe*.

CHO'-BA, [Χωβὰ.] A place in the land of *Palestine*.

CHO-RA'-SIN or CHO-RA'-SHAN or CHO-RA'-ZIN, [Χωραζὶν, i. e. *the secret.*] A town of *Judæa* in the half tribe of *Manasseh*, on the sea coast of *Galilee* near to *Capernaum*.

CHOS-A-ME'-US (SI'-MON) [Χοσαμαῖος.] One whose family returned from the babylonish captivity.

CHO-ZE'-BA, [Χωζηβα, i. e. *men liers.*] A town of *Palestine* in the tribe of *Judah*.

CHRIST, [Χρισός, i. e. *anointed, or the chosen of God.*] The *Saviour* of mankind—the anointed, answering to the hebrew *Messiah*.

CHRON'-I-CLES, [Παραλειπομενα.] Two canonical books of the Old Testament, so called: supposed to have been written by *Ezra*; they contain a short *chronology* for the space of 2985 years from the creation.

CHRY'-SOL-ITE, [Χρυσόλιθ⊕.] A precious stone, of a dusky green colour, with a cast of yellow.

CHRY-SOP'-RA-SUS, [Χρυσόπρασ⊕.] A precious stone of a yellow colour approaching to green; the *second* stone in the *first* row in the breast-plate of the Jewish high priest: called also a *Topaz*.

CHUB. A province of *Egypt*, in *Africa*.

CHUN,

CHUN, [i. e. *making ready.*] A city of antient *Syria,* in *Asia.*

CHU'-SA or CHU'-ZA, [Χυζᾶ, i. e. *the feer, or prophet.*] A fteward to *Herod Agrippa.*

CHUSH'-AN RISH-A-THA'-IM, [Χυσαρσαθαιμ, i. e. *ethiopian, or blackneſs of iniquities.*] A king of *Meſopotamia,* who oppreſſed the Iſraelites for eight years.

CHUS'-I, [Χυσι.] A place in the land of *Paleſtine.*

C before I.

CI-LIC'-I-A, [Κιλικία, i. e. *which rolls or overturns.*] A country in the fouth caft of *Aſia Minor,* over againſt *Cyprus* Iſle: its capital *Tarſus,* where St. *Paul* was born.

CIN'-NER-ETH or CIN'-NER-ŌTH, [Χενερὲθ. Χενερὼθ, i. e. *as a candle.*] A fenced city of *Paleſtine,* in the tribe of *Zebulun:* fuppoſed to be the fame as *Tiberias,* as the lake of *Genneſareth, Cinneroth* and *Tiberias* are the fame.

CIR'-A-MA, [Κιραμᾶ.] A place in *Paleſtine.*

CI'-SAI, [Κισαῖⓢ.] An anceſtor of *Mardocheus,* or *Mordecai,* of the tribe of *Benjamin.*

CIS'-LEU. See *Chiſleu.*

CIT'-TIM, [Κιτίοι.] The people of *Perſia* fo called.

C before L.

CLAU'-DA, [Κλαύδη, i. e. *a broken, or lamentable voice.*] An iſland near the iſle of *Crete.*

CLAU'-DI-A, [Κλαυδία, i. e. *lame.*] A *Roman* lady, and a convert of the apoſtle *Paul.*

CLAU'-DI-US CÆ'-SAR, [Κλαύδιⓢ Καῖσαρ.] An emperor of *Rome,* fucceſſor to *Caligula;* he died A. D. 54, Æt. 64.

CLAU'-DI-US LYS'-I-AS, [Κλαύδιⓢ Λυσίας.] A *Roman* captain who wrote to *Felix* the deputy governor, relating to St. *Paul.*

CLE'-MENT, [Κλημεντⓢ, i. e. *mild, good, modeſt, merciful.*] One mentioned by St. *Paul;* fuppoſed afterwards to have been biſhop of *Rome.*

CLE-OP'-

CLE-OP'-A-TRA, [Κλεοπάτρα. L. *Cleo'patra*, i. e. *the glory of the country.*] An *Ægyptian* queen, fifter and wife to the laft *Ptolemy.*

CLE'-OPH-AS or CLE-O'-PAS, [Κλέοπας, Κλώπας. L. *Cle'ophas*, i. e. *the whole glory.*] A difciple of our *Saviour*, and faid to be brother of *Jofeph* the reputed father of our *Saviour.*

CLO'-E, [Χλόη, i. e. *green herb.*] One mentioned by the apoftle *Paul* as a convert.

C before N.

CNI'-DUS, [Κνίδος, i. e. *age.*] A city and promontory of *Caria*, in *Afia.*

C before O.

COCK'-A-TRICE. A venomous ferpent of the oviparous kind, in *Afia* and *Africa*—it is fometimes called a *bafilifk*, of which many fabulous ftories are told.

CÆ'-LĒ SYR'-I-A, [Κοίλη Συρία, i. e. *crooked, or low Syria.*] A part of *Syria* in *Afia*, lying between *Libanus* and *Antilibanus.*

COL-HOZ'-EH, [Χολεζὲ, i. e. *every prophet.*] A ruler of part of the city of *Jerufalem.*

COL'-LI-US, [Καλλίος. Κάλιος. Καλιτὰς.] See *Calitas.*

COL-OS'-SE, [Κολοσσαὶ, i. e. *punifhment, or correction.*] A capital city of *Phrygia* in *Afia*, to the inhabitants of which St. *Paul* wrote two epiftles.

COL-OS'-SI-ANS, [Κολοσσαιοί.] Two of the canonical books of the *New Teftament*, fo called—alfo the inhabitants of *Colaffe.*

CON-I'-AH, ['Ιεχονίας, i. e. *ftrength or ftability of the lord.*] See *Jeconiah.*

CO-NON-I'AH, [Χωνενίας, i. e. *the ftrength of the Lord.*] The name of one of the *Levites.*

CO'-OS or COS, [Κόs, i. e. *top.*] An ifland and city of the *Archipelago.*

COR. An *hebrew* meafure; the fame as *Homer.*

COR'-BE, [Χορβὲ.] One who returned from the babylonifh captivity.

COR'-BAN,

COR'-BAN, [Κ⸳ρϐᾶν.] The *hebrew* word for a gift or offering to GOD—alfo the treafury where the gifts in money were depofited.

COR'-E, [Κορὲ.] See KORAH.

COR'-INTH, [Κορινϑ⸳, i. e. *fatisfied, ornament, or beauty.*] The capital city of *Achaia* in *Greece*.

CO-RINTH'-I-ANS, [Κορινϑιοι.] The inhabitants of *Corinth*—alfo *two* canonical books of the *New Teftament*, viz. the epiftles of St. *Paul* to the *Corinthians*.

COR'-MO-RANT. A fpecies of the *pelican*, almoft as large as a goofe, with fourteen long feathers in its tail; the under part of the body is whitifh —it is a fea-fowl and lives upon fifh, and dives very rapidly after its prey—the *hebrew* and *greek* name of this bird is expreffive of its impetuofity.

COR-NE'-LI-US, [Κορνηλι⸳, i. e. *an horn.*] A *Roman* centurion, who was converted to Chriftianity by the apoftle *Peter*.

COS. See *Coos.*

CO'-SAM, [Κωσὰμ, *divining.*] One of our *Saviour's* anceftors.

COU'-THA, [Κⱥϑὰ.] One whofe family returned from the babylonifh captivity.

CŌZ, [Κῶς, i. e. *a thorn.*] A defcendant from the patriarch *Afher.*

COZ'-BI, [Χασϐι, i. e. *a liar, or as fliding away.*] A *Midianitifh* woman whom *Phinehas* flew for her ignominious conduct with *Zimri.*

C *before* R.

CRA'-TĒS, [Κρⱥτης, i. e. *an harrow, or hurdle.*] A *Grecian* philofopher of *Thebes*—alfo a governor of the *Cyprians.*

CRES'-CENS, [Κρησκης, i. e. *growing, increafing.*] One mentioned by St. *Paul*, who was a preacher of Chriftianity.

CRE'-TE, [Κρητε, i. e. *carnal, flefhly.*] An ifland of the Mediterranean fea, now *Candi: Titus* was bifhop of this ifland: it is 270 miles long, but not 50 miles broad.

G

CRE'-TES

GRE'-TES or GRE'-TI-ANS, [Κρῆτες.] The inhabitants of *Crete* Isle.
CRIS'-PUS, [Κρίσπ⊙, i. e. *curled.*] A chief ruler of
the synagogue who was baptized by St. *Paul.*
CROC'-O-DILE. See LEVIATHAN.

C before U.

CU'-BIT. A *jewish* measure about one *foot and nine
inches* in length.
CUSH, [Χὺς, i. e. *blackness or heat.*] The eldest son
of *Ham,* and the father of *Nimrod*—also the
name of a country supposed to be *Æthiopia*; and
another in *Arabia Petræa,* on the east coast of the
red sea towards *Ægypt* and *Palestine.*
CUSH'-AN or *the land* of Cush, [Αἰθίοποι, i. e. *blackness, heat.*] The same with Æthiopian *Cush.*
CUSH-AN RISH-A-THA'-IM, [Χυσαρσαθαίμ, i. e.
blackness of iniquities.] A king of *Mesopotamia.*
CUSH'-I, [Χυσὶ, i. e. *black or an Æthiopian.*] *Joab*'s
messenger to king *David,* on his son *Absalom*'s
being slain.
CUTH or CUTH'-AH, [Χυθὰ, i. e. *burning.*] A
province of *Assyria,* and supposed to be the same
with *Cush*; as also *Susiana,* which is now called
Cuthestan in *Persia.*
CUTH'-E-ANS. A people who were carried captives to *Babylon* from *Cuthah.*

C before Y.

CY'-A-MON, [Κυαμάνος.] A place opposite *Esdraelon.*
CYM'-BAL, [Κυμβάλ⊙.] A brass instrument of mu-
sick, something like a *kettle drum,* but smaller.
CYP'-RI-ANS, [Κυπρίοι.] The inhabitants of *Cyprus*
Isle.
CY'-PRUS, [Κύπρ⊙, i. e. *fair, or fairness.*] A famous
island in the *mediterranean sea,* between *Cilicia*
and *Syria,* 200 miles long and 60 miles broad.
CY-RE'-NE, [Κυρήνη, i. e. *a wall, coldness, meeting, or
a floor.*] A celebrated city of *Lybia* in *Africa.*

CY-REN-

CY-REN'-I-AN, [Κυρεναῖος.] An inhabitant of *Cyrene.*

CY-REN'-I-US, [Κυρηνίος, i. e. *who governs.*] A governor of *Syria* in *Asia.*

CY'-RUS, [Κῦρ⊙, i. e. *as a wretch or as an heir.*] The son of *Cambyses* king of *Persia,* by *Mandane* the daughter of *Astyages* king of *Media:* he died A. M. 3475.

D.

D *before* A.

DAB'-A-REH, [Δεββὰ, i. e. *the word, or the thing, or a bee.*] One of the cities of *Palestine* in the tribe of *Issachar.*

DAB'-BA-SHETH, [Βαιθάραβα, i. e. *flowing with honey, or causing infamy.*] A town of *Palestine* in the tribe of *Zebulun.*

DAB'-E-RATH, [Δαβιρὼθ, i. e. *word, thing, obedient.*] Two towns of *Palestine,* one in the tribe of *Zebulun,* the other in the tribe of *Issachar.*

DA'-BRI-A. A scribe mentioned in the *second* book of *Esdras.*

DA-CO'-BI, [Δακὴβ. Δακηβί.] One whose family returned from the babylonish captivity.

DAD-DE'-US, [Δοδθαι⊙.] One who returned from the babylonish captivity.

DA'-GŌN, [Δαγὼν, i. e. *corn or fish.*] An idol of the *Philistines* represented as half *man* and half *fish.*

DAI'-SAN, [Δαισὰν.] One whose sons were servants of the temple.

DA-LA'-I-AH, [Δαλαία, i. e. *the poor of the Lord.*] A descendant from *David* king of *Israel.*

G 2   DAL-MA-

DAL-MA-NU'-THA, [Δαλμανθά, i. e. *a bucket, lean-*
nefs, branch.] A country of *Judæa* or *Palefine.*

DAL-MA'-TIA, [Δαλμαῖία, i. e. *deceitful lamps, or vain*
brightnefs.] A country, now of *Eurspæan Turkey,*
on the gulph of *Venice,* where *Titus* preached
the gofpel.

DAL'-PHON, [Δελφὰν, i. e. *the houfe of caves.*] A fon
of *Ham* the patriarch—alfo one of *Haman's* fons.

DAM'-A-RIS, [Δάμαρις, i. e. *a little woman*] A convert of the apoftle *Paul:* fome think that fhe was
the wife of *Dionyfius* the *Areopagite.*

DA-MAS-CENES', [Δαμασκηνοι.] The people of
Damafcus.

DA-MAS'-CUS, [Δαμασκὸς, i. e. *a fack full of blood.*]
A large city of antient *Syria* in *Afia:* now *Damas.*

DAN, [Δὰν, i. e. *judgment, or he that judges.*] The
fifth fon of *Jacob* the patriarch by *Bilhah, Rachel's*
handmaid—alfo a diftrict and city of *Palefine,* in
the tribe of *Naphtali.*

DAN-ITES. Defcendants from *Dan.*

DAN-JA'-AN, [Δαν Ιαςὰν. Δανιὀὰν Ουδαν.] A city in
the land of *Palefine.*

DAN'-I-EL, [Δανιὴλ, i. e. *judgment of God, or God is*
my judge.] One of the greater prophets, from
whom the canonical book of *Daniel* took its
name: he was carried captive to *Babylon* when
young, in the reign of *Jeboiakim* king of *Judah,*
A. M. 3393—alfo a fon of king *David* by *Abi-*
gail the *Carmelitefs.*

DAN'-NAH, ['Ρεννὰ, i. e. *judging.*] A city in the
mountains of the land of *Palefine,* in the tribe
of *Judah.*

DA'-O-BRATH. See *Daburch.*

DAPH'NE, [Δαφνη, i. e. *bay tree.*] A grove near
Antioch the capital of *Syria.*

DA'-RA, [Δαράδ. Δαρά, i. e. *generation, or the houfe of*
the shepherd, or the race of wickednefs.] A defcendant from the patriarch *Judah.*

DAR'-DA, [Δαρδα, i. e. *the dwelling place of know-*
ledge.] A wife man mentioned in the book of
Kings.

DA-RI'-

DA-RI'-AN. One who returned from the babylonish captivity.

DA-RI'-US, [Δαρει⊙, i. e. *he that inquires or informs himself.*] The name of several kings: as *Darius* the *Mede*, uncle to *Cyrus:* he is called *Cyaxares*, and succeeded *Belshazzar* in *Babylon*, A. M. 3468 —also *Darius* the son of *Hystaspes*, whom some suppose to be *Ahasuerus* queen *Esther*'s husband —also others of that name.

DAR'-KŌN, [Δαρκὼν, i. e. *of generation, or the possession.*] One who returned from the babylonish captivity.

DA'-THAN, [Δαθὰν, i. e. *laws or rites.*] One of the sons of *Eli* the high priest—also one, who with *Korah*, *Abiram*, and *On*, rebelled against *Moses* and *Aaron.*

DATH'-EM-AH or DATH'-MAN, [Δάθεμα.] A fortress in the land of *Gilead.*

DA'-VID, [Δαυιδ, i. e. *beloved or dear.*] A king of *Israel*, the son of *Jesse*, of the tribe of *Judah* and town of *Bethlehem*; he died A. M. 2990, Æt. 71, after forty years' reign.

DAY. The *Jews* began their day in the *evening:* the *Babylonians* reckoned from one *sun-rising* to another.

D before E.

DE'-BIR, [Δαβὶν. Δαβὶρ, i. e. *an orator, or word.*] A king of *Eglon*—also a city of the tribe of *Judah* near to *Hebron:* it is sometimes called *Kirjath-sepher* or *Kirjath-sannah*—also another in the tribe of *Gad.*

DEB-O'-RAH, [Δεββῶρα. Δεβόρρα. L. Deb'orah, i. e. *a word, or a bee.*] A prophetess and *judgess* of *Israel*, A. M. 2691 ; the wife of *Lapidoth*—also *Rebecca*'s nurse.

DEC'-A-LOGUE. The ten commandments, given by GOD to *Moses*, so called.

DEC-AP'-OL-IS, [Δεκαπόλις.] A country of *Palestine*, partly in *Palestine*, and partly in *Cœle Syria*, on both sides of the river *Jordan:* so called because it contained *ten* cities.

DED'-

DED'-AN, [Δεδὰν. Δαδαν, i. e. *their friendship or a judge.*] One of the posterity of *Ham*, a grandson of *Abraham*—also a city near to *Edom*.

DED'-AN-IM, [i. e. *the beloved of those.*] Uncertain whether he was a descendant from *Japhet* or *Ham*.

DED'-AN-IMS. The posterity of *Dedan*, descended from *Dedanim* the son of *Javan*.

DE-HA'-VITES, [Δαυαΐοι.] People whom the king of *Assyria* brought from *Ava* into *Samaria*.

DE'-KAR, [Δακὰρ, i. e. *force.*] Father to one of king *Solomon*'s houshold.

DEL-A-I'-AH, [Δαλαΐα, i. c. *the poor of the Lord.*] A *Levite* son to *Elixneai*, of king *David*'s family.

DEL'-I-LAH, [Δαλιδὰ. Δαλιλά, *poor, small, or head of hair.*] A concubine of *Samson* a judge of *Israel*.

DE'-LUS or DE'-LOS, [Δῆλ©.] An island in the *Ægean* sea, reputed to be the birth place of *Apollo* and *Diana*.

DE'-MAS, [Δημᾶς, i. e. *popular.*] A disciple of St. *Paul*; but afterwards fell from him.

DE-ME'-TRI-US, [Δημήτρι©, i. e. *belonging to Ceres or to corn.*] The name of two kings of *Syria*— also a silversmith of *Ephesus*, mentioned in the book of *Acts*—also a virtuous Christian, mentioned by St. *John* in his third epistle.

DE'-MOPH-ŌN, [Δημοφῶν, i. e. *slaying the people.*] A governor appointed by *Antiochus*; in the *Apocrypha*.

DER'-BE, [Δέρβη, i. e. *a sling.*] A city of *Lycaonia* in *Greece*; is now Asiatick *Turkey*.

DES'-SAU. A town mentioned in the *second* book of *Maccabees*.

DE-U'-EL, ['Ραγυὴλ, i. e. *the knowledge or science of God.*] A descendant from the patriarch *Gad*: called also *Reuel*.

DEU'-TER-ON-OM-Y, [Δευϊερονομιον.] A canonical book of the *Old Testament*, being the *fifth* and last of the *Pentateuch* or five books of *Moses*: so called, because it was a recapitulation of the laws in the preceding books; or a second law.

D *before*

D *before* I.

DI'-A-MOND, [῎Ιασπις.] The moſt valuable of all gems; when it is pure, it is perfectly clear and pellucid as the pureſt water: it was the *third* ſtone in the *ſecond* row, in the Jewiſh high prieſt's breaſt-plate.

DI-A'-NA, [῎Αρτέμις, i. e. *luminous.*] The heathen goddeſs of chaſtity; principally worſhipped at *Epheſus* in *Aſia*; her temple there was one of the *ſeven* wonders of the world.

DI-AS-COR-INTH'-I-US, [Διοσκορινθίος, i. e. *an heavenly ornament.*] Suppoſed to be the name of a *Corinthian* month, about our *March* or *April.*

DIB'-LA-IM, [Δεϭηλαὶμ, i. e. *a cluſter of figs.*] The name of a man mentioned by the prophet *Hoſea.*

DIB'-LATH, [Δἰϭλαθὰ, i. e. *paſte of dry figs.*] A deſart on the borders of *Moab.*

DI'-BŌN, [Δαιϭὼν. Δηϭὼν, i. e. *underſtanding.*] A city of *Paleſtine*, in the tribe of *Reuben.*

DI'-BŌN GAD, [Δαιϭὼν Γὰϭ, i. e. *great underſtanding.*] A place of *Midian* where the *Iſraelites* encamped the 39th time; in the wilderneſs.

DIB'-RI, [Δαϭρεὶ, i. e. *an orator.*] The name of one belonging to the tribe of *Dan.*

DIB'-ZA-HAB or DI'-ZA-HAB, [i. e. *where much gold is.*] A place in the wilderneſs where the *Iſraelites* paſſed.

DI'-DRACHM. A Jewiſh coin, worth about *fourteen pence* Engliſh money.

DID'-Y-MUS, [Δἰδυμ☉, i. e. *a twin.*] The ſurname of *Thomas* the apoſtle.

DIK'-LAH or DIL'-DAH, [Δεκλὰ, i. e. *his diminiſhing.*] A deſcendant from the patriarch *Shem.*

DI'-LE-AN, [Δαλὰϭ, i. e. *that is poor.*] A city of *Paleſtine*, in the tribe of *Judah* in the valley.

DIM'-NAH, [Δαμνὰ, i. e. *dung.*] A *Levitical* city of *Paleſtine*, in the tribe of *Zebulun.*

DI'-MŌN, [Δειμὼν, i. e. *where it is red.*] A place in the land of *Moab* in *Aſia.*

DI-MO'-

DI-MO'-NAH, [Διμωνὰ, i. e. *a dunghill.*] A city of *Palestine*, in the tribe of *Judah*.

DI'-NAH, [Δεῖνα, i. e. *judgment.*] The daughter of *Jacob* and *Leah*, who was ravished by the *Shechemites*.

DI-NA'-ITES, [Δειναῖοι.] A people of *Assyria* in *Asia*.

DIN'-HA-BAH, [Δενναβά, i. e. *his judgment in those things.*] A city of *Edom* or *Idumæa*.

DI-ON-YS'-I-US, [Διονίσιος, i. e. *from heaven,* or *moved forward.*] A man who was a member of the *Areopagus* at *Athens*, and who disputed with, and was converted by St. *Paul*, and was burnt as a martyr at *Athens*, A. D. 95.

DI-OT'-REPH-ĒS, [Διοτρεφὴς, i. e. *nourished of Jupiter.*] One who refused hospitality to those whom St. *John* sent to him.

DIS'-CUS, [Δίσκος.] A game among the *Athenians*, by throwing a round piece of iron or other metal, or a stone, with an hole in the center: it depended upon strength and flight to throw it to the greatest distance: it was like our game of *quoits*.

DI'-SHAN, ['Ρισών, i. e. *a threshing.*] One of the children of *Seir*, a descendant from *Esau*.

DI'-SHŌN, [Δησῶν, i. e. *fatness, or ashes.*] A descendant from *Esau*.

DI'-ZA-HAB. See *Dibzahab*.

D *before* O,

DO'-CUS, [Δώx.] An hold or fortress built by *Abubus* the father of *Ptolemy*; in the *second* book of *Maccabees*.

DO'-DA-I, [Δωδία, i. e. *beloved.*] An officer of king *David*.

DO'-DA-NIM, [Δωδανὶν. Δωδανείμ, i. e. *beloved.*] A descendant from *Japhet* the patriarch: he was the youngest son of *Javan*.

DO'-DA-VAH, [Δωδία, i. e. *love.*] The father of the prophet *Eliezer*.

DO'-DO,

DO'-DO, [Δωδὰς. Δωδαῖ, i. e. *his uncle.*] One of the tribe of *Iſſachar* the patriarch, the father of *Elea-zer* one of king *David*'s heroes.

DO'-ĒG, [Δωήχ, i. e. *careful.*] An *Edomite*, chief herdſman to king *Saul.*

DOPH'-KAH, [Ραφαχά, i. e. *a knocking.*] The *ninth* encampment of the *Iſraelites.*

DŌR, [Δώρ, i. e. *generation or habitation.*] A country on the *weſt* ſide of the river *Jordan*; in the half tribe of *Manaſſeh.*

DO'-RA, [Δωρᾶ.] An iſland and fountain of the *Perſian* gulph in *Aſia.*

DOR'-CAS, [Δορχάς, i. e. *a female roe or doe.*] A woman converted to Chriſtianity, mentioned in *Acts* ix. 36.

DOR-Y'-MEN-ES, [Δορυμέν℗.] The father of *Ptolemy* in the *firſt* book of *Maccabees.*

DO-SITH'-E-US, [Δωσίθε℗, i. e. *giving to God.*] One who pretended to be a prieſt of the tribe of *Levi*—alſo an officer in the army of *Judas Maccabees.*

DO'-THA-IM or DO'-THAN, [Δωθχείμ, i. e. *the law or cuſtom.*] A town of *Paleſtine*, about twelve miles from *Jeruſalem*, in the tribe of *Zebulun.*

DOVES DUNG. It is ſaid in the ſecond book of *Kings*, chap. vi. ver. 24. that, in the famine of *Samaria*, the fourth part of a cab of *doves-dung* ſold for five pieces of ſilver or near *two ſhillings* ſterling. There is ſome diſpute what is meant by *doves-dung*; ſome ſuppoſe it to be the real excrement of the dove—others, that it was the contents of the crop of the dove; but *Bochartus* ſays, that the *Arabians* have a kind of vetches or lentiles called *doves-dung*; which was the cheapeſt of food.

D *before* R.

DRACH'-MA. A *grecian* ſilver coin, about *ſeven-pence three farthings* value ſterling.

DROM'-E-DA-RY. See CAMEL.

DRU-

DRU-SIL'-LA, [Δρουσίλλα, i. e. *sprinkled over with dew.*] Wife to *Felix* governor of *Judæa.*

DU'-MAH, [Δυμὰ, i. e. *silence or likeness.*] A city of *Palestine* in the tribe of *Judah* in the mountains— alfo a fon of *Ishmael.*

DU'-RA, [Δεειρὰ. Δῶρα, i. e. *generation or habitation.*] A great plain near *Babylon,* where *Nebuchadnezzar* fet up his golden image.

E.

E *before* A.

E-A'-NAS, [Μάνης.] One who returned from the babylonifh captivity.

E *before* B.

E'-BAL, [Γαιβὰλ, i. e. *an heap of antientnefs.*] One of the pofterity of *Efau*—alfo a mountain of the *Canaanites* beyond *Jordan* in the tribe of *Ephraim,* oppofite *Gerizim.*

E'-BED, [Ωβὴδ, i. e. *a fervant.*] The names of two men, one a *Gentile,* and the other a *Jew.*

E-BED'-MEL-ECH, ['Αβδεμέλεχ, i. e. *fervant of the king.*] An *æthiopian* or *arabian* eunuch in the court of king *Zedekiah,* who delivered the prophet *Jeremiah* from the dungeon.

EB-EN-EZ'-ER, ['Αβενεζὲρ, i. e. *the ftone of help.*] The name of the field in *Philiftia,* where the *Ifraelites* were defeated by the *Philiftines* when the *Ark of the Lord* was taken.

EB'-ER, [Εβὲρ, i. e. *paffage, or anger.*] A defcendant from the patriarch *Shem,* he died A. M. 2187, Æt. 464.

EB-I'-

EB-I'-A-SAPH, ['Αϐιασὰφ, i. e. *a gathering father.*]
A fon of *Korah*—alfo a fon of *Elkanah.*

EB-RO'-NAH, ['Εϐρωνὰ, i. e. *paffing over, or being
angry.*] The *thirty-firft* encampment of the *Ifraelites,* in the wildernefs.

E *before* C.

E-CA'-NUS. A fcribe mentioned in the *fecond* book
of *Efdras.*

EC-BAT'-A-NA, ['Εϰϐατάνα, i. e. *the brother of death.*]
The chief city of *Media* in *Afia.*

EC-CLE-SI-AS'-TĒS, ['Εϰϰλησιαςὴς, i. e. *the preacher.*] A canonical book of the *Old Teftament,*
written by king *Solomon.*

EC-CLE-SI-AS'-TI-CUS, ['Εϰϰλησιαςιϰὸς.] An apocryphal book written by *Jefus* the fon of *Sirach.*

E *before* D.

ED, [i. e. *witnefs.*] An altar erected by the *Ifraelites*
in the time of *Jofhua.*

ED'-AR, [i. e. *a flock.*] A place to which the patriarch
Jacob fojourned.

ED'-EN, ['Εδὲμ, i. e. *pleafure or delight.*] A place
in *Chaldæa,* now afiatic *Turkey,* where *Paradife*
was fituated—alfo a *Levite.*

ED'-ER, ['Εδερ, i. e. *a flock.*] One of the pofterity
of the patriarch *Levi*—alfo a city of *Judah.*

E'-DĒS, ['Ηδαῒς.] One who returned from the babylonifh captivity.

ED'-I-AS, ['Εδδίας.] One who returned from the
babylonifh captivity; a porter or guard of the
temple.

ED'-NA, ['Εδνὰ, i. e. *everlafting reft, or pleafure.*] The
wife of *Raguel* in the book of *Tobit.*

ED'-ŌM, ['Εδώμ, i. e. *earthly, bloody, or red.*] The
name of *Efau*—alfo the land of *Seir* in *Afia,* fo
called from *Efau* or *Edom*; it is part of *Arabia
Petræa,* and is alfo called *Idumæa.*

ED'-ŌM-

ED'-ŌM-ITES, ['Ιδυμαῖοι.] The inhabitants of *Edom*, or *Idumæa*.

ED'-RE-I, ['Εδραὶμ, i. e. *the heap of strength or might.*] A place in the land of *Bashan*, beyond *Jordan*, in the tribe of *Manasseh*—also a town of the tribe of *Naphtali*.

E *before* G.

EG'-LAH, ['Αιγὰλ, i. e. *an heifer, or chariot.*] The *sixth* wife of king *David*, and mother of *Ithream*.

EG'-LA-IM, ['Αγαλεὶμ, i. e. *drops of the sea.*] A city beyond *Jordan*, in the land of *Moab*, by the east of the *dead sea*.

EG'-LŌN, ['Εγλὼμ, i. e. *a calf, or chariot.*] A place and a king of it, in the land of *Moab*—also a city of *Judah* in the valley.

E'-GYPT, ['Αιγύπτ⊙; i. e. *anguish, or tribulation.*] It is called, in Hebrew, *Mizraim*, after *Mizraim* the son of *Ham*: it is a large kingdom in *Africa*, on the famous river *Nile*.

E *before* H.

E'-HI, ['Αῖχις. 'Αῖχεις, i. e. *my brother.*] A son of the patriarch *Benjamin*.

E'-HŪD, ['Αὼδ, i. e. *praising.*] The *third* judge of Israel, A. M. 2611, a *Benjaminite*, who slew *Eglon* king of *Moab*.

E *before* K,

EK'-ER, ['Ακόρ. 'Ικάρ, i. e. *barren, feeble.*] One of the posterity of *Judah* the patriarch.

EK-REB'-ĒL, ['Εκρεβὴλ.] A place in the land of *Palestine*.

EK'-RŌN, ['Ακκαρὼν, i. e. *barrenness.*] A city of the *Philistines*, afterwards in the tribe of *Dan*: the god of it was supposed to be the god of *Flies*, by the name of *Beelzebub*: it was about *thirty-four* miles west of *Jerusalem*.

EK-RŌN

EK'-RON-ITES, ['Αχχαρωνίτοι.] The inhabitants of *Ekron.*

E *before* L.

E'-LA, ['Ηλά.] One who returned from the baby-lonifh captivity.

EL'-A-DAH, ['Ελαδά, i. e. *the eternity of God.*] One of the pofterity of *Ephraim* the patriarch.

E'-LAH, ['Ηλᾶ, i. e. *an elm, oak, or curfe.*] A place in the land of *Judæa,* where David flew *Goliah*—alfo a king of *Ifrael*—alfo others.

E'-LAM, ['Ηλάμ. 'Αιλάμ, *a young man, or a virgin.*] The eldeft fon of *Shem* the patriarch, who fettled in *Elam,* a kingdom to the eaft of the river *Ti-gris,* afterwards *Sufiana,* or *Perfia*—alfo others.

E'-LAM-ITES, ['Ηλαμῖται.] The inhabitants of *Elam.*

EL-A'-SAH, ['Ελεαςά, i. e. *the doings of God.*] One of the pofterity of *Saul* king of *Ifrael.*

E'-LATH, ['Αιλάν, i. e. *firength.*] A place in the wildernefs where the *Ifraelites* fojourned—alfo the emporium of *Syria* in *Afia.*

EL-BETH'-EL ['Ελ Βαιθηλ, i. e. *the God of Bethel.*] A place where the patriarch *Jacob* built an altar, in the land of *Canaan.*

EL'-CI-A, ['Ελκία, i. e. *the portion or gentlenefs of the Lord.*] An anceftor of *Judith* in the *Apocrypha.*

EL'-DA-AH, ['Ελδαγά, i. e. *the knowledge of God.*] A grandfon of the patriarch *Abraham.*

EL'-DAD, ['Ελδάδ, i. e. *loved of God.*] One of the feventy elders appointed by *Mofes.*

EL'-DERS of IS'-RAEL. The heads of the tribes, or of the great families in *Ifrael.*

EL'-E-AD, ['Ελεάδ, i. e. *witnefs of God.*] One of the grandfons of *Ephraim,* who was killed in the city of *Gath.*

EL-E-A'-LEH, ['Ελεαλή, i. e. *God's afcenfion.*] A city of *Judæa,* in the tribe of *Reuben.*

EL-E-A'-SAH, ['Ελεαςά, i. e. *the work or doings of God.*] A place of *Palefine,* in the tribe of *Ben-*
jamin

jamin—alfo one of king *Saul's* pofterity, the fon of *Helez.*

EL-E-A'-ZER, ['Ελεάζαρ, i. e. *the help, or aid of God.*] The *third* fon of *Aaron* the high prieft of the *Jews*—alfo others.

EL-E-AZ-U'-RUS, ['Ελιάζυρ⊙.] One who returned from the babylonifh captivity.

EL-EL-O'-HE IS'-RA-EL, [i. e. *God, the God of Ifrael.*] The name of an altar erected in *Canaan* by the patriarch *Jacob.*

EL'-EPH, ['Ελἐθ, i. e. *learning.*] A city of *Palefine* in the tribe of *Benjamin.*

EL-EU'-THER-US, ['Ελευθέρ⊙.] A river of *Syria,* the boundary between *Syria* and *Phœnicia*; its fource is between mounts *Libanus* and *Anti-libanus.*

EL-EU-ZA'-I, ['Αξαΐ. 'Ελιωζί.] One who reforted to king *David* at *Ziklag.*

EL-HA'-NAN, ['Ελεανὰν, i. e. *gift or mercy of God.*] One of king *David's* warriors; the fon of *Dodo.*

E'-LI, ['Ηλὶ, i. e. *the offering or lifting up.*] An high prieft of the Jews; the *fixteenth* Judge of *Ifrael:* he died A. M. 2909, Æt. 98.

E'-LI E'-LI LA'-MA SA-BAC-THA'-NI, ['Ηλί 'Ηλί Λαμὰ Σαβαχθαί.] The words ufed by our *Saviour* at his crucifixion, fignifying, *my God! my God! why haft thou forfaken me?*

EL'-I-AB, ['Ελιάβ, i. e. *God my father.*] One who reforted to king *David* at *Ziklag,* and his brother —alfo others.

EL-I'-A-DA, ['Ελιαδαὲ, i. e. *the knowledge of God.*] One of the fons of *David* king of *Ifrael* by one of his concubines.

E-LI'-A-DAH, ['Ελιαδαὲ.] The father of *Rezin* a king of *Damafcus* in *Syria.*

EL-I'-A-DAS, ['Ελιαδὰs.] One who returned from the babylonifh captivity.

EL-I'-A-DUN, ['Ηλιαδέν.] One who returned from the babylonifh captivity.

EL-I'-AH, ['Ηλία, i. e. *God the Lord.*] One of the pofterity of the patriarch *Benjamin.*

EL-I'-

EL-I'-AH-BA, ['Ελιαϐὰ.] A *Shaalbonite,* one of king *David's* worthies.

EL-I'-A-KIM, ['Ελιακίμ, i. e. *the refurrection of God, or God arifeth.*] A fon of *Jofiah* king of *Judah,* who was made king—alfo the fon of *Hilkiah,* fteward to king *Hezekiah.*

EL-I'-A-LI, ['Ελιαλì; i. e. *God's afcenfion.*] One who returned from the babylonifh captivity.

EL-I'-AM, ['Ελιαϐ, i. e. *the people of God.*] The father of *Bathfheba* the wife of *Uriah*—alfo a fon of *Achitophel,* and one of king *David's* worthies.

EL'-I-AS. See *Elijah.* L. *El'ias.*

EL-I'-A-SAPH, ['Ελισὰφ, i. e. *the Lord increafeth.*] The fon of *Deuel:* he was put over the hoft of *Gilead,* and was prince of the tribe of *Gad* in the time of *Mofes.*

EL-I'-A-SHIB, ['Ελιασìϐ, i. e. *the Lord returneth.*] A *jewifh* high prieft.

EL-I'-A-SIS, ['Ελιàσις.] One whofe family returned from the babylonifh captivity.

EL-I'-A-THA or EL-I'-A-THAH, ['Ελιαθὰ, i. e. *my God cometh, or thou art my God.*] The fon of *Heman;* he was one of the fingers in the temple of *Solomon.*

EL-I-AZ'-AR, ['Ελεάζερ.] One who returned from the babylonifh captivity.

EL-I'-DAD, ['Ελδαδ, i. e. *the beloved of God.*] The fon of *Chiflon,* of the tribe of *Benjamin.*

EL'-I-ĒL, ['Ελιήλ, i. e. *God, my God.*] One who reforted to king *David* at *Ziklag*—alfo one of the *Levites,* and others.

EL-I-E'-NA-I, ['Ελιωναῒ, i. e. *the God of mine eyes.*] One of the pofterity of the patriarch *Benjamin.*

EL-I-EZ'-ER, ['Ελιέζερ, i. e. *the help of God.*] A native of *Damafcus* and fteward of *Abraham's* houfhold—alfo one of the pofterity of the patriarch *Benjamin.*

EL-I'-HA-BA, ['Ελιαϐὰ, i. e. *my God the father.*] One of king *David's* worthies.

EL-I-HÆ'-NA-I, [Ελιωναι, i. e. *the God of mine eyes.*] One who returned from the babylonish captivity.

EL-I-HOR'-EPH, ['Ελιχόρεφ, i. e. *the God of youth.*] One of the jewish *Scribes.*

EL-I'-HU, ['Ελιή. 'Ηλιής, i. e. *my God himself, or he is my God.*] One of king *David*'s brethren, who followed his fortune when he fled from *Saul*—also one of *Job*'s friends, descended from *Nahor*—also the grandfather of *Elkanah.*

EL-I'-JAH or EL'-I-AS, ['Ηλίας, i. e. *God the Lord, or a strong Lord.*] A famous prophet of *Israel*, a native of the city of *Tishbe* in the land of *Gilead*, who was translated.

EL'-I-KA, ['Ελικά, i. e. *the pelican of God.*] One of king *David*'s thirty worthies.

E'-LIM, ['Αιλείμ, i. e. *rams.*] The *sixth* encampment of the *Israelites*, in the wilderness.

EL-IM'-EL-ECH, ['Ελιμέλεχ, i. e. *my God the king, or the counsel of God.*] One of *Bethlehem Judah*, the husband of *Naomi.*

EL-I-Æ'-NA-I, ['Ελιωναι, i.e. *to him mine eyes.*] One of the posterity of the patriarch *Benjamin*; a son of *Neariah.*

EL-I-O'-NAS, ['Ελιωνας.] One who returned from the babylonish captivity.

EL-I'-PHAL, ['Ελιφάλ, i. e. *a miracle of God.*] One of king *David*'s warriors; the son of *Ur.*

EL-I'-PHAL-EH, ['Ελιφενα. 'Ελιφάλ., i. e. *the God of judgment.*] One who was a singer and porter of the temple of *Jerusalem.*

EL'-I-PHAZ, ['Ελιφαζ, i. e. *the endeavour of God.*] A son of *Esau* and his wife *Ada*—also one of *Job*'s friends.

EL-I'-PHEL-ET, ['Ελιφαλάθ. 'Ελιφαλὲτ, i.e. *the God of deliverance.*] One of the sons of *David* king of *Israel*—also others of that name.

EL-IS'-A-BETH, ['Ελισάβετ.] See *Elizabeth.*

EL-I-SÆ'-US. See *Elisha.*

EL-I'-

EL-I'-SHA, ['Ελισαιὲ, i. e. *my God saveth, or the health of my God.*] The son of *Shaphat*, a disciple of and successor to the prophet *Elijah*.

EL'-I-SHAH, ['Ελισὰ, i. e. *it is God; or the lamb of God.*] One of the sons of *Javan*, and grandson of *Japhet*.

EL-I'-SHA-MA, ['Ελισαμὰ, i. e. *the God of hearing.*] A prince of the tribe of *Ephraim* in the time of *Moses*—also one of the sons of *David*, king of *Israel*.

EL-I'-SHA-PHAT, [Ελισαφαν, i. e. *my God judgeth.*] The son of *Zichri*; one of king *Jehoiada's* captains.

EL-I'-SHE-BA or EL-IS'-A-BETH, ['Ελισαβὲθ, i.e. *the oath or fulness of God.*] The daughter of *Amminadab*, and wife to *Aaron* the high priest.

EL-I-SHU'-A, ['Ελισυὲ, i. e. *God keeping safe.*] One of king *David's* sons.

EL-IS'-I-MUS, ['Ελάσιμ⊙.] One who returned from the babylonish captivity, and a porter or guard of the temple.

EL-I'-U, ['Ηλιῦ.] Grandfather to *Elkanah* the father of *Samuel*.

EL'-I-UD, ['Ελιώδ, i. e. *God of praise.*] One of the ancestors of *Joseph*, husband to the virgin *Mary*; in St. *Matthew*'s genealogy.

EL-IZ'-A-BETH, ['Ελισάβετ, i. e. *the oath or fulness of God.*] The wife of *Zechariah* a jewish priest, and mother of *John* the baptist.

EL-IZ'-A-PHAN, ['Ελισαφὰν, i. e. *God of the north-east wind.*] The son of *Uzziel* and uncle to *Aaron* —also others.

EL-I-ZE'US, ['Ελισαιός.] The *New Testament* name of *Elisha*.

EL-I'-ZUR, ['Ελισὲρ, i. e. *the strength of God.*] The son of *Shedeur*, and head of the tribe of *Reuben* in the time of *Moses*.

EL'-KA-NAH, ['Ελκανὰ, i. e. *the zeal of God.*] A son of *Korah*—also the husband of *Hannah*, and father to *Samuel* the prophet and judge.

H

EL-KO'-

EL-KO'-SHITE, [i. e. *in the evening, hardiness, or rigour of God.*] An inhabitant of *Elkoshai*, a village of *Galilee.*

EL'-LA-SAR, ['Ελλασὰρ, i. e. *revolting from God.*] A city of the *Canaanites.*

EL-MO'-DAM, [Ελμωδάμ, i. e. *the God of measure, or of the garment.*] One of the ancestors of *Joseph,* husband to the virgin *Mary.*

EL'-NA-AM, [Ελναάμ.] One of king *David's* worthies.

EL'-NA-AN, ['Ελναάμ, i. e. *God's fairness.*] One of king *David's* worthies.

EL'-NA-THAN, ['Ελνανάθαμ, i. e. *the gift of God.*] Grandfather to *Jehoiakim* king of *Judah.*

EL'-ON, ['Αλλὼν. 'Αιλὼμ. Ελὼν, i. e. *strong.*] Father in law to *Esau* the patriarch—also a place in the tribe of *Dan* in *Palestine*—also the *thirteenth* judge of *Israel*; he died A. M. 2831—also a son of *Zebulun.*

EL'-ON-ITES. Descendants from *Elon,* of the posterity of the patriarch *Esau.*

EL'-ON BETH'-HA-NAN, ['Ελὼν Βηθαναν, i. e. *the house of grace or mercy.*] A place in the land of *Judæa.*

EL-O'-HI or EL-O'-I, The *hebrew* name for GOD.

E'-LOTH, ['Αιλὰθ, i. e. *olives.*] A sea port of *Edom,* on the *red sea.*

EL'-PA-AL, ['Ελφαὰλ, i. e. *God's work.*] One of the posterity of the patriarch *Benjamin.*

EL'-PA-LET, ['Ελιφαλὴθ, i. e. *the God of deliverance.*] A son of *David* king of *Israel.* See ELIPHALET.

EL-PA'-RAN, [Φαρὰν.] A place in the wilderness, through which the *Israelites* journeyed.

EL'-TE-KETH or EL'-TE-KEH, ['Αλκαθὰ, i. e. *the case of God.*] A city of *Palestine,* in the tribe of *Dan.*

EL-TEK'-ON, [Θεκὰμ, i. e. *God's correction.*] A city of the tribe of *Judah* in *Edom.*

EL-TO'-LAD, ['Ελϛωὐδαδ, i. e. *the generation of God.*] A city of *Palestine,* in the tribe of *Judah.*

EL'-UL,

EL'-ŪL, ['Ελɕλ, i. e. *cry, or outcry.*] The jewiſh *twelfth* month, anſwering to part of our *Auguſt* and part of *September.*

EL-U-ZA'-I, ['Αζαὶ. 'Ελιωζί, i. e. *God my ſtrength.*] One of the officers of king *David,* who reſorted to him at *Ziklag.* See ELEUZAI.

EL-Y-MA'-IS, ['Ελυμαὶs, i. e. *ſudden fears.*] The capital city of antient *Perſia,* or *Elam.*

EL'-Y-MAS, ['Ελύμας, i. e. *a corrupter or ſorcerer.*] A magician or ſorcerer who reſiſted the preaching of St. *Paul,* and was ſtruck blind.

EL'-ZA-BAD, 'Ελσαϐαδ, i. e. *the dowry of God.*] One who reſorted to king *David* at *Ziklag.*

EL'-ZA-PHAN, ['Ελισαφὰν, i. e. *God of the north-eaſt wind.*] One of the poſterity of the patriarch *Levi.*

E before M.

E-MAL-CU'-ĒL, ['Ειμαλκɕαὶ, i. e. *the meſſenger of God.*] One mentioned in the *firſt* book of the *Maccabees,* who *educated Antiochus* the ſon of *Alexander.*

EM'-E-RALD, ["Ανθραξ. Σμάραγδϴ.] A gem of a lively *green* colour: it was the *firſt* ſtone in the *ſecond* row, in the *jewiſh* high prieſt's breaſt-plate.

EM'-IMS, ['Ομμὶν, i. e. *fears or fearful.*] A people who dwelt in the land of *Moab,* to the eaſt of the river *Jordan.*

EM-AN-U'-ĒL, ['Εμμανɕήλ. L. *Eman'uel,* i. e. *God with us.*] A name given to the *Meſſiah,* by the prophet *Iſaiah.*

EM'-MA-ŪS, ['Εμμαɕs. 'Εμμὰυs, i. e. *fearful, counſel, or abjeɕt people.*] A village *ſeven* or *eight* miles north of *Jeruſalem,* in the tribe of *Judah.*

EM'-MĒR, ['Εμμὴϱ, i. e. *ſaying, ſpeaking; a lamb.*] One who returned from the babyloniſh captivity.

EM'-OR, ['Εμμὸϱ, i. e. *an aſs.*] See HAMOR.

EM'-OR-ITES. See AMORITES.

H 2

E *before* N.

E'-NAM, ['Μzιανὶ, i. e. *a fountain or open place.*] A city of *Palestine*, in the tribe of *Judah*, in the valley.

E'-NAN, ['Aινάν, i. e. *a cloud.*] One of the posterity of *Naphtali.*

EN-CAMP'-MENT. See CAMP.

EN-'DŌR, ['Ενδώϱ, i. e. *a well or habitation.*] A town in the lot of *Manasseh* on the *west* side of the river *Jordan*, noted for the *witch*, or *sorceress*, whom king *Saul* consulted.

E'-NE-AS, ['Aιναάς.] See ÆNEAS.

EN EG'-LA-IM, ['Εναγαλλείμ, i. e. *the fountain of calves.*] A town, antiently on the *east* side of *Sodom*, or the *dead sea.*

EN-E-MES'-SAR, ['Ενεμεσσάρ⊙.] A king of *Assyria.*

EN-E'-NI-AS, ['Εννέος.] One who returned from the babylonish captivity.

EN-GAN'-NIM, ['Εγγανείμ, i. e. *the eye of protection, or well of gardens.*] A city of *Palestine*, in the tribe of *Judah* in the valley.

EN-GED'-I, ['Εγγαδδί, i. e. *the well of a kid, or of felicity.*] A town on the *east* side of the lake of *Sodom*, or *dead sea*, about *thirty one* miles from *Jerusalem.*

EN HAD'-DAH, ['Αυναδά, i. e. *quick sight, or the well of gladness.*] A city of *Palestine*, belonging to the tribe of *Issachar.*

EN HAK'-KO-RE, [i. e. *the fountain of him who prayed.*] A place so named by *Samson*, where he found water to quench his thirst after slaying the *Philistines.*

EN HA'-ZOR, ['Ασὸϱ, i. e. *a well, or the grass of the well.*] A city of *Palestine*, in the tribe of *Naphtali.*

EN MISH'-PAT, [i. e. *the well of judgment.*] See KADESH.

EN'-ŌCH, ['Ενώχ, i. e. *taught, or dedicated.*] The son of *Cain*; the *first* city mentioned in scripture

ture was called *Cain* by his father *Cain*; it was
to the *eaſt* of *Eden*—alſo a ſon of *Jared* and father of *Methuſelah*; he lived 365 years and was
trnnſlated.

E'-NŌN, ['Αιναν, i. e. *a cloud, or well.*] A place near
Salim, by the river *Jordan*, where *John* baptized:
in the tribe of *Gad*.

EN'-ŌS or EN'-ŌSH, ['Ενως, i. e. *fallen man, or deſpe-
ration.*] The ſon of *Seth* and father of *Cainan*,
was born A. M. 235, died A. M. 1140, Æt. 905:
his poſterity were called *the ſons of God*.

EN RIM'-MON, [Ρεμμαυν, i. e. *the well of height.*]
A city of *Judæa*, where ſome of the children of
Judah ſettled, after the babyloniſh captivity.

EN RO'-GEL, [Ρωγηλ, i. e. *the well or fountain of
ſearching out.*] A place in the tribe of *Judah*,
to the *eaſt* of *Jeruſalem*, at the foot of mount
Zion.

EN SHE'-MESH, [Βαιθσαμας, i. e. *the well or fountain
of the ſun.*] A place or fountain on the frontiers
of the tribe of *Judah* and *Benjamin*.

EN TAP-PU'-AH, [Θαφθωθ. Ταφωθ, i. e. *the well or
fountain of an apple, or inflation.*] A place of *Paleſtine* in the tribe of *Manaſſeh*.

E before P.

EP'-A-PHRAS, [Επαφρας, i. e. *covered with foam.*]
An inhabitant of *Coleſſe*, converted to Chriſtianity by St. *Paul*; he was ſuppoſed to be the
firſt biſhop of *Coleſſe*.

EP-APH-ROD-I'-TUS, [Επαφροδιτ©., i. e. *fair or
pleaſant.*] A fellow labourer with St. *Paul*; the
emperor *Nero*'s ſecretary.

EP-E'-NET-US, [Επαινετ©., i. e. *praiſe worthy.*] A
diſciple of St. *Paul*, whom the apoſtle calls the
firſt fruits of *Achaia*.

EPH'-AH, ['Οιφι. Γεφας. Γαιφα, i. e. *weary.*] A
jewiſh dry, and liquid meaſure; the dry containing *three pecks and three pints:* the liquid, about
three pints wine meaſure—alſo one of the ſons of
H 3

Midian

Midian—also a place in *Arabia*—also a concubine of *Caleb*—and others.

EPH'-AI, ['Ιωφέ, i. e. *weary; tired.*] A *jew* men-tioned by the prophet *Jeremiah*.

EPH'ER, ['Αφειϱ. 'Οφὲϱ, i. e. *duſt or lead.*] A ſon of *Midian* and grandſon of the patriarch *Abraham*.

EPH'-ES DAM'-MIM, [Αφεσδομμείν, i. e. *the portion or effuſion of blood.*] A place in *Canaan* where the *Philiſtines* encamped.

EPH'-ES'-I-ANS, ['Εφεσίοι.] The inhabitants of *Epheſus*, to whom St. *Paul* wrote that canonical epiſtle in the *New Teſtament*.

EPH'-ES-US, ["Εφεσ☉, i. e. *deſirable.*] A celebrated city of *Ionia* in *Greece*, famed for the temple of *Diana*, one of the ſeven wonders of the world : here St. *Paul* preached and made many converts: now *Aiaſalouch*.

EPH'-LAL, ['Εφάελ, i. e. *judging or praying.*] The name of one of the poſterity of the patriarch *Judah*.

EPH'-ŌD, ['Επωμίδα. Σεφί, i. e. *an ornament.*] A kind of garment worn by the *jewiſh* high prieſt, brought from behind the neck and over the two ſhoulders ; and hanging down before, was put acroſs the ſtomach, and made uſe of as a girdle to the tunic; on this garment was faſtened the breaſt-plate—alſo the father of *Hanniel*.

EPH'-OR, [i. e. *duſt or lead.*] Several perſons of that name. See EPHER.

EPH'-PHA-THA, ['Εφφαθὰ.] The *hebrew* word for, *be opened*.

EPH'-RA-IM, ['Εφϱαὶμ, i. e. *fruitful or increaſing.*] The *ſecond* ſon of the patriarch *Joſeph* by *Aſenath* the daughter of *Potiphar*—alſo a diviſion and a city of *Judæa*.

EPH'-RA-IM-ITES. The poſterity of the patriarch *Ephraim*.

EPH'-RA-TAH, ['Εφϱαθὰ, i. e. *abundance or fertility.*] A place near to *Bethlehem* in *Judæa:* it alſo de-notes the tribe of *Ephraim*—alſo the founder of *Bethlehem*.

EPH'-

EPH'-RATH, ['Εφραθ, i. e. *abundance or fertility*.] A wife of *Caleb*—also the same place as *Bethlehem*.

EPH'-RATH-ITES. The inhabitants of *Ephrath*.

EPH'-RŌN, ['Εφραν, i. e. *dust*.] An *Hittite*, the son of *Zoar*, who sold to *Abraham* the land for a burial place—also a city of *Palestine* between the lands of *Gilead* and *Judah*.

EP-I-CU-RE'-ANS, ['Επικυρειοι, i. e. *aiders or helpers*.] A sect of *Greek* philosophers who held the supreme good to be pleasure, and the supreme evil to be pain: they believed in a GOD, but denied a Providence.

EP-IPH'-A-NĒS, ['Επιφανης, i. e. *illustrious*.] The surname of *Antiochus*, a king of *Syria*.

E *before* R.

ĒR, ['Ηρ, i. e. *a watchman*.] The first-born son of the patriarch *Judah*.

ER'-AN, ['Εδεν, i. e. *a follower*.] One of the posterity of the patriarch *Ephraim*.

ER'-AN-ITES. The posterity of *Eran*.

ER-AS'-TUS, ['Εραςο, i. e. *amiable*.] Chamberlain of the city of *Corinth*, converted by St. *Paul*, and supposed to be bishop of *Macedonia*.

ER'-ECH, ['Ορεχ, i. e. *length, or health*.] Part of *Nimrod's* kingdom in *Mesopotamia* in *Asia*.

E'-RI, ['Αχδεις. 'Αδδι, i. e. *my city*.] A son of *Gad* the patriarch.

E *before* S.

E-SA-I'-AH or E-SA-I'-AS. See ISAIAH.

E-SAR-HAD'-DON, ['Ασαραδαν, i. e. *binding, chearfulness*.] A son of and successor to *Senacherib* king of *Assyria*; he died, A. M. 3336.

E'-SAU, ['Ησαυ, i. e. *doing, or working*.] Twin brother to *Jacob* by *Rebeckah*: son to the patriarch *Isaac*.

ES'-DRAS, ['Εσδρας, i. e. *an helper*.] The name of *two* of the apocryphal books—also a *jewish* chief priest.

ES-DRE'-

ES-DRE'-LON, ['Εσδρηλώμ, i. e. *the helper of strength*.] A king of antient *Asia*—also a city in the tribe of *Issachar*.

ES'-EB-ŌN, ['Εσεβών.] A place in the land of *Palestine*.

ES-EB-RI'-AS, ['Εσερεβίας.] A priest who returned from the babylonish captivity.

E'-SEK, ['Αδικία, i. e. *contention*.] A well of *Gerar*, so named by *Isaac* the patriarch.

ESH'-BA-AL, ['Ασαβάλ, i. e. *the fire of the ruler*.] The same with *Ishbosheth* the *fourth* son of king *Saul*.

ESH'-BAN, ['Ασβάν, i. e. *fire of the sun*.] A city of *Palestine*, in the tribe of *Judah*—also a descendant from *Esau*.

ESCH'-COL, ['Εσχώλ, i. e. *grapes, or a cluster*.] The name of an *Amorite*—also a valley and brook in the land of *Canaan*—also the brother of *Mamre* and *Aner*.

ESH'-E-AN, ['Εσάν, i. e. *held up*.] A mountainous place of *Palestine*, in the tribe of *Judah*.

E'-SHEK, ['Ασέκ, i. e. *violence, or force*.] One of king *Saul*'s posterity.

ESH'-KA-LŌN, ["Ασκάλων, i. e. *the fire of slander*.] The same with *Askalon*; which see.

ESH'-KA-LŌN-ITES, ['Ασκαλωνίται.] The people of *Eshkalon* or *Ascalon*.

ESH'-TA-ŌL, ['Αγαώλ, i. e. *a strong woman*.] A city of *Palestine*, in the tribe of *Dan*, but first in the tribe of *Judah* in the valley.

ESH'-TAUL-ITES, [i. e. *strong women*.] Descendants from *Caleb* the son of *Hur*.

ESH-TE'-MO-A or ESH-TE'-MOTH, ['Εσθημοὰ, i. e. *which is heard, or the bosom of a woman*.] A levitical city of *Palestine*, in the tribe of *Judah*.

ESH'-TON, ['Ασσαθών.] One of the posterity of *Judah* the patriarch.

ES'-LI, 'Εσλὶ, i. e. *near me*.] The son of *Nagge*, mentioned by St. *Luke* in his genealogy of *Christ*.

ES-MA-CHI'-AH. See *Ismachiah*.

ES-O'-RA, ['Αισωρὰ.]   The name of a place in *Pale-stine.*

ES'-RIL, ['Εσρὶλ.]   One who returned from the ba-bylonish captivity.

ES'-ROM, ['Εσρὼμ, i. e. *the dart of joy.*]   The name of one mentioned by St. *Matthew* and St. *Luke,* in their genealogies of *Christ.*

ES'-SENES.   A very strict sect of the *Jews.*

EST'-HA-ŌL.   See ESHTAOL.

EST'-HĒR, ['Εσθὴρ, i. e. *secret, or hidden.*]   A *first* cousin to *Mord·cai* the Jew; of the tribe of *Ben-jamin,* and wife to king *Ahasuerus;* after whose name the *seventeenth* canonical book of the *Old Testament* is called—also one of the books of the *Apocrypha.*

E *before* T.

E'-TAM, ['Αιτὰμ. 'Ητάμ, i. e. *their bird, or their covering.*]   A village of *Palestine,* in the tribe of *Judah.*

ETH'-AM, ['Οθωμ, i. e. *their strength.*]   The *first* encampment of the *Israelites* in the wilderness.

ETH'-AN, ['Εθάν, i. e. *strength.*]   An *Ezrahite,* one of the wisest men of his time—also others.

ETH'-A-NIM, ['Αθανίν, i. e. *strong, or valiant.*]   The *seventh jewish* month, answering to part of our *September* and part of *October:* after the captivity it was called *Tizri.*

ETH'-BA-AL, ['Ιεθεβαὰλ, i. e. *unto an image.*]   A king of *Zidon,* and father to *Jezebel.*

ETH'-ER, ['Ιεθὲρ, i. e. *talk.*]   A city of *Palestine,* in the tribe of *Judah,* in the valley; also of *Simeon.*

E-THI-OP'-I-A, ['Αιθιοπία.]   See ÆTHIOPIA.

E-THI-OP'-I-ANS, ['Αιθιοπες.]   See ÆTHIOPI-ANS.

ETH'-MA, ['Εθμὰ.]   One whose sons returned from the babylonish captivity.

ETH'-NAN, ['Εθνάν, i. e. *a gift.*]   One of the pos-terity of *Asher* the son of patriarch *Jacob.*

ETH'-NI, ['Αθανὶ, i. e. *strong.*]   One of the descend-ants of *Levi* the patriarch.

E before

E *before* U *and* V.

EU-AS'-I-BUS, ['Ευάσιϐ©.]   One who returned from the babyloniſh captivity.

EU-BU'-LUS, ["Ευϐϵλ©, i. e. *prudent or wiſe.*] One of the apoſtle *Paul's* converts.

EVE, ["Ευα, i. e. *living, or enlivening.*] The *firſt* woman, or the *mother* of mankind.

E'-VI, ['Ευὶ, i. e. *unjuſt.*]   A king of *Midian* in *Aſia*.

E'-VIL ME-RO'-DACH, ['Ευιαλμαρωδὲκ, i. e. *the food of Merodach.*]   A king of antient *Babylon*, who ſucceeded *Nebuchadnezzar* the great: he died A. M. 3445.

EU'-MEN-ES, ['Ευμένης.]   A king of *Bythinia* and *Pergamus* in *Aſia*.

EU'-NA-TAN, ['Εννατὰν.]   A principal man among the *jews* after the babyloniſh captivity.

EU-NI'-CE, ['Ευνίκη, i. e. *good victory.*]   A *jeweſs* by birth, married to an *heathen*; ſhe was mother to *Timothy* who was a favourite of St. *Paul*, who wrote two epiſtles to him.

EU-O'-DI-AS, ['Ευωδίας, i. e. *a good ſmell.*]   A female convert of the apoſtle *Paul*, who mentions her in his epiſtle to the *Philippians*.

EU'-PA-TŌR, ['Ευπάτωρ, i. e. *good father.*]   The ſurname of king *Antiochus*.

EU-PHRA'-TES, [Ευφράτης, i. e. *fruitful.*]   A large river of *Aſia*, riſing in the mountains of *Armenia*, running through *Cappadocia*, *Syria*, *Arabia Deſerta*, *Chaldæa*, and *Meſopotamia*; and emptying into the *Perſian gulph*.

EU-POL'-EM-US, ['Ευπόλεμ©, i. e. *fighting well.*]   One of the embaſſadors of *Judas Maccabæus*.

EU-ROC'-LY-DŌN, ['Ευροκλυδων, i. e. *a north eaſt wind.*]   A *north eaſt wind* in the *mediterranean ſea*, now called a *Levantor*.

EU'-TY-CHUS, ['Ευτυχ©, i. e. *happy, or fortunate.*]   A youth, who fell from a window whilſt St. *Paul* was preaching, but was recovered by the apoſtle.

E *before* X.

EX'-OD-US, ['Εξοδος.] The second canonical book of the *Old Testament*; called so, from the *going out*, or *departure* of the children of *Israel* from *Ægypt*; this book treating, chiefly, upon that subject.

EX-OR'-CIST, ['Εξορχιστης.] Is one who hath the power of casting out devils, or diseases. This power was given by our *Saviour* to his disciples; which they exercised for the benefit of mankind; and is supposed to have continued about 200 years in the christian church. This power was also pretended to by others.

E *before* Z.

EZ'-AR, ['Ασαρ.] A son of *Seir*, a descendant from the patriarch *Esau*.

EZ'-BA-I, ['Ασβαι.] The name of one of king *David*'s worthies.

EZ'-BON, ['Εσεβων, i. e. *hastening to understand*.] One of the posterity of the patriarch *Benjamin*—also a son of *Gad*.

EZ-EK'-I-EL, ['Ιεζεκιηλ. L. *Ezek'iel*, i. e. *the strength of God*.] The son of *Buzi*, of the house of *Aaron*: he was carried captive to *Babylon* with *Jehoiakim* king of *Judah*: he was one of the greater prophets, and his prophecy makes one of the canonical books of sacred writ.

E'-ZEL, [i. e. *a walking, or of the way*.] The name of a stone mentioned in the agreement between *Jonathan* and *David*.

E'-ZEM or A'-ZEM, ['Αισεμ, i. e. *a bone*.] A place of *Palestine*, in the tribe of *Simeon*.

EZ'-ER, ['Εζερ, i. e. *an help*.] One of the sons of *Ephraim* the patriarch, who was slain at *Gath*— also a son of *Seir*.

EZ-ER-I'-AS, ['Εζεριας.] The grandfather of *Esdras* in the *Apocrypha*.

EZ-I'-

EZ-I'-AS, ['Oζίος.]   An anceſtor of *Eſdras.*

EZ'-I-ŌN GE'-BAR or EZ'-I-ŌN GA'-BAR, [Γε-σιὼν Γάβεϱ, i. e. *counſel of man.*]   A city and ſea-port of *Idumæa,* on the coaſt of the *red ſea*—alſo the *thirty-ſecond* encampment of the *Iſraelites,* in the wildernefs.

EZ'-NITE.   The name of a *jewiſh* family.

EZ'-RA, ['Eσϱὶ. 'Eσδϱὰς, i. e. *an helper.*]   A *jewiſh* ſcribe, the ſon of *Seraiah,* who wrote one of the canonical books of the *Old Teſtament,* which is entitled *Ezra.*

EZ'-RA-HITE, [Eζϱαναΐτης.]   The meaning un-certain.

EZ'-RI, [Eζϱaì, i. e. *my help.*]   An overſeer of tillage in *Judæa,* appointed by king *Solomon.*

EZ'-RI-ĒL, ['Eσϱιὴλ, i. e. *the help of God.*]   See AZRIEL.

EZ'-RIL, ['Eσϱὶλ.]   One who returned from the ba-byloniſh captivity.

EZ'-RŌN or HEZ'-RŌN, ['Aσϱὼμ, i. e. *the arrow of joy.*]   A ſon of *Reuben* the patriarch—alſo a ſon of *Pharez*—alſo a city called *Hazor.*

EZ'-RŌN-ITES.   The defcendants from *Ezron.*

F.

F *before* A.

FAIR-HAVENS.   Mentioned in the book of the *Acts:* ſuppoſed to be on the coaſt of the iſle of *Crete.*

FAT VALLEY.   The vallies in the tribe of *Ephraim,* in the land of *Paleſtine,* were ſo called from the richneſs and fertility of their ſoil.

F *before* E.

FEASTS. The *jews* obferved fundry feftivals—as the feaft of unleavened bread, or the *paffover*. See *Paffover*. The feaft of *tabernacles*. See *Tabernacles*. The feaft of *weeks* or *pentecoft*. See *Pentecoft*. The feaft of *trumpets*, which was celebrated on the firft and fecond day of the month *Tifri*, or the firft month of the civil year—the *jews* in general believe that it was inftituted in memory of the creation, which, they fay, was in that month—fome fay, that it was in memory of *Ifaac*'s deliverance from being facrificed—others, that it was in commemoration of the law being given from mount *Sinai*, when the trumpet and thunder were heard—and others, that it was in preparation, to put mankind in mind of the *general refurrection*, which is to be ufhered in by the found of a trumpet—but the moft probable reafon feems to be, the proclaiming the entrance of the *civil* year; as all contracts, mortgages, &c. were to be regulated by it.

The feaft of the *new moons* was obferved on the firft day of every moon; and thofe who obferved or thought they obferved the *new moon*, were to repair with all fpeed to the grand council, and give notice of it: and according to the credibility of the witneffes, the prefident proclaimed the *new moon* by found of trumpet. All thefe feafts were obferved by facrifices.

The foregoing feafts were appointed by the *mofaic* law; but in procefs of time, the *jews* added others: as the feaft of *Purim* or of *lots*, in memory of their deliverance from *Haman*'s cruelty —alfo the feaft of the *dedication* of the temple; and others.

FE′-LIX, [Φῆλιξ, i. e. *happy, or profperous*.] The *Roman* procurator of *Judæa*, A. D. 54, who fent for St. *Paul* and heard him difcourfe on the doctrines of Chriftianity.

FES′-TUS

FES'-TUS (*Por'-ti-us*) [i. e. *joyful.*] The *Roman* governor of *Judæa*, who succeeded *Felix*, A. D. 60.

F *before* O.

FOR-TU-NA'-TUS, [i. e. *happy, or prosperous.*] One mentioned by St. *Paul* in his first epistle to the *Corinthians*, who came from *Corinth* to *Ephesus* to visit the apostle.

FOX'-ES.   It is by no means probable that those animals which in sacred writ are called *foxes*, were of the same species which are *now* called *foxes*—the *hebrew* word *Shual*, translated *fox*, will comprehend other animals, and perhaps all other beasts of prey of the same size—these creatures were exceeding numerous in *Judæa*, and several places received their names from them, as *Hazar-Shual, the. gate of the fox, &c.*—they went together in large herds, so that *two hundred* have been seen in a company, whereas *our* fox is not a gregarious animal—besides, they were very fond of grapes, and destroyed their vineyards; in allusion to which is that verse in chap. ii. of *Solomon's song*, viz. *take us the foxes, the little foxes, that spoil the vines: for our vines have tender grapes.*

F *before* R.

FRONT'-LET.   A square piece of calf's skin, including four pieces of parchment, on each side of which the *Jews* wrote a passage of their law, and which were worn on their foreheads.

G.

G before A.

GA'-AL, [Γααλ, i. e. *contempt, or abomination.*] The son of *Ebed,* suppofed to be a *gentile,* who was defirous of having the *Canaanites* eftablifhed again in *Shechem.*

GA'-ASH, [Γαάς, i. e. *a ftorm.*] An hill of *Paleftine* near to mount *Ephraim,* from whence a brook arofe, and near to the burial place of *Joshua.*

GA'-BA, [Γαβαὰ, i. e. *an hill.*] A city in the north of *Paleftine,* in the tribe of *Benjamin.* See *Geba.*

GAB'-A-ĒL, [Γαβαήλ.] One mentioned in the book of *Tobit,* the brother of *Gabrias.*

GAB'-A-THA, [Γαβαθὰ.] An eunuch of *Artaxerxes* king of *Perfia.*

GAB'-BAI, [Γηβὲ, i. e. *the back.*] One of the chiefs of the tribe of *Benjamin.*

GAB'-BA-THA, [Γαββαθᾶ, i. e. *high, or elevated, or paved with ftone.*] The place from which *Pilate* pronounced judgment againft our *Saviour;* called *the pavement.*

GA'-BRI-AS, [Γαβρία.] One mentioned in the book of *Tobit,* the brother of *Gabael.*

GA'-BRI-ĒL, [Γαβρίηλ, i. e. *a man of God, or the ftrength of God.*] One of the principal angels of Heaven.

GAD, [Γαδ, i. e. *a band, a garrifon, happy, or ready.*] The fon of the patriarch *Jacob* by *Zilpah* the handmaid of *Leah:* his allotment was beyond the

the river *Jordan*—alſo the name of a prophet
who followed *David*'s fortune when he was perſe-
cuted by *Saul*.

GAD'-A-RA, [Γαδαρα.] A famous city beyond the
river *Jordan*.

GAD'-A-RENES, [Γαδαρηνοῖ, i. e. *walled, or hedged
about.*] The people of *Gadara*.

GAD'-DĒS, [Γαδδῆς.] The name of a place in *Paleſtine*.

GAD'-DI, [Γαδδὶ, i. e. *my army, or a kid.*] One of
the tribe of *Joſeph*, i. e. of *Ephraim* or *Manaſſeh*,
ſent by *Moſes* to view the land of *Canaan*.

GAD'-DI-EL, [Γαδιὴλ, i. e. *the God of felicity.*] The
ſon of *Sodi*, of the tribe of *Zebulun*, ſent by *Moſes*
to view the land of *Canaan*.

GAD'-I, [Γαδδι.] Father to *Menahim*, who ſlew *Shallum* the king of *Samaria*.

GAD'-ITES. The deſcendants from *Gad* the patriarch.

GA'-HAM, [Γααμ.] A ſon of *Nahor*, *Abraham*'s
brother, by his concubine *Reumah*.

GA'-HAR, [Γααρ.] One whoſe children were *Nethinims*, when the *Jews* returned from the *babyloniſh* captivity.

GA-I'-US, [Γαῖος, i. e. *Lord, or an earthly man.*] A
diſciple of St. *Paul*, and his hoſt at *Corinth*;
he is ſaid to have been made biſhop of *Theſſalonica*.

GA'-LA-AD, [Γαλααδ.] A place in the land of
Moab.

GA'-LAL, [Γαλαλ, i. e. *a role, or wheel.*] A *Levite*
who ſettled firſt in *Judæa*, after the *babyloniſh*
captivity.

GA-LA'-TI-A, [Γαλατια, i. e. *white, or of the colour
of milk.*] A province of *Aſia Minor*, ſo called
from the *Galetæ* or *Gauls*: now *Chiagare*.

GA-LA'-TI-ANS, [Γαλάται.] The people of *Gala-
tia*, to the Chriſtians of which St. *Paul* wrote
his epiſtle, which is part of the canon of
Scripture.

GAL'-BA-

GAL'-BA-NUM, [Γαλβάνη.] A gum of a plant growing in *Arabia* and other parts of *Afia*, which flows by incifion of the plant.

GA'-LE-ED, [i. e. *the heap of witnefs*.] A *pillar of ftones* fet up as a witnefs of a covenant between *Laban* and *Jacob:* called fo by *Jacob.* See *Jegar-fahadutha.*

GAL'-GA-LA, [Γάλγαλα.] A city of *Affyria* in *Afia.*

GAL'-I-LEE, [Γαλιλαία, i. e. *turning, rolling, or a wheel.*] A province of *Paleftine,* divided into upper and lower *Galilee*; the upper called *Galilee of the Gentiles,* becaufe bordering upon gentile nations.

GAL-I-LE'-ANS, [Γαλιλαῖοι.] The people of *Galilee.*

GAL'-LIM, [Γαλλείμ, i. e. *heaping up together.*] A place mentioned in the *firft* book of *Samuel,* and by the prophet *Ifaiah.*

GAL'-LI-O, [Γαλλίων, i. e. *he who lives upon milk.*] The brother of *Seneca* the philofopher, and pro-conful of *Achaia.*

GA'-MA-ĒL, [Γαμαήλ.] A fon of *Ithamar.*

GA-MA'-LI-ĒL, [Γαμαλιήλ, i. e. *God's reward, or camel of God.*] Prince of the tribe of *Manaffeh* when the *Ifraelites* came out of *Egypt*—alfo a *pharifee* who was tutor to St. *Paul* when he was called *Saul.*

GAM'-MA-DIMS, [Γαμμαδείμ, i. e. *dwarfs, or a cubit.*] Uncertain who they were: fome fuppofe them to be *Africans,* others *Phœnicians,* &c.

GA'-MUL, [Γαμùλ, i. e. *a recompence.*] One, who by the *twenty-fecond lot* was of the priefthood in king *David's* reign.

GAR, [Γὰρ.] One of the fervants of *Solomon.*

GA'-REB, [Γαρήβ, i. e. *a fcab.*] An *Ithrite,* one of king *David's* worthies—alfo an hill near to or at *Jerufalem.*

GA-RIZ'-IM, [Γαριζὶν.] See GERIZIM.

GAR'-MITES, [i. e. *bones, or my caufe.*] A people uncertain who they were.

GASH'-MU, [Γησάμ.] Suppofed to be the fame with *Gefhem.*

GAT'-AM, [Γοθὼμ, i. e. *their bellowing.*] The son of *Eliphaz* and grandson of the patriarch *Esau.*

GATH, [Γἐθ, i. e. *a wine press.*] A noted city, and one of the *five* principalities of the *Philistines,* about thirty-two miles *west* of *Jerusalem.*

GATH HEPH'-ER, [Γαιθεφἑϱ.] A city of the tribe of *Zebulun* in *Palestine,* where the prophet *Jonah* was born.

GATH RIM'-MŌN, [Γεθϱεμμὰν, i. e. *the high wine press.*] A city of *Palestine,* in the tribe of *Dan.*

GAU'-LAN or GAU'-LON. A famous city beyond the river *Jordan,* from whence the province *Gaulonitis* was named.

GA'-ZA, [Γαζὰ, i. e. *strong, or a goat.*] A city of the *Philistines,* made part of the tribe of *Judah,* in the valley.

GA'-ZA-BAR, [i. e. *a treasurer.*] A prince of the tribe of *Judah:* the same with *Sheshbazzar.*

GA-ZA'-RA, [Γαζήϱα.] A place of *Palestine,* in the tribe of *Dan.*

GA'-ZATH-ITES, [Γαζαίοι.] The inhabitants of *Gaza.*

GA'-ZER, [Γαζηϱά, i. e. *dividing, or a sentence.*] A city of the *Philistines,* in the tribe of *Ephraim.*

GA'-ZE'-RA, [Γαζηϱά.] One whose sons returned from the babylonish captivity, and were servants of the temple.

GAZ'-EZ, [Γεζὲ, i. e. *a passing over.*] The name of a son and grandson of *Caleb.*

GAZ'-ITES, [Γαζαίοι.] The inhabitants of *Gaza.*

GAZ'-ZAM, [Γαζὲμ, i. e. *the fleece of them.*] One who returned from the babylonish captivity.

G before E.

GE'-BA, [Γαϐαὶ. Γαϐαὶ, i. e. *an hill.*] A city of *Palestine,* given to the *Levites.*

GEB'-AL, [Γεϐὰλ, i. e. *the end.*] A city of *Syria.*

GEB'-AR or GEB'-ER, [Ναϐὲϱ, i. e. *manly, strong.*] One of king *Solomon's* principal officers over *Israel.*

GEB'-

GEB'-IM, [Γιββεὶρ, i. e. *grafshoppers*.] A place in *Paleſtine*, mentioned by the prophet *Iſaiah*.

GED-AL-I'-AH, [Γοδολίας, i. e. *the greatneſs of the Lord*.] The ſon of *Ahikam*, a governor of the *Jews*, whom *Nebuchadnezzar* had left to govern in *Judæa*—alſo others.

GED'-DŬR, [Γεδδὴρ.] One whoſe ſons were ſervants of the temple.

GED'-ĒR. See *Gedir*.

GED-E'-RAH, [Γαδηρα, i. e. *a wall*.] A city of *Paleſtine*, in the tribe of *Judah*, in the valley.

GED-E'-RATH-ITE, [Γαδαραθαιὸς.] An inhabitant of *Gederah*.

GED'-ĒR-ITE. An inhabitant of *Gederah*.

GED-E'-ROTH, [Γεδηρώθ.] See *Gedir*.

GED-E-ROTH-A'-IM, [Γαδαραθεὶμ, i. e. *hedges*.] A city of *Paleſtine*, in the tribe of *Judah*, in the valley.

GED'-IR, [Γαδὲρ, Γεδώρ, i. e. *a wall*.] A place which *Joſhua* took in *Canaan*, in the tribe of *Judah* in the valley.

GED'-ŌR, [Γεδώρ. Γεδδώρ, i. e. *hedges*.] A city of *Paleſtine*, in the tribe of *Judah*, in the mountains —a deſcendant from *Benjamin*—and others.

GE-HAZ'-I, [Γιεζὶ, i. e. *valley of ſight*.] The ſervant of *Eliſha* the prophet, who received preſents from *Naaman* the *Syrian*, and was ſtruck with a leproſy for it.

GEL'-I-LŌTH, [Γαλιλώθ.] See GILGAL.

GE-MAL'-LI, [Γαμαλί, i. e. *wares, or a camel*.] One of the tribe of *Dan*, whoſe ſon was ſent to ſpy out the land of *Canaan*.

GEM-A-RI'-AH, [Γαμαρίος, i. e. *perfection, or conſuming of the Lord*.] The ſon of *Hilkiah*: he was ſent to *Babylon* by king *Zedekiah*, to carry the tribute money to *Nebuchadnezzar*.

GEN-E'-SAR, [Γεννησὰρ.] See *Geneſareth*.

GEN-E'-SA-RETH, [Γεννσαρέτ. Γεννσὰρ, i. e. *the garden of a prince*.] A lake of *Judæa*, the ſame with the lake of *Tiberias*, or ſea of *Cinnereth*.

GEN'-ES-IS [Γενεσις, i. e. *in the beginning.*] The *firſt* canonical book of the *Old Teſtament,* and the *firſt* of the *Pentateuch.*

GEN-NE'-US, [Γενναιος.] The father of one of the *Appollonius's,* an oppreſſor of the *jews.*

GEN-U'-BATH, [Γαυνϐαϑ, i. e. *theft, or garden of the daughter.*] The ſon of *Hadad,* the *Edomite*; born in *Egypt,* of royal parentage.

GEN'-TILES. Thoſe who had not received the faith and law of GOD, were ſo called by the *Hebrews.*

GE'-ŌN, [Γηων.] A river of *Canaan.*

GE'-RA, [Γηρα, i. e. *a pilgrim, or ſtranger.*] A *Benjamite,* the father of *Ehud* who ſlew *Eglon* king of *Moab.*

GE'-RAH. A *jewiſh* coin, about *one penny half penny* in our ſterling money.

GER'-AR, [Γεραρα, i. e. *a pilgrimage, or a ſtriving.*] A royal city of the *Philiſtines*; in the tribe of *Simeon.*

GE'-RA-SA. A city to the *eaſt* of the *dead ſea,* either in *Cœlo-Syria,* or in *Arabia.*

GER'-GASH-I. See GIRGASHI.

GER'-GASH-ITES, [Γεργεσαιοι, i. e. *who arrive from pilgrimage.*] An antient people of *Canaan* beyond the ſea of *Tiberias*; deſcended from *Canaan* the ſon of *Ham.*

GER-GES-ENES', [Γεργεσηνοι.] The ſame as *Gergaſhites.*

GE-RIZ'-IM, [Γαριζιν, i. e. *hatchets.*] A famous mountain of *Samaria,* on which the *Levites* were commanded to bleſs the *Iſraelites.*

GER-RIN'-I-ANS or GER-RÆ'-ANS, [Γερρηνοι.] Probably the inhabitants of *Gerar.*

GER'-SHOM, [Γηρσαμ, i. e. *a ſtranger there.*] The ſon of *Moſes* and *Zipperah.*

GER'-SHŌN, [Γηρσων, i. e. *his baniſhment.*] A ſon of the patriarch *Lvi,* and prince of one of the families of the *Levites.*

GER'-SHŌN-ITES. The poſterity of *Gerſhon.*

GER'-SHŪR, [Γεσσηρ.] A country of *Syria :* king *David* married a daughter of their king, by whom he had *Abſalom.*

GES'-EM,

GES'-EM, [Γεσὲμ.] See GOSHEN.

GE'-SHAN or GE'-SHĒN, [Γηροὰμ, i. e. *drawing near*.] One of the defcendants from *Hezron*.

GE-SHEM, [Γησὰμ, i. e. *rain*.] An *Arabian* who oppofed *Nehemiah* in building the walls of *Jerufalem*.

GESH'-ŪR, [Γεδσὰρ. Γεσσὶρ, i. e. *a walled valley*.] A city of *Syria* where *Talmai* was king.

GESH'-UR-I, [Γαργασὶ.] A place of *Syria*, near the river *Jordan*; probably the fame with *Geſhur*.

GESH'-UR-ITES, [Γεσιρὶ.] The inhabitants of *Geſhur*.

GETH'-ER, [Γαθὲρ. Γεθὲρ, i. e. *the valley of fearching out*.] The fon of *Aram*, and grandfon of *Shem*, who fettled in *Syria*.

GETH-OL-I'-AS, [Γοδολίας.] One who returned from the babylonifh captivity.

GETH-SE'-MA-NE, [Γεθσημανῆ, i. e. *a plentiful valley*.] A village in the mount of *Olives*: in the tribe of *Benjamin*.

GĒ-U'-ĒL, [Γεδιὴλ, i. e. *God's redemption*.] One of the tribe of *Gad*, fent to fpy out the land of *Canaan*.

GEZ'-ER, [Γαζὲρ, i. e. *dividing or a fentence*.] A place which *Joſhua* took in the land of *Canaan*. See *Gedir*.

GEZ'-RITES, [Γεσιρὸι.] A people of *Philiſtia*, towards *Ægypt*.

G *before* I.

GI'-AH, [Γαὶ, i. e. *a figh or a groan*.] A place of *Canaan*, near to the wildernefs of *Gibeon*.

GIB'-BAR, [Γαβὲρ, i. e. *ſtrong or manly*.] One who returned from the babylonifh captivity.

GIB'-BETH-ŌN, [Βεγεθῶν, i. e. *a back or an high houſe*.] A city of *Paleſtine* in the tribe of *Dan*, allotted to the *Levites*.

GIB'-E-A or GIB'-E-AH, [Γαβαὰ, i. e. *an hill*.] A city of the tribe of *Benjamin*, about three miles north of *Jerufalem*—alfo one of *Caleb*'s grandfons —alfo a city of *Judah*.

I 3   GIB'-

GIB'-E-ATH, [Γαβαὰθ, i. e. *an hill.*] A city of the tribe of *Benjamin* in *Paleſtine.*

GIB'-E-ŌN, [Γαβαὼν, i. e. *an hill.*] A city about *five* miles from *Jeruſalem*, near to *Gibeah :* in the tribe of *Benjamin.*

GIB'-E-ŌN-ITES, [Γαβαωνῖται.] The inhabitants of *Gibeon :* the remnant of the *Amorites.*

GIB'-LITES. A people of the land of *Canaan.*

GID-DAL'-TI, [Γοδολλαϑι.] The ſon of *Heman* the *Levite.*

GID'-DĒL, [Γεδδὴλ, i. e. *great.*] One who returned from the babyloniſh captivity.

GID'-E-ŌN, [Γεδεὼν, i. e. *a breaker or deſtroyer.*] The ſon of *Joaſh* of the tribe of *Manaſſeh :* the ſame with *Jerubbaal ;* the ſeventh judge of *Iſrael*, A. M. 2731, died A. M. 2770.

GID'-E-O'-NI, Γαδεωνί, i. e. *a breaker or deſtroyer.*] One of the tribe of *Benjamin.*

GID'-OM, [Γεδὼν.] A place in the land of *Paleſtine.*

GI'-ER EA'-GLE. It is the *vulture-eagle*, a bird between the vulture and the eagle : *gier* is the old engliſh word for *vulture.*

GI'-HŌN, [Γεῶν, i. e. *a breaſt, or valley of grace.*] The name of one of the *four* rivers of *Paradiſe.*

GIL-A-LA'-I, [Γελὼλ, i. e. *a wheel or marble.*] A *Levite* who officiated at the dedication of the new walls of *Jeruſalem.*

GIL-BO'-A, [Γελβυέ, i. e. *revolution of enquiry.*] A mountain of *Paleſtine* in the half tribe of *Manaſſeh*, famous for the death of *Saul* and his ſon *Jonathan.*

GIL'-E-AD, [Γαλαὰδ, i. e. *the heap of witneſs.*] Mountains of *Paleſtine*, in the tribes of *Reuben*, *Gad*, and the half tribe of *Manaſſeh*—alſo the name of *Jephtha's* father—alſo a ſon of *Manaſſeh.*

GIL'-EAD-ITE, [Γαλααδίτ℗.] An inhabitant of *Gilead.*

GIL'-GAL, [Γολγὸλ. Γαλγαλὰ, i. e. *a wheel or revolution.*] A place to the *weſt* of the river *Jordan*, where the *Iſraelites* encamped : in the half tribe of *Manaſſeh.*

GI'-LOH,

GI'-LOH, [Γηλώμ, i. e. *a rejoicing, or discovering.*]
A city of *Palestine* in the tribe of *Judah,* in the
mountains.

GIL-O'-NITE, [Γελωνίτ☉.]   An inhabitant of
Gileh.

GIM'-ZO, [Γαμζὼ, i. e. *that bulrush.*] A city of *Palestine* to the south of the tribe of *Judah.*

GI'-NATH, [Γανὰθ, i. e. *a garden.*] Father to *Tibni*
whom the *Israelites* desired for their king.

GIN'-NE-THO or GIN'-NE-THŌN, [Γανναθὼν,
i. e. *a garden.*] One of the *Levites* who sealed the
covenant, together with *Nehemiah* the governor.

GIR'-GASH-I, [Γεργεσαῖος, i. e. *drawing near to pilgrimage.*]   A son of *Canaan.*

GIR'-GASH-ITES, [Γεργεσαῖοι.   See *Gergashites.*

GIS'-PA, [Γεσφὰς, i. e. *coming hither.*]   One who
superintended the *Nethinims* or labourers in the
temple service.

GIT'-TAH HEPH'-ER, [Γεθαεφέρ, i. e. *digging a
wine press.*]   A place of *Palestine* in the tribe of
Zebulun.

GIT'-TA-IM, [Γεθαὶμ, i. e. *a wine press.*] A city of
Palestine in the tribe of *Benjamin.*

GIT'-TITES, [Γετθαῖοι, i. e. *wine presses.*]   The inhabitants of the city of *Gath.*

GIT'-TITH.   In the title of some of the *Psalms,* is
supposed to be an harp or instrument of musick,
used by the inhabitants of *Gath* and *Philistia.*

GI-ZO'-NITE, [i. e. *shaving.*] The appellation uncertain.

G *before* L.

GLEDE.   A bird of the *kite* species.

G *before* N.

GNI'-DUS.   See *Cnidus.*

G *before* O.

GO'-AT *(fcape)* The goat which was fet at liberty on the day of folemn expiation (among the *jews*) bearing away or efcaping with the fins of the people.

GO'-ATH, [i. e. *his touching, or, his roaring.*] A place in or near to *Jerufalem.*

GOB, [Γὸβ, i. e. *grafshoppers.*] A place in the land of *Palefiine*, called alfo *Gezar.*

GŌG, [Γὼγ, i. e. *a roof of an houfe.*] Son to *Shemaiah*, of the pofterity of *Reuben*—alfo *Gog* and *Magog* in an allegorical fenfe, are fuppofed to be the enemies of the church and faints.

GO'-LAN, [Γαυλὼν, i. e. *a paffing over.*] A city of refuge in the half tribe of *Manaffeh*, given to the *Levites.* See *Bafhan.*

GOL'-GOTH-A, [Γολγοθὰ, i. e. *an heap of fkulls.*] The *hebrew* word for *the place of a fkull*; where they crucified our *Saviour*; alfo called *Calvary.*

GOL'-I-AH or GOL'-I-ATH, [Γολιὰθ, L. *Gol'-i-ath.* i. e. *a captivity, or paffing over.*] A famous *phili-fline* champion, flain by king *David; about eleven feet and three inches in fiature.*

GOM'-ER, [Γομὲρ, i. e. *confuming, or wanting.*] The fon of *Japhet* and grandfon of *Noah*—alfo *Hofeah's* figurative wife.

GOM-OR'-RAH, [Γομόρρα, i. e. *a rebellious people.*] One of the *five* cities deftroyed by fire in *Lot's* time.

GO'-PHER WOOD. Suppofed to be the wood of the *cyprefs tree.*

GOR'-GI-AS, [Γοργίας, i. e. *terrible or fwift.*] A famous captain in the troops of *Antiochus Epiphanes.*

GOR'-TY-NA, [Γορτυνα.] An inland city of the ifland of *Crete.*

GOSH'-EN, [Γεσὲμ. Γοσὸμ, i. e. *a drawing near.*] A canton of *Ægypt*, which *Jofeph* procured for his father and brethren to dwell in—alfo a city of *Palefiine*, in the tribe of *Judah*, in the mountains.

GOTH-

GOTH-ON-I'-ĔL, [Γοθονιηλ.] Father of *Chabris* a governor of *Bethulia.*

GO'-ZAN, [Γωζὰν, i. e. *fleece of wool, or paſſing over.*] A place ſuppoſed to be in *Aſſyria.*

G *before* R

GRA'-BA, ['Αγραβὰ.] One whoſe ſons were ſervants of the temple.

GRE'-CI-A or GREECE, [i. e. *deceiving, or making ſad.*]   A large country of *Aſia.*

GRE'-CI-ANS or GREEKS, [Γραικοὶ.]   The inhabitants of *Greece.*

G *before* U.

GUD'-GO-DAH, [Γαδγὰδ, i. e. *the happineſs of felicity.*]   A place in the wilderneſs through which the *Iſraelites* marched.

GU'-NI, [Γυνὶ, i. e. *garden or covering.*]   One of the ſons of the patriarch *Naphtali.*

GU'-NITES.   The deſcendants from *Guni.*

GŪR, [Γαὶ. Γὺρ, i. e. *a whelp.*]   The place near to which *Jehu* ſlew *Ahaziah* king of *Judah.*

GŪR BA'-AL, i. e. *the whelp of the governor.*]   A place where the *Arabians* dwelt.

H *before*

H.

H *before* A.

HA-A-HASH'-TA-RI, [i. e. *a runner.*] A fon of the patriarch *Afher.*

HAB-AI'-AH, [Δαϭεία, i. e. *the hiding of the Lord.*] One of the priefts in the time of *Ezra.*

HAB-AK'-KUK, ['Αμϭακύμ, i. e. *a wreftler.*] The *eighth* of the leffer prophets, of the tribe of *Simeon,* a native of *Bethcar:* one of the canonical books of *Scripture* was named after him.

HAB-A-ZIN'-I-AH, [Χαϭαοίν, i. e. *a hiding of the fhield of the Lord.*] One of the defcendants of *Rechab*; the father of *Jeremiah.*

HA-BER'-GE-ON. A corflet, or coat of mail.

HA'-BŌR, ['Αϭώϱ, i. e. *a fellow or partaker.*] A city of the *Medes* in *Affyria.*

HACH-A-LI'-AH, [Χελχία, i. e. *wanting of the Lord.*] The father of *Nehemiah* the governor.

HACH'-IL-AH, [Εχελᾱ, i. e. *hope in that.*] A place in the land of *Paleftine.*

HACH'-MON-I, ['Αχαμὶ, i. e. *a wife man.*] The father of *Jehiel* the tutor to king *David's* fons.

HACH'-MON-ITE. A defcendant from *Hachmoni.*

HAD'-A, [Χοδδὰν, i. e. *power, greatnefs.*] One of *Ifhmael's* fons.

HA'-DAD, ['Αδὰδ, i. e. *joy, or rejoicing.*] A king of *Moab.*

HAD-AD-EZ'-ER, ['Αδαδἑζεϱ, i. e. *comelinefs, or beautiful help.* A king of *Zobah,* who was defeated by king *David.*

HA'-DAD,

HA'-DAD-RIM'-MŌN, ['Αδαδρεμμὰν, i. e. *the voice of height.*] A town or plain near to *Jezreel* where king *Josiah* was slain.

HAD'-AR. See *Hada.*

HAD'-A-SHAH, ['Αδασὰν, i. e. *news, or a month.*] A town of *Palestine,* in the tribe of *Judah.*

HAD-AS'-SA, ['Αδασσὰ, i. e. *a myrtle tree.*] The *jewish* name for queen *Esther*; *Esther* being her *persian* name.

HAD-AT'-TAH, A city of *Palestine,* in the tribe of *Judah.*

HAD'-ID, ['Αοδαδ, i. e. *rejoicing, or sharp.*] A city in the tribe of *Benjamin.*

HAD'-LA-I, ['Ελδαὶ, i. e. *loytering, or letting.*] One of the patriarch *Ephraim*'s posterity.

HAD-O'-RAM, ['Οδοῤῥὰ. 'Αδωράμ, i. e. *their praise.*] One of the posterity of the patriarch *Shem*—also a son of *Tou* king of *Hamath.*

HAD'-RACH, [Σεδρὰχ, i. e. *joy of tenderness.*] A country of *Syria.*

HA'-GAB, ['Αγὰβ, i. e. *a grasshopper.*] One of the children of the order of *Nethinims.*

HAG'-A-BAH, ['Αγαβὰ, i. e. *a grasshopper.*] See AGABA.

HAG'-A-I, ['Αγιὰ.] A servant of *Solomon.*

HA'-GAR, ['Αγαρ, i. e. *a stranger, chewing of the cud, or fearing.*] Wife to the patriarch *Abraham* and mother of *Ishmael.*

HA-GAR-ENES', ['Αγαρηνοὶ.] The posterity of *Ishmael.*

HA'-GAR-ITES, ['Αγαρίται.] A people who possessed the country *east* of *Gilead,* chiefly belonging to the *Gadites* and *Manassites.*

HAG'-GAI, ['Αγγὶς. 'Αγγαῖος, i. e. *pleasant, or turning in a circle.*] The son of *Shimea,* a descendant from *Merari:* he was the *tenth* of the *twelve* lesser prophets; and a canonical book of *Scripture* is so named from him — also a son of the patriarch *Gad.*

HAG'-GER-I, ['Αγαρὶ, i. e. *a stranger.*] The father of *Mibhar* one of king *David*'s worthies.

HAG'-GI,

HAG'-GI, ['Αγγὶ, i. e. *a stranger.*]   One of the pofterity of the patriarch *Gad.*

HAG'-GI-AH, ['Αγγία, i. e. *the Lord's feaſt.*]   One
of the poſterity of the patriarch *Levi.*

HAG'-GITES.   The poſterity of *Haggi.*

HAG'-GITH, ['Αγγιθ, i. e. *rejoicing.*]   The father of
king *Adonijah.*

HA'-I or HAI, [Γαὶ. Αἶα. Αἶ. Γαὶ.]   See AI.

HAK'-KA-TAN, ['Ακκαταν, i. e. *little.*]   The father
of *Jonathan* an high prieſt of the *Jews.*

HAK'-KŌZ, ['Ακκώς, i. e. *a thorn, the ſummer, or an
end.*]   One of the prieſts in king *David*'s time.

HAK-U'-PHA, ['Ακυφά, i. e. *a commandment of the
mouth.*]   One whoſe children were of the order
of *Nethinims.*

HA'-LAH, ['Αλά. 'Αλαὲ, i. e. *a moiſt table.*]   A city
of the *Medes,* in *Aſſyria.*

HAL'-AC, [Χελχὰ, i. e. *part.*]   A mountain of
Paleſtine.

HAL'-HŪL, ['Αιλυὰ, i. e. *grief, or the looking for
grief.*]   A city of *Paleſtine,* in the tribe of *Judah,*
in the mountains.

HA'-LI, ['Αλὲφ, i. e. *ſickneſs, a beginning, or precious
ſtone.*]   One of the boundaries of the tribe of
Aſher.

HAL-I-CAR-NAS'-SUS, ['Αλικαρνασσὸς, i. e. *the
chief dwelling place by the ſea ſide.*]   A maritime
city of *Curia* in *Greece:* the country of *Herodotus,*
of *Dionyſius* the roman hiſtorian, and of *Heraclitus*
the poet: famous for the mauſoleum of *Mauſolus*
king of *Caria,* one of the ſeven wonders of the
world.

HAL-LE-LU'-JAH, ['Αλληλυΐα, i. e. *praiſe ye the
Lord.*]   A diſtinguiſhed note of praiſe.

HAL-LO'-ĒSH, ['Αλωὴς, i. e. *ſaying nothing, or an
enchanter.*]   One who returned from the babyloniſh captivity, and ſealed the covenant with
Nehemiah.

HAM, [Χὰμ, i. e. *crafty, or heat.*]   One of the ſons
of the patriarch *Noah*—alſo a place in the country
of *Egypt.*

HA'-MAN,

HA'-MAN, ['Aμὰν, i. e. *making an uproar, or troubling.*]
A prime minifter of *Ahafuerus*, king of *Perfia*.

HA'-MATH or HE'-MATH, ['Aιμάϑ, i. e. *anger,
heat, or a wall.*] A city of *Syria*, and capital of
a province of the fame name.

HA'-MATH-ITE. A defcendant from *Canaan* the
fon of *Ham*.

HA'-MATH ZO'-BAH, ['Aιμάϑ Σωβά. Baισωβὰ, i. e.
the anger, heat; or the wall of an army.] A place
which king *Solomon* took, fuppofed to be in *Syria*.

HAM'-MATH, ['Aμμάϑ.] A city of *Palefline*, in
the tribe of *Naphtali*.

HAM-MED'-A-THA, ['Aμαδαϑõς, i. e. *troubling the
law.*] The father of *Haman*, of the race of *Agag*
an *Amalekite*.

HAM'-MEL-ECH, [Mαλκίος, i. e. *a king, or counfellor.*] One mentioned by the prophet *Jeremiah*;
he was the father of *Malchiah*.

HAM'-MO-LEK'-ETH, [Mαλεκέϑ.] A woman of
the tribe of *Manaffeh*.

HAM'-MON, [Eμεμαὺν, i. e. *heat, or the fun.*] A
city of *Palefline* in the tribe of *Naphtali*, given
to the *Levites*, a boundary of the tribe of *Afher*.

HAM-O'-NAH, [i. e. *his multitude, or his uproar.*] A
city where *Ezekiel* prophefied that *Gog* and his
people fhould be buried.

HAM'-ON GŌG, [Γώγ, i. e. *the multitude of the roof
of an houfe.*] A valley where *Gog* was buried.

HAM'-OR, ['Eμμὰρ, i. e. *an afs or dirt.*] The father
of *Shechem*, who ravifhed *Dinah* the daughter of
Jacob.

HA'-MOTH. See HAMATH.

HAM'-OTH DŌR, [Nεμμάϑ. 'Eμμαϑδůρ, i. e. *indig-
nation.*] A city of refuge in *Palefline*, in the tribe
of *Naphtali*.

HAM-U'-EL, ['Iεμυήλ. 'Aμυήλ.] One of the pofterity of the patriarch *Simeon*.

HAM'-ŪL, [Xαμůλ, i. e. *godly or merciful.*] A grandfon to the patriarch *Judah* by *Tamar*.

HAM'-ŪL-ITES. The pofterity of *Hamul*.

HAM-U'-

HAM-U'-TAL, ['Αμιτὰλ. Αμειτάαλ, i. e. *heat of the dew*.] The wife of king *Josiah*.

HAN-AM'-E-EL, ['Αναμεήλ, i. e. *the mercy of God.*] The son of *Shallum*, and kinsman of the prophet *Jeremiah*.

HAN'-AN, ['Ανὰν, i. e. *full of grace.*] One of the descendants from *Benjamin*, whose children were of the order of *Nethinims*—also others.

HAN-AN'-E-EL, ['Αναμεήλ, i. e. *grace from God.*] A tower of the city of *Jerusalem*, so named.

HAN'-AN-I, ['Ανανì, i. e. *giving, merciful, or godly.*] Father to the prophet *Jehu*—also a prophet of that name—and others.

HAN-AN-I'-AH, ['Ανανία, i. e. *the grace or mercy of the Lord.*] The name of a false prophet mentioned in *Jeremiah*—also one of the singers of the temple of *Jerusalem*—also a captain under king *Uzziah*—also the son of *Pedaiah*.

HA'-NES, [Τάνης, i. e. *banishment of grace.*] A city or garrison on the borders of *Ægypt*, next to *Judæa*.

HAN'-I-EL, [Ανιὴλ, i. e. *the gift of God.*] One of the posterity of the patriarch *Asher*.

HAN'-NAH, ["Αννα, i. e. *merciful or taking rest.*] The wife of *Elkanah*, and mother of the prophet and judge *Samuel*.

HAN'-NA-THON, ['Αναθών, i. e. *the gift of grace.*] A town of *Palestine* in the tribe of *Zebulun*.

HAN'-NI-EL, ['Ανιὴλ, i. e. *grace or the mercy of God.*] The son of *Ephod*, of the tribe of *Manasseh*.

HAN'-OCH, ['Ενὼχ, i. e. *dedicated.*] The son of *Midian*, *Abraham*'s son—also a son of the patriarch *Reuben*.

HAN'-OCH-ITES. Descendants from *Hanoch*.

HAN'-UN, ['Αννὼν, i. e. *merciful, or giving.*] The son of *Nahash* king of the *Ammonites* who insulted *David*'s ambassadors.

HAPH'-AR-A-IM, ['Αφεραείμ, i. e. *searching or digging.*] A city of *Palestine* in the tribe of *Issachar*.

HA'-RA, [i. e. *an hill, or a shewing forth.*] The name of the country of *Media*.

HAR'-A-DAH, [Χαραδὰθ, i. e. *the well of great fear.*] The *twenty-first* encampment of the *Ifraelites*, in the wildernefs.

HAR-AI'-AH. See *Harhata.*

HAR'-AN, ['Αράν. Χαῤῥὰν, i. e. *anger.*] A fon of *Terah, Abraham's* father, and father of *Lot*—alfo a fon of *Caleb* of the pofterity of *Judah*—alfo a city where *Terah* died, and from whence *Abraham* went to *Canaan*—afo a fon of *Shimei.*

HAR'-A-RITE, ['Αραχαῖος.] Probably an inhabitant of *Hara.*

HAR-BO'-NAH, [Χαρθωνὰ, i. e. *deftruction.*] One appointed by king *Ahafuerus* to fee to the execution of *Haman.*

HA'-REPH, ['Αρὶμ, i. e. *winter, or reproach.*] A fon of *Caleb*, of the pofterity of *Judah.*

HA'-RETH, [Σαρὶχ, i. e. *liberty.*] A foreft of *Judah* to which king *David* fled.

HAR'-HAS, ['Αρὰs, i. e. *anger, or the heat of confidence.*] A keeper of king *Jofiah's* wardrobe.

HAR-HA'-TA, ['Αραχίας, i. e. *heat or anger of the Lord.*] A goldfmith who worked for the new temple of *Jerufalem.*

HAR'-HŪR, ['Αρὰϱ, i. e. *made warm, or the heat of liberty.*] One whofe children were of the order of *Nethinims.*

HA'-RIM, ['Ηρὰμ, i. e. *deftroyed, or dedicated to God.*] A prieft who fealed the covenant with *Nehemiah* the governor.

HA'-RIPH, ['Αρὶφ.] One who returned from the babylonifh captivity.

HAR'-NE-PHER, ['Αρναφὰϱ, i. e. *the anger of a bull, or anger increafing.*] A defcendant from the patriarch *Afher.*

HA'-ROD, ['Αραδ, i. e. *fear.*] A *well* and place in *Midian.*

HA'-ROD-ITE. An inhabitant of *Harod.*

HAR'-O-EH, ['Αραὰ.] One of the pofterity of the patriarch *Judah.*

HA-RO'-RITE, ['Αρωρὶ.] Uncertain whom.

HAR'-O-

HAR'-O-SHĒTH, ['Αρισὼθ, i. e. *workmanship or a wood.*] A city where *Sisera dwelt.*

HARP. An instrument of musick with several strings, to be played upon with the fingers.

HAR'-SHA, ['Αρσά, i. e. *workmanship, or a wood.*] One whose children were of the order of *Nethinims.*

HA'-RUM, [Ιαρίν. 'Αρίμ, i. e. *high, or throwing down.*] One of the posterity of the patriarch *Judah.*

HAR-U'-MAPH, ['Ερωμὰφ, i. e. *destruction.*] One who returned from the babylonish captivity.

HAR-U'-PHITE, [ο'Αρнφί, i. e. *slander, or youth, or sharp.*] *Shephatiah* one of king *David's* brave officers, was stiled the *Haruphite.*

HA'-RUZ, ['Αρῶς, i. e. *careful.*] The grandfather of king *Amon.*

HAS-A-DI'-AH, ['Ασαδία, i. e. *the mercy of the Lord.*] The son of *Zerubbabel.*

HAS-EN-U'-AH, ['Ασινῶς. 'Ασανῆα, i. e. *a bramble or an enemy.*] One of the posterity of the patriarch *Benjamin.*

HASH-AB-I'-AH, ['Ασεβἰ. 'Ασαβίας, i. e. *the estimation of the Lord.*] The son of *Amaziah* the *Levite.*

HASH-AB'-NAH or HASH-AB-NI'-AH, ['Εσσαβανὰ. 'Ασαβανία, i. e. *the silence of the Lord.*] One of the order of the *Levites.*

HASH-BAD'-A-NA, ['Ασαβαδμὰ] A *Levite* who was at *Ezra's* left hand whilst he read the law.

HA'-SHEM, ['Ασὰμ, i. e. *named, or a putting to.*] A *Gizonite* of the land of *Canaan.*

HASH-MO'-NAH, [Σελμωνᾶ, i. e. *the hasting of a gift, or embassy.*] The *twenty-sixth* encampment of the *Israelites;* in the wilderness.

HASH'-ŪB, ['Ασὼβ, i. e. *esteemed, or numbered.*] One who sealed the covenant with *Nehemiah* the governor.

HASH-U'-BAH, ['Ασнβἐ, i. e. *estimation or thought.*] A descendant from king *David.*

HASH'-ŪM, ['Ασὺμ, i. e. *silence or their hasting.*] One who returned from the babylonish captivity.

HASH-U'-

HASH-U'-PHA, ['Ασειφὰ, i. e. *spent or made bare.*] The fon of *Zerubbaal*—and others.

HAS'-RAH, ['Αϱὰs. 'Εσϱῆ.] See *Harhas.*

HAS'-SE-NA'-AH, [Ασανα.] One who returned from the babylonifh captivity.

HAS-U'-PHA, ['Ασυφὰ, i. e. *forgiving.*] One whofe children were of the order of *Nethinims.*

HAT'-ACH, ['Αϑαχ, i. e. *fmiting.*] One who was chamberlain to king *Ahafuerus.*

HATH'-ATH, ['Αθαϑ, i. e. *fear.*] One of the pofterity of the patriarch *Judah*, a fon of *Oth-niel.*

HAT-I'-TA, ['Αʔιτὰ, i. e. *a bending of fin.*] One whofe children were of the order of *Nethinims.*

HAT'-TIL, ['Αʔιλ, i. e. *an howling for fin.*] One whofe children were king *Solomon*'s fervants.

HAT-TI'-PHA, ['Ατυφὰ, i. e. *robbery.*] One whofe children were of the order of *Nethinims.*

HAT'-TUSH, [Χαʔὺs. 'Αʔὺs, i. e. *forfaking fin.*] A prieft who fealed the covenant with *Nehemiah* the governor.

HV'-I-LAH, ['Εὒιλὰ. 'Ευιλὰτ, i. e. *grieving, or fpeaking to him.*] The fon of *Cufh*—alfo the fon of *Joktan*— alfo fuppofed to be a part of *Arabia.*

HA'-VOTH JA'-IR, ['Επαύλεις Ιαὶϱ, i. e. *town of light.*] The name given to feveral towns which *Jair*, the *Manaffite*, took.

HAU'-RAN, ['Αυϱανίτιδ☉, i. e. *a hole, liberty, or whitenefs.*] A city of *Damafcus* in *Syria.*

HAZ'-A-EL, ['Αζαὴλ, i. e. *feeing God.*] The prime minifter of *Benhadad* king of *Syria*, and his fuc-ceffor in the kingdom.

HAZ-AI'-AH, ['Οξία, i. e. *feeing the Lord.*] ne who returned from the babylonifh captivity.

HA'-ZAR AD'-DAR, [i. e. *an imprifoned generation, or fairnefs.*] One of the boundaries of the land of *Canaan.*

HA'-ZAR EN'-AN, ['Αϱσεναὶν, i. e. *imprifoned.*] One of the eaft boundary cities of the land of *Pale-ftine.*

HA'-ZAR GAD'-DAH, ['Ασεργαδδα, i. e. *imprisoned* or *bond.*] A city of the land of *Palestine*, in the tribe of *Judah.*

HA'-ZAR HAT'-TI-CON, [i. e. *middle, between the middle, or preparation.*] A place towards *Egypt.*

HA'-ZAR MA'-VETH, ['Ατερμαθ, i. e. *court, or entry, or dwelling of death.*] A descendant of the patriarch *Shem*; son of *Joktan.*

HAZ-A'-ROTH, ['Ασηρωθ, i. e. *palaces.*] A place in the country of *Moab.*

HA'-ZAR SHU'-EL, ['Εσερουαλ, i. e. *a wolf's house.*] A city of *Palestine*, in the tribe of *Simeon.*

HA'-ZAR SU'-SAH, [Σαρουσιν, i. e. *the hay paunch, or entry of an horse.*] A city of *Palestine*, in the tribe of *Simeon:* called also *Hazar Sufim.*

HA'-ZAR SU'-SIM, ['Εσερουσιμ, i. e. *the porch, or entry of an house.*] A city of *Palestine*, in the tribe of *Simeon:* called also *Hazar Sufah.*

HAZ'-EL EL-PO'-NI, ['Εσηλεββων. 'Εσηλελφων, i. e. *the shadow of the countenance.*] A woman of the posterity of *Judah.*

HA-ZE'-RIM, ['Ασηδωθ, i. e. *porches.*] The antient habitation of the *Avims* before they were driven off by the *Caphtorims.*

HA-ZE'-ROTH, ['Ασηρωθ, i. e. *palaces, or villages.*] The *fourteenth* encampment of the *Israelites.*

HA'-ZER SHU'-SHIM, ['Ημισησεωσιν.] A city of *Palestine*, in the tribe of *Judah.*

HAZ'-E-ZON TA'-MAR, ['Ασασονθαμαρ, i. e. *drawing near to bitterness.*] A place where the *Ammonites* dwelt; on the *western* coast of the *dead sea:* it is the same as *Engedi.*

HAZ'-I-EL, ['Αζιηλ, i. e. *seeing God.*] The son of *Shimei*, a *Levite* and a singer at the temple.

HAZ'-O, ['Αζαυ, i. e. *seeing, or prophesying.*] The son of *Abraham's* brother *Nahor* by his wife *Milcah.*

HAZ'-OR or HEZ'-RON, ['Ασωρ, i. e. *hay, or court.*] Cities of *Palestine*, in the tribes of *Naphtali* and of *Judah.*

HAZ'-UB

HAZ'-UB-AH, ['Ασουβὲδ, i. e. *forsaken.*] The wife
of *Caleb*—also the mother of king *Jehosaphat.*

H *before* E.

HEAVE OFFERINGS. See OFFERINGS.

HEB'-ER, [Χαβὲϱ. 'Εβὲϱ, i. e. *a companion, or partaker.*]
A son of *Beriah* and grandson to *Asher*—also one
of the posterity of *Benjamin.*

HEB'-ER-ITES, [Χαβεϱί.] The descendants from
Heber.

HEB'-REWS, ['Εβϱαίοι.] The *jewish* nation, so called
from *Heber*—also one of the canonical books of
the *New Testament,* so named.

HEB'-RŌN, [Χεβϱὰν, i. e. *fellowship.*] A cave in the
land of *Canaan,* which *Abraham* bought for a burial place—also an antient city of *Palestine,* in the
tribe of *Judah, twenty* miles south of *Jerusalem,*
and *twenty* miles north from *Beersheba,* a city of
refuge — also a son of *Koath* — also a son of
Mareshah.

HEB'-RŌN-ITES. The people of *Hebron,* descendants from *Heber* the *Levite.*

HEG'-A-I or HEG'-E, ['Αγαΐ, i. e. *sighing, or speech.*]
Keeper of the women of king *Ahasuerus's* seraglio,
and his chamberlain.

HEL'-AH, ['Αλαὰ.] One of the posterity of the
patriarch *Judah,* the wife of *Tekoah.*

HE'-LAM, ['Αίλαμ, i. e. *the army of the mother.*] A
place in *Syria.*

HEL'-BAH, [Χεβδὰ, i. e. *milk, fat, or grief in that.*]
A place in the land of *Canaan,* in the tribe of
Asher.

HEL'-BON, [Χελβὼν, i. e. *milk, or fat.*] A place
mentioned by the prophet *Ezekiel.*

HEL-CHI'-AH, [Χελχίος, i. e. *the portion or gentleness
of the Lord.*] An ancestor of *Esdras.*

HEL'-DA-I, [Χολδία, i. e. *the world, or rustiness.*] One
who supplied *Zechariah* with gold and silver to
make crowns for *Joshua* the son of *Josedeck.*

HEL'-EB, ['Ελὰϐ, i. e. *the world, or ruſtineſs.*] A *Netophathite,* one of king *David's* worthies.

HEL'-ED, ['Ελὰδ, i. e. *the world, or ruſtineſs.*] One of king *David's* worthies.

HEL'-EK, [Χελέγ, i. e. *a part, or portion.*] A deſcendant from the patriarch *Manaſſeh.*

HEL'-EK-ITES. Deſcendants from *Helek.*

HEL'-EM, ['Ελέμ, i. e. *dreaming, or healing.*] One of the poſterity of the patriarch *Aſher.*

HEL'-EPH, [Μαλεφ, i. e. *changing, or paſſing over.*] A city of *Paleſtine,* in the tribe of *Naphtali.*

HEL'-EZ, [Χελλῆς, i. e. *armed, or ſet free.*] A *Paltite,* one of king *David's* worthies—alſo others.

HE'-LI, ['Ηλὶ, i. e. *aſcending.*] The father of *Joseph* the virgin *Mary's* huſband.

HE-LI-OD-O'-RUS, ['Ηλιόδωρⓢ, i. e. *the gift of the ſun.*] Treaſurer to *Seleucus* king of *Syria.*

HEL'-KA-I, ['Ελκαὶ, i. e. *part, or portion.*] The name of one of the *Levites.*

HEL'-KATH, ['Εζαλεκὲθ, i. e. *a portion, or dividing.*] One of the border towns of the tribe of *Aſher,* given to the *Levites.*

HEL'-KATH HAZ'-ZU-RIM, [i. e. *the field of ſtrong men.*] A field mentioned in the *ſecond* book of *Samuel.*

HEL-KI'-AS, [Χελκίας.] A governor of the temple in king *Joſiah's* reign.

HELL, ['Αδης.] In ſacred writ it means generally the *grave,* and ſometimes the *future ſtate of puniſhment.* In the hebrew it is *Sheol:* in the ſaxon language it is *Helle.* The *Saxons* deified (after his death) their famous warrior, *Woden;* they alſo ſuppoſed a goddeſs, whom they named *Hel,* and who, by *Woden,* received dominion over the infernal regions, there to puniſh the bad: *Woden* had the diſtribution of rewards to the good, or thoſe who died in battle, where they were to drink *ale* out of the ſkulls of their enemies.

HE'-LON, [Χαιλὼν; i. e. *a window or grief.*] The father of *Eliab,* of the tribe of *Zebulun.*

HE'-MAN,

HE'-MAN, ['Αιμὰν, i. e. *much, or making an uproar.*] The son of *Joel:* he was a celebrated singer in the temple of *Jerusalem*—also a descendant from *Esau.*

HE'-MATH or HA'-MATH, ['Αιμὰθ, i. e. *anger, heat, or a wall.*] The father of the house of *Rechab.*

HEM'-DAN, ['Αμαδὰ, i. e. *desire, or heat of judgment.*] One of the posterity of *Esau.*

HEN, [i. e. *grace, quiet, or rest.*] The son of *Zephaniah.*

HE'-NA, ['Ανὰ, i. e. *a troubling.*] A country conquered by the *Assyrians.*

HE'-NA-DAD, ['Ηναδὰδ, i. e. *grace of the beloved.*] A *Levite* who sealed the covenant with *Nehemiah.*

HEN'-OCH, ['Ενὼχ, i. e. *taught or dedicate.*] Son of *Midian,* and grandson to the patriarch *Abraham.*

HEPH'ER, ['Οφὲρ, i. e. *a digger, or delver.*] The father of *Zelophehad,* one of king *David's* worthies —also a country.

HEPH'-ER-ITES. The posterity of *Hepher.*

HEPH'-ZI-BAH, ['Αψιβὰ, i. e. *my pleasure; or delight in her.*] The mother of *Manasseh* king of *Judah.*

HE'-RAM. A city of *Palestine* in the tribe of *Naphtali.*

HER'-CU-LES, ['Ηρακλὴς, i. e. *Juno's glory.*] In heathen fable was the son of *Jupiter* and *Alcmena:* there were many of that name who were deified.

HE'-RES, ["Αρες, i. e. *the son, or an earthen pot.*] A mountain of *Ajalon* where the *Amorites* dwelt, until the family of *Joseph* made them tributaries.

HE'-RESH, ['Αρὴς, i. e. *a carpenter.*] The name of one of the *Levites.*

HER'-MAS, ['Ερμᾶς, i. e. *Mercury, or gain.*] A convert whom the apostle *Paul* salutes in his epistle to the *Romans.*

HER'-MES, ['Ερμῆς, i. e. *Mercury, or gain.*] One of the *seventy* disciples and made bishop of *Dalmatia.*

HER-MOG'-EN-ES, ['Ερμογένης, i. e. *begotten by Mercury.*] One, of whom St. *Paul* complains that he had deserted him.

K 3

HER'-

HER'-MŌN, [Αερμὼν. Ἑρμὼν, i. e. *dedicated to God.*] An high mountain on the *eaſt* ſide of the river *Jordan,* which was the northern boundary of the land of *Paleſtine.*

HER'-MŌN-ITES. The inhabitants about mount *Hermon.*

HĒR'-ŌD, [Ἡρώδης, i. e. *the mount of pride.*] The roman king of *Judæa* at our *Saviour's* birth—alſo *Herod Antipas* the tetrarch, the ſon of king *Herod,* who beheaded *John* the baptiſt — alſo *Herod Agrippa,* grandſon to king *Herod.*

HER-O'-DI-ANS, [Ἡρωδιανοὶ.] A ſect of Jews, who followed the ſentiments of *Herod* the great, that they might comply with many of the heathen uſages.

HE-RO'-DI-AS, [Ἡρωδιὰς, i. e. *the mount of pride.*] Siſter to king *Agrippa,* and grand-daughter to *Herod* the great: ſhe firſt married her uncle *Herod Philip,* then deſerted him and married his brother.

HE-RO'-DI-ŌN, [Ἡρωδίων, i. e. *Juno's ſong.*] A couſin of the apoſtle *Paul.*

HER'-ON. A fierce bird of the *eagle* kind, which feeds upon fiſh.

HES'-EB, [Ἀσδὶ.] One whoſe ſon was one of king *Solomon's* twelve principal officers, or purveyor of proviſions.

HES'-ED. See *Heſeb.*

HESH'-BŌN, [Ἀσεβὼν, i. e. *a number, or thought.*] A famous city of the *Amorites* beyond *Jordan* in the tribe of *Reuben*—alſo a city of the *Levites,* in the tribe of *Gad*—alſo a deſcendant from *Eſau.*

HESH'-MŌN, [i. e. *an haſty meſſage.*] A city of *Paleſtine* in the tribe of *Judah.*

HETH, [Χὲτ, i. e. *fear, or aſtoniſhed.*] The *ſecond* ſon of *Canaan* and the father of the *Hittites.*

HETH'-LŌN, [Ἀιθαλὼν, i. e. *an houſe to be feared.*] A place near to *Damaſcus* in *Syria.*

HEZ'-E-KI, [Ἀζακὶ.] One of the poſterity of the patriarch *Benjamin.*

HEZ-

HEZ-EK-I'-AH, ['Aζεκίας. L. *Ezech'ias*, i. e. *the strength of the Lord.*] A king of *Judah* and son of *Ahaz* and *Abi:* he died A. M. 3306—also a son of *Neariah*, a descendant from king *David*.

HE'-ZER or HE'-ZIR, ['Hζὶρ. Xηζεὶρ, i. e. *a hog, or converted.*] One of the priests in king *David's* reign.

HEZ'-I-ON, ['Aζὶν.] A king of *Syria*.

HEZ'-RA-I, ['Aσαραὶ, i. e. *an entry, or hay.*] One of king *David's* valiant men.

HEZ'-RO, ['Hσερὲ. 'Aσραὶ, i. e. *an entry, or hay.*] One of king *David's* valiant men.

HEZ'-RŌN, ['Aσραὶν. 'Eσρώμ, i. e. *the arrow of joy, or division of a song.*] A grandson of the patriarch *Judah*—also a city of *Palestine* in the tribe of *Judah*.

HEZ-RŌN'-ITES, ['Aσωνοῖ.] The descendants from *Hezron*.

H *before* I.

HID'-DA-I, [i. e. *a praise, or a cry.*] One of king *David's* worthies.

HID'-DEK-EL, ['Eδδεκὲλ. Tίγρις, i. e. *a sharp voice.*] One of the *four* rivers of *Paradise*; supposed to be the river *Tigris* in *Asia*.

HI'-ĒL, ['Aχιὴλ, i. e. *the Lord liveth, or the life of God.*] A *Bethelite* who rebuilt *Jericho*.

HI-ER-AP'-OL-IS, ['Ieραπόλις, i. e. *an holy or sacred city.*] A city of *Phrygia* in *Asia*, near to *Colosse* and *Laodicea*.

HI-ER'-E-ĒL, ['Ieρεὴλ.] One who returned from the babylonish captivity.

HI-ER'-EM-ŌTH, ['Ieρεμὼϑ, i. e. *he that fears, sees, or rejects death.*] One who returned from the babylonish captivity, and was a porter or guard of the temple. See *Jerimoth*.

HI-ER-I E'-LUS, ['Ieζριὴλ⊙.] One who returned from the babylonish captivity.

HI-ER'-MAS, ['Ieρμὰς.] One who returned from the babylonish captivity, and was a guard or porter of the temple.

 HI-ER.

HI-ER-ŌN'-Y-MUS, ['Ιερώνομ☉, i. e. *an holy name.*]
A governor, who with *Timotheus,* &c. troubled
the Jews, mentioned in the *second* book of the
Maccabees.

HIG-GAI'-ON, [i. e. *meditation, or confideration.*] A
jewifh mufical inftrument.

HIL'-ĒN, [Χελών, i. e. *a window, or grief.*] A city
of *Paleftine,* in the tribe of *Judah,* given to the
Levites.

HIL-KI'-AH, [Χελχείας, i. e. *the Lord's gentlenefs.*]
The father of *Eliakim*—alfo the father of *Jeremiah,* a prieft, and others.

HIL'-LĒL, ['Ελλήλ, i. e. *praifing, or. foolifhnefs.*]
The father of *Abdon,* a judge of *Ifrael.*

HIN, [Εἴν.] A jewifh *liquid* meafure, fomething
above a *quart.*

HIN'-NOM, ['Εννόμ, i. e. *there they are, or their riches.*]
A valley of *Paleftine,* fo called after *Hinnom.*

HI'-RAH, ['Ειράς, i. e. *liberty, or anger.*] An *Adul-
lamite,* a friend to the patriarch *Judah.*

HI'-RAM, [Χειράμ; i. e. *the height of life.*] A king
of *Tyre,* in league with king *David* and *Solomon*
—alfo a famous artificer in brafs and copper—
alfo one of the pofterity of *Benjamin.*

HIR-CA'-NUS, (*John*) ['Υρκάν☉, i. e. *the poffeffor
of a city.*] A jewifh high prieft, fon to *Simon
Maccabæus.*

HIS-KI'-JAH, ['Εζεκία, i. e. *the ftrength of the Lord.*]
One who fealed the covenant with *Nehemiah* the
governor.

HIT'-TITĒS, [Χετταῖοι, i. e. *broken afunder; aftonifh-
ing.*] The defcendants from *Heth.*

HI'-VITES, ['Ευαῖοι, i. e. *living or declaring.*] A
people defcended from *Canaan* the patriarch:
fuppofed from a fon of *Canaan* named *Hivi.*

H *before* O.

HOB'-A or HOB'-AH, [Χοβά, i. e. *an hiding.*] A
place on the left hand of *Damafcus* in *Syria,*
whither *Abraham* purfued the four kings who
had taken *Lot* prifoner.

HOB'-AB,

HOB'-AB, ['Οβὰβ, i. e. *beloved.*] The son of *Reuel* father in law to *Moses.*

HŌD, ['Ωδ, i. e. *praise, or confession.*] One who was a defcendant from the patriarch *Afher.*

HO-DA-I'-AH, ['Ωδηΐα, i. e. *the praife of the Lord.*] A brave man of the tribe of *Manaffeh*—alfo one of king *David's* pofterity, the fon of *Eliœnai.*

HO-DA-VI'-AH, ['Ωδηΐα, i. e. *the praife of the Lord.*] One of the pofterity of the patriarch *Benjamin.*

HO'-DESH, ['Αδὰ, i. e. *a table, or news.*] The wife of *Shaharaim,* who was of the pofterity of *Benjamin.*

HO-DE'-VA or HO-DE'-VAH, ['Οωδηΐα.] One of the *Levites* who returned from the babylonifh captivity.

HO-DI'-AH, ['Ωδΐα, i. e. *the praife of the Lord.*] A woman of the pofterity of *Judah.*

HO-DI'-JAH, ['Ωδηΐα, i. e. *praife the Lord.*] One who fealed the covenant with *Nehemiah* the governor.

HOG'-LAH, ['Εγλὰ, i. e. *pleafantnefs, or his compaffing.*] One of the daughters of *Zelophehad.*

HO'-HAM, ['Ελὰμ, i. e. *woe be to them.*] One who was a king of *Hebron.*

HOL'-EN, [Γελλὰ.] A city of refuge in the land of *Palefine.* See *Holon.*

HOL-OF-ER'-NĒS, ['Ολοφέρνης, i. e. *a ftrong captain.*] Lieutenant general of the armies of *Nebuchadnezzar* king of *Affyria.*

HO'-LON, [Χαλὴ, i. e. *a window, or grief.*] A city of *Palefine* in the tribe of *Judah,* in the mountains.

HO'-MAN or HE'-MAN, ['Αιμὰν, i. e. *much, or making an uproar.*] One of the defcendants of *Efau.*

HOM'-ER, [Γομὸρ.] A *jewifh* meafure of capacity, about *fix pints.*

HOPH'-NI, ['Οφνὶ, i. e. *a fift, or a little fift.*] A fon of *Eli* the high prieft, who was flain in battle by the *Philiftines.*

HOPH'-

HOPH'-RAH, ['Ουαφρά.]　A king of *Egypt* in king *Hezekiah*'s time, the fame with *Apries*.

HŌR, ['Ωρ, i. e. *an hill, or fhewing.*]　A mountain on the north border of the land of *Canaan*; where was the *thirty-fourth* encampment of the *Ifraelites*; in the wildernefs.

HO'-RAM, [Ωράμ, i. e. *their hill.*]　A king of *Gezer*.

HO'-RĒB, [Χωρηβ, i. e. *all alone, or forfaken.*]　A mountain of *Arabia Petræa*, near to mount *Sinai*.

HO'-REM, ['Ωρὲμ, i. e. *an offering dedicated to God.*]　A city of *Palefine*, in the tribe of *Naphtali*.

HOR-HA-GID' GAD, [Γαδγαδ, i. e. *the hill of felicity.*]　The *twenty-ninth* encampment of the *Ifraelites*; in the wildernefs.

HOR'-I, [Κορρὶ, i. e. *a prince, chief, or free-born.*]　One of the defcendants from *Efau*.

HOR'-IMS, [Χορραῖοι, i. e. *princes, or being angry.*]　A people who antiently dwelt in *Seir*.

HOR'-ITES, [Χορραῖοι, i. e. *a prince, or chief.*]　A people of mount *Seir* beyond the river *Jordan*.

HOR'-MAH, ['Ερμᾶ, i. e. *dedicated, or confecrated.*]　A city of *Palefine*, in the tribe of *Judah*.

HO-RŌ-NA'-IM, ['Ωρωναὶμ, i. e. *angers, or ragings.*]　A city of the *Moabites*.

HO-RŌN'-ITES, ['Αρωνοὶ, i. e. *anger.*]　A people about mount *Seir*.

HŌS'-A or HAS'-AH, ['Οσᾶ, i. e. *trufing, or having fure confidence.*]　One of the porters of the temple of *Jerufalem*—alfo a city of *Palefine*, in the tribe of *Afher*.

HO-SAN'-NA, ['Ωσαννὰ, i. e. *fave I pray thee, or keep, or preferve I befeech 'thee, or give falvation.*]　A form of benediction made ufe of by the *Jews*, and particularly applied to *Chrif* at his laft entry into *Jerufalem*.

HO-SE'-A, ['Ωσηὲ, i. e. *falvation, or a faviour.*]　The fon of *Beeri*, and the firft of the leffer prophets, from whom the canonical book *Hofea* took its name.

HO-SHA-

HO-SHA-I'-AH, ['Ωσαϊα, i. e. *the salvation of the Lord.*] One who was at the dedication of the walls of *Jerusalem:* the father of *Jaazaniah.*

HO'-SHA-MA, ['Ωσαμὰθ, i. e. *heard, or obeying.*] One of the posterity of king *David.*

HO-SHE'-A, ['Ωσηὲ, i. e. *salvation, or a saviour.*] The son of *Elah,* and the last king of *Israel,*

HO'-THAM, [Χωθὰμ, i. e. *a seal.*] The son of *Heber,* and one of the posterity of the patriarch *Asher.*

HO'-THAN, [Χωθὰμ, i. e. *a seal.*] One of the cities of *Aroer,* in the tribe of *Dan,* in *Palestine.*

HO'-THIR, ['Ωθηρὶ, i. e. *excelling, or remaining.*] One of the singers of the temple of *Jerusalem;* the son of *Heman.*

HOUR. The *Hebrews* divided the day into *four* parts, *viz.* morning, high day or noon, the first evening, and the last evening: the *night* was divided into *three* parts, *viz.* night, midnight, and the morning watch. When the *Jews* became subject to the *Romans,* they followed them in dividing the night into *four* parts, called *watches,* because the *Romans* relieved their centinels every *three* hours: so that the *fourth* watch of the night was about *three* hours before sunrising. After the manner of the *Greeks* and *Romans,* their day was divided into *twelve* hours: the *first* hour was at sun-rise, answering to our *six* of the clock at the *Equinox;* the *third* hour at *nine* of the clock in the morning; the *sixth* hour at noon; the *ninth* hour at *three* of the clock afternoon, and so on.

H *before* U.

HUK'-KOK, ['Ακὰκ, i. e. *an engraver, scribe, or lawyer.*] A city of *Palestine,* in the tribe of *Asher.*

HUL, ["Ούλ, i. e. *sorrow; iniquity; sand.*] A son of *Aram* and grandson to *Shem* the patriarch.

HUL'-DAH, ["Ολδα, i. e. *the world, circle of the world, or west.*] A prophetess, the wife of *Shallum,* to whom king *Joseph* sent for counsel.

HUM+‑

HUM'-TAH, ['Eυμὰ.] A city of *Palestine*, in the tribe of *Judah*, in the mountains.

HUPH'-AM, ['Oφὰμ, i. e. *their chamber, or bank.*] A son of the patriarch *Benjamin*.

HUPH'-AM-ITES. The descendants from *Hupham*.

HUP'-PAH, ['Oπφᾶ, i. e. *a chamber, cover, or bank.*] One of the priest's in king *David*'s time.

HUP'-PIM, ['Aπφὶν, i. e. *a chamber covered, or the sea shore.* One of the descendants from the patriarch *Benjamin*, supposed to be the same with *Hupham*.

HŪR, [Oὺρ. 'Ωρ, i. e. *liberty, prince, or whiteness.*] A son of *Judah*—also *Ephratah*'s eldest son—also a king of *Midian*, whom the *Israelites* slew.

HU'-RAI, ['Oυρὶ.] One of king *David's* worthies.

HU'-RAM, ['Oυρὰμ, i. e. *their liberty, their whiteness, or their hole.*] One of the posterity of *Benjamin*. See *Hiram*.

HU'-RI, ['Oυρὶ, i. e. *being angry, liberty, witeness, or a hole.*] A son of *Abihail*, one of the posterity of *Gad*.

HU'-SHAH, [Oὺσὰ. 'Ωσὰν, i. e. *hasting, or holding peace.*] The son of *Ezra*, one of the posterity of the patriarch *Judah*.

HU'-SHAI, [Xυσὶ, i. e. *a meaning, or hasting.*] A great friend to king *David*; he defeated the counsel of *Achitophel*.

HU'-SHAM, ['Aσόμ, i. e. *their hasting, or their silence.*] The *third* king who reigned in *Edom*.

HU'-SHATH-ITE, [i. e. *hasting, holding peace, or sensuality.*] Is one who descended from *Hushah*.

HU'-SHIM, ['Ωσίμ, i. e. *hasting, holding peace, or sensuality.*] One of the patriarch *Dan*'s sons—also a wife of *Shaharaim* who was of the posterity of *Benjamin*.

HUZ, ["Oυζ, i. e. *counsel, woods, or fastened.*] The first born son of *Nahor*, *Abraham*'s brother, by his wife *Milcah*.

HUZ'-OTH, [i. e. *streets, or populous.*] See KIR-JATH HUZOTH.

HUZ'

HUZ'-ZAB.   Some suppose her to be a queen of
Assyria: others that it was the metaphorical
name of the city of Nineveh.
HY-DAS'-PĒS, [Ὑδάσπης, i. e. *the knowledge of a
sheep, or knowledge of change.*]   A king of antient
Media—also a river in *East India*, in *Asia.*
HY-MEN-E'-US, [Ὑμέναιⓞ, i. e. *a wedding song.*]
Probably a citizen of *Ephesus*, and a convert of
St. *Paul*, but afterwards fell off and denied the
resurrection of the body.

J and I.

J before A.

JA'-A-KAN, ['Ιαχίμ, i. e. *tribulation, labour, or violent taking away possession.*]   One whose descendants
lived at *Beeroth* in the wilderness.
JA-A'-KO-BAH, ['Ιωχαβὰ, i. e. *a supplanter, deceiver,
or the heel.*]   A prince of the tribe of *Simeon.*
JA-AL'-A, ['Ιεηλὰ. 'Ιελά, i. e. *ascending, a little doe,
or a little goat.*]   One whose children were of the
order of *Nethinims.*
JA-AL'-AH.   The same with *Jaala.*
JA-AL'-AM, ['Ιεγλὸμ, i. e. *heir, or little goat.*]   The
son of the patriarch *Esau*, by *Aholibamah.*
JA'-A-NAI, ['Ιαναί. 'Ιανὶν, i. e. *answering, afflicting,
or making poor.*]   One of the posterity of the patriarch *Gad.*
JA-AR-E-ŌR'-A-GIM, ['Αριωργίμ.]   A *Bethlemite*
whose son slew the giant *Goliah*'s brother.
JA-AS'-

JA-AS'-AU, [i. e. *doing, or my doer.*] One who had married a ſtrange wife in the babyloniſh captivity and afterwards put her away.

JA-AS'-I-ĒL, ['Ιασιήλ, i. e. *God's work, or the doings of God.*] A prince of the half tribe of *Manaſſeh*, in *Paleſtine.*

JA-AZ'-AH, ['Ιαζὴρ, i. e. *helper, or aider.*] A *levitical* city in the tribe of *Reuben*, in *Paleſtine.*

JA-AZ-AN-I'-AH, ['Ιεζονίας, i. e. *the nouriſhment of the Lord, or the weapons of the Lord.*] The ſon of *Shaphan*, ſhewn to *Ezekiel* in a viſion as an idolater.

JA-AZ'-AR, ['Ιαζὴρ, i. e. *an helper.*] A city of the *Amorites.*

JA-AZ-I'-AH, ['Οζία, i. e. *the ſtrength of the Lord.*] One of the poſterity of the patriarch *Levi.*

JA-AZ-I'-ĒL, ['Οζιήλ, i. e. *the ſtrength of the Lord.*] One who was a porter or guard of the temple.

JA'-BAL, ['Ιϐϐάλ. 'Ιαϐήλ, i. e. *falling away, bringing, building, or a cheek.*] The ſon of *Lamech* and *Adah*, the father of ſhepherds.

JAB'-BOK, ['Ιαϐώκ, i. e. *making empty, a ſcattering, or a wreſtling.*] A brook on the *eaſt* ſide of the river *Jordan*, near to which the patriarch *Jacob* wreſtled with the angel.

JA'-BĒSH or JA'-BĒSH GIL'-E-AD, ['Ιαϐεῖs Γαλαὰδ, i. e. *drought or confuſion.*] A city in the half tribe of *Manaſſeh*, on the *eaſt* ſide of the river *Jordan.*

JA'-BESH, ['Ιαϐις, i. e. *drought; confuſion.*] The father of *Shallum* who uſurped the throne of *Judah.*

JA'-BĒZ, ['Ιαϐὴs. 'Ιαϐις, i. e. *ſadneſs; ſorrow; grief.*] One mentioned in the *firſt* Chron. chap. iv. ver. 9.—alſo a city *firſt* Chron. chap. ii. ver. 55, perhaps *Jabeſh-Gilead.*

JA'-BIN, ['Ιαϐείν, i. e. *underſtanding, or building.*] A king of *Hazor* in the north *Canaan*, ſlain by *Joſhua*—alſo another king of *Hazor* delivered into the hands of *Deborah* the propheteſs.

JAB'-

JAB'-NEEL, ['Ιαϐνήλ., i. e. *God's building or understanding.*] A town of *Palestine* on the frontiers of the tribe of *Naphtali*—another in the tribe of *Judah.*

JAB'-NEH, ['Ιαϐνὲ, i. e. *building or understanding.*] A city of the *Philistines.*

JA'-CHAN, ['Ιαχἀν, i. e. *wearing out, or pressing.*] One of the posterity of the patriarch *Gad.*

JA'-CHIN, ['Ιαχὶν, i. e. *preparing or stability.*] The *fifth* son of the patriarch *Simeon*—also the name of a priest—also one of the pillars which king *Solomon* placed in the porch of the temple of *Jerusalem.*

JA-CHIN-ITES, ['Ιαχεναῖ.] The descendants of *Jachin.*

JA'-CINTH, ['Υάκινϑ©.] A precious stone of a cloudy colour.

JA'-CŌB, ['Ιακώϐ, i. e. *a supplanter, deceiver, the heel or the footstep.*] The son of *Isaac* and *Rebecca,* and father of the twelve post-diluvian patriarchs, he died A. M. 2315, Æt. 147.

JA-CU'-BUS, ['Ιάκυϐ©.] A *Levite* who returned from the babylonish captivity.

JA'-DA, ['Ιαδαὲ, i. e. *knowing.*] The son of *Anam* of the tribe of *Judah.*

JAD-A'-U, [Ιεδδụα, i. e. *his hand, or his confession.*] The son of *Nebo,* one who returned from the babylonish captivity.

JAD-DU'-A, ['Ιεδδύα, i. e. *known.*] An high priest of the *Jews* in the time of *Alexander* the great— also one who sealed the covenant with *Nehemiah.*

JA'-DON, ['Ευάρων.] One who repaired the walls of *Jerusalem.*

JA'-ĒL, ['Ιαήλ, i. e. *a little doe or goat, or ascending.*] The wife of *Heber* the *Kenite:* she slew *Sisera* the Canaanitish general.

JA'-GUR, ['Ασὼρ. 'Ιαγὴρ, i. e. *husbandman, stranger, fearing, or gathering together.*] A city of *Palestine* in the tribe of *Judah.*

JAH, [i. e. *the everlasting.*] A word expressive of the attributes of GOD.

JA-HAL'-

JA-HAL'-E-ĒL, ['Αλελεήλ, i. e. *praiſing God, or the clearneſs or light of God.*] One of the poſterity of *Judah* and father of *Ziph.*

JA-HAL'-EL-ĒL, ['Ιλαελήλ.] One of the poſterity of the patriarch *Levi.*

JA'-HATH, ['Ιέθ. 'Ιαὰθ, i. e. *broken in pieces, or fearing, or deſcending.*] The ſon of *Gerſhom* and grandſon to *Levi*—alſo *Banaiah's* ſon—alſo an overſeer of the work of the temple at *Jeruſalem*—alſo others.

JA'-HAZ, ['Ιασσὰ, i. e. *brawling or ſtrife.*] A city beyond the river *Jordan,* in the tribe of *Reuben,* where *Sihon* king of the *Amorites* was diſcomfited.

JA-HAZ'-AH, ['Ιαζῆρ, i. e. *ſcolding, contention, or the end of the Lord.*] A city beyond *Jordan,* the ſame with *Jahaz.*

JA-HAZ-I'-AH, ['Ιαζιάς. Ιασζιας, i. e. *the viſion of the Lord.*] The ſon of *Tikvah.*

JA-HAZ'-I-ĒL, ['Ιεζιήλ, i. e. *ſeeing God.*] A ſon of *Naphtali*—alſo a brave man who deſerted king *Saul* to join *David.*

JAH'-DA-I, ['Αδδαὶ.] One of the poſterity of the patriarch *Judah.*

JAH'-DI-ĒL, ['Ιεδιήλ, i. e. *the unity, joy, ſharpneſs, or revenge of God.*] One of the poſterity of the patriarch *Manaſſeh.*

JAH'-DO, ['Ιεδδαὶ. 'Αδαὶ, i. e. *I alone, his joy, ſharpneſs of wit, or his newneſs.*] One of the poſterity of the patriarch *Gad.*

JAH'-LEEL, ['Αχοήλ. 'Αλλήλ, i. e. *waiting for, or beſeeching, or hope, or beginning in God.*] The *third* ſon of the patriarch *Zebulun.*

JAH'-LEEL-ITES. The deſcendants of *Jahleel.*

JAH'-MA-I, ['Ιαμαὶ, i. e. *warm or making warm.*] The ſon of *Tola,* and grandſon of *Iſſachar* the patriarch.

JAH'-ZAH, ['Ιασὰ.] A city of *Paleſtine* in the tribe of *Zebulun,* given to the *Levites.*

JAH'-

JAH'-ZE-ĒL or JAH'-ZI-ĒL, ['Aσιήλ, i. e. *God hasteth or divideth.*] One of the sons of the patriarch *Naphtali.*

JAH'-ZE-ĒL-ITES. The posterity of *Jahzeel.*

JAH'-ZER-AH, ['Aζεφά.] One of the posterity of the patriarch *Levi.*

JA'-IR, ['Iaìϱ, i. e. *illuminated, or a river.*] The son of *Segub*, of the tribe of *Manasseh*, the *tenth* judge of *Israel*, he died A. M. 2818—also a son of *Manasseh.*

JA'-IR-ITES. The descendants from *Jair.*

JA-I'-RUS, ['Iάειϱ⊙, i. e. *illuminated, or a river.*] Chief ruler of the jewish synagogue at *Capernaum*, whose daughter our *Saviour* restored to life.

JA'-KAN, ['Iaxάν, i. e. *weeping out, or pressing.*] A son of *Ezer* a descendant from *Abraham.*

JA'-KEH. The father of *Agur*, mentioned in the book of *Proverbs.*

JA'-KIM, ['Iaxìμ, i. e. *rising, confirming, or establishing.*] One of the posterity of the patriarch *Benjamin.*

JAK'-KIM. One of the priests of king *David*'s appointment.

JA'-LŌN, ['Iaλών, i. e. *tarrying or murmuring.*] One of the posterity of the patriarch *Judah.*

JAM'-BRĒS, ['Iaμϭϱῆs, i. e. *a rebel, bitter, or changing, or the sea, with poverty or want.*] A famous magician who, with *Jannes*, opposed *Moses* in *Egypt.*

JAM'-BRI, ['Iaμϭϱì, i. e. *rebellious; waxing bitter; changing.*] By the children of *Jambri* is meant a people of *Arabia* who were plundering robbers.

JAMES, ['Iάxωϭ⊙, i. e. *a supplanter or maintainer.*] *James* the greater was son of *Zebedee* and *Salome*, and brother to *John* the evangelist; he suffered martyrdom A. C. 44. *James* the less was son of *Cleophas* and of *Mary* sister to the virgin *Mary:* he wrote the epistle of his name, in the *New Testament*, was bishop of *Jerusalem* and was martyred.

L

JA'-MIN,

JA'-MIN, ['Ιαμὶν, i. e. *right hand, or south wind.*] The son of *Ram*, and grandson to *Jerahmeel*—also a son of *Simeon*.

JA'-MIN-ITES. The posterity of *Jamin.*

JAM'-LECH, ['Ιεμολὸχ, i. e. *reigning or asking counsel.*] A prince of the tribe of *Simeon.*

JAM'-NA-AN, ['Ιεμναάν.] A place mentioned in the *Apocrypha.*

JAM-NI'-A, ['Ιαμνείας, i. e. *building or understanding.*] A place not far from *Judæa,* a sea-port town.

JAM'-NITES, ['Ιαμνίται.] The inhabitants of *Jamnia.*

JAN'-NA. ['Ιαννὰ, i. e. *answering, beginning to speak, afflicted, or poor.*] The father of *Melchi*; an ancestor of *Joseph* the husband of the virgin *Mary,* in St. *Luke*'s genealogy.

JAN'-NES, ['Ιαννῆς, i. e. *answering, afflicted, humble, or poor.*] A magician who with *Jambres* opposed *Moses* in *Egypt.*

JAN-O'-AH or JAN-O'-HAH, ['Ιανωκᾶ, i. e. *resting, tarrying, or deriving.*] A city of *Palestine* in the tribe of *Ephraim,* on its borders.

JA'-NUM, ['Ιεμαΐν, i. e. *sleeping.*] A city of *Palestine,* in the tribe of *Judah* in the mountains.

JA'-PHET or JA'-PHETH, ['Ιάφεθ, i. e. *enlarged, fair, persuading or enticing.*] A son of *Noah,* whose descendants peopled *Europe.*

JAPH'-I-AH, ['Ιεφθα, i. e. *making see, appearing or lightening.*] A city of *Palestine* in the tribe of *Zebulun*—also a son of king *David.*

JAPH'-LET, ['Ιαφλὴτ, i. e. *delivered or banished.*] A son of *Heber,* the grandson of *Asher.*

JAPH'-LET-I, ['Απ'λαλὶμ, i. e. *delivered or banished.*] One of the borders of the children of *Joseph.*

JAPH'-O, ['Ιοππῆς, i. e. *fairness or comeliness.*] A city of *Palestine* in the tribe of *Dan.*

JAR. An hebrew *month,* which answers to about our *April.*

JA'-RAH, ['Ιαδὰ, i. e. *a wood, honeycomb, pouring out, or watching diligently.*] One of the posterity of king *Saul.*

JA'-REB, ['Ιαρειμ, i. e. *a revenger.*] The name of
a king of *Affyria.*

JA'-RED, ['Ιαρεδ, i. e. *ruling or coming down.*] One
of the patriarchs who lived 962 years, the father
of *Enoch:* he died A. M. 1422—alfo others.

JA-RE-SI'-AH, ['Ιαρασία, i. e. *the bed of the Lord;
the Lord hath taken away; poverty.*] One of the
pofterity of the patriarch *Benjamin.*

JAR'-HA, ['Ιερεε.] An ægyptian fervant to *Shefhan,*
of the tribe of *Judah,* who married his mafter's
daughter.

JA'-RIB, ['Ιαριϐ, i. e. *fighting, chiding, multiplying or
avenging.*] A fon of the patriarch *Simeon*—alfo
a prieft of that name.

JAR'-MUTH, ['Ιερμὰϑ, i. e. *fearing, feeing, or throwing down death.*] A city of *Palestine,* in the tribe
of *Judah* in the valley—alfo one of the tribe of
Manaffeh — alfo one of *Iffachar,* given to the
Levites.

JA-RO'-AH, ['Ιωρά, i. e. *making a fweet fmell, breathing, or the moon.*] One of the pofterity of the
patriarch *Gad.*

JAS'-A-EL, ['Ιασαῆλϴ.] One who returned from
the babylonifh captivity.

JA'-SHEM or JA'-SHEN, ['Ιασὶν, i. e. *antient or fleeping.*] The father of one of king *David's* worthies.

JA'-SHER, ['Ευϑός, i. e. *righteous.*] One who is
fuppofed to have written a book of hymns or
odes on the battles of the *Ifraelites.*

JASH-OB'-E-AM, ['Ιεσϐαάμ. Σοϐοκὰμ, i. e. *the people
fitting, or the controverfy, or the captivity of the people.*] An *Hachmonite* or *Tachmonite,* a captain
over *thirty* men in king *David's* army.

JASH'-UB, ['Ιασὺϐ, i. e. *a returning, a controverfy, or
a dwelling place.*] A fon of the patriarch *Iffachar*
—alfo one who returned from the babylonifh
captivity.

JASH-U'-BI LE'-HEM. A place mentioned in the
firft book of *Chronicles,* but uncertain where.

JA'-SHUB-ITES. The defcendants from *Jafhub.*

JAS'-I-ĒL, ['Ισσιηλ, i. e. *the strength of God.*] One of king *David's* warriors.

JA'-SŌN, ['Ιασων. L. *I-a'-son,* i. e. *healing.*] An high prieſt of the *Jews*—alſo an hoſt and kinſman of St. *Paul* in *Theſſalonica.*

JAS'-PER, ["Ιασπις.] A precious ſtone of a beautiful bright green, but ſometimes clouded with white, yellow, blue and brown: it was the *third* ſtone of the *fourth* row of ſtones in the jewiſh high prieſt's breaſt-plate.

JA-SU'-BUS, ['Ιασϐ☉.] One who returned from the babyloniſh captivity.

JAT'-AL, ['Αλαλ.] One whoſe ſons were porters or guards of the temple.

JATH'-NI-ĒL, ['Ιενηηλ. 'Ιαθαναηλ, i. e. *a gift of God.*] The *fourth* ſon of *Meſhelemiah,* and one of the porters of the temple of *Jeruſalem.*

JAT'-TIR, ['Ιατθειρ. 'Ιεθερ, i. e. *a remnant, or excellent.*] A city of *Pal ſtine,* in the tribe of *Judah,* in the mountains, given to the *Levites.*

JA'-VAN, ['Ιωϋάν, i. e. *making ſad.*] The *fourth* ſon of *Japhet,* and father of the *Ionians* in *Greece.*

JAZ'-AR, ['Ιαζηρ.] An high prieſt of the *Jews* when our *Saviour* was born.

JAZ'-ĒR, ['Ιαζηρ, i. e. *an aid, or helper.*] A city of *Paleſtine,* in the tribe of *Gad,* given to the *Levites.*

JAZ'-I-ĒL, ['Οζιηλ, i. e. *the strength of God.*] One of the *Levites,* a porter or guard of the temple.

JAZ'-IZ, ['Ιαζιζ, i. e. *brightneſs, or a departing.*] One who ſuperintended the flocks of king *David.*

I before B.

IB'-HAR, ['Εϐεαρ, i. e. *choſen.*] One of the ſons of king *David.*

IB'-LE-AM, ['Ιεϐλαάμ, i. e. *the antient of the people, or the people decreaſing.*] A city of *Paleſtine,* in the tribe of *Manaſſeh.*

IB-NEI'-AH or IB-NI'-JAH, ['Ιεϐναά, i. e. *the building, or underſtanding of the Lord, or a ſon by adoption.*]
The

The ſon of *Reuel*, one of the poſterity of *Benjamin* the patriarch.

IB'-RI, ['Αϐαρί, i. e. *paſſing over, being angry, or being
with young.*] One of the poſterity of the patriarch *Levi.*

IB'-ZAN, ['Αϐαισσὰν, 'Εσεϐὰν, i. e. *the father of a target, or of coldneſs.*] One of the tribe of *Judah,*
and the *twelfth* judge of *Iſrael:* he died A. M.
2831.

I *before* C.

ICH'-A-BŌD, ['Ιωχαϐὴδ, i. e. *where is glory? or,
no glory, or woe unto glory.*] The ſon of *Phinehas,*
and grandſon of *Eli* the high prieſt of the *Jews.*

I-CON'-I-UM, ['Ικόνιον, i. e. *coming.*] Now *Cogni:*
the capital of *Lycaonia* in *Aſia Minor,* where St.
Paul preached.

I *before* D.

ID'-A-LAH, ['Ιεδαλα, i. e. *the hand of ſlander, or of
God, or an oath, or curſing.*] A city of *Paleſtine,*
in the tribe of *Zebulun.*

ID'-BASH, ['Ιεϐδάς, i. e. *flowing with honey, or the
hand of deſtruction.*] One of the poſterity of the
patriarch *Judah.*

ID'-DO, [Σαδδώ. 'Αδδώ, i. e. *his hand, his power, or his
confeſſion.*] One of the poſterity of the patriarch
Levi—alſo a prophet, grandfather of the prophet
Zechariah.

ID-U'-ĒL, ['Ιδυὴλ.⊙.] A principal man among
the *Jews* after the babyloniſh captivity.

ID-U-MÆ'-A, ['Ιδυμαία, i. e. *red, earthy, or bloody.*]
A province of *Arabia,* where *Edom* or *Eſau* fixed
his abode: it lay ſouth of *Paleſtine.*

ID-U-MÆ'-ANS, ['Ιδυμαῖοι, i. e. *red; earthy; bloody.*]
The people of *Idumæa.*

J befort

J before E.

JE'-A-RIM, ['Ιαριμ, i. e. *a leap, or woods.*] A mountain of *Palestine*, in the tribe of *Judah*; it is also called *Chesalon*.

JE-AT'-ER-AI, ['Ιεθρι, i. e. *searching out.*] One of the posterity of the patriarch *Levi*.

JE-BER-E-CHI'-AH, [Βαραχιος, i. e. *speaking well of the Lord. or bowing the knee to the Lord.*] The father of *Zechariah* the priest.

JE'-BUS, ['Ιηβûs, i. e. *a treading underfoot, tumbling, rolling, or a manger.*] The city of *Jerusalem*; so called antiently, from *Jebusi* the son of *Canaan*.

JEB-U'-SI, ['Ιεβυσαι, i. e. *tredden underfoot, tumbled, or manglers.*] A son of *Canaan*, and father of the *Jebusites*—also a border of the tribe of *Benjamin*.

JEB'-US-ITES, ['Ιεβυσαιοι.] The descendants from *Jebusi*, inhabitants of *Jebus*.

JEC-A-MI'-AH, ['Ιεκιμια, i. e. *the resurrection, confirmation, or revenge of the Lord.*] The son of *Jeconiah*, of the royal family of *Judah*.

JEC-OL-I'-AH. ['Ιεχελια, i. e. *the perfection, or power of the Lord.*] The wife of *Amaziah* king of *Judah*, and mother of *Azariah*.

JEC-ON-I'-AH, ['Ιεχονιας, i. e. *stability of the Lord.*] Son of *Jehoiachin* king of *Judah*, he succeeded his father. A. M. 3406.

JED-AI'-AH or JED-AI'-A, ['Ιεδυα, i. e. *the hand of the Lord, or confessing the Lord.*] The name of one of the *jewish* priests, and of others.

JED-DE'-US, ['Ιεδαιος.] One who returned from the babylonish captivity.

JED'-DU, ['Ιεδδος.] A priest who returned from the babylonish captivity with his family.

JED-EI'-AH: See *Jehdeiah*.

JED-I'-A-EL, ['Ιεδιηλ, i. e. *the science or the knowledge of God.*] A brave man, who quitted king *Saul's* army and joined king *David*—also others.

JED-I'-DAH, ['Ιεδδιδα, i. e. *beloved.*] The daughter of *Adaiah* and mother of *Josiah* king of *Judah*.

JED-ID-

JED-ID-I'-AH, ['Ιεδδεδι, i. e. *beloved of the Lord, our loving to the Lord.*] A fon of king *David* by *Bathsheba*.

JED'-I-ĒL, [Γεδιηλ, i. e. *the knowledge, or unity, or joy, or renewing of God.*] One who repaired unto king *David* at *Ziklag:* the fame with *Jediael*.

JED'-U-THŪN, ['Ιδιθυν, i. e. *belonging to the law, or giving praife.*] A *Levite* of *Merari's* family, and one of the *four* great mafters of mufick of the temple of *Jerufalem*.

JE-E'-LI, ['Ιεηλι.] One of the fervants of *Solomon*.

JE-EZ'-ER, ['Αχιεζερ, i. e. *the ifle of help, or woe be to help.*] The fon of *Naphtali*—alfo the fon of *Gilead* chief of the family of the *Jeezerites*.

JE-EZ'-ER-ITES. The defcendants from *Jeezer*.

JE'-GAR SA-HA-DU'-THA, [i. e. *the heap of witnefs.*] An heap of ftones, where *Jacob* and his brethren did eat together: called fo by *Laban*. See *Galeed*.

JE-HAL'-E-ĒL, ['Αλεηλ, i. e. *praifing God; the clearnefs of God.*] One of the porters or guards of the temple.

JE-HAL'-EL-ĒL, ['Ιλαελ̇ηλ.] A defcendant from *Merari*.

JE-HAZ'-I-ĒL. See *Jehaziel*.

JEH-DEI'-AH, ['Ιεδια, i. e. *joy; together; one Lord.*] A *Meronothite* who had the care of the affes in king *David's* reign.

JE-HEI'-ĒL, [Ιεηλ, i. e. *God liveth, God hath taken away, or God heaping up.*] One who returned from the babylonifh captivity—alfo others.

JE-HEZ'-EK-ĒL, ['Εζεκηλ, i. e. *the ftrength of God.*] One of the twenty-four families of the priefts.

JE-HI'-AH, ['Ιεια, i. e. *the Lord liveth.*] A doorkeeper of the ark, in king *David's* time.

JE-HI'-ĒL, ['Ιεηλ.] One of king *David's* valiant men.

JE-HI'-ĒL-I, ['Ιεηλ, i. e. *the fame with Jeheiel.*] One of the pofterity of the patriarch *Levi*.

JE-HI'-SHA-I, [Ιεσαι.] One of the tribe of *Gad*. See *Jefhifhai*.

JE-HIS-KI'-AH, ['Εζεκίας, i. e. *the strength or taking of the Lord.*] One of the posterity of the patriarch *Ephraim.*

JE-HO'-A-DAH, ['Ιαδὰ, i. e. *the congregation; passing over; the testimony or taking away of the Lord.*] The son of *Achaz,* of the posterity of king *Saul.*

JE-HO-AD'-DAN. ['Ιωαδαὲν, i. e. *the pleasure or delights or the time of the Lord.*] The mother of *Amaziah* king of *Judah.*

JE-HO'-A-HAZ, ['Ιωάχαζ, i. e. *the taking possession of the Lord, or the Lord seeing.*] The son of *Josiah* king of *Judah,* who succeeded his father, but reigned only *three months:* he is called *Shallum*—also the son of *Jehu,* king of *Israel.*

JE-HO'-ASH, ['Ιωὰς. i. e. *the fire of the Lord, or the offering of the Lord.*] A king of *Judah,* son to king *Ahaziah*; he died A. M. 3166. See *Joash.*

JE-HO'-HA-DAH, ['Ιωιαδὰ, i. e. *the congregation, or the passing over, or the testimony, or the decking, or the prey, or the taking away of the Lord.*] One of the posterity of king *Saul.*

JE-HŌ-HAN'-AN, ['Ιωανὰν, i. e. *the grace, mercy, or gift of the Lord.*] One of the porters or guards of the temple of *Jerusalem.*

JE-HOI'-A-CHIN, ['Ιωαχὶμ.] See *Jeconiah.*

JE-HOI'-A-DA, ['Ιωδαὲ, i. e. *the knowledge of the Lord.*] The successor of *Azariah* in the high priesthood.

JE-HOI'-A-KIM or EL-I'-A-KIM, ['Ιωαχὶμ, i. e. *the rising, avenging, or establishing of the Lord.*] The son of king *Josiah,* and brother and successor of *Jehoahaz* king of *Judah.*

JE-HOI'-A-RIB, ['Ιωαρεὶβ, i. e *the fighting, chiding, or multiplying of the Lord.*] The head of the *first* family of the priests, established by king *David.*

JE-HO'-NA-DAB, ['Ιωναδὰβ, i.e. *voluntary or willing.*] The son of *Shimeah, David*'s nephew—also the son of *Rechab,* father of the *Rechabites.*

JE-HO'-NA-THAN, ['Ιωναθὰν, i. e. *the gift of the Lord, or the gift of a dove.*] The son of *Uzziah*—also the son of *Shimeah*—also king *David*'s uncle.

JE-HO'-

JE-HO'-RAM, ['Ιωράμ, i. e. *the height, or the throwing down of the Lord.*] Son and fucceffor to *Jehofaphat* king of *Judah*—alfo a fon of *Ahab* king of *Ifrael.*

JE-HO-SHAB'-E-ATH, ['Ιωσαβεὲθ.] A daughter of king *Joram* or *Jehoram.* See *Jehofheba.*

JE-HO'-SHA-PHAT, ['Ιωσαφὰτ, i. e. *the Lord is the Judge.*] Son and fucceffor to *Afa* king of *Judah* —alfo a fon of king *Solomon,* who died A. M. 3115—alfo others.

JE-HO'-SHE-BA, ['Ιωσαβεὲ, i. e. *the fullnefs, or oath of the Lord.*] The wife of *Jehoiada* the high prieft; a daughter of king *Joram.*

JE-HO'-SHŪ-A, ['Ιησὲ.] See JOSHUA.

JE-HO'-VAH, [i. e. *the Lord, felf exifting.*] The incommunicative name of GOD.

JE-HO'-VAH JI'-RETH, [i. e. *the Lord feeth, or will fee, or provideth.*] The place where *Abraham* was about to offer up his fon *Ifaac.*

JE-HO'-VAH NIS'-SI, [i. e. *the Lord my banner.*] An altar fo named, built by *Mofes.*

JE-HO'-VAH SHAL'-LOM, [i. e. *the Lord of peace.*] An altar fo named, built by *Gideon.*

JE-HO'-VAH SHAM'-MAH, [i. e. *the Lord is there.*] The name of *Ezekiel's* prophetick city.

JE-HO'-VAH TSID'-KE-NU, [i. e *the Lord our righteoufnefs.*] The name which *Jeremiah* faid fhould be given to *Jerufalem.*

JE-HO'-ZA-BAD, ['Ιωζαβάδ, i. e. *the Lord's dowry, or having a dowry.*] One of the murderers of king *Joafh*—and others.

JE-HO'-ZA-DAK, ['Ιωσαδάκ, i. e. *the juftice of the Lord.*] One of the pofterity of *Levi*—and others.

JE'-HU, ['Ιὲ. 'Ιηὲ, i. e. *he, he that, or being.*] A prophet fent to *Baafha* king of *Ifrael,* and flain by his order—alfo a captain who was anointed king of *Ifrael* A. M. 3120 by *Elifha,* and reigned *twenty-eight* years—alfo others of that name.

JE-HUB'-BAH, ['Ιαβὰ, i. e. *an hiding, a beloved, fin or binding.*] One of the pofterity of the patriarch *Afher.*

JE-HU'-

JE-HU'-CAL, ['Ιωαχαλ, i. e. *mighty, perfect, or wasted.*] The son of *Shelemiah* in king *Zedekiah*'s reign.

JE'-HUD, ['Ιϑϑ, i. e. *praising, or confessing.*] A city of *Palestine*, in the tribe of *Dan.*

JE-HU'-DI, ['Ιηδις, i. e. *praising, or confessing.*] A grandson of *Shelemiah*, of the priest's order.

JE-HU-DI'-JAH, ['Ιηδεια, i. e. *a praising, or confessing of the Lord.*] The mother of *Jered*, of the tribe of *Judah.*

JE-HUSH, ['Ινης, i. e. *keeping counsel, or fastened.*] One of the posterity of king *Saul.*

JE-I'-EL. See *Jehiel.*

JE-KAB'-ZE-EL, ['Καϐσειλ, i. e. *the congregation of God.*] A village of the land of *Canaan.*

JEK-AM-E'-AM, ['Ιεκεμιας, i. e. *the people shall arise.*] One of the posterity of the patriarch *Levi.*

JEK-AM-I'-AH, ['Ιεκεμιας, i. e. *the establishing or revenging of the Lord.*] The son of *Shallum*, of the posterity of *Judah.*

JEK-UTH'-I-EL, [Ιεκυτιηλ. Χετιηλ, i. e. *the hope, or congregation of God.*] One of the posterity of the patriarch *Judah.*

JEM-I'-MAH, ['Ιεμιμα, i. e. *handsome as the day.*] The eldest of *Job*'s three daughters which he had after his misfortunes.

JEM-U'-EL, ['Ιεμυηλ, i. e. *God's day, or the sea of God.*] One of the sons of the patriarch *Simeon.*

JEPH'-THAH, ['Ιεφθαε, i. e. *opening.*] The *eleventh* judge of *Israel*, who devoted his daughter to the *Lord*, either by sacrifice or celibacy; he died A. M. 2824, the son of *Gilead.*

JEPH-UN'-NAH, ['Ιεφουνη, i. e. *beholding.*] One of the posterity of the patriarch *Judah*, *Caleb*'s father.

JE'-RAH, ['Ιαραχ. 'Ιαδερ, i. e. *the moon, or month, or smelling sweet.*] A descendant from the patriarch *Shem.*

JE-RAH'-ME'-EL, ['Ιεραμεηλ, i. e. *the mercy of God, or the beloved of God.*] The first born son of *Hezron* who was grandson of the patriarch *Judah.*

JE-RAH'-

JE-RAH'-ME-ĒL-ITES. The posterity of *Jerah-meel.*

JER-ECH'-US, ['Ιεϱεχὸς.] One whose family returned from the babylonish captivity.

JE'-RED, ['Ιάϱεδ, i. e. *ruling, or coming down.*] The son of *Mahaleel*—also the son of *Ezra* by *J.hudijah*; of the tribe of *Judah.*

JER'-E-MAI, ['Ιεϱαμί, i. e. *my height, or fearing, or throwing forth waters.*] One who returned from the babylonish captivity.

JER-EM-I'-AH, ['Ιεϱεμίας. L. *Jer-em'-i-as*, i. e. *exalting the Lord, or the Lord's height.*] One of the greater prophets, after whom the canonical book of *Jeremiah* is named: he was the son of *Hilkiah*, of the race of priests; he prophesied in the fourteenth year of his age and thirteenth year of the reign of *Josiah* to A. M. 3575—also others of that name.

JER'-E-MŌTH, ['Ιεϱιμώθ, i. e. *eminences, or he that fears, or sees death.*] One of the posterity of the patriarch *Benjamin.*

JER'-E-MOUTH, ['Αϱμώθ. 'Ιαϱμώθ.] One who returned from the babylonish captivity.

JER'-I-AH, ['Ιεϱιὰ, i. e. *the fear, vision, or throwing down of the Lord.*] One of the posterity of the patriarch *Levi.*

JER'-I-BAI, ['Ιεϱιβαί, i. e. *fighting, chiding, or multiplying.*] One of king *David*'s valiant men—also one who returned from the babylonish captivity.

JER'-I-CHO, ['Ιεϱιχώ, i. e. *the moon, month, or his sweet smell.*] A city about *six* miles from the river *Jordan* in *Palestine*, in the tribe of *Benjamin:* about *twenty-three* miles from *Jerusalem.*

JER'-I-ĒL, ['Ιεϱιὴλ, i. e *the fear, or vision of God.*] A son of *Tola*, and grandson to the patriarch *Issachar.*

JER-I'-JAH, ['Ιωϱίας.] An *Hebronite*, one of king *David*'s officers.

JER'-I-MŌTH, ['Ιεϱιμώθ, i. e. *he that fears, sees, or rejects death.*] The name of several persons in sacred writ—also a city in the tribe of *Judah.*

JER-'I-

JER'-I-ŌTH, ['Ιεριώθ, i. e. *kettles, cauldrons, or breaking asunder,*] A wife of *Caleb,* a defcendant from the patriarch *Judah.*

JER'-O-AM or **JER'-O-HAM,** ['Ιροάμ, i. e. *high, merciful, or beloved.*] One of the pofterity of the patriarch *Levi.*

JER-OB'-O-AM, ['Ιεροβοάμ, i. e. *fighting againft, chiding, or encreafing the people.*] The fon of *Nebat,* and *firft* king of *Ifrael;* he reigned twenty-two years—alfo the fon of *Jehoafh* king of *Ifrael,* who fucceeded his father A. M. 3179, and reigned *forty-one* years.

JER-UB'-BA-AL or **JER-UB'-E-SHETH,** ['Ιεροβααλ, i. e. *let Baal avenge, or an idol overcome.*] The furname of *Gideon.*

JER'-U-ĒL, ['Ιεριήλ, i. e. *the fear or vifion of God.*] A wildernefs of that name, to the weft of the *dead fea.*

JE-RU'-SA-LEM, ['Ιερυσαλήμ, i. e. *the vifion of peace, or the perfect vifion, or perfect fear.*] It was antiently called *Jebus,* and inhabited by the *Jebufies:* it was the metropolis of the land of *Paleftine,* in the tribe of *Benjamin:* fome fuppofe it was the antient *Salem,* built by king *Melchifedeck;* it lies in 31 deg. 50 min. North Lat. and 36. o deg. E. Long. now *Cudfembaric.*

JER-U'-SHA, ['Ιερυσά, i. e. *poffeffion, or banifhment.*] The mother of *Jotham* king of *Judah,* and daughter of *Zadok.*

JES-AI'-AH, ['Ισαίας, i. e. *the health, or falvation of the Lord.*] One of the tribe of the patriarch *Benjamin.*

JESH-A-I'-AH, ['Ισαΐα, i. e. *the health or falvation of the Lord.*] The fon of *Jeduthun* the *Levite.*

JESH'-A-NAH, ['Ισυννί.] A city of *Paleftine,* in the tribe of *Ephraim.*

JESH-AR-EL'-AH, ['Ισαρελά.] The *feventh* of the *twenty-four* families of the *Levites.*

JESH-EB'-E-AH or **JESH-EB'-E-AB,** ['Ισβααλ, i. e. *the fitting, or captivity of the father.*] Chief of the *fourteenth* family of the priefts who waited at the temple.

JESH'-

JESH'-ER, ['Ιασὰρ, i. e. *right, singing, having a regard, or ruling.*] The fon of *Caleb*, a defcendant from the patriarch *Judah*, by his wife *Azubah*.

JESH-I'-MON, ['Ιεσσαιμὸς, i. e. *folitude, or defolation.*] A city of *Paleftine*, in the tribe of *Simeon*.

JESH-I-SHA'-I, ['Ιεσαὶ, i. e. *antient, or rejoicing exceedingly.*] One of the pofterity of the patriarch *Gad*.

JESH-O-HA'-I-AH, ['Ιασηία, i. e. *the Lord preffing, or the meditation of God.*] A prince of the tribe of *Simeon*.

JESH-U'-A, ['Ιησᾶ, i. e. *a faviour.*] One who returned from the babylonifh captivity—alfo an high prieft of the *Jews*.

JESH-U'-RUN, [i. e. *upright or righteous.*] The people of *Ifrael* are fo called by *Mofes* and *Ifaiah*.

JES-I'-AH, ['Ιεσσιά, i. e. *a fprinkling of the Lord.*] One who repaired to king *David* at *Ziklag*.

JES-IM'-I-EL, ['Ισμαὴλ, i. e. *the naming, or aftonifhment of God.*] A prince of the tribe of *Simeon*.

JES'-SE, ['Ιεσσαί, i. e. *a gift, oblation, or being.*] The fon of *Obed*, and father of king *David*.

JES-U'-A. The fame with *Jefhua*.

JES-U'-I, ['Ιεσσυὶ, i. e. *who is equal, or proper, or flat country.*] The third fon of *Afher*, and head of the family of the *Jefuites*.

JES-U'-ITES, ['Ιεσυὶ.] The defcendants from *Jefui*.

JE'-SUS, [ΙΗΣΟΥΣ, i. e. *Saviour, or the Lord the Saviour, or the falvation of the Lord.*] The name of *Chrift*, from his coming to fave mankind from their fins: he was born on the *twenty-fifth* of December, A. M. 4000: he died by crucifixion, April *third* Æt. *thirty-three*—alfo *Jefhua* or *Jofhua* the fon of *Jofedeck*, and high prieft of the *Jews*—alfo the fon of *Sirach*, author of the *apocryphal* book of *Ecclefiafticus*.

JETH'-ER, ['Ιεθὲρ, i. e. *excelling, remaining, fearching out diligently, or a fmall ftring.*] The eldeft fon of *Gideon*—alfo others of that name.

JETH'-ETH, ['Ιεθὲρ, i. e. *giving.*] The name of a duke, a defcendant from the patriarch *Efau*.

JETH'-

JETH'-LAH, [Σιλαθὰ, i. e. *hanging up*; *heaping up*.] A city of *Palestine*, in the tribe of *Dan*.

JETH'-RO, ['Ιοθὸρ, i. e. *his excellence, his remains, or his posterity*.] A priest or prince of *Midian*; the father in law of *Moses*.

JET'-ŪR, ['Ιέτὸρ, i. e. *an order, or keeping, or mountainous*.] A son of *Ishmael*—also a place which *Reuben* the patriarch warred against.

JE'-U-ĒL, ['Ιεήλ, i. e. *God hath taken away, or God heaping up*.] A descendant from *Terah*.

JE'-ŪSH, ['Ιεὸς. 'Ιωὰς, i. e. *he that is devoured, or gnawed by the moth, or gathered together*.] A son of the patriarch *Esau*—also a descendant from the patriarch *Benjamin*.

JE'-ŪZ, ['Ιεὸς, i. e. *the same with Jeush*.] One of the posterity of the patriarch *Benjamin*.

JEWS, ['Ιὸδαῖοι, i. e. *praising, or confessing*.] The people of *Israel* so called, from the patriarch *Judah* the son of *Jacob* or *Israel*.

JEW'-RIE, ['Ιὸδαὶα.] The land of *Canaan* so called, when possessed by the *Jews*.

JEZ-AN-I'-AH, ['Εζονίας, i. e. *the nourishment or weapons of the Lord*.] One who persuaded the *Israelites* to go into *Egypt* contrary to the advice of *Jeremiah*.

JEZ'-A-BEL, ['Ιεζάϐελ, i. e. *woe to thee or to the dunghill*.] A daughter of *Ethbaal*, a king of *Sidon*, and wife of *Ahab* king of *Israel*: she caused the prophets of the Lord to be slain, and was slain herself by order of *Jehu*.

JEZ-E'-LUS, ['Ιεζήλ⊙.] One who returned from the babylonish captivity.

JEZ'-ER, ['Ιεσὲρ, i. e. *the isle of help, or woe be to help*.] A son to the patriarch *Naphtali*—also a son of *Gilead*, of whom came the *Jezerites*, or *Izrites*.

JEZ'-ER-ITES. Descendants from *Jezer* the son of *Gilead*.

JEZ'-I-AH, ['Αζία, i. e. *a sprinkling of the Lord*.] One who returned from the babylonish captivity.

JEZ'-I-ĒL, ['Αζιὴλ, i. e. *the sprinkling of God*.] One who repaired to king *David* at *Ziklag*.

JEZ-LI'.

JEZ-LI'-AH, ['Ιεξλίας.] One of the posterity of the patriarch *Benjamin*.

JEZ'-O-AR, [Σααρ, i. e. *clear or white.*] One of the posterity of the patriarch *Judah*.

JEZ-RA-HI'-AH, ['Ιεζρίας, i. e. *brightness of the Lord.*] Chief of the singers of the temple in the time of *Nehemiah*.

JEZ'-RE-EL, ['Ιεζραέλ, i. e. *seed of God.*] A famous city of *Palestine*, in the valley of *Jezreel*, in the tribe of *Judah*—also one of the posterity of *Judah*.

JEZ'-RE-EL-ITE. An inhabitant of the city of *Jezreel*.

JEZ'-RE-EL-I'-TESS, ['Ιεζραηλίτις.] A woman of the city of *Jezreel*.

I *before* G.

I'-GAL, [Γάαλ, i. e. *redeemed or defiled.*] One of king *David*'s worthies—also a prince of the tribe of *Issachar*.

IG-DAL-I'-AH, [Γοδόλιας, i. e. *the greatness of the Lord.*] One who had the care of the wine cellar of the temple of *Jerusalem*.

I GE-AB'-A-RIM. See IIM.

IG-E'-AL, ['Ιωήλ. Γεγαάλ, i. e. *redeemer, or redeemed, or defiled.*] One of the posterity of king *David*.

J *before* I.

JIB'-SAM, ['Ιεμαοὰν, i. e. *their drought or their confusion.*] The sons of *Tola*, and grandson to *Issachar*.

JID'-LAPH, ['Ιελδαφ, i. e. *a distilling from the head, or the dropping of an house.*] One of the sons of *Nahar* (*Abraham*'s brother) by his wife *Milcah*.

J'-IM, [Γαῒ, i. e. *heaps of Hebrews, or passers over.*] A city of *Palestine* in the tribe of *Judah*: it was the 38th encampment of the *Israelites*, in the land of *Moab*.

JIM'-LA

JIM'-LA or IM'-LA, ['Ιεμλά, i. e. *a replenishing, or circumcision*.] The father of the prophet *Micaiah*.

JIM'-NA or JIM'-NAH or IM'-NAH, ['Ιεμνὰ, i. e. *the right hand, numbering or preparing*.] A son of *Asher*—also a *Levite*.

JIM'-NITES. The descendants from *Jimna*.

I'-JŌN, [Αὶν. 'Αὶνὼν, i. e. *a beholding, a fountain, or eye*.] A city of *Palestine* in the tribe of *Naphtali*.

JIPH'-TAH, ['Ιανὰ, i. e. *opening*.] A city of *Palestine* in the tribe of *Judah*, in the valley.

JIPH'-THAH-ĒL, [Γαιφαὴλ, i. e. *God opening*.] A valley of *Palestine*, which bounded the tribes of *Zebulun*, and of *Asher*.

I *before* K.

IK'-KESH, ['Εχχὶς, i. e. *forward or wicked*.] A *Tekoite*, son of *Ira* one of king *David*'s captains.

I *before* L.

I'-LAI, ['Ηλὶ.] An *Ahohite*, one of king *David*'s worthies.

IL-LY'-RI-CUM, ['Ιλλυρικὸν i. e. *a making merry*.] A country or province to the north west of *Macedonia*, on the coast of the *adriatic sea*, in *Asia*, opposite *Italy*.

I *before* M.

IM'-LAH. See JIMLA.

IM'-MAH, ['Ιεμνὰ.] The name of one of the *Levites*. See JIMNA.

IM'-NA or IM'-NAH. See JIMNA.

IM or EM-MAN-U'-ĒL, ['Εμμανυὴλ, i. e. *God with us*.] The prophetic name of *Jesus Christ*, or the *Messiah*.

IM'-MER, [Εμμὴρ, i. e. *saying, speaking, or a lamb*.] One of the priests in king *David*'s time—also a city of *Babylon*.

IM'-RAH,

IM'-RAH, ['Ιμρὰν, i. e. *a rebel, waxing bitter, or changing.*] One of the pofterity of *Afher* the patriarch.

IM'-RI, ['Εμϐρὶ, i. e. *faying, fpeaking, exalting, or bitter, or a lamb.*] One of the pofterity of *Judah* the patriarch.

I *before* N.

IN'-DI-A, ['Ινδικῆ, i. e. *a praifing, confeffing, comely, fair.*] A large country in the eaft of *Afia*, being a *third* part of it: eaft of *Perfia*; fouth of great *Tartary*; weft of *China*, and north of the *indian ocean*.

J *before* O.

JO'-AB, ['Ιωὰϐ, i. e. *willing, or fatherhood.*] The fon of *Zeruiah* king *David's* fifter, and brother to *Abifhai* and *Afahel:* he was *David's* firft general— alfo others.

JO'-A-CHAZ, ['Ιεχονίας, i. e. *the preparing or ftability of the Lord.*] The fon of king *Jofias, firft* Efdras, chap. i. ver. 34; the fame with *Jehoahaz.*

JO-A-DA'-NUS, ['Ιωαδάν℗.] A prieft who returned from the babylonifh captivity, and had married a ftrange wife.

JO'-AH, ['Ιωαά, i. e. *brotherhood, or having a brother.*] A fon of *Gerfhom*, and grandfon to *Levi* the patriarch—alfo the fon of *Afaph* the recorder—alfo others.

JO'-A-HAZ, ['Ιάαχαζ, i. e. *apprehending, poffeffing, or feeing.*] A fon of *Joah* the recorder in king *Jofiah's* reign.

JO'-A-KIM, ['Ιωακὶμ, i. e. *the rifing or eftablifhing of the Lord.*] Said to be the hufband of *Anna*, and father of the virgin *Mary*—alfo the hufband of *Sufanna.*

JO-AN'-NA, ['Ιωάννα, i. e. *the grace, gift, or mercy of the Lord.*] The wife of *Chuza, Herod's* fteward: fhe followed our *Saviour* in his travels.

M

JO-AN'-

JO-AN'-NAN, ['Ιωαννὰν.] The son of *Mattathias*, in the *Apocrypha*.

JO'-ASH, ['Ιωᾶς, i. e. *difagreeing, defpairing, or burning*.] A king of *Ifrael*, fon of *Ahaziah* king of *Ifrael*.

JO'-A-THAM, ['Ιωάθαμ.] See JOTHAM.

JO-A-ZAB'-DUS, ['Ιωζαβδῳ.] A *Levite* who returned from the babylonifh captivity.

JŌB, ['Ιὼβ, i. e. *forrowful, hated, howling out, or abiding enmity*.] A great man of the land of *Uz*, in eaft *Edom*, not far from *Bozra*; remarkable for his patience; fuppofed to be contemporary with *Mofes*, and from whom the canonical book of *Job* was named—alfo one of the fons of the patriarch *Iffachar*.

JO'-BAB, ['Ιωβὰβ, i. e. *forrowful, or hated*.] A fon of *Joktan*—alfo a king of *Edom*.

JO'-CHE-BED, ['Ιωχαβὶδ, i. e. *glorious*.] The wife of *Amram*, and mother of *Miriam, Mofes* and *Aaron*.

JO'-DA, ['Ιωδὰ.] One who returned from the babylonifh captivity.

JO'-ED, ['Ιωὰδ, i. e. *witneffing, robbing, or paffing over*.] One who returned from the babylonifh captivity.

JO'ĒL, ['Ιωὴλ, i. e. *willing, beginning, or fwearing*.] The fon of *Pethuel*, the *fecond* of the *twelve* leffer prophets, from whom the canonical book of *Joel* was named; he was of the tribe of *Reuben*—alfo others of that name.

JO-E'-LAH, ['Ιωὴλά, i. e. *a lifting up, profiting, or taking away flander*.] The fon of *Jeroboam*; one who took king *David*'s part.

JO-EZ'-ER, ['Ιοεζὲρ, i. e. *helping*.] A gallant officer in the army of king *David*.

JOG'-BE-HAH, ['Ιεγεβάλ, i. e. *an exalting or high*.] A city of the *Amorites*.

JOG'-LI, ['Εγλί, i. e. *a declaring, paffing over, turning back, or a rejoicing*.] The father of *Bukki* a prince of the tribe of *Dan*.

JO'-HA, ['Ιωδὰ. 'Ιωχά, i. e. *making lively*.] One of the pofterity of the patriarch *Benjamin*.

JO-HAN'-

JO-HAN'-AN, ['Iωαναν, i. e. *the grace, gift, or mercy of the Lord.*]   An high prieſt of the *Jews* and ſon of *Azariah*—alſo a ſon of *Eliænai*, of king *Solomon*'s race—alſo a *Gadite* who reſorted to king *David* at *Ziklag.*

JOHN (*the baptiſt*) ['Iωαννης Βαπλστῆς, i. e. *gracious, holy, or merciful.*]   The forerunner or herald of our *Saviour*; he was the ſon of *Zechariah* the prieſt and *Eliſabeth* his wife; he was about *ſix* months older than our *Saviour*, and baptized him about A. D. 28; and was beheaded by *Herod Antipas.*

JOHN (*the evangeliſt*) ['Iωαννης.]   A native of *Bethſaida* in *Galilee*, by profeſſion a fiſherman, and ſon of *Zebedee* and *Salome*; he lived to near an *hundred* years of age: the goſpel and epiſtles of *John* were named from him.

JOI'-AD-A, ['Iωοδαὲ. 'Iωαδά.]   See JEHOIADA.

JOI'-A-KIM, ['Iωακιμ, i. e. *the riſing, avenging, or eſtabliſhing of the Lord.*]   A jewiſh *prieſt*, the ſon of *Jeſua.*

JOI'-A-RIB, ['Iωαριϐ, i. e. *the battle, chiding, or multiplying of the Lord.*]   One who returned from the babyloniſh captivity.

JOK'-DE-AM, ['Aρικὰμ, i. e. *the crookedneſs or burning of the people.*]   A city of *Paleſtine*, in the tribe of *Judah*, in the mountains.

JO'-KIM, ['Iωακιμ, i. e. *that made the ſun ſtand.*]   One of the poſterity of the patriarch *Judah.*

JOK'-ME-AM, ['Iεχμαάμ, i. e. *the riſing, confirmation, or revenge of the people.*]   A city of *Paleſtine* in the tribe of *Ephraim.*

JOK'-NE-AM, ['Iεχμανιμ, i. e. *poſſeſſing or building up of the people.*]   A city of *Paleſtine* in the tribe of *Zebulun*, given to the *Levites.*

JOK'-SHAN, ['Iεζὰν, i. e. *hardneſs, an offence, or a knocking.*]   The ſon of the patriarch *Abraham* by *Keturah.*

JOK'-TAN, ['Iεκτὰν, i. e. *a little one, wearineſs, or ſtrife.*]   A grandſon of *Arphaxad* the ſon of *Shem* the patriarch.

                   JOK'-

JOK'-THE-ĒL, ['Ιεκθαὴλ, i. e. *the rock*.]　A city of
　　Paleſtine in the tribe of *Judah* in the valley.

JO'-NA, *(Bar)* ['Ιωνὰ, i. e. *the ſon of a dove, or the ſon
　of Jonas.*]　*Simon* the ſon of *Jonas* ſo called, the
　ſurname of St. *Peter: Bar* ſignifies *ſon.*

JO'-NA-DAB, ['Ιωναδὰϐ.]　See *Jehonadab.*

JO'-NAH, ['Ιωνᾶς, i. e. *a dove, deſtroyer, or rooting
　up, or multiplying of the people.*]　　The ſon of
　Amittai: he was the *fifth* of the leſſer prophets;
　was a native of *Gath-hepher* in *Galilee*; and from
　him the canonical book *Jonah* was named.

JO'-NAN, ['Ιωνὰν, i. e. *a dove or multiplying of the peo-
　ple.*]　An anceſtor of *Joſeph* huſband to the vir-
　gin *Mary*, in St. *Luke*'s genealogy.

JO'-NAS, ['Ιωνᾶς.]　See *Jonah.*

JO'-NA-THAN, ['Ιωναθὰν, i. e. *the gift of the Lord.*]
　The ſon of *Saul* king of *Iſrael*, and a moſt faith-
　ful friend of king *David* — alſo others of that
　name.

JO'-NATH EL'-IM RE-CHO'-CHIM.　A word in
　the title of the *fifty-ſixth* Pſalm: it is uncertain
　whether it means an inſtrument of muſick or the
　beginning of a ſong.

JOP'-PA, ['Ιὸππα, i. e. *fairneſs or comelineſs.*]　A ſea
　port town of *Paleſtine*, ſouth of *Cæſarea*; in the
　tribe of *Zebulun.*

JO'-RAH, ['Ιωρὰ, i. e. *ſhewing, caſting forth, or a caul-
　dron.*]　One who returned from the babyloniſh
　captivity.

JO'-RA-I, ['Ιωϱεῖ. 'Ιωϱεὶ, i. e. *declaring, throwing forth,
　a cauldron.*]　A deſcendant from the patriarch
　Gad.

JO'-RAM, ['Ιωϱὰμ, i. e. *the height, or throwing down
　of the Lord.*]　A ſon and ſucceſſor of *Ahab* king
　of *Iſrael*; was ſlain by *Jehu*, A. M. 3120.—
　alſo a ſon of *Toi* king of *Hamath*—alſo a cap-
　tain under king *Joſiah.*

JOR'-DAN, ['Ιοϱδάνης, i. e. *the river of or caſting forth
　judgment; or a cauldron of judgment.*]　A river of
　note, riſing in mount *Libanus*, runs 150 miles
　through *Paleſtine*, and empties itſelf into the
　　　　　　　　　　　　　　　　　　　　　dead

dead fea: its ordinary breadth is not above 60 feet; its name is from *Jor* a fpring, and *Dan* a town near to its fource.

JO'-RI-BAS, ['Ιωριβ⊙.] One whofe family returned from the babylonifh captivity; a principal man among the *Jews.*

JO'-RIM, ['Ιωρειμ, i. e. *the exaltation of the Lord.*] The fon of *Matthat* in St. *Luke's* genealogy.

JOR'-KO-AM, ['Ιερκαάν.] A fon of *Raham,* of the pofterity of *Judah.*

JO'-SA-BAD, ['Ιωζαβαθ. 'Ιωζάβ⊙.] One who repaired to king *David* at *Ziklag*—alfo one who returned from the babylonifh captivity.

JO'-SA-PHAT, ['Ιωσαφὰτ.] See *Jehefaphat.*

JO-SA-PHI'-AS, ['Ιωσαφίας, i. e. *the increafe of the Lord; the Lord finifhing.*] One who returned from the babylonifh captivity.

JO'-SE, ['Ιωσὴ, i. e. *fparing, being, or lifting up.*] The fon of *Eliezer,* an anceftor of *Jofeph* the hufband of the virgin *Mary,* in St. *Luke's* genealogy; he is called *Achaz* by St. *Matthew.*

JO'-SED-ECH, ['Ιωσεδὲκ.] An high prieft the father of *Jefus* or *Jofhua,* in the *Apocrypha,* and in *Haggai.*

JO'-SE-EL. One who returned from the babylonifh captivity.

JO'-SEPH, ['Ιωσὴφ, i. e. *increafing or perfect.*] The fon of the patriarch *Jacob* by *Rachel;* he was fold by the *Midianites* to *Potiphar,* and afterwards was prime minifter to *Pharaoh* king of *Egypt*— alfo the hufband of the virgin *Mary*—alfo *Jofeph* of *Arimathea* who buried our *Saviour*—alfo others.

JO'-SES or JO'-SEPH, ['Ιωσῆς, *fparing; exalted.*] The fon of *Mary* and *Cleophas;* brother of *James* the lefs, and a near relation to our *Saviour.*

JO'-SHA-BAD, ['Ιωζὰβαδ, i. e. *having a dowry.*] One of the chief of the *Levites.*

JO'-SHAH, ['Ιωσία, i. e. *being, forgetting, or owing.*] A prince of the tribe of *Simeon,* the fon of *Amaziah.*

JO'-SHA-PHAT, ['Ιωσαφὰτ, i. e. *the judgment of the Lord.*] One of king *David's* valiant men, and his recorder.

M 3

JO-SHA-

JO-SHA-VI′-AH, [Ωσωΐα, i. e. *the seat, alteration or captivity of the Lord.*] One of king *David*'s valiant men.

JOSH-BEK′-A-SHA, ['Ιεσϐασαχὰ, i. e. *it is requiring, beseeching, or an hard sitting.*] One of the singers of the temple of *Jerusalem.*

JOSH′-U-A, ['Ιησȣ̃ς, i. e. *a Saviour.*] The son of *Nun*, of the tribe of *Ephraim*, the commander of the *Israelites* after the death of *Moses*; supposed to be the author of the canonical book of *Joshua*: he died A. M. 2570, Æt. 110—also others of that name.

JO-SI′-AH or JO-SI′-AS, ['Ιωσίας. L. *Jo′-si-as*, i. e *the fire or burning of the Lord.*] The son of *Amon* king of *Judah* by *Jedidah*: he began his reign at eight years of age, A. M. 3364, and died A. M. 3395, or 640 years B. C.

JO-SI-BI′-AH, ['Ιωσαϐία, i. e. *the seat or captivity of the Lord.*] A prince of the tribe of *Simeon.*

JO-SIPH-I′-AH. ['Ιωσεφία, i. e. *the increase of the Lord, or the Lord's finishing.*] One who returned from the babylonish captivity.

JO-SI′-PHUS, ['Ιώσηφος.] One who returned from the babylonish captivity.

I-O′-TA. A letter of the *greek* alphabet; signifying smallness or the least part of a thing.

JOT′-BAH, ['Ιεϑϐα.] A city of *Judah.*

JOT′-BATH or JOT′-BATH-A, ['Ετεϐαθά, i. e. *his goodness, or a desert turning away.*] The *thirtieth* encampment of the *Israelites*, in the wilderness.

JO′-THAM, ['Ιωάθαμ, i. e. *absolute, or perfect.*] The youngest son of *Gideon*—also the son and successor of *Uzziah* king of *Judah*; he died A. M. 3262—also others of that name.

JO′-ZAB-AD, ['Ιωζαϐὲδ, i. e. *endowed, or having a dowry.*] One who returned from the babylonish captivity.

JOZ′-ACH-AR, ['Ιεζιρχὰρ, i. e. *remembering, or of the male kind.*] One who slew king *Joash.*

JO′-ZAD-AK, ['Ιωσεδὲκ.] One who returned from the babylonish captivity.

I *before* P.

IPH-ED-EI'-AH, ['Ιεφαδία, i. e. *the redemption of the Lord.*] One of the defcendants from the patriarch *Benjamin.*

I *before* R.

IR, ['Ωρ, i. e. *a watchman, city, or an heap of vifion.*] One of the pofterity of the patriarch *Benjamin.*

I'-RA, ['Ιρὰ. 'Ιρὰς, i. e. *a watchman, making bare, pouring out.*] An *Ithrite,* one of king *David*'s worthies—alfo *Ira* the *Tekoite,* another of his worthies.

I'-RAD, [Γαϊδαδ, i. e. *a wild afs, a heap of government, or a dragon.*] A fon of *Enoch.*

I'-RAM, ['Ηρὰμ, i. e. *a city of them, the pouring out of them, or an high heap.*] A duke of *Edom,* defcended from *Efau.*

I'-RI, ['Ουρὶ, i. e. *fire, or light.*] A grandfon of the patriarch *Benjamin.*

I-RI'-JAH, [Σαρεία, i. e. *the fear, vifion, or throwing forth of the Lord.*] One who arrefted the prophet *Jeremiah,* and delivered him to king *Zedekiah,* who imprifoned him.

IR-NA'-HASH, ['Ηρναὰς. Ναὰς.] One of the pofterity of the patriarch *Judah;* or a country.

IR'-ON, ['Κερωὲ.] A city of *Paleftine,* in the tribe of *Naphtali.*

IR'-PE-ĒL, ['Ιερφανλ, i. e. *the health, medicine, or exalting of God.*] A city of *Paleftine,* in the tribe of *Benjamin.*

IR-SHE'-MISH, ['Σαμμὼς, i. e. *a city of the fon, or a city of bondage.*] A city of *Paleftine,* in the tribe of *Dan.*

I'-RU, [Ηρ. 'Ιρὰ, i. e. *a city of the fon, or a city of bondage.*] A fon of *Caleb* the fon of *Jephunneh.*

M 4   I *before*

I *before* S.

I'SA-AC, ['Ισαὰκ, i. e. *laughter.*] The son of *Abra-ham* and *Sarah*, and father of the patriarch *Jacob:* he died A. M. 2288, Æt. 180.

I-SA-I'-AH or E-SA-I'-AS, ['Hσαίας, i. e. *the health, or salvation of the Lord.*] The *first* of the four greater prophets, after whom the canonical book, *Isaiah*, was named: he was of royal extract: being the son of *Amos* king *Josiah*'s son, and brother to king *Amaziah:* he is called the *evangelical prophet.*

IS'-CAH, ['Ιεχά, i. e. *anointing, covering, shadowing.*] or *espying.*] A daughter of *Haran* father in law to *Nahor.*

IS-CAR'-I-ŌT, ['Ισκαριώτης, i. e. *an hireling, or a man of death.*] The name of that disciple who betrayed our *Saviour:* he was called *Iscariot*, probably as belonging to *Karioth* or *Cerioth*; that is, a man of *Kerioth.*

IS'-DA-ĒL, ['Ιοδαὴλ.] One whose family returned from the babylonish captivity—also one of the servants of *Solomon.*

ISH'-BAH, ['Ιεσβὰ.] One of the posterity of the patriarch *Judah.*

ISH'-BAK, [Ιεσβὼκ, i. e. *it is void, or made void, or forsaking.*] A son of the patriarch *Abraham* by *Keturah.*

ISH-BI BE'-NOB, ['Ιεσβὶ, i. e. *fitting, or taking captivity, in prophecy.*] One who was of the race of giants, and was killed by *Abishai* the son of *Zeruiah.*

ISH'-BOSH-ETH, ['Ιεβοϑὲ, i. e. *a man of shame, or the delay of a man.*] The son and successor of king *Saul*, and slain by *Rechab* and *Baanah.*

ISH'-I, ['Ιεσὶ. Σεὶ, i. e. *salvation, or having regard.*] The son of *Appaim*, of the tribe of *Judah*—also others.

ISH-I'-AH, ['Ισία. 'Ιεσία, i. e. *it is the Lord.*] The great grandson of the patriarch *Issachar*, and the son of *Uzzi.*

ISH-

ISH-I'-JAH, ['Ιεσία, i. e. *it is the Lord.*] One who returned from the babylonish captivity.

ISH'-MA, ['Ιεσμὰν, i. e. *named, put unto, a marvelling, or desolation.*] One of the posterity of the patriarch *Judah.*

ISH'-MA-EL, ['Ισμαήλ, i. e. *God hath heard, or the hearing of God.*] The son of *Abraham* and *Hagar*, who dwelt in *Paran*, and was father of a numerous posterity—also others.

ISH'-MA-EL-ITES, ['Ισμαηλῖται.] The descendants from *Ishmael* who dwelt in *Arabia.*

ISH-MA-I'-AH, ['Σαμαίας, i. e. *hearing, or obeying the Lord.*] The son of *Obadiah*, and chief of the tribe of *Zebulun* in king *David*'s time.

ISH'-ME-RAI, ['Ισαμαρὶ, i. e. *keeper, or keeping.*] One of the descendants from the patriarch *Benjamin.*

ISH'-OD, ['Ισὼδ, i. e. *a comely man.*] One of the posterity of the patriarch *Manasseh.*

ISH'-PAN, ['Ιεσφὰν, i. e. *hid, or broken asunder.*] One of the posterity of the patriarch *Benjamin.*

ISH'-TOB, ['Ιςὼβ, i. e. *good man.*] A place in *Syria.*

ISH-U'-A, ISH-U'-AI, or IS-U'-I, ['Ιεσσιὺ. Συιὰ. Γεσσιὺ, i. e. *plainness, equal, or putting.*] A son of the patriarch *Asher*, of whom came the *Isuites.*

IS-MA-CHI'-AH, [Σαμαχία, i. e. *cleaving to, leaning upon, or joined to the Lord.*] A priest or *Levite* in the time of king *Hezekiah.*

IS-MA-I'-AH, [Σαμαῖος.] One who went to king *David* at *Ziklag.*

IS'-PAH, ['Ιεσφὰ, i. e. *a jasper stone.*] One of the posterity of the patriarch *Benjamin.*

IS'-RA-EL, ['Ισραήλ, i. e. *a prince of God, or prevailing, or wrestling with God.*] The name given to the patriarch *Jacob* by the angel who wrestled with him. *Israel* sometimes means *Jacob*; sometimes his progeny; and sometimes the kingdom of *Israel* as distinct from the tribe of *Judah.*

IS'-RA-ĒL-ITES, ['Ισραηλῖται.]   The defcendants
  from *Jacob* or *Ifrael*.

IS'-SA-CHAR, ['Ισσάχαρ, i. e. *wages, or reward.*]
  The *fifth* fon of the patriarch *Jacob* by *Leah*.

IST-AL-CU'-RUS, ['Ισαλκήρ☉.] One whofe family
  returned from the babylonifh captivity.

IS-U'-I, ['Ιεϐλ.]   See *Ifhuah*.

IS-U'-ITES.   Defcendants from *Ifui*.   See *Ifhuah*.

I *before* T.

IT'-A-I or ITH'-A-I, ['Εθι. Ιθαι, i. e. *ftrong, my fign,
  a ploughfhare, or a coming to.*]   A *Benjamite*, the
  fon of *Riba*, and a moft faithful fervant to king
  David.

IT'-AL-Y, ['Ιταλία, i. e. *with calves.*]   A large
  country of *Europe*, of which *Rome* is the metropolis.

ITH'-A-MAR, ['Ιθάμαρ, i. e. *woe to the change or to
  the hand, or the ifle of the hand or finger, or the change
  of an ifle.*]   He was the fourth fon of *Aaron* the
  high prieft.

ITH'-I-ĒL, ['Εθιηλ. 'Αιθιηλ, i. e. *God with me, or the
  figh of God, the coming to of God, or the ploughfhare
  of God.*]   The fon of *Jefaiah*, of the tribe of
  Benjamin—alfo a fon of *Hachmoni*, and tutor to
  king *David*'s fons.

ITH'-MAH, ['Ιεθαμὰ, i. e. *an orphan, or marvelling.*]
  One of king *David*'s valiant men.

ITH'-NAN, [Μαινὰμ.]   A city of *Palefine* in the tribe
  of *Judah*.

ITH'-RA.   See *Jether*.

ITH'-RAN, ['Ιθρὰν, i. e. *excelling, remaining, fearching out diligently, or a fmall rope.*]   One of the defcendants from the patriarch *Afher* and alfo from
  Efau.

ITH'-RE-AM, ['Ιεθεραὰμ, i. e. *the excellency or remnant of the people.*]   The fon of king *David* by
  Eglah.

ITH'-RITES, ['Εθεραῖοι, i. e. *excelling; a remaining.*]
  The family of *Ithra*.

IT'-TAH

IT'-TAH KA'-ZIN, [Κατασὲμ, i. e. *an hour or time of a prince.*] A city of *Palestine* in the tribe of *Zebulun*, on its borders.

IT'-TAI, [ΕϿ.] See *Itai.*

IT-U-RE'-A, ['Ιτυραία, i. e. *kept, or of a mountain, or full of hills.*] A province of *Syria* beyond the river *Jordan*, near to the desart of *Arabia*, whereof *Philip* was tetrarch.

I *before* V *and* U.

I'-VAH, ['Aἡα. 'Aνὰ, i. e. *iniquity.*] A country conquered by the *Assyrians*, with a city of the same name.

JU'-BAL, ['Ιηϐὴλ, i. e. *bringing, or fading, or a trumpet.*] A son of the patriarch *Lamech*; the inventor of musical instruments.

JU'-BI-LEE, [i. e. *bringing, or fading, or a trumpet.*] The year of *Jubilee* was every *fiftieth* year among the *Jews*, which fell out after seven weeks of years: in this *fiftieth* year none sowed or reaped; all estates reverted to their *first* owners, and all *hebrew* slaves were set free.

JU'-CAL, ['Ιωάχαλ, i. e. *mighty or perfect.*] The son of *Shelemiah*, mentioned in *Jeremiah's* prophecy.

JU'-DA, ['Ιηδα, i. e. *confession or praise.*] The name of two persons in St. *Luke's* genealogy; one the son of *Joanna*, the other the son of *Joseph.*

JU'-DAH, ['Ιηδας, i. e. *confession or praise.*] The fourth son of the patriarch *Jacob* by *Leah*; from him the tribe of *Judah* was named.

JU'-DAS, ['Ιηδας, i. e. *confession; praise.*] A *Levite* who returned from the babylonish captivity.

JU'-DAS IS-CAR'-I-OT, ['Ιηδας 'Ιηκαριώτης.] See *Iscariot.*

JU'-DAS MAC-CA-BÆ'-US. The son of *Mattathias* the priest; a famous jewish warrior.

JUDE or JU'-DAS, ['Ιηδας, i. e. *confessing or praising.*] He was surnamed *Thaddeus* or *Lebbeus*, and the *Zealot* or *Zelotes:* he was brother to *James* the
less,

lefs, who was fuppofed to be fon to the virgin *Mary*'s fifter *Mary*—alfo the name of a canonical book of the *New Teftament*.

JU-DÆ'-A, ['Ιυδαία, *i. e. confeffing or praifing.*] A province of *Afia*, called, antiently, *Canaan*; *Paleftine*; the *land of promife*; the *land of Ifrael*; and laftly, the *land of Judæa*.

JUDG'-ES, ['Κριται.] The *feventh* canonical book of the *Old Teftament*, fuppofed to have been written by *Samuel* the prophet and judge; it contains the fpace of about 299 years from the death of *Jofhua* to the government and high priefthood of *Eli* the *fixteenth* judge of *Ifrael*.

JU'-DITH, ['Ιυδιθ, *i. e. confeffing or praifing.*] She was of the tribe of *Reuben*, and daughter of *Merari*, and widow of *Manaffeh*—alfo the name of one of the books of the *Apocrypha*—alfo the wife of *Efau*.

JU-EL, ['Ιυηλ. Γευηλ.] One who returned from the babylonifh captivity.

JU'-LI-A, ['Ιυλία, *i. e. full of foft cotton, or downy.*] One whom the apoftle *Paul* falutes in his epiftle to the *Romans*.

JU'-LI-US, ['Ιυλιۥ, *i. e. downy, or foft.*] The centurion into whofe hands St. *Paul* was committed, to be conveyed to *Rome*.

JU'-NI-A, ['Ιυνία, *i. e. of Juno.*] A woman whom St. *Paul* falutes in his epiftle to the *Romans*; his kinfwoman.

JU'-PI-TER, [*i. e. the father that helpeth.*] The fupreme god of the antient pagans.

JU-SHAB'-HE-SED, ['Ιωσαβεσεδ, *i. e. a dwelling place, the feat, or changing of mercy.*] One of the pofterity of king *David*, a fon of *Zerubbabel*.

JUS'-TUS, ['Ιουστۥ, *i. e. juft, or virtuous.*] One appointed by the apoftles to be chofen in the room of *Judas*; but the lot fell upon *Matthias*.

JUT'-

JUT'-TAH, ['Ιτὰν, i. e. *turning away.*] A city of *Paleſtine*, in the tribe of *Judah*, in the mountains.

I *before* Z.

IZ'-HAR or IZ'-E-HAR, ['Ισσαὰρ, i. e. *clearneſs, oil, or pertaining to none.*] The ſon of *Kohath*, and father of the *Izharites.*

IZ'-HAR-ITES, [i. e. *the ſame as Izhar.*] The deſcendants from *Izhar.*

IZ'-RA-HITE. *Shammuth* is called ſo.

IZ-RA-I'-AH or IS-RA-I'-AH, ['Ιεζαραΐα, i. e. *the Lord ariſeth or the clearneſs of the Lord.*] A grandſon of the patriarch *Iſſachar.*

IZ'-RE-ĒL, ['Ιαζηλ.] See JEZREEL.

IZ'-RI, ['Ιεσρὶ, i. e. *faſting, tribulation, or making narrow.*] One of the ſingers of the temple of *Jeruſalem.*

IZ'-RITES, [i. e. *faſting; tribulation; ſorrowful.*] Deſcendants from *Jezer.*

K.

K *before* A.

KAB. See *Cab* and the *table of meaſures* at the end.

KAB'-ZE-ĒL, [Καβεσεὴλ, i. e. *the congregation of God.*] A city of *Paleſtine* in the tribe of *Judah.*

KA'-DĒS, [Καδης.] See *Cades.*

KA'-DĒSH or CA'-DĒSH, [Καδης, i. e. *holineſs.*] The ſame city with *En-Miſhpat*—alſo the *thirty-third*

third encampment of the *Israelites*; in the wildernefs.

KA'-DĒSH BAR-NE'-A, [Καδης Βαρνη, i. e. *holinefs
of an inconftant fon or of corn or of troubled clamour.*]
A city of *Paleftine* in the tribe of *Judah*, to the
fouth of *Hebron*.

KAD'-MI-ĒL, [Καδμιηλ, i. e. *God of antientnefs, or
God of rifing.*] A *Levite* who returned from the
babylonifh captivity with his family.

KAD-MO'-NITES, [Κεδμωναιοι, i. e. *antients or chief.*]
Antient inhabitants of the land of *Canaan*.

KAL'-LA-I, [Καλλαι, i. e. *light, refting by fire, or my
voice.*] A prieft who returned from the babylonifh captivity.

KA'-NAH, [Χελχανα, i. e. *of reeds.*] The name of
a river; one of the borders of the tribe of *Afher*,
and *Ephraim*.

KA-RE'-AH, [Καρηθ. Κασηε.] See *Careah*.

KAR'-KA-A, [Καρκε, i. e. *a floor, or diffolving coldnefs.*]
A city of *Paleftine*, on the borders of the tribe of
Judah.

KAR'-KOR, [Καρκαρ.] A place mentioned in the
book of *Judges*.

KAR'-NA-IM, [Καρναιν.] See *Carnaim*.

KAR'-TAH, [Καδης, i. e. *calling, or a meeting.*] A
city of *Paleftine* in the tribe of *Zebulun*, given to
the *Levites*.

KAR'-TAN, [Καρθαν, i. e. *a calling, or meeting, or
reading.*] A city of the *Levites* in *Paleftine*, in the
half tribe of *Manaffeh*.

KAT'-TAH, [Καταναθ.] A city of *Paleftine*, in the
tribe of *Zebulun*.

K *before* E.

KE'-DAR, [Κηδαρ, i. e. *blacknefs, or fadnefs.*] The
fon of *Ifhmael*, and father of the *Kedarinians*.

KED'-E-MAH, [Κεδμα, i. e. *antient, or the firft.*]
The youngeft fon of *Ifhmael*.

KED'-E-MŌTH [Κεδαμωθ, i. e. *the chief, or a burning, or the crookednefs of death.*] A town of *Paleftine*, in the tribe of *Reuben*.

KE'-DĒSH

KE′-DĒSH or **KE′-DĒSH NAPH′-TALI,** [Καδης Νεφθαλειμ, i. e. *holiness.*] A city of *Palestine,* in the tribe of *Naphtali,* given to the *Levites,* as a *city of refuge,* on the *west* side of the river *Jordan.*

KE-HEL′-ATH-AH, [Μακελλαθ, i. e. *an whole, or a congregation, or a church.*] The *eighteenth* encampment of the *Israelites* in the wilderness.

KEI′-LAH, [Κειλα, i. e. *dissolving, dividing, or his fastening.*] A town of *Palestine,* in the tribe of *Judah,* in the valley — also one of *Judah's* posterity.

KE-LAI′-AH, [Κωλια. Κωλαα, i. e. *the voice of the Lord, or resting of the Lord, or succour, or gathering together.*] A *Levite* who returned from the babylonish captivity, and sealed the covenant with *Nehemiah.*

KE′-LI-TA, [Κωλιτας.] See *Kelaiah.*

KEM-U′-ĒL, [Καμυηλ, i. e. *God hath raised up, or established him.*] The *third* son of *Nahor* the brother of *Abraham* by his wife *Milcah*—also others of that name.

KE′-NAH, [Καναθ, i. e. *a buying, possession, or bewailing.*] A city which was taken by *Nobah,* in the land of *Gilead,* in the tribe of *Manasseh.*

KE′-NAN, [Καιναν, i. e. *a buyer or owner.*] The name of one of the patriarchs before the flood.

KE′-NATH, [Καναθ.] See *Kenah.*

KEN′-AZ, [Κενεζ, i. e. *this bird's nest, or this bewailing possession, or buying.*] The son of *Eliphaz,* and grandson of *Esau.*

KEN′-ITES, [Κεναιοι, i. e. *possession, a bird's nest, or bewailing.*] A people descended from *Keni,* who dwelt westward of the *dead sea* in *Arabia Petræa.*

KEN′-IZ-ZITES, [Κενεζαιοι, i. e. *a possession, or buying.*] An antient people of *Canaan,* whose land GOD promised to *Abraham.*

KER-EN-HAP′-PŪCH, [Καρναφυχ, i. e. *the horn, or child of beauty.*] The *third* of *Job's* daughters after his misfortunes.

KER′-

I

KER'-I-ŌTH, [Καριω'θ, i. e. *cities, callings, or meetings.*] A city of *Paleſtine*, one of the boundaries of the tribe of *Judah*.

KE'-ROS, [Χειραός, i. e. *crooked, or crookedneſs.*] One who returned from the babyloniſh captivity.

KET-U'-RAH, [Χετ'ϑρα, i. e. *ſmelling ſweet, perfuming, or contended for.*] The *ſecond* wife of the patriarch *Abraham*, by whom he had ſix ſons.

KEZ-I'-A, [Κασίαν. Κεσίαν, i. e. *as pleaſant as caſſia, or fine ſpices.*] The *ſecond* daughter of *Job* after his misfortunes.

KEZ'-IZ, ['Αμεκασίς, i. e. *a valley.*] A city of *Paleſtine*, in the tribe of *Benjamin*.

K *before* I.

KIB'-ROTH HAT-TA'-A-VAH, [i. e. *the graves of luſt.*] The *thirteenth* encampment of the *Iſraelites*.

KIB'-ZA-IM, [Καβσεὶμ, i. e. *congregation.*] A city of *Paleſtine*, in the tribe of *Ephraim*, given to the *Levites*.

KID'-RŌN, [Κέδρων, i. e. *making black, or ſad.*] A brook in the valley of *Jehoſaphat*, on the eaſt ſide of *Jeruſalem*, between the city and the mount of *Olives*, or mount *Olivet*.

KI'-NAH, ['Ικὰμ, i. e. *poſſeſſion, buying, a bird's neſt, or bewailing.*] A city of *Paleſtine*, in the tribe of *Judah*.

KINGS, [Βασιλεῖς.] *Two* canonical books of the *Old Teſtament* ſo called; ſuppoſed to be compiled by *Ezra:* they contain a hiſtory of the *hebrew* ſtate from king *David* to the time of the babyloniſh captivity, including about 417 years.

KIR, [Κυρήνη, i. e. *a wall, black, coldneſs, or a meeting.*] A place of *Media* in *Aſia*.

KIR-HA'-RA-SETH, [i. e. *a wall of workmanſhip.*] A royal city of the *Moabites*.

KIR-HE'-RESH, [Κειρἁδας, i. e. *a wall of workmanſhip.*] The ſame with *Rabbath-Moab*, otherwiſe called *Aer*, the capital of *Moab*.

KIR'-

KIR'-I-ATH, or KIR'-JATH, ['Ιαρὶμ, i. e. *cities, callings, or meetings.*] A city of *Paleſtine* in the tribe of *Benjamin*.

KIR'-JATH AR'-BA, [Καριαϑὰρϭὸμ, i. e. *the fourth city.*] A place built by *Arba*, being the ſame as *Hebron*, in the land of *Canaan*.

KIR'-JATH A'-IM, [Καριαϑαὶμ, i. e. *the two cities, the callings, the meetings.*] A city to the eaſt of the river *Jordan*, in the tribe of *Naphtali*.

KIR-I-ATH-A'-IM. See *Kirjathaim*.

KIR'-JATH A'-RIM, [Καριαϑὰμ, i. e. *city of cities, or the city of thoſe who watch.*] A city of *Paleſtine* in the tribe of *Benjamin*.

KIR-I-ATH-A'-RI-US, [Καριαϑαρίος.] The name of a place in the land of *Paleſtine*.

KIR'-JATH BA'-AL, [Καριαθ Βαὰλ, i. e. *a city of an idol, of a ruler, or poſſeſſor.*] A city of *Paleſtine* in the tribe of *Judah* in the mountains: the ſame as *Kirjath Jearim*.

KIR'-JATH HUZ'-OTH, [i. e. *à city of ſtreets, or populous.*] A place in the land of *Moab*.

KIR'-JATH JE'-A-RIM, [Πόλις 'Ιαρὶμ, i. e. *a city of woods.*] A city of *Paleſtine* in the tribe of *Ju-dah*, founded by *Shobal* one of *Judah*'s poſterity. See *Baalah*.

KIR'-JATH SAN'-NAH, [Δαϭὶϱ, i. e. *a city of a blackberry tree, or a city of enmity.*] A city of *Pa-leſtine* in the tribe of *Judah*, in the mountains: called alſo *Debir*.

KIR'-JATH SEPH'-ER, [Καριαθσεφὲϱ, i. e. *a city of letters.*] The antient name of the city *Debir*: in the tribe of *Naphtali*.

KIR'-I-ŌTH, [Καριωθ.] A city of the *Moabites*.

KISH, [Κὶs, i. e. *hard, ſore, or ſtraw to thatch.*] The ſon of *Ner*, a *Benjamite*, and father of king *Saul*.

KISH'-I, [Κιϭὰ, i. e. *hardneſs, his gravity, or his of-fence.*] The ſon of *Abdi*, and father of *Ethan*.

KISH'-I-ŌN, [Κιϭὼν, i. e. *hardneſs or ſoreneſs.*] A place of *Paleſtine* in the tribe of *Iſſachar*, yielded to the *Levites* of *Gerſhom*'s family.

N

KI'-SHŌN

KI'-SHŌN or KI'-SŌN, [Κισὼν, i. e. *hard, sore.*] A brook whofe fource is in the valley of *Jezreel* in *Paleſtine*—alfo a city in the half tribe of *Manaſſeh*, given to the *Levites*.

KITE. A fpecies of the *Falcon*, with a forked tail, a brown body, and a whitifh head; and about the fize of a large tame pigeon.

KITH'-LISH, [Καθαλίς, i. e. *it is a wall, or the company of a lionefs.*] A city of *Paleſtine*, in the tribe of *Judah*.

KIT'-RŌN, [Κἑδρων, i. e. *making fweet, or a binding together.*] A city of the *Canaanites*.

KIT'-TIM, [Χετίιμ, i. e. *breaking fmall, or gold.*] The fon of *Javan* and grandfon of *Noah*.

K *before* N.

KNOPS. Ornaments of a round figure, like to apples or pomegranates.

K *before* O.

KO'-A, [Ύχὴὲ, i. e. *hope, a congregation, a line, or a rule.*] Suppofed to be a title or degree of honor among the *Babylonians*.

KO'-HATH, [Κἀθ, i. e. *a congregation, wrinkle, or bluntnefs.*] The *fecond* fon of the patriarch *Levi*, died A. M. 2422, Æt. 133.

KO'-HATH-ITES. The pofterity of *Kohath*.

KO-LA-I'-AH, [Χωλεία, i. e. *the voice of the Lord.*] One who returned from the babylonifh captivity.

KOR'-AH, [Κορἑ, i. e. *baldnefs, ice, or froſt.*] The fon of *Izhar* and grandfon of *Levi*, who was fwallowed alive by the earth, for his rebellion againſt *Mofes* and *Aaron*—alfo others of that name.

KOR'-AH-ITES, [Κορῖται.] The family of *Korah*.

KOR'-ATH-ITES or KOR'-HITES. The pofterity of *Korah*.

KOR'-E, [Κορἑ.] A grandfon of *Korah*.

KOZ,

KOZ, ['Ακκὸς.] One who returned from the babylonifh captivity.

K before U.

KUSH-AÏ'-AH, [Κισαϊ©.] See KISHI.

L.

L before A.

LA'-A-DAH, [Λααδὰ, i. e. *to affemble together, to
teftify, paffing over, or robbing.*] One of the tribe
of *Judah*; the fon of *Shelah*—alfo a defcendant
from the patriarch *Ephraim.*

LA'-A-DAN, [Λεαδὰν, i. e. *for pleafure, devouring,
judgment, for a witnefs.*] A fon of *Gerfhom*—alfo
others.

LA'-BAN, [Λάβαν, i. e. *white, fhining, gentle, or brittle.*] The fon of *Bethuel*, grandfon of *Nahor*,
brother to *Rebecca* and father of *Rachel* and *Leah*
—alfo a wildernefs where *Mofes* publifhed the
Law.

LA'-BA-NA, [Λαβανὰ, i. e. *the moon; whitenefs;
frankincenfe.*] One who returned from the babylonifh captivity, and whofe fons were fervants
of the temple.

LA-CED-Æ'-MŌN or SPAR'-TA, [Λακεδαιμων.
Σπάρτα, i. e. *a lake of devils, or a well of mad men.*]
A famous city of *Peloponnefus* in *Greece*: now
Mifitra in european *Turkey.*

                    LA-CED-

LA-CED-E-MON'I-ANS, [Σπαρίιαταὶ. Λακεδαιμό-
νιοι.] The people of *Lacedæmon*.

LA'-CHISH, [Λαχὶς, i. e. *walking, or being to thyself.*]
A city of *Palestine* to the south of the tribe of
Judah; in the tribe of *Dan*—also a city of *Judah*
in the valley.

LAC-U'-NUS, [Λακκῦνℰ.] One who returned from
the babylonish captivity.

LA'-DAN, [Λαδὰν, i. e. *the same as Laadan.*] One
who returned from the babylonish captivity.

LA'-ĒL, [Λαὴλ, i. e. *to God, or to the mighty.*] One
of the family of the *Levites*.

LA'-HAD, [Λααδ, i. e. *praising, or to confess.*] One
of the posterity of the patriarch *Judah*.

LA-HAI'-ROI. A well, near to which the patriarch
Isaac dwelt.

LAH'-MAN or LAH'-MAS, [Λαμμάς, i. e. *the bread
of them, or the fight or war of them.*] A city of
Palestine, in the tribe of *Judah*, in the valley.

LAH'-MI, [Λαομί. Λαχμὶ, i. e. *my bread, or my fight.*]
The brother of *Goliah* the giant.

LA'-ISH, [Λαΐσα. Λαῒς, i. e. *a lion.*] A city of *Palestine*, near to the river *Jordan*; afterwards *Le-
shem*, in the tribe of *Reuben*—also the father of
Phaltiel.

LA'-KŪM, [Λακκύμ.] A city of *Palestine*, in the
tribe of *Naphtali*.

LA'-MECH, [Λάμεχ, i. e. *poor, humbled or smitten.*]
The son of *Methuselah* and father of *Noah*, he died
A. M. 1651, Æt. 777.

LA-MENT-A'-TI-ONS, [Θρῆνοι.] A canonical book
of the *Old Testament*, being a mournful poem of
the prophet *Jeremiah*, on the destruction of *Jerusalem* by *Nebuchadnezzar*.

LA-OD-I-CE'-A, [Λαοδιχεία, i. e. *just people.*] A
city of *Phrygia* in *Asia*, near to *Colosse*: formerly
Diospolis.

LA-OD-I-CE'-ANS. The inhabitants of *Laodicea*.

LAP-ID'-ŌTH, [Λαφιδὼθ, i. e. *lightnings, or lamps.*]
The husband of *Deborah* the prophetess.

LAP'-

LAP'-WING. A bird about the fize of a common
   pigeon, with a piercing eye, a fmall beautiful
   head, elegantly variegated and ornamented with
   a beautiful creft hanging over the hinder part of
   the neck—it is a bird almoft continually on the
   wing, and feeds upon infects.

LA-SE'-A, [Λασαία, i. e. *thick, or wife.*] A city near
   to the *fair havens,* on the ifle of *Crete.*

LA'-SHAH, [Λασά, i. e. *to call, or to anoint.*] A
   city not far from *Sodom.*

LA-SHA'-RON, [Ἀσώμ.] A city of *Canaan,* on the
   weft fide of *Jordan.*

LAS'-THEN-ĒS, [Λασθένει, i. e. *the ftrength of a ftone.*]
   The name of a prince of the ifle of *Crete.*

LAZ'-A-RUS, [Λάζαρ☉, i. e. *the help of God.*] The
   brother of *Martha* and *Mary,* whom our *Saviour*
   raifed from the dead—alfo another mentioned
   with *Dives,* in a parable of our *Saviour.*

L before E.

LE'-AH, [Λεία, i. e. *painful, or wearied.*] The wife
   of the patriarch *Jacob* and eldeft daughter of
   Laban.

LEB'-A-NAH, [Λαβανὶς, i. e. *the moon, whitenefs,
   frankincenfe, brittle.*] One whofe children were
   of the order of *Nethinims.*

LEB'-A-NON, [Λιβάν☉, i. e. *the fame as Lebanah.*]
   A place of *Syria,* fo called from the great ftore
   of frankincenfe there.

LEB'-A-ŌTH, [Λαβώς, i. e. *a lionefs, or fign of the
   heart.*] A town of *Paleftine,* in the tribe of
   Judah.

LEB-BE'-US, [Λεββαῖος, i. e. *praifing, or confeffing.*]
   One of the twelve difciples of our *Saviour,* fur-
   named *Thaddeus:* St. *Luke* calls him *Judas* or
   Jude.

LEB-O'-NAH, [Λεβωνᾶ, i. e. *the moon, frankincenfe,
   brittle.*] A place mentioned in the book of
   Judges, fuppofed by fome to be fix miles from
   Bethel.

LE'-CHAH, [Ληχὰ̀. Λάιχά, i. e. *walking, or going.*]
One of the defcendants from the patriarch *Judah.*

LE'-GI-ŌN, [Λεγεὼν.] In the roman army, was a
body, of foot confifting of *ten* cohorts or *fix thoufand* men.

LE'-HA-BIM, [Λαβιειμ, i. e. *enflamed, or fwords.*]
The *third* fon of *Mizraim* and grandfon to *Ham*;
Mizraim is fuppofed to have peopled *Lybia* in
Africa.

LE'-HI, [Λεχί, i. e. *the jaw.*] A place of the
Philiftines, where *Samfon* flew a thoufand of them
with the jaw bone of an afs: in the tribe of
Dan.

LEM'-U-ĒL, [i. e. *God to them*; *God with them.*]
Suppofed to be king *Solomon.*

LEP'-RO-SY, [Λέπρα.] A filthy and infectious dif-
eafe, particularly defcribed in the book of *Leviticus*;
but. is not that which is *now* called the leprofy—
it infected walls and wood of houfes, and garments, and is fuppofed to have procceded from
infects.

LE'-SHEM, [Λαχὶς, i. e. *a name, putting, a precious
ftone.*] Formerly *Laifh,* before it was taken by
the *Danites.*

LET'-TUS, [Λατ]ὺς.] One who returned from the
babylonifh captivity.

LET-U'-SHIM, [Λατουσιειμ, i. e. *hammermen, or file
men.*] The *fecond* fon of *Dedan* the grandfon of
Abraham and *Keturah.*

LE'-VI, [Λευὶ, i. e. *joined, coupled, or added to him.*]
The *third* fon of the patriarch *Jacob,* by *Leah*;
he died A. M. 2392, Æt. 137—alfo a publican
mentioned in the 5th chap. of *Luke.*

LE-VI'-A-THAN, [Λευιάθαν, i. e. *a coupling together; his fellowfhip.*] The *Leviathan* is generally
fuppofed to be intended for the *whale*; and is
really meant fo in the 104th *Pfalm :* but in the
74th *Pfalm,* and in the 27th chapter of the prophet *Ifaiah,* it means the *crocodile,* as emblematical
of the *Ægyptians* whofe river *Nile* abounded with
crocodiles

crocodiles—but more efpecially in the book of *Job*, the *crocodile* feems to be intended; as the defcription of the *leviathan*, there, anfwers to the character of the *crocodile*, but by no means is defcriptive of the *whale*.

The river *Nile* in *Egypt* is remarkable for *crocodiles*. It is an amphibious animal; it hath four legs; its upper parts are covered with impenetrable fcales, like to a coat of mail—it is generally about *eighteen feet* long, and fome are much longer—it is an oviparous animal; but its multiplication is leffened by the *ichneumon*, an animal of the *rat* kind, who devours its eggs.

LE'-VIS, [Λɛυὶς.] One who returned from the babylonifh captivity.

LE'-VITES, [Λɛυῖται.] Defcendants from *Levi* and chofen for the fervice of the temple.

LE-VIT'-I-CUS, [Λɛυῖτικ⊙.] The *third* book of the *Pentateuch* of *Mofes*, which treats chiefly of the regulation of the priefts, Levites and facrifices.

LE-ŪM'-MIM, [Λαωμɛὶμ, i. e. *countries, or without waters.*] A great grandfon of the patriarch *Abraham*.

L before I.

LIB'-A-NUS, [Λιϐάν⊙, i. e. *whitenefs, frankincenfe, moon, brittle.*] A celebrated mountain which feparates *Syria* from *Paleftine:* noted for its cedar trees: *Solomon's* palace was called the houfe of the foreft of *Lebanon.*

LIB'-NAH, [Λɛϐνὰ. Λɛϐωνᾶ, i. e. *the fame with Lebanon.*] A city in the fouthern part of the tribe of *Judah*, in *Paleftine*, appointed one of the cities of refuge—alfo the *feventeenth* encampment of the *Ifraelites.*

LIB'-NI, [Λοϐɛνὶ, i. e. *the fame with Lebanon.*] A fon of *Gerfhom* and grandfon to the patriarch *Levi.*

LIB'-NITES. The defcendants from *Libni.*

LIB'-Y-A, [Λιϐύη, i. e. *grofs*, *or fat.*] A province of *Egypt* in *Africa*, fuppofed to have been peopled by *Lehabim* the fon of *Mizraim.*

LIB'-Y-ANS, [Λιϐυες.] The people of *Lybia.*

LIGN'-ALOES, [Pronounced *Line-Aloes.*] A tree growing in feveral parts of *Afia*, called *Lignum-Aloes* or *Xylo-Aloes:* the wood of it is fweet-fcented.

LI'-GURE, [Λιγύριον.] The *firft* precious ftone in the *third* row of the jewifh high prieft's breaftplate; and on it was engraven the name of GOD: it was of a bright fparkling colour refembling a *carbuncle.*

LIK'-HI, [Λακίμ.] One of the pofterity of the patriarch *Manaffeh.*

LI'-NUS, [Λῖνⓢ, i. e. *a net.*] One mentioned by St. *Paul* in his *fecond* epiftle to *Timothy*; and faid, by fome of the fathers, to have fucceeded St. *Peter* in the fee of *Rome.*

L *before* O.

LO-AM'-MI, [Ὀυ λαός μη, i. e. *not my people.*] The metaphorical fon of the prophet *Hofea.*

LO'-CUST, [Ἀκρίδα.] The *locuft* is a large winged infect, in fhape like to a grafshopper; very common in *Europe, Afia,* and *Africa—Thevenot,* the traveller, fays, that they live about fix months, and lay about 300 eggs in autumn, which are hatched in the following fpring—it is faid, that in *Arabia*, the whole air hath been darkened by their flight for 18 or 20 miles—they devour the fruits of the earth in a very rapid manner, fo as to occafion a famine. In *Afia* and *Africa* it is common for people to eat them, and to preferve them in falt and pickle, and in feveral other ways—the common way of dreffing them, was by plucking off their legs and wings, and then putting them over a blaze, in a pan full of holes; or elfe, to knock them down and lay them in heaps, and then kindle a fire

about

about them—it is fuppofed that *John the Baptiſt* made this fort of locuſts a part of his food in the wildernefs.

LŌD, [Λὼδ, i. e. *nativity, or generation.*] A city of *Paleſtine*, in the tribe of *Benjamin*.

LOD'-E-BAR, [Λοδαϐὰϱ.] A city of the land of *Paleſtine*.

LOG. An *hebrew* meafure, containing about *five ſixths* of a pint engliſh. wine meafure.

LO'-IS, [Λωὶς, i. e. *better.*] The grandmother of *Timothy*, or whom St. *Paul* fpeaks with commendation as a Chriſtian.

LO RU-HA'-MAH, [i. e. *that hath not obtained mercy.*] The metaphorical daughter of the prophet *Hoſea*.

LŌT, [Λὼτ, i. e. *wrapped, joined, covered, or bound together.*] The ſon of *Haran*, and nephew to *Abraham*.

LO'-TAN, [Λωτὰν, i. e. *the ſame meaning as Lot.*] A duke of the *Horites*, a defcendant from *Efau*, and ſon of *Seir*.

LO-THA-SU'-BUS, [Λωθασυϐ☉.] One whofe family returned from the babyloniſh captivity.

LOZ'-ŌN, [Λοζὼν.] One who was a fervant to *Solomon*.

L before U.

LUB'-IM, [Λίϐυη, i. e. *the heart of a man, or the heart of the ſea.*] The name of *Lybia* in *Africa*; fuppofed to have been peopled by *Lehabim*.

LUB'-IMS, [Λίϐυεs.] The people of *Lybia*.

LU'-CAS, [Λυκᾶs, i. e. *a riſing to him, or luminous.*] A fellow labourer with St. *Paul*.

LU'-CI-FER, ['Εωσφόρ☉, i. e. *bringing light.*] He is fometimes taken for the *morning ſtar:* fometimes for *Jeſus Chriſt*, as the light of the world; and fometimes for the *Devil*.

LU'-CI-US, (*of Cyrene*) [Λυκίos, i. e. *of light.*] Suppofed to be one of the prophets of the chriſtian church, or one of the feventy difciples and archbiſhop of *Cyrene*—alfo a roman Conful.

LŪD,

LŪD, [Λὸδ, i. e. *nativity or generation.*] The *fourth* son of *Shem* the patriarch; suppofed to have peopled *Lydia* in *Afia: Lydia* is alfo called *Lud.*

LUD'-IM, [Λυδιείμ, i. e. *the fame meaning as Lud.*] The fon of *Mizraim* and grandfon to *Ham* the patriarch.

LU'-HITH, [Λυΰϑ, i. e. *a floor made of boards, or greenneſs.*] A place or canton in the land of *Moab.*

LUKE, [Λυκᾶς, i. e. *a rifing to him.*] A phyfician, a *Syrian,* and a native of *Antioch,* who wrote the *third* canonical book of the *New Teſtament* bearing his name; and alfo the other canonical book of the *Acts of the Apoſtles.*

LŪZ, [Λυζὰ, i. e. *an almond, a departing, or a bending.*] The antient name of *Bethel.*

L before Y.

LYB'-I-A, [Λιϐυη.] See LIBYA.

LYB'-I-ANS. See LIBYANS.

LY-CA-ON'-I-A, [Λυκαὸνία, i. e. *a wolf.*] A province of *Afia Minor* where *Paul* and *Barnabas* preached.

LYC'-CA. A province in *Afia Minor.*

LYD'-DA, [Λύδδα, i. e. *a ſtanding pond of water.*] A city of the *Philiftines,* on the banks of the mediterranean fea, called *Diofpolis;* in the tribe of *Ephraim.*

LYD'-I-A, [Λυδία, i. e. *a ſtanding pond of water.*] A woman of *Thyatira* converted by St. *Paul;* fhe was his hoftefs—alfo a province of *Afia Minor,* peopled by the fons of *Lud.*

LYD'-I-ANS, [Λυδοὶ.] The inhabitants of *Lydia.*

LY-SA'-NI-AS, [Λυσανίας, i. e. *diffolving fadneſs.*] A tetrarch of *Abilene.*

LY'-SI-A, [Λύκια, i. e. *a wolf.*] A province of *Afia Minor.*

LY'-SI-AS, [Λυσίας, i. e. *diffolving.*] A general of *Antiochus Epiphanes,* defeated by *Judas Maccabeus.*

LY-'SIM'-

LY-SIM'-A-CHUS, [Λυσίμαχ☉, i. e. *diſſolving battle.*] The brother of *Menelaus*, high prieſt of the *Jews*, in the time of the *Maccabees.*

LYS'-TRA, [Λύϛρα, i. e. *diſſolving.*] A city of *Lycaonia*, a province of *Aſia Minor:* the inhabitants of it ſuppoſed Sᵗ. *Paul* and *Barnabas* to have been *gods*; but they were afterwards ſtoned out of it.

M.

M *before* A.

MA'-AC-AH, [Μααχὰ, i. e. *preſſed down, worn, or faſtened.*] A ſmall province of *Syria*, north eaſt of the river *Jordan*, on the road to *Damaſcus.* See *Maachathi* — alſo the mother of *Abſalom.*

MA'-ACH-AH, [Μοχὰ. Μααχὰ, i. e. *preſſed down, worn, or faſtened.*] A concubine of *Caleb*, a deſcendant from *Judah*—alſo *Abiſhalom's* daughter.

MA-A-CH'-ATH-I, [Μαχαϑί, i. e. *broken.*] A place in *Syria*, in the half tribe of *Manaſſeh.*

MA-ACH'-ATH-ITES, [Μαχατοὶ.] The people of *Maachathi.*

MA-AD-A'-I, [Μοοδία, i. e. *pleaſant, teſtifying, paſſing over, taken away.*] One who returned from the babyloniſh captivity.

MA-AD-I'-AH, [Μοοδίας, i. e. *pleaſantneſs, or the teſtimony or covenant of the Lord.*] One of the prieſts at the new dedication of the walls of *Jeruſalem.*

MA-A'-I,

MA-A'-I, [Μαïα, i. e. *a belly, or heaping up.*] The name of a jewiſh prieſt.

MA-AL'-EH AC-RAB'-BIM, ['Αxραϐίν.] One of the borders of the tribe of *Judah* in *Paleſtine.*

MA-AN'-AI, [Βαανì.] One who returned from the babyloniſh captivity.

MA'-A-RATH, [Μαγαρὼθ, i. e. *a den, making empty, or watching.*] A city belonging to the tribe of *Judah*, in the mountains.

MA-AS-E-I'-AH, [Μαασαïα, i. e. *the work of the Lord.*] The ſon of *Ahaz*, king of *Iſrael*—alſo a porter of the temple.

MA-AS-I'-AH, [Μαασαïα, i. e. *the defence, ſtrength, or ſure truſt of the Lord.*] A chief of the laſt of the twenty-four families of the prieſts.

MA'-ATH, [Μαὰϑ, i. e. *wiping away, breaking, fearing, ſmiting.*] One of the anceſtors of *Joſeph*, the huſband of the virgin *Mary*, in St. *Luke's* genealogy.

MA'-AZ, [Μαὰς, i. e. *wood, or of wood.*] The grand-ſon of *Jerahmeel*, of the tribe of *Judah.*

MA-AZ-I'-AH, [Μοοϛία. Μααϛία.] See *Maaſiah.*

MAB'-DA-I, [Μαϐδαì.] One who returned from the babyloniſh captivity.

MAC'-A-LŌN, [Μαxαλὼν.] A place in *Paleſtine.*

MAC'-CA-BEES, [Μαxxαϐαιοι.] Two of the *Apocryphal* books ſo called after *Judas Maccabæus* and his family.

MAC-CA-BÆ'-US, [Μαxxαϐαïος, i. e. *ſmiting, or a warrior.*] The ſurname of *Judas*, the ſon of *Mattathias* the jewiſh high prieſt; ſo called, becauſe the motto of his ſtandard was the firſt letters of that hebrew ſentence, *Mi lamoka Baalim Jehovah* (i. e. *who is like to thee among the gods, among the lords,*) which letters were formed into the artificial word *Maccabi*; and all who fought under his ſtandard were called *Maccabees*: the title of two of the apocryphal books is *Maccabees*, being a hiſtory of the family and wars of the *Maccabees.*

MA-CED-

MA-CED-ON'-I-A, [Μακεδονία, i. e. *burning, wor-shipping, crookedness, lofty.*] A large province of now european *Turkey.*

MA-CED-ON'-I-ANS. The people of *Macedonia.*

MACH'-BEN-AH or MACH'-BEN-AI, [Μαχα-εννὰ. Μελχαβαναὶ, i. e. *poverty, the smiting of his son.*] A valiant man of king *David's* army—alſo others.

MAC'-HI, [Μαχχὶ, i. e. *poor, or a ſmiter.*] One of the tribe of *Gad.*

MAC'-HIR, [Μαχεὶς, i. e. *ſelling, or knowing.*] The father of *Gilead,* and ſon of *Manaſſeh*—alſo a ſon of *Ammiel.*

MAC'-HIR-ITES. The deſcendants from *Machir.*

MACH'-MAS, [Μάχμας.] See *Michmaſh.*

MACH-NA-DE'-BAI, [Μαχναδααβὴ. Μαχαδναβὴ, i. e. *a ſmiter, or a poor man vowing of his own accord.*] One who returned from the babyloniſh captivity.

MACH-PE'-LAH, [i. e. *double.*] The name of the field or the cave which the patriarch *Abraham* purchaſed of *Ephron* to bury his wife *Sarah.*

MACK-HE'-LŌTH, [Μακηλώθ.] See *Makheloth.*

MAC'-RŌN, [Μάκρων.] A ſurname of one of the *Ptolomies.*

MA'-DA-I, [Μαδαῖμ, i. e. *a meaſure, judging, or a garment.*] The *third* ſon of the patriarch *Japhet.*

MA-DI'-A-BUN, [Μαδιαβὴν.] One who returned from the babyloniſh captivity.

MAD-I'-AH, [Μααδίας.] A prieſt in *Zerubbabel's* time. See *Maadiah.*

MAD'-I-AN, [Μαδιαν.] See *Midian.*

MAD-MAN'-NAH, [Μαδεβανὰ. Μαδμηνὰ, i. e. *a meaſure of a gift, the preparation of a garment, or a dunghill.*] A city of *Paleſtine,* in the tribe of *Judah*—alſo a ſon of *Shaaph,* of the poſterity of *Judah.*

MA'-DON, [Μαρων, i. e. *a chiding, a garment, or his meaſure.*] A city in the north of *Caanan,* which fell to the tribe of *Naphtali.*

MA-E'-LUS, [Μαῆλ©.] One who returned from the babyloniſh captivity.

MAG'-

MAG'-BISH, [Μαγεβις, i. e. *excelling other, or height.*] A place of *Palestine,* suppofed to be in the tribe of *Benjamin.*

MAG'-DA-LA, [Μαγδαλα, i. e. *a tower, or greatnefs.*] A town of *Palestine,* in the tribe of *Manaffeh.*

MAG'-DA-LĒN. See *Magdalene.*

MAG-DA-LE'-NE, (*Mary*) [Μαγδαληνη, i. e. *magnified, exalted, or a tower.*] A woman of the town of *Magdala*; out of whom our *Saviour* caft feven devils.

MAG'-DI-ĒL, [Μαγεδιηλ, i. e. *preaching or declaring God, or the apple or chofen fruit of God.*] A prince of the *Idumæans,* who fucceeded *Mibzar.*

MA'-GI, [Μαγοι.] Suppofed to be philofophers who ftudied aftronomy: The *Chaldeans* were well fkilled in that fcience, and it was their wife-men, who having obferved the new ftar at our *Saviour*'s birth, waited upon the new born infant with their offerings.

MA-GI'-CI-AN. One who deals in divination, pretending to know the fecrets of futurity — the word fignifies, to *fee fecrets.*

MA'-GŌG, [Μαγωγ, i. e. *covering or melting.*] The fon of *Japhet,* and grandfon of *Noah*; fuppofed to be the father of the *Scythians* or *Tartars.*

MA'-GOR MIS'-SA-BIB, [i. e. *terror on every fide.*] The name given to *Pafhur,* one of the jewifh priefts.

MAG'-PI-ASH, [Μεγαφης, i. e. *a body thruft hard together, or the moth of the body or of the garment.*] A *Levite* who fealed the covenant with *Nehemiah* the governor.

MA-HAL'-AH, [Μαελα, i. e. *ficknefs, a company of dancers, a harp.*] One of the pofterity of the patriarch *Manaffeh.*

MA-HAL'-ATH, [Μαελεθ, i. e. *infirmity, a harp, a company of dancers, or pardon.*] *Efau*'s wife, the daughter of *Ifhmael,* the fon of *Abraham*—alfo the wife of *Rehoboam* king of *Judah.*

MA-HAL'-

MA-HAL'-ATH LE-AN'-NŌTH. In the title of the eighty-eighth *Pfalm*, means, that one *chorus* was to fing one verfe, and anfwered with the next verfe by another *chorus*, accompanied with flutes and pipes.

MA-HAL'-ATH MAS'-CHIL. The words in the title of the 53d *Pfalm*—the word *mahalath* fignifies a flute or pipe; and *mafchil* the tune or fong.

MA-HAL'-E-ĒL, [Μαλελεήλ, i. e. *praifing God, or God's illumination.*] A fon of *Cainan*, of the race of *Seth*, died A. M. 1290, Æt. 895.

MA-HAL'-I, [Μοολεɩ, i. e. *infirmity; ficknefs; an harp; pardon.*] A fon of *Merari*. See *Mahli*.

MA-HA-NA'-IM, [Μαναεμ. Μααναὶμ, i. e. *tents, camps, a company of foldiers, two armies.*] The place where the angels met *Jacob*—alfo a city of the *Levites*, in the tribe of *Gad*.

MA-HA'-NEH DAN, [i. e. *the tents of judgment.*] Or *Kirjath Jearim*; fo called from the patriarch *Dan* who pitched there.

MA-HA'-NEM, [ΜαναΥιν, i. e. *a comforter.*] The *fixteenth* king of *Ifrael*, who flew *Shallum*, and reigned in his ftead.

MA-HA-RA'-I, [Μαραὶ. Μαχαραὶ, i. e. *hafting, a hill, from my hill.*] One of the chief of king *David's* guards.

MA'-HATH, [Μααθ, i. e. *wiping away, breaking, fearing, fmiting.*] One of the *Levites*.

MA'-HA-VITES, [i. e. *declaring a meffage, blotting out, the marrow in bones.*] A people, but uncertain whom.

MA'-HAZ, [Μαχès, i. e. *an end, or ending, or waxing hope.*] A place mentioned in the book of *Kings*, uncertain where: but fuppofed to be in *Canaan*.

MA-HAZ'-I-ŌTH, [Μεαζώθ, i. e. *feeing a fign, or feeing a letter.*] The fon of *Heman*, chief of the 23d family of the *Levites*.

MA-HER-SHAL'-AL-HASH'-BAZ, [i. e. *making fpeed to the fpoil.*] A prophetic name mentioned
by

by the prophet *Ifaiah*, as a fign of the fpeedy deftruction of *Syria* and *Ephraim*.

MAH'-LAH, [Μαλὰ, i. e. *ficknefs, an harp, pardon.*]
One of the daughters of *Zelophehad*.

MAH'-LI, [Μοολὶ, i. e. *the fame meaning with Mahlah.*]
A fon of *Merari*, of the pofterity of *Levi*.

MAH'-LITES. The pofterity of *Mahli*.

MAH'-LŌN, [Μααλὼν, i. e. *the fame meaning with
Mahlah.*] A fon of *Elimelech* and *Naomi*.

MA'-HOL, [Μὰλ, i. e. *the fame meaning as Mahalath.*]
One mentioned in the *firſt* book of *Kings*, but
uncertain whom: his fons are fuppofed to have
been wife men of the eaſt.

MAI-AN'-E-AS, [Μαιάννας.] A *Levite* who returned
from the babylonifh captivity.

MA'-KAS, [Μακὲς, i. e. *an end; ending; waxing
hope.*] A place of *Paleſtine* where one of king
Solomon's officers refided, who had the care of the
provifions for the royal houfhold. See *Mahaz*.

MA'-KED, [Μακὲδ.] A city of *Paleſtine*.

MAK-HE'-LŌTH, [Μακηλὼθ, i. e. *churches, compa-
nies, congregations.*] The *twenty-fecond* encampment of the *Ifraelites*, in the wildernefs.

MAK-KE'-DAH, [Μαχηδάν, i. e. *burning, worfhip-
ping, crookednefs.*] A city of *Paleſtine*, in the tribe
of *Judah* in the valley.

MAK'-TESH. A place near to *Jerufalem*.

MAL'-A-CHI, [Μαλαχίας, i. e. *my meffenger, or angel.*] The laſt of the *twelve* lefſer prophets;
after whom the canonical book *Malachi* was
named.

MAL'-CHAM, [Μελχάμ, i. e. *their king, their counfellor.*] One of the pofterity of the patriarch
Benjamin—alfo *Moloch*.

MAL-CHI'-AH, [Μελχία. Μελχίας, i. e. *the Lord
my king or my counfellor.*] The chief of the *fifth*
family of the *twenty-four* prieſts' family — alfo
others of that name.

MAL'-CHI-ĒL, [Μελχιήλ, i. e. *God is my king, or my
kingdom, or my counfellor.*] The fon of *Beriah*,
and grandfon to *Afher*.

MAL'-

MAL'-CHI-ĒL-ITES. The posterity of *Malchiel*.

MAL-CHI'-JAH. See *Malchiah*.

MAL-CHI'-RAM, [Μελχιράμ.] A son of *Jecaniah*.

MAL-CHI-SHU'-AH, [Μελχισυὲ, i. e. *my king the Saviour, the king of health, the mighty king.*] The third son of king *Saul*.

MAL'-CHOM, [Μελχάμ, i. e. *their king, their counsellor.*] The god of the *Ammonites*, the same as *Moloch*.

MAL'-CHUS, [Μαλχ☉, i. e. *my king, kingdom, or my counsellor.*] A servant of the high priest, whose ear *Peter* cut-off, in the garden of *Olives*, when our *Saviour* was apprehended.

MAL'-LAS, [Μαλλίος.] A place mentioned in the *second* book of the *Maccabees*.

MAL'-LO-THI, [Μαλλιϑὶ, i. e. *fullness, circumcision.*] One of the singers of the temple of *Jerusalem*.

MAL'-LUCH, [Μαλὼχ. Μαλὸχ, i. e. *reigning, or counselling.*] One of the priests who sealed the covenant with *Nehemiah* the governor.

MA-MAI'-AS, [Σαμαίας.] A principal man among the *jews*, who returned from the babylonish captivity.

MAM'-MŌN, [Μαμμῶνα.] A *Syriac* word signifying *Riches*.

MAM'-NI-TA-NAI'-MUS, [Μαμνιτάναιμ☉.] One whose family returned from the babylonish captivity.

MAM'-RE, [Μαμϐρῆ, i. e. *a rebel, bitter, changing, or set with trees.*] An *Amorite*, brother of *Aner* and *Eshcol*, and a friend of the patriarch *Abraham* —also a plain near to *Hebron*, where *Abraham* dwelt.

MA-MU'-CUS, [Μαμὸχ☉.] One who returned from the babylonish captivity.

MA'-NA-ĒN, [Μαναὴν, i. e. *their comforter, or leader, or a gift not registered.*] A person who had been brought up with *Herod* the tetrarch.

MA'-NA-HATH, [Μαναχὰϑ. Μαχανὰθ.] One of the descendants from *Esau*.

MA-NA'-HEM. See *Mahanem*.

O

MA-NA'-

MA-NA'-HETH-ITES, [i. e. *my lady, my prince of rest.*] Of the posterity of *Judah.*

MA-NAS-SE'-AS, [Μανασσίας.] One who returned from the babylonish captivity.

MA-NAS'-SEH, [Μανασσῆς, i. e. *forgotten, or forgetfulness.*] The eldest son of *Joseph,* and grandson of the patriarch *Jacob*—also the son and successor of *Hezekiah* king of *Judah,* who died A. M. 3361—also others of that name.

MA-NAS'-SITES. Descendants from *Manasseh* the son of *Joseph.*

MAN'-DRAKE, [Μανδραγόρας.] A plant very common in the east countries, which bears a very large leaf and has a fruit like an apple: it is said to render barren women fruitful.

MA'-NEH, [Μνᾶ.] A jewish coin of *sixty* shekels, worth about *seven pounds, and ten shillings* sterling.

MA'-NI, [Μανί.] One whose sons returned from the babylonish captivity.

MAN'-NA, [Μάν. Μαννα. τί ἐςι τῆτο;] A sweet dew, which, through the coolness of the night and morning, was congealed into little corns like coriander seeds—the hebrew word which we translate *manna* is a question, viz. *what is this?* for the *Israelites* had no name for it; for they wist not what it was; and therefore asked this question.

MA-NO'-AH, [Μανωὲ, i. e. *rest or a gift.*] The father of *Samson,* of the tribe of *Dan,* and of the city *Zorah.*

MA'-OCH, [Ἀμμὰχ, i. e. *holden together.*] A king of *Gath* in *Philistia.*

MA'-ON, [Μαών, i. e. *a dwelling place, a place of offence or of sin.*] A city of *Palestine,* in the tribe of *Judah* in the mountains — also the son of *Shammai.*

MA'-ON-ITES. The inhabitants of the city *Maon.*

MAR'-A, [i. e. *bitter or bitterness.*] *Naomi* was called *Mara.*

MAR'-AH, [Μεῤῥὰ, i. e. *bitter or bitterness.*] A name given by the *Israelites* to the place in the wilderness nefs where they found the water bitter: it was their *fifth* encampment.

MAR'-A-LAH, [Μαραλά, i. e. *fleep, a facrifice of myrrh, afcenfion.*] A city of *Paleftine*, in the tribe of *Zebulun.*

MAR-AN-ATH'-A, [Μαράναθα.] A *Syriack* word, being a form of curfing among the Jews, fignifying, *the Lord comes, or is come.*

MAR'-CUS, [Μάρκ⊙, i. e. *filled, or made fine.*] The fon of *Barnabas's* fifter; St. *Peter* calls him his fon.

MAR-DOCH-E'-US, [Μαρδοχαιος.] See MORDE-CAI.

MAR-E'-SHAH, [Μαρησά. Μαρισά, i. e. *from the beginning, an inheritance, or the bitterness of the field.*] A city of *Paleftine* in the tribe of *Judah*, in the valley—alfo the father of *Hebron*, of the tribe of *Judah.*

MARK, [Μάρκ⊙, i. e. *the fame with Marcus.*] The *fecond* canonical book of the *New Teftament*, Mark, was written by him: he was one of the *four* evangelifts.

MAR-I'-SA, [Μαρισά.] See *Marefhah.*

MAR'-MŌTH, [Μαρμώθ.] A prieft who returned from the babylonifh captivity.

MAR'-OTH, [i. e. *bitternefs.*] Suppofed to be fome place which repined at the profperity of *Jerufalem.*

MARS. The god of war among the *Romans.*

MAR'-SE-NA, [Μαρσανὰ, i. e. *the bitternefs of a bramble, or enemy.*] A prince of *Perfia* and *Media.*

MARS HILL. A place in *Athens*, from whence St. *Paul* preached to the *Athenians.*

MAR'-TE-NA. See *Marfena.*

MAR'-THA, [Μάρθα, i. e. *ftirring up, bitter, provoking, a lady.*] The fifter of *Lazarus* and *Mary*, of *Bethany.*

MA'-RY, [Μαρία, i. e. *exalted, the fon of bitternefs, miftrefs or lady of tho fea.*] The mother of our *Saviour*, daughter of *Joachim* and *Anna*, of the tribe of *Judah*—alfo the mother of *James* and

Simon

Simon, the brethren of our *Saviour*—alfo the fifter of *Lazarus* and *Martha*.

MAS'-CHIL. A title of feveral Pfalms, fignifying an inftructive fong.

MA'-SEL-ŌTH, [Μαισαλὼθ.] A city of *Affyria*.

MASH, [Μοσόχ.] A fon of *Aram* and grandfon to the patriarch *Shem*.

MA'-SHAL, [Μαασάλ, i. e. *a parable, governing or ruling.*] A city of *Paleſtine*, in the tribe of *Aſher*, given to the *Levites*.

MAS'-MAN, [Μαασμὰν.] A principal man among the *jews* after their captivity.

MAS'-MŌTH. A prieſt who returned from the babyloniſh captivity.

MAS'-REK-AH, [Μασσεκκάς, i. e. *hiffing, touching vanity, a vine.*] A city mentioned in the *firſt* book of *Chronicles* and in *Geneſis*, being in the land of *Edom*.

MAS'-A, [Μασσὴ, i. e. *a burden, fometimes, or prophecy.*] The name of one of *Iſhmael*'s fons.

MAS'-SAH, [i. e. *temptation.*] *Rephidim* was fo called by the *Iſraelites*.

MAS-SI'-AS, [Μασσίας.] One who returned from the babyloniſh captivity.

MAT'-RED, [Ματραἲθ, i. e. *the wand of government, labour.*] The mother of *Mehitabel*, the wife of king *Hadad*.

MAT'-RI, [Ματ7αρί, i. e. *rain, heaping, cuſtody, or a priſon.*] One of the tribe of *Benjamin*.

MAT'-TAN, [Ματθὰν, i. e. *his gift, the death of them, expectation, hope.*] A fon of *Eleazar*, father of *Jacob* and grandfather of *Joſeph* the huſband of the virgin *Mary*—alfo a prieſt of *Baal*.

MAT'-TAN-AH, [Ματθανέω, i. e. *the fame as Mattan.*] A place through which the *Iſraelites* paffed in the wilderneſs.

MAT-TAN-I'-AH, [Ματθανίαν, i.e. *the gift, or hope of the Lord.*] Chief of the *ninth* family of the *Levites*.

MAT'-TA-THA, [Ματθαθὰ, i. e. *his gift.*] The fon of *Nathan* and grandfon of king *David* by *Bathſheba*.

MAT-

MAT-TA-THI'-AS, [Ματΐαθίας, i. e. *a gift of the Lord.*] An anceſtor of *Joſeph* the huſband of the virgin *Mary*—alſo the ſon of *John*, of the race of the prieſts.

MAT-TE-NA'-I, [Μεΐθανία, i. e. *the ſame as Mattan.*] One of the valiant men of king *David's* army.

MAT'-THAN, [Ματθὰν, i. e. *the death of them, his gift, expeſtation, hope.*] One who is mentioned in St. *Matthew's* genealogy of *Chriſt.*

MAT'-THAT, [Ματθατ, i. e. *a gift or giving.*] An anceſtor of *Joſeph* the huſband of the virgin *Mary*, mentioned by St. *Luke.*

MAT-THE'-LAS, [Μαθήλας.] A jewiſh prieſt who had married a ſtrange wife during the babyloniſh captivity.

MAT'-THEW, [Ματθαῖος, i. e. *given, or a reward.*] One of the *four* evangeliſts, after whom the canonical book *Matthew*, of the *New Teſtament*, was named: he was a *galilean jew* and a publican, and the ſon of *Alpheus.*

MAT'-THI-AS, [Ματθιὰς, L. *Mat'-thi-as,* i. e. *the gift of the Lord.*] An apoſtle of *Jeſus Chriſt*, ſuppoſed to be one of the ſeventy diſciples: he was choſen to fill the vacancy by the death of *Judas Iſcariot.*

MAT-TI-THI'-AH, [Ματθαθίας, i. e. *the gift of the Lord.*] One of the ſingers of the temple of *Jeruſalem.*

MAZ-I-TI'-AS, [Μαζιτίας.] One whoſe family returned from the babyloniſh captivity.

MAZ-ZA'-ROTH, [Μαζυρὼθ.] The *chaldee* name for the *Zodiac.*

M before E.

ME'-AH, [Μανὶ, i. e. *an hundred cubits.*] A tower on the walls of *Jeruſalem.*

ME-A'-NI. One who returned from the babyloniſh captivity.

ME-A'-RAH, [i. e. *a den, cave, making empty, or watching.*] A place in antient *Canaan*, near to *Sidon:* alſo the river *Magoras* running into the *mediterranean ſea.*

O 3

MEAS'-

MEAS'-URE. A *jewish* measure was about eight bushels and an half.

MEAT OFFERING. See OFFERINGS.

MEB-UN'-NAI, [Μεβηναι, i. e. *a son, building, understanding.*] An *Hushathite,* one of king *David's* worthies.

MECH-E'-RATH, [Μεχωραθι, i. e. *selling, or knowledge.*] The native place of *Hepher,* one of king *David's* worthies.

MECH-E'-RATH-ITE. An inhabitant of *Mecherath.*

ME'-DAD, [Μαδαδ, i. e. *measuring, or the waters of the beloved.*] One of the seventy elders appointed by *Moses.*

ME'-DA-LAH. A city of *Palestine,* in the tribe of *Zebulun.* See *Igdalah.*

ME'-DAN, [Μαδαλ, i. e. *strife, judging a measure, or a garment.*] The *third* son of the patriarch *Abraham* by *Keturah.*

ME'-DE-BA, [Μηδαβα, i. e. *the waters of grief, or waters springing up.*] A city of *Palestine,* in the southern parts of the tribe of *Reuben,* beyond the river *Jordan.*

MEDES, [Μηδοι, i. e. *measure, abounding, or a garment.*] The people of the kingdom of *Media.*

ME'-DI-A, [Μηδια, i. e. *the same as Medes.*] The country of the *Medes* in *Asia,* in hebrew *Madai,* supposed to be peopled by the posterity of *Madai,* the *third* son of *Japhet.*

ME'-DI-AN. An inhabitant of *Media.*

ME-ED'-A, [Μεεδδα.] One whose sons were servants of the temple after the babylonish captivity.

ME-GID'-DO or **ME-GID'-DON,** [Μαγεδδω, i. e. *a declaring of a message, an apple, or the chosen fruit.*] A city of *Palestine,* in the half tribe of *Manasseh.*

ME-HAL'-I, [Μοολει.] See MAHLI.

ME-HET'-AB-EL, [Μετεβεηλ, i. e. *how good is God, or God doing well.*] The wife of *Hadar* a king of *Edom.*

ME-HI'-

I

ME-HI'-DA, [Μαηδὰ, i. e. *a riddle, sharpnefs of wit, or the hand fmitten.*] One whofe children were of the order of *Nethinims.*

ME'-HIR, [Μαχίρ, i. e. *a reward.*] One of the pofterity of the patriarch *Judah.*

ME-HO'-LATH-ITE. *Barzillai* was a *Meholathite,* but the term is uncertain.

ME-HU'-JA-EL, [Μαλελεήλ., i. e. *teaching, declaring God, or fmitten of God.*] The fon of *Irad* and father of *Methufael,* of the race of *Cain.*

ME-HU'-MAN, [Μαημάν, i. e. *troubled, making an uproar, a multitude.*] Chief of the eunuchs or officers of king *Ahafuerus.*

ME-HU'-NIM, [Μοηνίμ.] One whofe children were of the order of *Nethinims.*

ME-HU'-NIMS, [Μιναίοι.] A people who dwelt on the borders of *Ægypt.*

ME-JARK'-ŌN, [i. e. *the waters of Jordan.*] A city of *Palefine,* in the tribe of *Dan.*

MEK-O'-NAH, [Μαβνῆ, i. e. *a foot of a pillar, or provifion.*] A city of *Palefine,* in the tribe of *Judah.*

MEL-A-TI'-AH, [Μαλτίας, i. e. *deliverance of the Lord.*] One who returned from the babylonifh captivity.

MEL'-CHI, [Μελχὶ, i. e. *my king, or my counfel.*] An anceftor of *Jofeph* the virgin *Mary's* hufband, in St. *Luke's* genealogy.

MEL'-CHI-AH, [Μελχία, i. e. *my king is the Lord.*] The father of *Pafhur* the prieft.

MEL'-CHI-AS, [Μελχίας.] One who returned from the babylonifh captivity.

MEL'-CHI-EL, [Μελχιήλ, i. e. *God is my king.*] Father of *Charmis* a governor of *Bethulia.*

MEL-CHIS'-ED-EK, [Μελχισεδὲκ, i. e. *king of righteoufnefs.*] King of *Salem* and prieft of the moft high GOD, who met and refrefhed *Abraham,* after his return from the purfuit of the four kings who had defeated the kings of *Sodom* and *Gomorrah.*

MEL-CHI-SHU'-A, [Μελχισηέ.] See *Malchifhuah.*

MEL'-

MEL'-E-A, [Μελεᾶ, i. e. *fupplying, or fupplied.*] The
fon of *Menan* in St. *Luke*'s genealogy.

MEL'-ECH, [Μελὰχ, i. e. *a king, or counfellor.*] One
of the defcendants from king *Saul.*

MEL'-LI-CU, [Μαλὰχ, i. e. *his kingdom, or counfel.*]
The fame perfon with *Malluch* the prieft.

MEL'-I-TA, [Μελίτη, i. e. *flowing with honey.*] An
ifland of the *mediterranean fea* where St. *Paul* was
fhipwrecked: now *Malta.*

MEL'-ZAR, [Μελσάρ, i. e. *the circumcifion of a narrow
place, of a bond, a fteward.*] One who was appointed to guard the prophet *Daniel,* by *Nebuchadnezzar*'s order.

MEM'-PHIS, [Μέμφις, i. e. *from the mouth, a cover
or overwhelmer.*] A celebrated city in *Ægypt,*
near the mouth of the river *Nile.*

MEM-U'-CAN, [Μαμυχὰν, i. e. *prepared, fure, made
poor, or fmitten.*] One of the principal counfellors of king *Ahafuerus.*

MĒ-NA'-HĒM, [Μαναὴμ, i. e. *their comforter, or
leader, or the preparation of heat.*] A king of *Judah,*
who flew *Shallum.*

ME'-NAN, [Μαινὰν, i. e. *numbered; rewarded; prepared.*] An anceftor of *Jofeph,* the virgin *Mary*'s
hufband, in St. *Luke*'s genealogy.

ME'-NE, [Μανὴ.] Signifies, GOD *hath numbered thy
kingdom and finifhed it.*

MEN-EL-A'-US, [Μενέλαⵀ, i. e. *power, or ftrength
of the people.*] An high prieft of the *Jews,* fometimes called *Onias.*

MEN-ES'-THE-ŪS, [Μενεθεώς, i. e. *chearfulnefs;
anger; or the ftrength of God.*] The father of
Apollonius, in the *fecond* book of *Maccabees.*

MEN'-ITH. One who returned from the babylonifh
captivity.

ME'-NO-THAI, [Μαναθὶ. Μαωναθέι.] A fon of
Othniel, father of *Ophrah,* of the tribe of *Judah.*

ME-O'-NEN-EM, [Μαωνενίμ, i. e. *charmers.*] A
place mentioned in the book of *Judges,* where
were *plains.*

ME'-PHA-

ME'-PHA-ATH, [Μωφαὰθ, i. e. *an appearance of waters, or the force of waters.*] A city of *Palestine*, in the tribe of *Reuben*, given to the *Levites*.

MEPH'-IB'-OSH-ETH, [Μεμφιϐοϑέ. Μεφιϐόσετ, i. e. *shame of mouth.*] A son of *Saul* by his concubine *Rizpah*—also a son of *Jonathan*, king *Saul's* son, whom king *David* took under his protection.

MER'-AB, [Μερὸϐ, i. e. *fighting, chiding, multiplying, or the office of a master.*] The eldest daughter of king *Saul*, promised to king *David*, but given to *Aduel* son of *Barzillai*.

MER-A-I'-AH, [Αμαριά, i. e. *bitter.*] A jewish priest in *Zerubbabel's* time.

MER-AI'-ŌTH, [Μαραὼθ, i. e. *bitterness, rebellious, changings.*] The son of *Ahitub*, a jewish high priest—also a son of *Zerahiah*, of the tribe of *Levi*.

MER'-AN, [Μεῤῥάν.] A city of *Arabia* in *Asia*.

MER-A'-RI, [Μεραρί, i. e. *bitter, stirred up, provoked.*] The *third* son of the patriarch *Levi*, and father of *Mahali* and *Mushi*.

MER-A'-RITES. The descendants from *Merari*.

MER-A-THA'-IM. A part of the babylonian empire.

MER-CU'-RI-US or MER'-CU-RY, [Ἑρμῆς, i. e. *of merchandise.*] In fable, the son of *Jupiter* and *Maia:* A god of the antient heathens, and whom the people of *Lystra* supposed St. *Paul* to represent.

MER'-CY SEAT. The cover of the ark of the covenant, or chest in which were deposited the *tables* of the law: it was covered with pure gold, and two golden *cherubim* stretched forth their wings to cover it; one at each end.

ME'-RED, [Μωράδ. Μωρήδ, i. e. *a rebel, rebellious, going down, bearing rule.*] A son of *Ezra*.

MER'-E-MŌTH, [Μεραμὼθ, i. e. *bitterness, myrrh of death.*] A jewish priest, the son of *Uriah*, and one who returned from the babylonish captivity.

MER'-

MER'-ES, [Μερὲς, i. e. *diſtilling down from the head, or an impoſthume.*] The name of a prince of *Perſia,* and *Media.*

MER'-I-BAH, [i. e. *ſtrife, or contention.*] *Rephidim,* ſo called by the *Iſraelites.*

MER'-I-BAH KA'-DĒSH. A place where the *Iſraelites* murmured in the wilderneſs.

MER-IB'-BA-AL, [Μεριβαὰλ, i. e. *rebellion, or fighting againſt Baal.*] The name of *Mephiboſheth* the ſon of *Jonathan.*

MER'-I-MŌTH, [Μεραμὼθ.] See *Meremoth.*

MER-O'-DACH, [Μαρωδὰχ, i. e. *bitter contention.*] a king of antient *Babylon* who was deified and worſhipped there.

MER-O'-DACH BA'-LA-DAN, [Μαρωδὰχ Βαλαδὰν, i. e. *bitter contrition without judgment.*] A king of *Babylon,* ſon of *Baladan.*

ME'-RŌM, [Μαρὼν, i. e. *heights.*] A river or lake mentioned in the book of *Judges*—alſo a city in the tribe of *Naphtali.*

ME-RO-NO'-THITE, [Μηρωνωθίτης, i. e. *my ſinging, rejoicing, bearing rule.*] One mentioned in the *firſt* book of *Chronicles,* but not deſcribed: *Jehdeiah* was a *Meronothite.*

ME'-RŌZ, [Μηρὼζ, i. e. *ſecret, or leanneſs.*] A city of *Galilee,* near to the brook *Kiſhon.*

ME'-RŪTH, ['Εμμηρὺθ.] A *prieſt* who returned from the babyloniſh captivity with his family.

MES'-ECH, [Μοσὸχ, i. e. *prolonging; drawing; or hedging in waters.*] Suppoſed not to be a place; but the meaning of the word is, *how long?*—ſome ſay, it was a country taking its name from *Meſhech* the ſon of *Japhet.*

ME'-SHA, [Μωσὰ, i. e. *a burden, a taking, or ſalvation.*] A king of the *Moabites*—alſo the firſt ſon of *Caleb* the ſon of *Hezron*—alſo others.

MESH'-A, [Μασσὴ, i. e. *a burden; a taking; ſalvation.*] A place mentioned in the book of *Geneſis;* the dwelling of the ſons of *Jokton.*

ME'-SHACH, [Μισὰχ, i. e. *prolonging, drawing, hedging in waters.*] The *chaldæan* name of *Miſhael,* one of the prophet *Daniel*'s companions.

MESH'.

MESH'-ECH, [Μοσὸχ, i. e. *the same etymon with Meshach*.] The *sixth* son of the patriarch *Japhet*.

MESH-EL-E-MI'-AH, [Μοσολλαμὶ, i. e. *the peace, the perfection or the recompencing of the Lord*.] The father of *Zechariah*; a *Levite* and a porter or guard of the temple of *Jerusalem*.

MESH-EZ'-A-BĒL or MESH-EZ'-A-BEĒL, [Μασεζηϐὴλ, i. e. *God taking away, flowing, or the salvation of God*.] A *Levite* who sealed the covenant together with *Nehemiah* the governor.

MESH-IL-LA'-MITH, [Μεσιλλημὶθ, i. e. *peaceable, perfect, giving again, the parables of death*.] The father of *Meshullam* the priest.

MESH-IL'-LE-MŌTH, [Μοσολαμὰθ, i. e. *making peace, perfection, giving again, the parables of death*.] One of the posterity of the patriarch *Ephraim*.

MESH-O'-BAH, [Μοσωϐὰϐ.] A prince of the tribe of *Simeon*.

MESH-UL'-LAM, [Μεσολλάμ, i. e. *peaceable, perfect, their parables, their power*.] A priest who sealed the covenant with *Nehemiah* the governor —also others of that name.

MESH-UL'-LEM-ETH, [Μεσολλὰμ.] The wife of *Manasseh* king of *Judah*, and mother of king *Amon*.

MES-O'-BAH, [Μεσωϐὶα.] The name of a place mentioned in the first book of *Chronicles*.

MES-O'-BA-ITE, [i. e. *the standing place of the Lord, or a little doe*.] One who was an inhabitant of *Mesobah*.

MES-OP-OT-A'-MI-A, [Μεσοποταμία, i. e. *middle of rivers*.] A famous country of *Asia*, between the rivers *Tigris* and *Euphrates*, formerly *Padan Aram* and *Aram Naharaim*, i. e. *Aram* of the two rivers; now *Diarbec proper* in Asiatic Turky.

MES-SI'-AH or MES-SI'-AS, [Μεσσίας, i. e. *in hebrew, anointed; in greek, Christ*.] A term peculiarly appropriated to our *Saviour*.

MET-E'-RUS, [Μετηρυς.] One who returned from the babylonish captivity with his family.

ME'-THEG

ME'-THEG AM'-MAH, [i. e. *the bridle of bondage.*] Supposed to be the city *Gath* in *Philistia*.

METH'-RE-DATH, [Μιθραδάτης, i. e. *beholding, or breaking the law, the going down of death.*] One who wrote to *Artaxerxes* king of *Persia*, against building *Jerusalem*; he was his treasurer.

ME-THU'-SA-EL or ME-THU'-SE-LAH or ME-THU'-SE-LA, [Μαθυσάλα, i. e. *he sent his death, the weapons of his death, the spoil of his death.*] The son of *Mehujael* or grandson of *Enoch*, and father of *Lamech*; the longest liver upon record; he died A. M. 1656, Æt. 969.

ME-U'-NIM, [Μεεινώμ, i. e. *dwelling places, afflicted, offending, answering.*] One whose children were of the order of *Nethinims*.

ME'-ZA-HAB, [Μαιζωὲβ, i. e. *gilded, the waters of gold.*] One who returned from the babylonish captivity—also the mother of *Matred*.

M before I.

MI'-AM-IN, [Μιαμεὶν, i. e. *the right hand, or preparing waters.*] One who returned from the babylonish captivity. See *Mijamin*.

MIB'-HAR, [Μαβὰρ, i. e. *chosen, or youth.*] One of king *David*'s valiant men.

MIB'-SAM, [Μαβασάν, i. e. *smelling sweet, or confounding them.*] One of the sons of *Ishmael*—also one of the posterity of the patriarch *Simeon*.

MIB'-ZAR, [Μαζὰρ. Βαβσὰρ, i. e. *defending, forbidding, taking away, gathering grapes.*] A duke, a descendant from *Esau*.

MI'-CAH, [Μιχαιας, i. e. *poor, smiting, or who is here in this place.*] One of the tribe of *Ephraim*, who occasioned a defection in religion among the *Israelites*—also the *sixth* of the twelve lesser prophets, who was an inhabitant of *Morasthi* or *Moresa*, in the tribe of *Judah*; and called *the Morashite*: he lived about the time of *Isaiah*.

MI-CAI'-AH, [Μιχαιας, i. e. *who is like the Lord? the poverty or smiling of the Lord.*] A prophet of
the

the tribe of *Ephraim*, in the reign of king *Ahab*.

MI'-CHA, [Μιχὰ, i. e. *the fame with Micah.*] One of the fons of *Mephibofheth* the fon of *Jonathan*, and grandfon to king *Saul*.

MI'-CHA-ĒL, [Μιχαὴλ, i. e. *who is like to God? the lowlinefs of God, or the fmiting of God.*] The name of an *Archangel*, fuppofed to have prefided over the jewifh nation—alfo one of the family of *Levi*; and another of the family of *Gad*.

MI-CHAH, [Μιχὰ, i. e. *poor; lowly.*] A fon of *Uzziel* and father of *Shamir*.

MI'-CHAL, [Μιχὸλ, i. e. *who is perfect?*] The daughter of king *Saul*, and wife of king *David*.

MICH'-MAS or MICH'-MASH, [Μαχμὰς, i. e. *a fmiter, a poor man, taken away.*] One who returned from the babylonifh captivity—alfo a city of that name, in *Palefine:* in the tribe of *Ephraim*.

MICH'-ME-THAH, [Μαχθωθ, i. e. *the gift or death of a fmiter, a poor man.*] A city of *Palefine*, in the tribe of *Ephraim* on the weft fide of the river *Jordan*.

MICH'-RI, [Μιχρὶ, i. e. *a felling, or knowledge.*] The father of *Uzzi*, the *fixth* high prieft of the Jews.

MICH'-TAM. The title of the *fixteenth* Pfalm, fignifying *a golden Pfalm*.

MID'-DIN, [Μαδδὶν, i. e. *judgment, ftriving or chiding.*] A city of *Palefine*, in the tribe of *Judah* in the wildernefs.

MID'-I-AN, [Μαδιὰν. Μαδιαμ, i. e. *judgment, ftriving, chiding.*] The *fourth* fon of *Abraham* by *Keturah*; and father of the *Midianites*—alfo the fon of *Cufh*, who peopled the country of *Midian* to the eaft of the *red fea*.

MID'-I-AN-ITES, [Μαδιηναῖοι.] The defcendants from *Midian*.

MIG'-DAL-ĒL, [Μαγδαλιὴλ, i. e. *the tower of God, or the greatnefs of God.*] A city of *Palefine* in the tribe of *Naphtali*.

MIG'-

MIG'-DAL GAD, [Μαγαδαλγὰδ, i. e. *a happy tower, a tower compaſſed about, the greatneſs compaſſed about.*] A city of *Paleſtine*, in the tribe of *Judah* in the valley.

MIG'-DOL, [Μαγδωλα, i. e. *a tower or greatneſs.*] A place before which the *Iſraelites* encamped in the wilderneſs, being their *third* encampment there.

MIG'-RON, [Μαγρὼν, i. e. *fear, a barn, or from the throat.*] A village of *Paleſtine*, near to *Gibeah*.

MI'-JA-MIN, [Μειαμιν, i. e. *the right hand, preparing waters.*] A prieſt who ſealed the covenant with *Nehemiah* the governor. See *Miamin*.

MIK'-LOTH, [Μαχελὰθ, i. e. *little wands, ſtaves, voices, looking downwards.*] One of the poſterity of the patriarch *Benjamin*.

MIK-NEI'-AH, [Μαχενιχ, i. e. *the poſſeſſion of the Lord, the buying the cattle or herd of the Lord.*] A *Levite* who was a porter of the temple of *Jeruſalem*.

MI-LA-LA'-I, [Ιαμαΐα, i. e. *circumciſion, my talk.*] The name of a jewiſh prieſt.

MIL'-CHAH or MIL'-CHA or MIL'-CAH, [Μελχὰ, i. e. *a queen, woman of counſel.*] The daughter of *Haran*; ſiſter of *Lot*, wife of *Nahor*, niece of *Abraham*, and mother of *Bethuel*—alſo a daughter of *Zelophehad*.

MIL'-COM, [Αμελχόμ, i. e. *their king, their counſellor.*] The god of the *Ammonites*; the ſame with *Moloch*.

MI-LE'-TUM or MI-LE'-TUS, [Μιλητου, i. e. *red kernels.*] A town on the continent of *Aſia Minor*, in the province of *Caria*: now *Palatſcha*.

MIL'-LO, [Μαλλώ. Μααλώ, i. e. *fullneſs, a filling.*] Suppoſed to be a deep valley between mount *Zion* and mount *Moriah*, which was filled up, or built over.

MI'-NA, [Μνᾶ.] See table of *coins*, at the end.

MIN-I'-A-MIM, [Βενιαμίν. Μιαμίν, i. e. *right hand, preparing waters.*] One of the *Levites*.

MIN'-NI, [i. e. *proviſion, a gift, number.*] The name of a country of the *Medes*.

MIN'-

MIN'-NITH, [Μεννίθ, i. e. *the same as Minni*.] A city of the *Ammonites*, to the east of the river *Jordan*, four miles from *Heshbon*.

MIN'-STREL. Is one who can play well upon an instrument of musick.

MIPH'-KAD, [Μαφεκάδ.] The name of a gate of the city of *Jerusalem*.

MIR'-I-AM, [Μαριάμ, i. e. *exalted, sea of bitterness, myrrh, the mistress or lady of the sea*.] The sister of *Aaron* and *Moses*, and daughter of *Amram* and *Jochebed* his wife: she was the eldest of the three children: and about *nine* or *ten* years older than *Moses*.

MIR'-MA, [Μαρμά, i. e. *deceit, highness, extolling himself*.] One of the posterity of *Benjamin* the patriarch.

MIS'-GAB, [Μασιγάθ.] Supposed to be a city of the *Moabites*.

MI'-SHA-EL, [Μισαηλ, i. e. *who demandeth, or who lent? God hath taken away or gone back*.] The son of *Uzziel* the *Levite*.

MI'-SHAL, [Μισαλλά. Μασαάλ, i. e. *parables, governing, ruling*.] A city of *Palestine*, in the tribe of *Asher*, given to the *Levites*.

MI'-SHAM, [Μεσοάμ. Μισαάλ, i. e. *their saviour, taking away, touching the people*.] One of the posterity of the patriarch *Benjamin*.

MI'-SHE-AL, [Μασαάλ, i. e. *requiring, lent, a grave, pit, taking away*.] A city of *Palestine*, one of the borders of the tribe of *Asher*.

MISH'-MA, [Μασμά, i. e. *a hearing, obeying*.] One of *Ishmael's* sons—also one of the posterity of the patriarch *Benjamin*.

MISH-MAN'-NA, [Μασμανά, i. e. *fatness, his oil, taking away, provision or a gift*.] One who resorted to king *David* at *Ziklag*.

MISH'-RA-ITES, [i. e. *spread abroad, taking away a friend or a shepherd, malice*.] A family mentioned in the *first* book of *Chronicles*, of *Kirjath-jearim*.

MIS'-PAR or MIS'-PER-ETH, [Μασφὰξ Μασφαραθ, i. e. *a numbering, shewing, the augmenting of tribute.*] One who returned from the babylonish captivity.

MIS'-PHA or MIS'-PHAH, [Μασύμα.] A city of *Palestine*, in the tribe of *Benjamin*.

MIS'-RA-IM. See *Mizraim*.

MIS'-RE-PHOTH-MA'-IM, [Μασρεὶθ Μεμφομαὶμ, i. e. *burning, hot waters.*] A city mentioned in the book of *Joshua*, supposed to be *Sarepta* or *Zarephath*.

MITE. A *roman* coin, which the *Scripture* calls *half of a farthing*: it was of the value of a quarter of a *roman* penny, and of *seven farthings* english money: others say it was the *third* part of a *farthing* english.

MITH'-CAH, [Μαθεκκά, i. e. *sweetness, pleasantness.*] The *twenty-fifth* encampment of the *Israelites*, in the wilderness.

MITH'-NITE, [i. e. *the loin; a gift, hope.*] *Jehosaphat*, one of king *David*'s warriors was so called, but uncertain why.

MITH-RI-DA'-TES, [Μιθριδάτης.] A king of *Pontus* in *Asia*—also a treasurer to *Cyrus* king of *Persia*.

MITH'-RI-DATH, [Μιθραδάτ☉, i. e. *assailing, beholding the law, breaking the law, the going down to death.*] One of those who signed the letter to *Artaxerxes* king of *Persia*, against building the walls of *Jerusalem*.

MIT-Y-LE'-NE, [Μιτυλήνη, i. e. *cleanliness, the wiping of the wine press.*] The capital of the isle of *Lesbos*.

MI'-ZAR, [i. e. *little.*] An hill mentioned in the book of *Psalms*.

MIZ'-PAH or MIZ'-PEH, [Μασφὰ, i. e. *a watch, tower, judgment, covering.*] A city of *Palestine*, in the tribe of *Benjamin*.

MIZ'-RA-IM, [Μασραὶμ, i. e. *straitness.*] A son of *Ham* the patriarch—also the *Ægyptians* were so called from *Misraim* who settled there.

MIZ'-

MIZ'-ZAH, [Μοζέ, i. e. *dropping, diftilling from the head, accuftoming, confumption.*] The fon of *Reuel*, and grandfon to *Efau*.

M *before* N.

MNA'-SON, [Μνάσων, i. e. *a diligent feeker, betroth-ing, remembering.*] A *jew* converted by *Jefus Chrift* himfelf, and one of the feventy difciples, at whofe houfe St. *Paul* lodged at *Jerufalem*, A. D. 58.

M *before* O.

MO'-AB, [Μωάβ, i. e. *of the father.*] The fon of *Lot* by his eldeft daughter: the father of the *Moabites*.

MO'-AB-ITES, [Μωαβῖται.] The pofterity of *Moab*, who dwelt to the eaft of the *dead fea*, on the river *Arnon*.

MO-AD-I'-AH, [Μααδαί.] The name of one of the *Levites*.

MOCH'-MUR. See *Mochram*.

MOCH'-RAM, [Μοχμήρ.] A river of *Paleftine*.

MO'-DIN, [Μωδεῖν.] A city or town of *Paleftine*, in the tribe of *Dan*, noted for being the dwelling and burial place of *Mattathias* and his fons the *Maccabees*.

MO'-ETH, [Μωέθ.] A *Levite*, who returned from the babylonifh captivity.

MO'-LA-DAH, [Μωλαδᾶ; i. e. *nativity, generation.*] A city of *Paleftine*, in the tribe of *Judah*.

MOL'-ECH or MOL'-OCH, [Μολόχ, i. e. *reigning, a counfellor.*] An idol of the *Ammonites*, to whom they dedicated their children by making them pafs through the fire in honour of him: fome fuppofe him to be *Saturn*, or the *Sun*.

MOL'-I, [Μοολὶ.] A fon of *Levi*.

MO'-LID, [Μωλίδ, i. e. *nativity, generation, a cir-cumcifed hand.*] One of the pofterity of *Caleb*.

MOL'-OCH, [Μολὸχ.] See *Molech*.

P   MOM'-

MOM'-DIS, [Μομδεις.] One who returned from the babylonifh captivity.

MONTH. See YEAR.

MON'-EY. For the jewifh money, fee the laft page.

MO-OS-I'-AS, [Μοοσιας.] One who returned from the babylonifh captivity.

MO'-RASH-ITE or MO'-RAS-THITE, [Μωραθί-της.] *Micah*, one of the twelve leffer prophets, was a *Morafhite*; of a place in the fouthern part of *Judæa*, called *Morafthi*.

MOR'-DEC-AI, [Μαρδοχαῖος, i. e. *bitter contrition, moft pure myrrh, teaching contrition.*] The fon of *Jair*, of king *Saul*'s race, and one of the chiefs of the tribe of *Benjamin*, and firft coufin to queen *Efther*.

MO'-REH, ['Αμωρὲ, i. e. *ftretching.*] A place on the eaft fide of the river *Jordan*.

MO'-RESH-ETH GATH, [Γαβααθμωραὶ.] Suppofed to be the king of *Affyria*, to whom the philiftine cities fent prefents.

MO-RI'-AH, ['Αμωρία, i. e. *the fear of God.*] A mountain of the country *Moriah* where *Abraham* defigned to have offered his fon *Ifaac*; and on which the temple of *Jerufalem* was afterwards built by king *Solomon*.

MO-SE'-RA, MO-SE'-RAH or MO-SO'-RŌTH; [Μασηρὼθ, i. e. *learning, difcipline, a bond, tradi-tion.*] A place in the wildernefs through which the *Ifraelites* marched, and where *Aaron* died and was buried, near to mount *Hor*; it was their *twenty-feventh* encampment.

MO'-SES, [Μωσῆs, i. e. *drawn up, drawn forth, taken out.*] The great jewifh lawgiver; the fon of *Amram* and *Jochebed*, of the tribe of *Levi*: he was born in *Ægypt* A. M. 2434, and died A. M. 2553, Æt. 120, after he had led the *Ifraelites* out of *Ægypt*, in the eightieth year of his age: he was about *nine* or *ten* years younger than his fifter *Miriam*, and *three* years younger than his brother *Aaron*.

MOS-OL'-LAM, [Μοσόλλαμ⊙.] One who returned from the babylonifh captivity. See *Mefhullam*.

MOS-

MOS-UL'-LA-MON, [Μοσόλλαμ☉.] A principal man among the *jews*, after the babylonish captivity.

MOZ'-A, [Μοσὰ, i. e. *found, unleavened, the end, expressing, making clean.*] The son of *Zimri*, of king *Saul's* family—also a son of *Caleb*.

MO'-ZAH, ['Αμωκὴ, i. e. *a chiding, a subtle invention; unleavened, pressing down.*] A city of *Palestine*, in the tribe of *Benjamin*.

M *before* U.

MUP'-PIM, [Μαμφίμ, i. e. *out of the mouth, a covering.*] A son of the patriarch *Benjamin*.

MU'-SHI, [Μησί. Ομμσεί, i. e. *departing, taking away, going back.*] The son of *Merari* chief of the family of the *Levites* called *Mushites*.

MU'-SHITES. The descendants from *Mushi*.

MUTH-LAB'-BEN. A word in the title of the 9th *Psalm*, supposed to be an instrument of *musick*, but uncertain what.

M *before* Y.

MYN'-DUS, [Μὺνδ☉.] A city of *Lower Asia*.

MY'-RA, [Μύρα, i. e. *I flow, pour out, weep.*] A city of *Lycia* in *Asia*, where St. *Paul* embarked for *Rome*.

MYS'-I-A, [Μυσία, i. e. *criminal, abominable.*] A province of *Asia Minor*, where St. *Paul* preached.

MYT-E-LE'-NE, [Μιτυλήνη.] See *Mitylene*.

N *before*

N.

N *before* A.

NA'-AM, [Ναὰμ. Νοὸμ, i. e. *fair, pleasant.*] The
son of *Caleb*, and grandson to *Jephunneh.*

NA'-AM-AH, [Νοεμά. Νααμὰ, i. e. *fair, comely,
greatly moving.*] An *Ammonitess*, wife of king
Solomon, and mother of king *Rehoboam*—also
Tubal—Cain's sister—also a city of *Palestine*, in
the tribe of *Judah*; in the valley.

NA'-A-MAN, [Ναιμὰν, i. e. *the same with Naamah.*]
General of the army of *Benhadad* king of *Syria*
—also a descendant from the patriarch *Benjamin.*

NA-AM'-ATH-ITES, [Μιναῖοι.] People of *Naamah*
or *Naamath*, on the borders of *Idumæa.*

NA'-AM-ITES. The posterity of *Naaman* the *Benjamite.*

NA-AR'-AH or NA-AR'-AI, [Νααραὶ. Νοορά, i. e.
a maid, young man, shaking off, watching.] One
of the valiant men of king *David*'s army; of the
posterity of *Judah*—also the wife of *Asher.*

NA-AR'-AN, [Νοαρὰν. Νααράν.] A city of *Palestine*,
in the tribe of *Ephraim.*

NA-AR'-ATH, [Νααραθά, i. e. *a maid, a young man,
shaking off, watching.*] A city of *Palestine*, in the
tribe of *Ephraim*, five miles from *Jericho.*

NA-ASH'-ON, [Ναασσὼν, i. e. *that foretells, that
conjectures, serpent, their auguries.*] *Aaron*'s brother in law, the son of *Amminadab* : a prince of
the tribe of *Judah.*

NA-ATH'-

NA-ATH'-US, [Νααθ⊙.] One who returned from
the babylonifh captivity.

NA'-BAL, [Ναβαλ, i. e. *a fool, mad.*] A churl of
the tribe of *Caleb*, who refufed king *David* and
his followers any refrefhment in their diftrefs:
his wife *Abigail* was afterwards married to king
David.

NAB-A-RI'-US, [Ναβαρίας.] One who returned from
the babylonifh captivity.

NAB-ATH-E'-ANS or NAB'-ATH-ITES, [Ναβα-
ταῖοι, i. e. *fpeaking, prophefying, budding forth.*]
Inhabitants of *Nabathæa* in *Arabia*.

NA'-BŌTH, [Ναβωθὶ, i. e. *a fpeech, prophecy, budding
forth.*] An *Ifraelite* of the city of *Jezreel*, who
refufed to give or fell his vineyard to king *Ahab*,
and was afterwards put to death.

NA'-CHŌN, [Ναχὼν, i. e. *ready, fure.*] One, at
whofe threfhing floor *Uzzah* was ftruck dead for
touching the ark.

NA'-CHŌR, [Ναχὼς, i. e. *hoarfe; angry; dry.*] A
fon of *Aaron*, and brother of *Abihu*—alfo a fon
of *Jeroboam*, and a king of *Ifrael*.

NA'-DAB, [Ναδὰβ, i. e. *a prince, liberal, vowing, of
his own accord.*] One of *Aaron's* fons, who with
his brother *Abihu* were flain for offering incenfe
with common fire—alfo a fon of *Jeroboam* and
king of *Ifrael*, who was affaffinated.

NA-DAB'-ATH-A, [Ναδεβὰθ.] A place in *Arabia*.

NAG'-GE, [Ναγγαὶ, i. e. *clearnefs, light.*] One of
the anceftors of *Jofeph*, the hufband of the virgin *Mary*, mentioned by St. *Luke*.

NA-HAL'-I-EL, [Νααλιὴλ, i. e. *the inheritance, flowing ftream, valley of God.*] A place through which
the *Ifraelites* paffed in the wildernefs.

NA-HAL'-LAL, [Ναβαὰλ, i. e. *praifed, bright, a
foot.*] A city of *Paleftine*, in the tribe of *Zebulun*,
given to the *Levites*.

NA-HAL'-ŌL, [Νααλωλ, i. e. *praifed, bright, a foot.*]
A city of *Paleftine*, in the tribe of *Zebulun*, perhaps *Nahalal*.

P 3   NA'-HAM,

NA'-HAM, [Ναχεμ. Ναχαϊμ, i. e. *a comforter, repentant, a leader or the reft of them.*] One of the pofterity of the patriarch *Judah.*

NA-HAM'-A-NI, [Ναεμανι, i. e. *the fame as Naham.*] One who returned from the babylonifh captivity.

NA-HAR-A'-I, [Νααραι. Ναχαραι, i. e. *a noife, a making warm, drynefs, ftrangling.*] A native of *Beeroth,* and armour bearer to *Joab;* one of great valour.

NA'-HASH, [Νααs, i. e. *a ferpent, prophefying, like brafs.*] A king of the *Ammonites,* killed by king *Saul*—alfo a king of the *Ammonites,* a friend to king *David;* probably, the fon of the other *Nahafh*—alfo the father of *Abigail* and *Zeruiah,* fuppofed to be the fame with *Jeffe, David's* father.

NA'-HATH, [Ναάθ, i. e. *reft, a leader, a going down.*] The fon of *Reuel,* and grandfon to *Efau*—alfo others of that name.

NAH'-BI or NA'-HA-BI, [Ναϐι, i. e. *very fecret, hid, my beloved, a leader with me.*] One of the fpies fent by *Mofes,* to view the land of *Canaan.*

NA'-HŌR, [Ναχωρ, i. e. *hoarfe, angry, dry, ftrangled.*] The fon of *Serug* and father of *Terah;* he died A. M. 1997, Æt. 148—alfo a fon of *Terah,* and brother of *Abraham.*

NAH'-SHŌN. See NAASHON.

NA'-HŪM, [Ναεμ, i. e. *a comforter, penitent, their guide.*] The *feventh* of the twelve minor prophets, a native of *Elkofhai.*

NA-I'-DUS, [Ναϊδⓢ,] One who returned from the babylonifh captivity.

NA'-IM or NA'-IN, [Ναϊν, i. e. *beauty, fairnefs, trouble.*] A city of *Paleftine,* near to mount *Tabor,* towards the fouth: in the tribe of *Iffachar.*

NAI'-OTH, [Ναυάθ, i. e. *comelinefs, a dwelling place.*] A place near to *Ramoth,* where the prophet *Samuel* and his fons dwelt: in the tribe of *Ephraim.*

NA-NE'-A, [Ναναια.] According to the perfian tongue, the goddefs *Diana*.

NA'-OM-I, [Νωεμὶν, i. e. *fair, beautiful, comely.*] The wife of *Elimelech*, and mother of *Ruth*.

NA'-PHISH, [Ναφὲς, i. e. *a foul, refting, multiplying.*] One of the fons of *Ifhmael*.

NAPH'-I-SI, [Ναφισὶ.] One who returned from the babylonifh captivity.

NAPH'-TA-LI, [Νεφθαλείμ, i. e. *my wreftling, likenefs, crookednefs.*] The *fixth* fon of the patriarch *Jacob*, by *Bilhah* the handmaid of *Rachel*.

NAPH'-THAR, [Νέφθαρ, i. e. *a cleanfing.*] A flame fo called in the 2d book of *Maccabees*. See *Nephi*.

NAPH'-TU-HIM, [Νεφθαλείμ, i. e. *open, an opening.*] The *fourth* fon of *Mizraim* the fon of *Ham* the patriarch.

NAR-CIS'-SUS, [Ναρκισσ©, i. e. *aftonifhed, neglecting.*] One mentioned by St. *Paul* in his epiftle to the *Romans*, whom the *Greeks* make to be one of the feventy difciples and bifhop of *Athens*.

NAS'-BAS, [Νασβὰς.] A nephew to *Achiacarus*, the cupbearer to *Sarchedonus* king of *Affyria*.

NA'-SHON, [Νααссὰν.] See NAASHON.

NA'-SITH, [Νασὶθ.] One whofe fons were fervants of the temple.

NA'-SOR, [Αζώρ.] See AZOR.

NA'-THAN, [Ναθαν, i. e. *given, giving, rewarded.*] A fon of king *David* by *Bathfheba*, and father of *Mattatha*—alfo a famous prophet in king *David's* reign, who reproved him in the affair with *Bathfheba*—alfo others of that name.

NA-THAN'-A-EL, [Ναθαναήλ, i. e. *the gift of God.*] A difciple of our *Saviour*, fuppofed to be the fame with *Bartholomew*.

NA-THAN-I'-AS, [Ναθανίας.] One who returned from the babylonifh captivity.

NA-THAN-MEL'-ECH, [Ναθανμέλεχ, i. e. *the gift of a king, the gift of counfel.*] One who was chamberlain to king *Jofiah*.

     NA'-VE,

NA'-VE, [Ναυῆ, i. e. *posterity; fairness; remaining for ever.*] The same person as *Joshua.*

NA'-UM, [Ναὺμ, i. e. *comforted.*] One who is mentioned in St. *Luke*'s genealogy of *Joseph* the virgin *Mary*'s husband.

NAZ'-A-RENES, [Ναζωραῖοι, i. e. *kept, a flower.*] A christian sect who were zealous observers of the law of *Moses* — also the inhabitants of *Nazareth* so called.

NAZ'-A-RETH, [Ναζαρὲτ, i. e. *separated, crowned, sanctified*] A city of lower *Galilee*, in the tribe of *Zebulun*, the usual place of residence of our *Saviour* for the first thirty years of his life; hence he was called a *Nazarene* or an inhabitant of *Nazareth.*

NAZ'-A-RITE. [Ναζαραῖος, i. e. *chosen, separated, distinguished.*] One who observed an uncommon degree of purity, abstaining from wine, letting his hair grow, not entering into an house where a dead body lay, and abstaining from being present at funerals.

N *before* E.

NE'-AH, [i. e. *moved, moving.*] A city of *Palestine*, in the tribe of *Zebulun.*

NE-AP'-OL-IS, [Νεάπολις, i. e. *a new city.*] A city of *Macedonia* in *Asia*, whither St. *Paul* went: now *Napoli.*

NE-AR-I'-AH, [Νεαρία, i. e. *the child of the Lord, the shaking of the Lord, the Lord watching.*] The fifth son of *Shecaniah*; he defeated the *Amalekites* in mount *Seir* — also one of king *David*'s posterity.

NE'-BA-I, [Ναβαὶ, i. e. *budding forth, speaking, prophesying.*] One of the chiefs of the people in *Nehemiah*'s time.

NE-BA'-JOTH, [Ναβαιὼθ, i. e. *buds, fruits, prophecies.*] The first born of *Ishmael.*

NE-BAL'-

NE-BAL'-LAT, [Ναϐαλάτ, i. e. *prophecy, hidden, budding forth.*] A city of *Palestine*, in the tribe of *Benjamin*.

NE'-BAT, [Ναϐὰτ, i. e. *beholding.*] The father of *Jeroboam* the firſt king of *Iſrael:* of the tribe of *Ephraim*, and race of *Joshua*.

NE'-BO, [Ναϐώ. Ναϐαῦ, i. e. *budding forth, speaking, prophesying.*] An idol of the *Babylonians*, ſuppoſed to be the ſame as *Bel* — alſo a mountain of *Palestine*, in the tribe of *Reuben* — alſo one who returned from the babyloniſh captivity.

NEB-U-CHAD-NEZ'-ZAR or NEB-U-CHOD-ON-OS'-OR or NEB-U-CHAD-REZ'-ZAR, [Ναϐχοδονόσορ, i. e. *the mourning of the generation, the ſorrowing of poverty.*] Began to reign at *Nineveh* A. M. 3335; he conquered the *Medes*; his father *Nebuchadnezzar* or *Nabopolaſſer* was founder of the babyloniſh empire.

NEB-U-CHAD-NEZ'-ZAR (*the great*) [Ναϐχοδονόσορ.] A ſon and ſucceſſor of *Nabopolaſſer*, who carried the children of *Iſrael* into captivity A. M. 3398, and died A. M. 3443, after a reign of 44 years.

NEB-U-SHAS'-BAN, [Ναϐυσαχὰν, i. e. *ſpeech, prophecy, ſpringing, flowing.*] A general of *Nebuchadnezzar*'s army.

NEB-U-ZAR'-A-DAN, [Ναϐυζαρδὰν, i. e. *a prophecy of foreign judgment, a budding forth.*] A general of *Nebuchadnezzar*'s army, and chief officer of his houſhold.

NECH'-O, [Νεχαὼ, i. e. *lame, ſmitten.*] A king of *Ægypt* who depoſed *Jehoahaz* king of *Judah*.

NEC-O'-DAN, [Νεχωδὰν.] One whoſe family returned from the babyloniſh captivity.

NE'-CRO-MAN-CER. One who enquires of the dead, or a conſulter of dead idols — their manner of conſulting the dead was, by viſiting their graves in the night, and there ſaying and muttering certain words with a low voice; by which means they pretended to have communion

nion with them by dreams, or by their appearing to them.

NED-A-BI'-AH, [Ναβαδιας, i. e. *the vow of the Lord, the prince of the Lord.*]. One of the posterity of king *David.*

NE-GI'-NOTH. Stringed instruments of musick to be played upon by the fingers of women musicians; and where *Neginoth* is mentioned, in the title of any Psalm, it means, *to the master of musick who presides over the stringed instruments.*

NE-HEL'-AM-ITE, [Νεαιλαμιτης, i. e. *a dreamer, a dream, a valley of waters.*] *Shemaiah* was a *Nehelamite*; but the name of the place or his origin is uncertain.

NE-HEM-I'-AH, [Νεεμια, i. e. *comfort, the rest of the Lord, direction of the Lord.*] He was son of *Hachaliah,* and governor of *Judah* after the return from the babylonish captivity, for about twelve years; he died A. M. 3580: one of the canonical books of the *Old Testament* is called after his name.

NE'-HUM, [Ναυμ, i. e. *a comforter, penitent, a leader of them.*] One who returned from the babylonish captivity.

NE-HUSH'-TA or NE-HUSH'-TAH, [Νεϑα, i. e. *brasen, soothsaying, a serpent.*] The mother of *Jehoiakim* king of *Judah.*

NE-HUSH'-TAN, [Νεεϑαν, i. e. *brasen, made of copper, given of the serpent, soothsaying.*] The name given by king *Hezekiah* to the brasen serpent made by *Moses.*

NE-I'-EL, ['Ιναηλ, i. e. *commotion, moving of God.*] A city of *Palestine,* in the tribe of *Asher.*

NEK'-EB, [Ναβοκ, i. e. *a pipe.*] A city of *Palestine,* in the tribe of *Naphtali.*

NEK-O'-DA, [Νεκωδα, i. e. *painted, inconstant, made crooked.*] One whose children were of the order of *Nethinims.*

NEM-U'-EL, [Ναμυηλ, i. e. *the sleeping of God.*] A son of *Eliab,* of the tribe of *Reuben*—also a son of the patriarch *Simeon.*

NEM-

NEM-U'-ĒL-ITES, [Ναμυηλοῖ.] The posterity of
Nemuel.

NEPH'-EG, [Νέφεγ. Ναφὲκ, i. e. weak, flacked.]
The son of Izhar—also a son of king David.

NEPH'-I, [Νεφθαεί.] The place where Nehemiah
found the muddy water, which was in the pit
where the holy fire had been hid. 2nd Maccabees, chap. 1. ver. 36. See Naphthar.

NEPH'-IS, [Νεφίs.] One who returned from the
babylonish captivity with his family.

NEPH'-ISH, [Ναφίσαιον, i. e. a foul.] A country of
Canaan, which Reuben warred against.

NEPH-ISH'-E-SIM, [Νεφωσκοὶ, i. e. diminished, torn
in pieces.] One whose children were of the order
of Nethinims.

NEPH'-TA-LI, [Νεφθαλείμ, i. e. the same as Naphtali.] A city of Palestine in Galilee, near to
Thisbe.

NEP-THO'-AH, [Ναφθὼ, i. e. open or an opening.]
The name of a fountain of Palestine, in the tribe
of Benjamin.

NEPH'-TU-IM, [Νεφθαλείμ, i. e. open or an opening.]
A son of Mizraim, and grandson to Ham the patriarch.

NEPH-U'-SIM, [Νεφυσίμ, i. e. diminished, torn in
pieces.] One whose children were of the order
of Nethinims.

NĒR, [Νὴρ, i. e. a candle, light, land sown every other
year.] The uncle of king Saul, and father of
Abner.

NE'-RE-US, [Νηρεας, i. c. the same meaning as Ner.]
One whom, with his sister, St. Paul salutes in
his epistle to the Romans.

NER'-GAL, [Εργὲλ, i. e. searching out, a footman, a
candle covered, land sown every other year.] A god
of the Cuthites.

NER'-GAL SHA-REZ'-ER, [Μαργανασὰρ.] A general in Nebuchadnezzar's army.

NE'-RI, [Νηρὶ, i. e. the light or candle of the Lord, land
sown every other year.] One of the ancestors of
Joseph

Joseph the virgin *Mary's* husband, in St. *Luke's* genealogy.

NE-RI'-AH, [Νηρίος, i. e. *the same as Neri.*] The father of the prophet *Baruch.*

NER'-O, [Νέρω.] An emperor of *Rome* who began to reign A. D. 54, and killed himself June 8, A. D. 68, Æt. 32, after a reign of 13 years, 7 months, and 28 days — he first persecuted the christians A. D. 64 — in his reign A. D. 67, St. *Paul* was beheaded and St. *Peter* crucified at *Rome.*

NETH-AN'-E-ĒL, [Ναθαναήλ, i. e. *the gift of God.*] The fourth son of *Jesse* the father of king *David* —also others of that name.

NETH-AN-I'-AH, [Ναθανίας, i. e. *the gift of the Lord.*] One of the royal race of *Judah*, the father of *Ishmael* who slew *Gedaliah*—also others of that name.

NETH'-I-NIMS, Ναθινέοι, i. e. *given, rewarded.*] Persons devoted to the meanest services of the tabernacle and temple; as the carrying of wood, water, &c.

NET-O'-PHAH, [Νετωφάθ, i. e. *dropping down from the head, the bending of the mouth.*] A country and city between *Bethlehem* and *Anathoth* — also one who returned from the babylonish captivity.

NET-O'-PHATH-I, Νετωφατί, i. c. *the same as Netophah.*] A country of the land of *Judæa.*

NET-O'-PHATH-ITES, [Νετωφαθῖτοι.] The inhabitants of *Netophathi.*

NEZ'-I-AH, [Νεσιά, i. c. *a conqueror, everlasting, strong.*] One whose children were of the order of *Nethinims.*

NE'-ZIB, [Νασίβ, i. e. *standing, a standing place, a plant.*] A city of *Palestine*, in the tribe of *Judah*, in the valley.

N before I.

NIB'-BAZ, [Ἐβλαζέρ. Ναιβὰς, i. e. *speaking, budding forth or prophesying a vision.*] A god of the *Avites*, supposed to be in the shape of a *Dog.*

NIB'-

NIB'-SHAN, [Νεβσὰν, i. e. *speech, prophecy, the springing forth of a tooth*.] A city of *Palestine*, in the tribe of *Judah*, in the wilderness.

NI-CA'-NOR, [Νικάνωρ, i. e. *a conqueror, victorious*.] A general of *Antiochus Epiphanes*, who was slain by *Judas Maccabæus*—also a christian deacon.

NIC-OD-E'-MUS, [Νικόδημ☉, i. e. *innocent blood, the victory of the people*.] A jew, a pharisee, and a senator of the *jewish sanhedrim*, who became a disciple of *Jesus Christ*.

NIC-OL-A'-I-TANS, [Νικολαῖτοι.] A sect of christians, founded by *Nicolas* one of the *first seven* deacons of the christian church; they allowed of adultery and the use of meats offered to idols.

NIC'-OL-AS, [Νικόλα☉, i. e. *overcomer, the victories of the common people*.] He was one of the *first* seven deacons of the church, and some suppose that he was the founder of the sect of the *Nicolaitans*: others think it to have been another *Nicolas*.

NIC-OP'-OL-IS, [Νικόπολις, i. e. *a city of victory*.] A city of *Epirus* in *Greece*, where St. *Paul* passed the winter A. D. 64.

NI'-GER, [Νίγερ, i. e. *black, purple, dark*.] A person surnamed *Simeon*, who is mentioned in the book of *Acts*—also a river of *Africa*, rising in *Æthiopia*.

NILE, [Νεῖλ☉.] See RIVER OF EGYPT.

NIM'-RAH or NIM'-RIM, [Ναμρὰ. Νεμηρείμ, i. e. *a leopard, rebellion, bitterness, a chance*.] A city in the land of *Palestine*, in the tribe of *Gad*.

NIM'-ROD, [Νεβρὼδ, i. e. *a rebel, sinner, an apostate*.] The *sixth* son of *Cush*, and the founder of *Babylon* and *Nineveh*.

NIM'-SHI, [Ναμεσσί, i. e. *rescued or touched*.] The grandfather of *Jehu*.

NIN'-E-VEH or NIN'-E-VE, [Νινευί. Νινευὴ, i. e. *fair, beautiful, a dwelling place*.] The capital city of *Assyria*, on the banks of the river *Tigris*; said to be founded by *Nimrod*, or *Ashur* the son of *Shem*.

NIN'-

NIN'-E-VITES, [Νινευῖται.] The inhabitants of *Nineveh*.

NI'-SAN, [Νισὰν, i. e. *a banner, a proving, trying flight, a miracle.*] A *jewish* month anſwering to about our *March*.

NIS'-ROCH, [Νεσρὰχ, i. e. *flight, a tender trying, banner, thy table.*] A god, worſhipped by the *Aſſyrians*.

N *before* O.

NO, [Νῶ, i. e. *a ſtirring up, a forbidding.*] The antient city of *Thebes* in *Ægypt*, which had an hundred gates: it is ſometimes called *No-Ammon* or *Hammon-No*, from *Ham* who ſettled in *Egypt*.

NO-AD-I'-AH, [Νωαδία, i. e. *the witneſſing of the Lord, the Lord taking way.*] The name of one of the *Levites*, in *Ezra* and *Nehemiah*.

NO'-AH or NO'-E, [Νῶε. Νουὰ, i. e. *ceaſing, reſt.*] The father of the poſtdiluvian world; the ſon of *Lamech*, born A. M. 1056: the deluge was A. M. 1656: he lived after the flood 350 years, and died A. M. 2006, Æt. 950—alſo a daughter of *Zelophehad*.

NOB, [Νομβᾶ, i. e. *ſpeech, prophecy, ſpringing forth, barking, barked at.*] A city of *Paleſtine*, in the tribe of *Benjamin*.

NOB'-AH, [Ναβαὺ, i. e. *barking, barked at.*] A city of *Paleſtine* beyond *Jordan*, which took its name from *Nobah* an *Iſraelite* who conquered it.

NOD, [Ναιδ, i. e. *fugitive.*] A country on the eaſt of *Eden*.

NOD'-AB, [Ναδαβαιης, i. e. *vowing of his own accord, principal.*] A country bordering upon *Iturea* and *Idumæa*.

NO-EB'-A, [Νοεβὰ.] One whoſe family returned from the babyloniſh captivity, and his ſons ſervants of the temple.

NO'-GA or NO'-GAH, [Νώγα. Ναγαὶ, i. e. *brightneſs, clearneſs.*] The name of one of king *David*'s ſons.

NO'-HAH,

NO'-HAH, [Νωὰ, i. e. *refting, a guide.*] The *fourth* fon of the patriarch *Benjamin.*

NŌM, [Νὰν.] A defcendant from the patriarch *Benjamin.*

NOM'-A-DES, [Νομάδες, i. e. *men wandering here and there.*] A name given to the people who tended their flocks, and fhifted from place to place.

NŌN, [Νὰν.] See *Nom.*

NOPH or MEM'-PHIS, [Μέμφεως, i. e. *a honey comb, a diftilling from the head, a lifting up, a furve.*] A famous city of *Ægypt,* the antient refidence of the kings of *Ægypt.*

NOPH'-AH, [i. e. *fearful, binding.*] A city of the *Moabites.*

N *before* U.

NUMBERS, ['Αριθμόι.] The *fourth* canonical book of the *Pentateuch* in the *Old Teftament;* fo called from the numbering of the families of *Ifrael* by *Mofes* and *Aaron.*

NU-ME'-NI-US, [Νεμηνι&.] A fon of *Antiochus Epiphanes.*

NŪN, [Ναυη. Νὲν, i. e. *fon, pofterity, flock, everlafting, a fifh.*] The fon of *Elifhama,* and father of *Jofhua,* of the tribe of *Ephraim.*

N *before* Y.

NYM'-PHAS, [Νυμφὰς, i. e. *a bride.*] One whom St. *Paul* falutes in his epiftle to the *Coloffians.*

O.

O *before* B.

OB-A-DI'-AH, ['Οϐδίας. 'Οϐδιϐέ, i. e. *servant of the Lord.*] A valiant man of king *David*'s army— also a fteward of king *Ahab*—alfo the *fourth* of the twelve lefter prophets, after whom the canonical book of the *Old Teftament, Obadiah,* was named—alfo a porter of the temple.

OB'-AL, [Γεϐαλ. 'Ευαλ, i. e. *the forwardnefs of antiquity, flowing.*] One of the pofterity of the patriarch *Shem.*

O'-BĒD, ['Ωϐηδ, i. e. *a servant, a workman.*] The fon of *Boaz* and father of *Jeffe* — alfo one of king *David*'s worthies—alfo others of that name.

O'-BĒD ED'-ŌM, ['Ωϐηθ Εδόμ. 'Αϐδεδόμ, i. e. *the servant of Edom, a servant Edomite.*] The fon of *Jeduthun* the *Levite.*

O'-BĒTH, ['Ωϐηθ.] One who returned from the babylonifh captivity.

O'-BIL, ['Ωϐιλ, i. e. *borne, brought, led away, sorrowful, waxing old.*] An *Ifhmaelite,* who had the care of king *David*'s camels.

O'-BŌTH, ['Ωϐωθ, i. e. *dragons, fathers, defires.*] The *thirty-feventh* encampment of the *Ifraelites,* in the wildernefs.

O *before* C.

OCH'-I-ĒL, ['Οχιϵ̄λ.] One of king *Jofiah's* captains over thoufands.

Ō-CID-E'-LUS, [Ωκόδηλ☉.] One whofe family returned from the babylonifh captivity.

OC'-I-NĀ, ['Oκινὰ.] A place mentioned in the book
of *Judith.*

OC'-RĀN, ['Εχράν, i. e. *troubling, troublefome.*]. One
of the tribe of *Afher*, the father of *Pagiel.*

O *before* D.

O'-DĒD, [Ωδηδ, i. e. *fuftaining, lifting up.*] A prophet of the Lord mentioned in the fecond book
of *Chronicles.*

OD-OL'-LAM, ['Oδολλάμ.] A city of *Idumæa.*

OD-ON-AR'-KES, ['Oδομηρᾶ. 'Oδοααρρης, i. e. *the
fon of praife, witnefs of a coffer.*] An ally of *Bac-
chides* the enemy of the *Jews.*

O *before* F.

OF'-FER-INGS. Among the *jews*, under the mofaic
law, there were a variety of offerings inftituted,
which are accurately defcribed in the beginning
of the book of *Leviticus,* as

Burnt-offerings: thefe were to confift, either of
the herd, and out of that the bullock only, and
he without blemifh—or of the flock, as the fheep
or the goat, and out of that the male only, and
he without blemifh—or laftly, of fowls, the turtle dove or the young pigeon — thefe *five* were
the only offering for a burnt facrifice, which
was to be wholly deftroyed by fire, and at the
door of the tabernacle only; except what was
thrown away of the legs and infides of the bullock, fheep or goat, and the crop and feathers
of the birds. There was no unclean beaft or
bird to be offered—and thefe were to be offered

Q   by

by way of atonement for fin. *Philo*, the learned
jew, obferves, that the offerer was to be like his
oblation; if fo, then induftry and innocence,
ufefulnefs and fimplicity are recommended, by
this inftitution, to the worfhippers of GOD.

Drink-offerings. With a *bullock, half a hin of
wine*, with three tenth deals of flour and half a
hin of oil.

With a *Ram, one third of an hin of wine*, with
two tenth deals of flour and one third of an
hin of oil.

With a *lamb* or a *kid* of the *goat, one quarter of
an hin of wine*, with one tenth deal of flour and
one quarter of an hin of oil.

With a *fheaf of the firft fruits, one quarter of an
hin of wine*, with one tenth deal of flour with oil.

Heave-offering. It is fo called, from the facrifice being lifted up towards heaven in token of
its being devoted to GOD.

Meat-offering. It might well be tranflated
wheat-offering, as it confifted, chiefly, of *flour*;
for no fort of flefh was to be offered in it—it
confifted of things inanimate, as *flour, bread, oil,
wine, falt, frankincenfe, &c.*—the wave fheaf and
the two wave loaves for the whole congregation,
and the others for private perfons according
to their ability in the expence of their offering
—the bread was to be *unleavened*, for *Maimonides*
fays, it was to diftinguifh the worfhippers of
the true God from the *Zabian* idolaters of thofe
times, who offered to their gods no bread but
leavened.

Peace-offering. It was an offering of thankf-
giving for peace, or for mercies received—fometimes it was offered by way of *vow*, in hope of
peace or future bleffings; and fometimes it was
offered without any antecedent obligation of a
vow, in which cafe it was called a *free-will-offering.*
The *fin* and *trefpafs-offering* fuppofed the offender
obnox-

obnoxious, and GOD difpleafed; but the *peace-offering* fuppofed GOD to be reconciled to the offerer, and him to be at peace with GOD. In the *fin* and *trefpafs-offering*, though the priefts partook of it, yet the offerer had no fhare; but in the *peace-offering* both prieft and offerer partook and feafted upon it. In the *burnt-offering* or *holocauft* the whole facrifice was confumed by fire, and neither prieft or offerer partook of them.

Sin-offering. Sin offerings were for expiation of particular fins or legal imperfections, called therefore, *fin-offerings*—the firft fort were for fins of ignorance or furprize, either by the high-prieft or body of the community, by the rulers, or by any one of the common people. The other fort of fin-offering was for *voluntary* fins; but as to the more capital violations of the *moral* law, as for *murder, adultery,* or the *worfhip of idols,* no expiatory facrifice was admitted.

Trefpafs-offering. It was for concealing the knowledge of a thing, as a witnefs; for touching an unclean thing; or in making a rafh oath —the offender, in this cafe, was to offer a female from the flock, a lamb or a kid; or two turtle-doves or two young pigeons—but if the trefpafs related to *holy things,* then the trefpaffer was to offer a ram without blemifh.

Wave-offering. It was fo called, becaufe it was waved *up* and *down,* and *eaft, weft, north,* and *fouth,* to fignify that he to whom it was offered, was Lord of the whole world, the GOD who fills all fpace, and to whom all things of right belong.

There were *annually* facrificed at the *national* charge,

1201 Lambs
132 Bullocks
72 Rams
21 Kids
2 Goats

befides *voluntary, vow* and *trefpafs* offerings.

O *before* G.

ŌG, ['Ωγ, i. e. *roasted bread, a mock, hindred.*]　A giant who was king of *Bashan:* his bed was *fifteen feet* and *nine inches* long, and *six feet* wide.

O *before* H.

O'HAD, ['Aωδ, i. e. *praising, confessing.*]　One of the sons of the patriarch *Simeon*.

O'-HEL, ['Oὸλ, i. e. *a tabernacle, tent, light.*]　One of the posterity of king *David*.

O *before* L.

O'-LA-MUS, ["Ωλαμὸs.]　One who returned from the babylonish captivity.

OL'-IVES (*mount of*) or OL'-I-VET.　An hill two miles to the east of *Jerusalem*, and parted from the city by the brook *Kidron* or *Cedron*.

OL-YM'-PHAS, ['Oλυμπάs, i. e. *heavenly.*]　A christian of note, whom St. *Paul* salutes in his epistle to the *Romans*.

OL-YM'-PI-US JU'-PI-TER, [Διὸs 'Oλυμπυ, i. e. *heavenly.*]　An heathen god whose statue *Antiochus Epiphanes* ordered to be erected in the temple of *Jerusalem*.

O *before* M.

O-MA-E'-RUS, ['Iσμαῆρ⊙.]　One who returned from the babylonish captivity.

O'-MAR, ['Ωμὰρ, i. e. *speaking, exalting.*]　A son of *Eliphaz*, and grandson of *Esau*.

O'-MEG-A, [Ω.]　The *last* letter of the greek alphabet: our *Saviour*, in the Revelation of St. *John*, is stiled the *Alpha* and *Omega*, or the first and the last: *Alpha* being the *first* letter in the same alphabet.

OM'-ER,

OM'-ER, [Γομὸϱ.] An hebrew meafure, fee *Homer*—alfo the name of a fon of *Eliphaz*, and grandfon of *Efau*; fee *Omar*.

OM'-RI, ['Αμϐρὶ. 'Αμρί, i. e. *a bundle, or a rebellicus or bitter people.*] A general of the army of *Elah* king of *Ifrael*, and fucceeded him: he died A. M. 3086, and was fucceeded by *Ahab*—alfo a grandfon of the patriarch *Benjamin*.

O before N.

ŌN, ['Αυν, i. e. *forrow, ftrength, iniquity.*] A country of *Ægypt*—alfo one of the rebels againft *Mofes*.

O'-NAM, ['Ωνάν, i. e. *forrow, ftrength, the iniquity of them.*] The fon of *Jerahmeel* by his wife *Atarah*—alfo the fon of *Shobal*.

O'-NAN, ['Αυάν, i. e. *the fame as On.*] A fon of the patriarch *Judah*.

ON-E'-SI-MUS, ['Ονησιμ☺, i. e. *as profitable.*] A *Phrygian* by birth, and flave of *Philemon*, to whom St. *Paul* wrote an epiftle: it is faid, *Onefimus* became a chriftian, and that St. *Paul* made him bifhop of *Berea* in *Macedonia*.

ON-E-SIPH'-OR-US, ['Ονησιφόρ☺, i. e. *bringing profit.*] A firm friend of St. *Paul*, who came to him at *Rome*, from *Afia*, and affifted him in his imprifonment.

ON-I'-A-RĒS, ['Ονιάρης.] The name of a *Lacedæmonian* king. See *Areus*.

ON-I'-AS, ['Ονίας, i. e. *the ftrength of the Lord, a fhip.*] The name of two high priefts, in the fecond book of *Maccabees*.

O'-NO, ['Ωνὼ, i. e. *grief, ftrength, iniquity of him.*] A city in the tribe of *Benjamin*, in *Palefline*.

O'-NŪS, ['Ωνὺς.] One who returned from the babylonifh captivity.

ON'-Y-CHA, ['Ονυχα.] An aromatic plant of *Arabia*: fome take it to be *bdellium*.

ON'-YX, [Ονὺξ.] A precious ftone: being the *fecond* ftone in the *fourth* row in the breaft-plate of the

jewifh

jewiſh high prieſt: the colour is of a whitiſh ground, of the colour of a human nail, with regular zones of brown.

O before P.

O'-PHEL, ['Oπὲλ. Ὦφὰλ, i. e. *a tower, darkneſs, a little white cloud.*] A place on the wall of *Jeruſalem*, or a tower near to it.

O'-PHER, ['Ουφεὶρ, i. e. *aſhes, a making fruitful.*] A ſon of *Joktan*, and grandſon of *Eber*.

O'-PHIR, [Ούφὶρ, i. e. *the ſame as Opher.*] A celebrated country for gold, but uncertain where: ſome ſuppoſe it to be the iſland *Taprobane*, now *Ceylon*, in *Eaſt India*; others ſuppoſe it to be the peninſula oppoſite the iſland *Sumatra* in *Eaſt India*—alſo the name of a deſcendant from the patriarch *Shem*.

OPH'-NI, ['Aφνεὶ, i. e. *fleeting, wearineſs, a folding together.*] A city of *Paleſtine*, in the tribe of *Benjamin*.

OPH'-RAH, ['Εφρὰ. Γοφερὰ, i. e. *duſt, lead, a fawn.*] A city of *Paleſtine*, in the tribe of *Benjamin*.

O before R.

O'-REB, ['Ὦρὴβ, i. e. *a crow, pleaſant, mingling together, a commander by faith, the evening.*] One of the princes of *Midian*, ſlain on the rock *Oreb*.

O'-REN or O'-RAN, ['Aρὰμ, i. e. *a coffer, rejoicing, the ſlander of them.*] The ſon of *Jehrameel*, and grandſon to *Hezron*, of the poſterity of *Judah*.

O-RI'-ON, ['Ὦρίων.] A conſtellation of the heavens, ſuppoſed to rule in *November*.

OR'-NAN, ['Oρνὰ. Oρνὰν.] See *Araunah*.

OR'-PHAH, ['Oρφᾶ, i. e. *a neck, ſtiff necked, making bare the mouth.*] The name of a *Moabitiſh* woman.

OR-THO'-SI-AS, ['Oρθωσιὰς, i. e. *upright, rectified.*] A town at the foot of mount *Libanus*.

O *before* S.

O-SAI'-AS, ['Ωσαιας.] The son of *Channuneus.*

O-SE'-AS or O'-SEE, ['Ωσηε.] The same with *Hosea*
the prophet.

O-SHE'-A, ['Αυση.] The same with *Joshua.*

OS'-PRAY. The *sea eagle,* a bird of prey, very
strong and swift.

OS'-SI-FRAGE. A species of *eagle,* so called from
its breaking the bones of its prey, which it car-
ries high in the air, and then lets it fall upon a
rock.

OS'-TRICH. An *african* bird, wild, and of the shape
of a goose, but much larger—it is very tall, so
that, sometimes, they are tutored to carry a person upon their backs—It is usually *seven feet* high
from the top of the head to the ground, the neck
being about three feet of the *seven* — when the
neck is stretched out in a right line, he is about
six feet from head to tail, and the tail is about
twelve inches long—the wings are short but strong
—it is very swift of foot, and its wings help in
running, but it cannot fly—the plumage is black,
white or grey — it devours almost any thing,
even metals, but as to its digesting iron, it is fabulous—it is bred in dry desarts, and the female
lays its eggs in the sand, ten or twelve together,
as large as a common bowl—it is said that she is
so forgetful as not to remember the place where
she lays them, so that when she comes to any
place where there are eggs, she sits upon them
and hatches them—when they are hunted, they
run with such velocity and strength so as to fling
the stones behind them which annoy their pur-
suers.

O *before* T.

OTH'-NI, ['Οθνι, i. e. *my time, my hour.*] One of
the porters of the temple of *Jerusalem.*

Q 4

OTH'-

OTH'-NI-ĒL, [Γοθουμλ, i. e. *the time or hour of God.*]
The *second* judge of *Ifrael*; he married *Achfa* the
daughter of *Caleb*; he was of the tribe of *Judah*,
and died A. M. 2610.

OTH-ON-I'-AS, [Oθovias.] One who returned from
the babylonifh captivity, a porter or guard of the
temple.

O *before* U.

OUCH'-ES. *Ouches* are the fockets in which ftones
are fet in any metals.

O *before* X.

ŌX, ['Ωξ, i. e. *pleafant, merry.*] The daughter of
Merari, mentioned in the book of *Judith*, in the
Apocrypha.

O *before* Z.

ŌZ, ['Ωζ.] See *Ox*.

O'-ZEM, ['Aπàμ, i. e. *the hafting of them, fafting.*]
The *fixth* fon of *Jeffe* the father of king *David*.

OZ-I'-AS, ['Oζias, i. e. *the ftrength or buck goat of the
Lord.*] The fon of *Micha*, of the tribe of *Simeon*,
and a governor of *Bethulia*.

OZ'-I-ĒL, ['Oζιηλ.] An anceftor of *Judith*.

OZ'-NI, ['Aζενí, i. e. *an ear, my hearkening, a goldfmith's balance.*] A fon of *Gad* the patriarch,
chief of the family of the *Oznites*.

OZ'-NITES. Defcendants from *Ozni*.

OZ-O'-RA, ['Eζωρà.] One who returned from the
babylonifh captivity.

P *before*

P,

P *before* A.

PA'-A-RAI, [Φααραì, i. e. *a gaping, an opening.*] The name of an *Arbite*, one of king *David*'s valiant men.

PA'-DAN. The father of one of the *Nethinims*.

PA-DAN A'-RAM. A city of *Syria* where *Laban* dwelt: now *Diarbec proper* in afiatic *Turkey*.

PA'-DŌN, [Φαδὼν, i. e. *his redemption, the yoke of an ox.*] One whofe children were of the order of *Nethinims*.

PA-GI'-EL, [Φαγαιηλ, i. e. *God hath met, the requiring pardon of God.*] A fon of *Ocran*, and head of the tribe of *Afher*.

PA'-HATH MO'-AB, [Φααθ Μωαϐ, i. e. *a duke of Moab.*] A place in the country of the *Moabites* —alfo one who returned from the babylonifh captivity.

PA'-I, [Φαὶ, i. e. *howling, fighing, appearing.*] A city in the land of *Edom*.

PAL'-AL, [Φολὰχ. Φαλάλι, i. e. *thinking, judging.*] One who repaired the walls of *Jerufalem*.

PAL'-EST-INE, [Φυλιϛιειμ, i. e. *ftrewed or covered with afhes or duft, the drink, decay, double decay.*] The antient country of the *Palefines*, extending from *Gaza* fouth, to *Lydda* north: in a more general

general fenfe, it is the whole land of *Promife,*
or *Canaan,* or the land of *Judæa:* it was about
200 miles long, and 80 miles broad about the
middle.

PAL'-LU, [Φαλλὸς, i. e. *marvellous, wonderful, hidden.*]
One of the fons of the patriarch *Reuben.*

PAL-LU'-ITES, [Φαλλμαῖ.]　The defcendants from
Pallu.

PALM'-TREE, ['Αμπελ⊙.] The *Palm-Tree* is a tall
ftrait tree, growing fometimes to the height of
an hundred feet—it is common in *Africa;* and
from its trunk the natives extract a liquor, called
palm-wine, refembling whey in colour, but very
fweet—it is extracted by making an incifion at
the top of the trunk, to which they apply *gourd-
bottles,* into which the liquor runs by pipes made
of its leaves—the wine is purgative when new;
but if kept two or three days, it ferments, grows
ftrong, and is palatable and wholefome—the *leaves,*
which are large, ferve for the coverings of houfes
—palm trees are common alfo in *Afia;* and *Jericho* was called *the city of palm-trees.*

PAL'-TI, [Φαλτὶ, i. e. *deliverance, banifhment.*] One
of the tribe of *Benjamin,* who went to fearch the
land of *Canaan.*

PAL'-TI-EL, [Φαλτιὴλ, i. e. *deliverance, banifhment
of God.*] A fon of *Azzan,* of the tribe of *Iffachar.*

PAL'-TITE. One who is of the pofterity of *Palti.*

PAM-PHYL'-I-A, [Παμφυλία, i. e. *a nation made up
of every tribe.*] A province of *Afia Minor,* whofe
coafts are wafhed by the *mediterranean fea.*

PAN'-NAG, [Φαννάγ.] A word mentioned in *Ezekiel's* prophecy; but it is uncertain whether it is
the name of a *place,* or of fome rich *ointment* or
gum.

PA'-PHOS, [Πάφ⊙.] A city of *Cyprus* Ifle, where
Venus, the heathen goddefs had a temple; and
where *Sergius Paulus,* the roman proconful, who
was converted to chriftianity by St. *Paul,* had a
feat: now *Baffa.*

PAR'-

PAR'-A-DISE, [Παραδεισ⊙.] The situation of it was supposed to be in *Chaldæa*, in *Asia*—metaphorically, it signifies a future state of happiness.

PA'-RAH, [Φαρὰ, i. e. *a cow, increasing, stirring up.*] A city of *Palestine*, in the tribe of *Benjamin*.

PA'-RAN, [Φαρὰν, i. e. *fairness, praise, springs.*] A desart of *Arabia Petræa*, to the south of the land of *Palestine*.

PAR'-BAR. A gate or building belonging to the city of *Jerusalem*.

PAR-MASH'-TA, [Φαρμοσθά, i. e. *the breaking of a foundation, a bull of one year old.*] The *seventh* son of *Haman*, who was hanged with his nine brethren, at the same time his father was.

PAR'-MEN-AS, [Παρμενᾶς, i. e. *continuing.*] One of the *first* seven deacons of the christian church.

PAR'-NATH or PAR'-NACH, [Φαρνάχ, i. e. *a bull smiting, smit, broken.*] One of the posterity of the patriarch *Zebulun*.

PA'-ROSH, [Φάρ⊙, i. e. *a flea, a gnat.*] One whose sons returned from the babylonish captivity.

PAR-SHAN'-DA-THA, [Φαρσανδαθά, i. e. *of his trouble, dung of impurity.*] The *eldest* son of *Haman*, who was hanged at the same time his father and nine brethren were.

PAR'-THI-ANS, [Πάρθοι, i. e. *fleers for fear, banished men.*] *Persians*, known in *Scripture* by the name of *Elamites*, until near the time of *Cyrus*.

PA'-RU-AH, [Φηασὺδ, i. e. *fresh, flourishing.*] One of the tribe of *Issachar*, father of *Jehosaphat*.

PAR-VA'-IM, [Φαρυίμ.] Supposed to be *Taprobane*, or what is now called the island *Ceylon*, in *East India*.

PA'-SACH, [Φασὲκ, i. e. *thy broken piece, thy diminishing.*] One of the posterity of the patriarch *Asher*.

PAS-DAM'-MIM, [Φασδαμίμ, i. e. *a portion, diminishing of blood.*] A place in *Palistia*.

PAS-E'-AH, [Φεσσή. Βεσσή, i. e. *a passing over, an halting.*] One whose children were of the order of *Nethinims*.

PASH'-ŬR, [Φασεὺρ, i. e. *increasing liberty, spreading out whiteness.*] A prieſt who ſealed the covenant with *Nehemiah.*

PASS-O'-VER, [Πάσχα.] An annual feſtival of the *Jews*, in commemoration of their departure from *Ægypt*; becauſe, the night before it, the angel, who deſtroyed the firſt born of the *Ægyptians*, paſſed over the houſes of the *Hebrews:* it is ſtill kept on the *fourteenth* day of the month next after the vernal equinox, or *April.*

PA'-TA-RA, [Πάταρα, i. e. *white limed, bringing death.*] A maritime city of *Lycia*, a province of *Aſia.*

PA-THE'-US, [Παθαῖος.] A *Levite* who returned from the babyloniſh captivity.

PATH'-RŌS, [Φαθωρῆς. Παθύρης, i. e. *a morſel of dough, a perſuaſion of decay.*] A canton and city of *Ægypt*, in *Africa.*

PATH-RŪ'-SIM, [Πατροσωνιεὶμ, i. e. *the ſame as Pathros.*] The *fifth* ſon of *Mizraim*, and grandſon of *Ham* the patriarch.

PAT'-MOS, [Πάτμ☉, i. e. *deadly, bringing death.*] An iſland of the *Ægean ſea*, to which St. *John* was baniſhed, A. D. 94.

PA'-TRI-ARCH, [Πατριάρχης, i. e. *a head of a family.*] *Adam, Lamech, Noah*, and other heads of families *before the flood* are called *ante-diluvian Patriarchs:* *Shem, Abraham* and other heads of families *after the flood* are called *poſt-diluvian Patriarchs.*

PAT'-ROB-AS, [Πατρόβας, i. e. *pertaining to the father.*] A diſciple of the Apoſtles.

PA-TROC'-LUS, [Πατρόκλ☉, L. *Pat'-roc-lus*, i. e. *of the father; the glory of the country.*] The father of *Nicanor* in the 2d book of *Maccabees.*

PA'-U. See PA'-I.

PAUL, (St.) [Παῦλ☉, i. e. *marvellous, entry into a flock, reſt, little.*] Formerly called *Saul*, of the tribe of *Benjamin*, a phariſee, a native of *Tarſus*, in *Cilicia*; firſt a great perſecutor of the chriſtian church, and then miraculouſly converted, on his way to *Damaſcus* in order to bring the chriſtians

tians, there, to *Jerufalem*; he was martyred by beheading, A. D. 66, Æt. 68.

PAUL'-US SER'-GI-US, [Παύλ🟐 Σεργίος, i. e. *Sergius fignifies a net.*] A proconful of *Cyprus* Ifle, and converted to chriftianity by St. *Paul*, about A. D. 44, or 45.

P *before* E.

PE-DA'-HĒL, [Φαδαήλ, i. e. *the redemption of God.*] A fon of *Ammihud*, of the tribe of *Naphtali*.

PE-DAH'-ZŪR, [Φαδασύρ, i. e. *a ftrong redeemer, a ftone redeeming.*] The father of *Gamaliel*, head of the tribe of *Manaffeh* when the *Ifraelites* came out of *Ægypt*.

PE-DA-I'-AH, [Φαδαϊάς, i. e. *the Lord's redeeming.*] A fon of *Feconiah* king of *Judah*, and father of *Zerubbabel* and *Shimei*—alfo others of that name.

PE'-KAH, [Φακεὲ, i. e. *opening.*] A fon of *Remaliah*, and general of the army of *Pekahiah* king of *Ifrael*; and fucceeded him.

PE-KA-HI'-AH, [Φακεσίας, i. e. *the Lord opening.*] Son and fucceffor of *Manahem* king of *Ifrael*.

PE'-KŌD, [Φακὺθ. Φακῦκ, i. e. *noble, rulers.*] Suppofed to be a title or degree of honour among the *Babylonians*; but it is mentioned as a city.

PEL-A-I'-AH, [Φαδαία. Φαλία, i. e. *the miracle, or fecret of the Lord.*] A *Levite* who fealed the covenant with *Nehemiah* the governor, the fon of *Eliænai*.

PEL-AL-I'-AH, [Φαλαλία, i. e. *thinking on the Lord, entreating the Lord, the judgment of the Lord.*] A fon of *Amzi* and father of *Jehoram*.

PEL-AT-I'-AH, [Φαλετῖα, i. e. *the deliverance, fetting free, or banifhment of the Lord.*] A fon of *Benaiah*, and prince of the people in the time of *Zedekiah* king of *Judah*, and who oppofed *Jeremiah*'s advice in fubmitting to king *Nebuchadnezzar*—alfo others.

PE'-LEG,

PE'-LEG, [Φαλὲγ, i. e. *a division.*] A grandſon of *Arphaxad* the ſon of *Shem,* he died A. M. 1996, Æt. 239.

PEL'-ĒT, [Φαλλήτ, i. e. *deliverance, baniſhment.*] A ſon of *Jahdai* of the poſterity of *Judah*—alſo one who reſorted to king *David* at *Ziklag.*

PEL'-ETH, [Φαλὲθ, i. e. *decay, judging.*] A ſon of *Jonathan,* a deſcendant from *Judah*—alſo a ſon of *Reuben.*

PEL'-ETH-ITES. Of the family of *Peleth,* famous warriors in the army of king *David*; and they, together with the *Cherethites,* had the guard of his perſon.

PEL'-I-AS, [Πεδίας.] One who returned from the babyloniſh captivity.

PEL'-I-CAN, [Πελεκὰν.] A bird both of *Aſia* and *Africa*—it is in the ſhape of and as large as a *ſwan,* and ſome of them much larger; the beak and feathers ſomething ſimilar—it hath a fleſhy bag at its throat to hold proviſions for its young, large enough to contain a man's head—it frequents freſh and ſalt waters, foreſts and groves— it principally feeds upon fiſh and water inſects— it builds its neſt in groves or buſhy places— after having fed itſelf, it then feeds its young, who eat out of the bag at its throat; from whence aroſe the vulgar error that its young fed on its *blood.*

PEL-O'-NITE, [i. e. *falling, hid, ſecret.*] *Helez* one of king *David's* valiant men was a *Pelonite*; but the origin of *Pelonite* is uncertain.

PEN-I'-ĒL, [Φανυὴλ, i. e. *ſeeing God, the face of God.*] A city of *Paleſtine,* to the eaſt of the river *Jordan,* near to the brook *Jabbok,* in the tribe of *Gad*— alſo the father of *Geder.*

PEN-IN'-NAH, [Φεννάνα, i. e. *a precious ſtone, our face.*] The ſecond wife of *Elkanah* the father of the prophet *Samuel.*

PENT-AP'-OL-IS. The name given to the *five* cities of *Sodom, Gomorrah, Admah, Zeboim,* and *Bela* or *Zoar.*

PENT'-

PENT'-A-TEUCH. The name given to the *five ca-nonical* books of *Moses*, viz. *Genesis, Exodus, Le-viticus, Numbers, Deuteronomy:* which contains the history of the world from the creation, for the first 2553 years.

PENT'-E-COST, [Πεντηκοςὸς.] A *jewish* feast, held in memory of the law given to *Moses* on mount *Sinai*, fifty days after the departure of the *Israel-ites* from *Ægypt:* it was celebrated fifty days after the *Pass-over*.

PEN-U'-EL, [Φανυηλ.] See PENIEL.

PE'-ŌR, [Φογὼϱ, i. e. *gaping, opening*.] A famous high place in the land of *Moab*.

PER'-A-ZIM, [Φαϱασὶν, i. e. *irruption*.] A mountain of *Palestine* where the *Philistines* were defeated.

PE'-RESH, [Φαϱές, i. e. *an horseman, casting out to be slain, declaring*.] The son of *Machir*, one of *Ma-nasseh's* posterity.

PE'-REZ, [Φαϱὲς.] It signifies, *thy kingdom is di-vided and given to the Persians*, who were called *Paros* by the *Chaldeans*—also one of king *Solomon's* captains.

PE'-REZ UZ'-ZA, [Φαϱὲς ʼΟζὰ, i. e. *the division of Uzzah, the division of strength or of a goat*.] The place so called, where *Uzzah* was struck dead for touching the ark.

PER'-GA, [Πέϱγη, i. e. *very earthly*.] A city of *Pamphylia* in *Asia*.

PER'-GA-MOS or PER'-GA-MUS, [Πέϱγαμ☉, i. e. *height*.] A celebrated city of *Troas* in *Asia*.

PER-I'-DA, [Φαϱεῖδα, i. e. *separation, division*.] One whose children were king *Solomon's* servants.

PER-IZ'-ZITES, [Φεϱεζαῖοι, i. e. *rural, dwelling in unwalled villages, dispersed*.] The antient inhabi-tants of *Palestine*, mixed with the *Canaanites*.

PER'-MEN-AS, [Παϱμεμᾶς.] See PARMENAS.

PER-SEP'-OL-IS, [Περσέπολις.] The capital city of antient *Persia*.

PER'-SE-US, [Περσέυς.] A king of the *Cittims* or *Macedonians*.

PER'-

PER'-SI-A, [Περσὶς, i. e. *breaking, dividing, a horse-hoof.*] An antient kingdom of *Asia*, its monarchy founded by *Cyrus:* the antient name of its inhabitants was, *Elamites:* the *Romans* called them *Parthians.*

PER'-SI-ANS, [Πέρσαι.] · The inhabitants of *Persia.*

PER'-SIS, [Περσὶς, i. e. *the same as Persia.*] A roman lady, saluted by St. *Paul,* in his epistle to the *Romans.* ·

PER-U'-DA, [Φαδκρὰ, i. e. *separation, division.*] One of the servants of king *Solomon.*

PE'-TER, (*Simon*) [Πέτρ⊙, i. e. *a stone, a rock.*] One of the apostles, son of *Jona* and brother of *Simon,* born at *Bethsaida,* was a fisherman; and was martyred at *Rome* by crucifixion, with his head downward at his own desire, A. D. 66: two of the books of the *New Testament* were named from him.

PETH-A-HI'-AH, [Φεταϊα. Βεθθεεὶα, i. e. *the Lord opening, the gate of the Lord.*] The head of the *nineteenth* family of the sacerdotal order.

PETH'-OR, [Φαθκρὰ, i. e. *a table.*] A city of *Mesopotamia,* where *Balaam* was born.

PETH-U'-EL, [Βαθκὴλ, i. e. *a persuasion of God, the enlarging of God.*] The father of the prophet *Joel.*

PE-UL'-THAI, [Φελαθὶ, i. e. *my works, my work.*] The *eighth* son of *Obed-Edom.*

P before H.

PHAC'-A-RETH, [Φαχαρὲθ.] One whose family returned from the babylonish captivity.

PHAI'-SUR, [Φαισὴρ.] One who returned from the babylonish captivity.

PHAL-DAI'-US, [Φαλδαῖος.] One who returned from the babylonish captivity.

PHA-LE'-AS, [Φαλαι⊙.] One whose sons were servants of the temple.

PHA'-LEG, [Φαλὲγ, i. e. *a division.*] One mentioned by St. *Luke* in his genealogical list.

PHAL'.

PHAL'-LU, [Φαλλὸs.] See *Pallu*.

PHAL'-TI or PHAL'-TI-ĒL, [Φαλτιnλ, i. e. *deliverance, banifhment.*] A fon of *Laifh*; he married *Michal*, after *Saul* had taken her from *David*; but *David* afterwards took her from *Phalti*.

PHAN-U'-ĒL, [Φανunλ, i. e. *feeing God, the face of God.*] Father of the prophetefs *Anna*; of the tribe of *Afher*.

PHA'-RA-CIM, [Φαραχὲμ.] One whofe family returned from the babylonifh captivity.

PHA'-RA-ŌH, [Φαραὼ, i. e. *fpreading abroad, uncovering, vengeance, a king.*] A common name of the kings of *Egypt*; as *Cæfar* was among the *Romans: ten* of that name are mentioned in *Scripture*.

PHA'-RA-ŌH HO'-PHRA, [Φαραω Ουαῤῥα.] A king of *Ægypt*, fometimes called *Apries*, he reigned 594 years before the birth of *Chrift*, in the reign of king *Zedekiah*.

PHA'-RA-ŌH NECH'-O, [Φαραὼ Νεχαὼ.] A king of *Ægypt*, in king *Jofiah's* reign, 616 years B. C. he is alfo called *Nechus*.

PHAR-A-THO'-NI, [Φαραϑὼν, i. e. *bearing fruit, increafing, a row.*] A city of *Palefine*, in the tribe of *Ephraim*.

PHA'-REZ, [Φαρὲs, i. e. *a divifion.*] A fon of *Judah* the patriarch, by *Tamar*.

PHA'-REZ-ITES, [i. e. *divided.*] The family of *Pharez*.

PHA-RI'-RA, [Φαριρὰ.] One whofe family returned from the babylonifh captivity.

PHAR'-I-SEES, [Φαρισαίοι, i. e. *a divifion, or fet apart.*] A fect of the *Jews* who pretended to a rigid exactnefs in the law of GOD; but, under that pretence, were very vicious.

PHA'-ROSH, [ΦάρΘ.] See PAROSH.

PHAR'-PHAR, [Φαρφὰρ, i. e. *diminifhed, a bull of a bull.*] A river of *Damafcus* in *Syria*.

PHAR'-ZITES, [i. e. *divided.*] A family defcended from *Pharez*.

R

PHAS-

PHAS-E'-AH, [Φεσὴ.] One whose children were
   of the order of *Nethinims*.

PHAS-E'-LIS, [Φασηλὶς, i. e. *a paffing over, a halting
   of nativity.*] A city of *Syria* in *Afia*.

PHAS'-I-RON, [Φασιρὰν.] A place, or people, mentioned in the *firft* book of *Maccabees*.

PHAS-SA'-RON, [Φασσηρ⊙.] One whose family
   returned from the babylonifh captivity.

PHE'-BE, [Φοίϐη, i. e. *clear, bright.*] A chriftian
   deaconefs, of the port of *Corinth* which is called
   Cenchrea.

PHE-NI'-CE, [Φοινίκη, i. e. *red, purple, palm.*] A
   port of the ifland of *Crete*.

PHE-NI'-CI-A, [Φοινίκη, i. e. *the fame as Phenice.*]
   A country of *Syria* in *Afia*.

PHIB'-ES-ETH, [Βηϐάς⊙, i. e. *defpite, from the
   mouth.*] A city of *Ægypt*, in *Africa*.

PHI'-COL, [Φιχὸλ, i. e. *the mouth of all, the perfection of the mouth.*] The chief captain of *Abimelech's* army.

PHI-LA-DEL-PHI'-A, [Φιλαδέλφεια, L. *the fame.*
   i. e. *the love of the brother, or of brotherhood.*] The
   capital city of the *Ammonites*; the fame with *Rab-
   bah* or *Rabbath:* now *Alla-Scheur*.

PHI-LAR'-CHES, [Φιλάρχης, i. e. *the lover of a
   prince.*] One who was an affociate with *Timotheus*,
   in the *fecond* book of *Maccabees*.

PHI-LE'-MON, [Φιλήμων, i. e. *who kiffes or is affec-
   tionate.*] A rich man of *Coloffe* in *Phrygia*, converted to the chriftian faith by *Epaphras* the
   difciple of St. *Paul:* to whom St. *Paul* wrote
   the canonical book of the *New Teftament*, called
   Philemon.

PHI-LE'-TUS, [Φιλητός, i. e. *beloved, amiable.*] One
   mentioned by St. *Paul*, in his *fecond* epiftle to
   Timothy, who fell from the faith, affirming that
   the refurrection was already paffed.

PHIL'-IP, [Φίλιππ⊙, i. e. *a warrior, warlike, a lover
   of horfes:*] An apoftle, a native of *Bethfaida*—
   alfo one of the feven deacons of the church, who
                                                  converted

converted the eunuch of queen *Candace*—also the father of *Alexander* the great.

PHI-LIP'-PI, [Φιλιπποι, i. e. *warlike men, lovers of horses.*] One of the chief cities of *Macedonia*, in *Asia*; formerly *Dathos*, but named *Philippi* after *Philip* king of *Macedon*.

PHI-LIP'-PI-ANS, [Φιλιππησιοι.] One of the canonical books of the *New Testament*; St. *Paul* wrote it to the *Philippians* or inhabitants of *Philippi*.

PHI-LIST'-I-A, [Φυλιςιειμ.] The country of the *Philistines*. See *Palestine*.

PHI-LIST'-I-IM, or PHI-LIST'-IM, [Φυλιςιειμ.] *Philistia* was so called.

PHI-LIST'-INES, [Αλλοφυλοι.] A people of *Palestine* who came from the isle *Caphtor*.

PHI-LOL'-OG-US, [Φιλολογ☉, i. e. *a lover of learning, a lover of the word.*] A person mentioned by St. *Paul* in his epistle to the *Romans*.

PHI-LO-ME'-TOR, [Φιλομητορ☉, i. e. *a lover of the mother.*] A surname of one of the *Ptolomies*.

PHIN'-NE-ES or PHIN'-E-HAS, [Φινεες, i. e. *a bold countenance.*] A son of *Eleazar*, and grandson of *Aaron*: he was the *third* high priest of the *Jews* and slew *Zimri* and *Cosbi*—also one of the sons of *Eli*.

PHI'-SON, [Φισων.] See *Pison*.

PHLEG'-ON, [Φλεγων, i. e. *zealous, turning.*] One mentioned by St. *Paul* in his epistle to the *Romans*; who, the Greeks say, was bishop of *Marathon* in *Greece*.

PHOR'-OS, [Φορ☉.] One who was a porter or guard of the temple, after his return from the babylonish captivity.

PHRYG'-I-A, [Φρυγια, i. e. *dry, barren.*] A country of *Asia*.

PHRYG'-I-A PA-CA-TI-AN'-A, [Φρυγια Παχατιανης.] A district of *Phrygia* in *Asia*, of which *Laodicea* was the capital: it was so called from *Pacatianus* who was the Roman prefect of it under the emperor *Constantine*.

PHUL, [Φυλ.] See *Pul*.

PHŪR. See *Pur*.

PHU'-RAH, [Φαρὰ, i. e. *that bears fruit, that grows.*] The servant of *Gideon*.

PHŪT, [Φȣδ.] One of the sons of the patriarch *Ham*—it also means the people of *Lybia* in *Africa*.

PHU'-VAH, [Φὰα, i. e. *a pair of bellows.*] One of the sons of *Issachar* the patriarch.

PHY-GEL'-LUS, [Φύγελλℴ, i. e. *fugitive.*] A christian of *Asia*, who, together with *Hermogenes*, left St. *Paul* in his distresses.

PHY-LAC'-TĒ-RIES, [Φυλακτήρια, i. e. *things to be especially observed.*] Were rolls of parchment on which were written certain words of the law, and which the *Jews* wore on their foreheads, their wrists, and the hems of their garments: the *Pharisees* wore theirs broader than the other *Jews*, out of ostentation.

P before I.

PI-HA-HI'-RŌTH, ['Ειρὼθ, i. e. *the mouth or pass of Hiroth, opening of liberty.*] A place in the wilderness, by which the *Israelites* passed near to the *red sea*; their *fourth* encampment.

PI'-LATE, [Πιλάτℴ, i. e. *who is armed with a dart.*] *Pontius Pilate* governor of *Judæa*, who delivered our *Saviour* to be crucified: the emperor *Caligula* banished him to *Vienne* in *Gaul*, where he died by suicide.

PIL'-DASH, [Φαλδές.] A son of *Nahor* the brother of the patriarch *Abraham*.

PI'-LE-THA, [Φαλαὶ.] A chief of the people who signed the covenant, with *Nehemiah* the governor.

PIL'-TA-I, [Φελεῆι.] One of the posterity of the patriarch *Levi*.

PI'-NŌN, [Φινὼν, i. e. *a precious stone, beholding, the mouth of the sun, the mouth of a fish.*] A duke of *Edom*, a descendant from *Esau*.

PI'-RA, [Πιρας.] A place in the land of *Palestine*.

PIR'-AM,

PIR'-AM, [Φεράμ. Φιδὼν, i. e. *a wild afs of them, the cruelty of them.*] A king of *Jarmuth*, in *Paleſtine*.

PIR'-A-THŌN, [Φαραθὼν, i. e. *his br aking, making bare, his revenge.*] A city of *Paleſtine*, in the tribe of *Ephraim*.

PIR'-ATH-ŌN-ITE, [Φαραθωνίτης.] An inhabitant of *Pirathon*.

PIS'-GAH, [Φασγὰ, i. e. *a hill, height, fortreſs, pro-viſion.*] A mountain of *Moab*, to the *eaſt* of the river *Jordan*.

PI-SID'-I-A, [Πισιδία, i. e. *a pitch tree, blacked with pitch.*] A province of *Aſia Minor*, where St. *Paul* preached.

PIS'-ON, [Φισὼν. Φεισῶν, i. e. *the changing greatneſs of the mouth, an enlarging.*] One of the *four* great rivers of *Paradiſe*, ſuppoſed by ſome to be the river *Phaſis* in *Colchis*.

PIS'-PAH, [Φασφὰ, i. e. *a mouth diminiſhed.*] One of the poſterity of the patriarch *Aſher*.

PI'-THŌM or PI'-THON, [Πιθώμ. Φιθὼν, i. e. *a mouthful of them, the perſuaſion of him, a gift of the mouth.*] One who was a deſcendant from king *Saul*—alſo a city of *Egypt*, built by the *Iſraelites* for *Pharaoh*.

P *before* L.

PLEI'-A-DES, [Πλειάδες.] The aſſemblage of the *ſeven ſtars*, in the neck of the conſtellation of *Taurus*, which appears at the beginning of the Spring.

P *before* O.

POCH'-ER-ETH, [Φαχεράθ, i. e. *the cutting of the mouth of warfare; the baniſhing of the mouth of drunkards.*] One of the ſervants of king *Solomon*.

POL'-LUX, [Πολυδεύκης.] A tutelar deity of mari-ners, in antient times, whoſe image was fixed at the ſtern of their veſſels.

POME'-GRAN-ATE. A fruit of the ſize of a large *apple*, growing in various parts of the world;

the

the covering is hard and the pulp agreeable, with many hard feeds in it—the hem of the jew-ish *high-prieſt*'s garment was to be adorned with the figures of *pomegranates.*

PON'-TI-US PI'-LATE, [Ποντιος Πιλατ⊙.] See PILATE.. *Pontius* ſignifies a *hand, or of the ſea.*

PON'-TUS, [Ποντ⊙, i. e. *the ſea.*] A province of *Aſia Minor;* to the faithful of which St. *Peter* wrote his *firſt* epiſtle.

PO'-RA-THA, [Φαραθά, i. e. *fruitful.*] One of the ſons of *Haman,* who ſuffered death at the ſame time when his father and nine brethren did.

POR'-TI-US FES'-TUS, [Πορχιος Φῆς⊙, i. e. *a feſ-tival calf.*] See *Feſtus.*

POS-I-DO'-NI-US, [Ποσιδωνιος, i. e. *giving drink.*] One of the officers of *Seleucus Nicanor.*

POT-IPH'-AR, [Πετεφρης, i. e. *a bull, a fat bull.*] An officer of *Pharaoh* king of *Ægypt,* captain of his guards, who bought *Joſeph.*

POT-IPH-E'-RA, [Πετεφρη, i. e. *ſcattering abroad fatneſs, the making bare of fatneſs.*] A prieſt of *On,* in *Ægypt.*

P before R.

PRE-TO'-RI-UM, [Πραι]ωριον.] The name of the *hall* into which they led our *Saviour* to be mocked.

PRIS-CIL'-LA or PRIS'-CA, [Πρισκιλλα, i. e. *an-tient.*] One, who, with her huſband *Aquila* (a maker of leathern tents for the army) entertained St. *Paul,* who worked at the ſame trade.

PROCH'-OR-US, [Προχορος, i. e. *he that preſides over the choirs.*] One of the ſeven *firſt* deacons of the church.

PROPH'-ET, [Προφητης.] In more antient times a prophet was called a *ſeer.* The *prophets* or *ſeers* were thoſe who foretold future events, which were diſcovered to them in dreams or in viſions, by divine inſpiration; although ſome of them were falſe prophets or pretenders to divine in-ſpiration — they were a ſociety by themſelves, and

and had an head prefiding over their fchool—they lived in the country, retired—they dreffed very plain, mean and coarfe—they were very bold in their addreffes to all orders of men—from their coarfe drefs and addrefs they were often accounted *mad-men*.

PROS'-E-LYTES, [Προσήλυτοι; i. e. *ftrangers.*] Among the *Hebrews* there were *two* forts of profelytes; the *firft* were *profelytes of the gate*, i. e. ftrangers who obferved the moral law and rules impofed on the children of *Noah*: the other fort were called *profelytes of Juftice*, who engaged themfelves to receive circumcifion and the whole law of *Mofes*.

PROV'-ERBS, [Παροιμίαι.] The book of the *Proverbs* of *Solomon* is the *twentieth* canonical book of the *Old Teftament*.

P before S.

PSALMS, [Ψαλμοὶ, i. e. *to touch.*] A canonical book of the *Old Teftament*, commonly called *the Pfalms of David*; although many of them were compofed by other perfons: it is fuppofed that they were collected by *Ezra* the fcribe—the *Jews* divided the book of *Pfalms* into *five* parts: the *firft* part contained the 42 firft *Pfalms*: the *fecond* part began with the 43d *Pfalm*, and ended with the 72d *Pfalm*: the *third* part began with the 73d *Pfalm* and ended with the 89th *Pfalm*: the *fourth* part began with the 90th *Pfalm* and ended with the 106th *Pfalm*: the *fifth* part began with the 107th *Pfalm*, and fo on to the end—the *Jews* alfo divided the 119th *Pfalm* into 22 parts, anfwering to the 22 letters in the *hebrew* alphabet; each part contained 8 verfes, and each verfe began with the letter under which it was placed, as the 8 verfes *under aleph* or *A* began *with aleph* or *A*, and fo on: this was fuppofed to have been done in order to preferve the fentences in the minds of learners—there are alfo 15 *Pfalms*, entitled *a*

fong

song of degrees, they begin with the 120th *Pfalm* and finifh with the 134th: why they are called *songs of degrees* is uncertain; fome fuppofe, that they were fung fucceffively on the 15 fteps of the afcent to the temple of *Jerufalem*, one on each ftep — others conjecture that the title denotes the elevation of the voice in finging, or the excellence of the compofure, or the mufick to which they were fet.

PSAL'-TE-RY, [Ψαλτήριον.] A mufical inftrument among the *Jews*, compofed of wood, with ftrings, and ufed in the folemnities of their religious worfhip.

P *before* T.

PTOL-OM-A'-IS, [Πτολεμαΐς.] A fea-port town of *Phœnicia*, in *Afia*, twenty miles fouth of *Tyre*.

PTOL-OM-E'-US or PTOL'-OM-Y, [Πτολεμαῖος, i. e. *a furrow, an affembly of waters, warlike.*] The name of many kings of *Ægypt*—alfo the high prieft *Abubus*'s fon, a captain in the *Maccabee* army.

P *before* U.

PU'-A or PU'-AH, [Φหά, i. e. *a mouth, a corner, a bufh of hair.*] The name of one of the *hebrew* midwives—alfo a defcendant from *Iffachar*.

PUB'-LIC-ANS, [Τελῶναι.] The farmers or receivers of the *Roman* revenues.

PUB'-LI-US, [Πόπλι☉, i. e. *common.*] The governor of the ifland *Melita*, or *Malta*, who treated St. *Paul* with great humanity when he was fhipwrecked there, A. D. 60.

PU'-DENS, [Πชδηs, i. e. *fhame faced.*] Suppofed to have been one of the *feventy* difciples, and to have fuffered martyrdom, in the reign of *Nero* the emperor of *Rome*.

PU'-HITES. The defcendants of *Puah*.

PŪL,

PŪL, [Φηλά, i. e. *decay, a bean.*]   A king of *Affyria,* in the time of *Menahem* king of the ten tribes of *Ifrael.*

PU'-NITES, [Φεαιοῖ, i. e. *beholding, my face.*]   A family defcended from *Puah.*

PU'-NON, [Φινών, i. e. *a precious ftone, beholding.*] The *thirty-fixth* encampment of the *Ifraelites*; in the wildernefs.

PŪR or PU'-RIM, [Φωρὶμ, i. e. *lot or lots.*]   A feaft of the jews on the 14th of their month *Adir,* or our *February*; in memory of lots caft by *Haman* the enemy of the jews.

PŪT, [Φυδ.]   See PHŪT.

PUT-E'-OL-I, [Ποτιόλοι.]   A city of *Campania* in *Italy,* now *Pozzuolo.*

PU'-TI-ĒL, [Φυτιὴλ, i. e. *the fatnefs of God.*]   The father in law of *Eleazar* the fon of *Aaron.*

P *before* Y.

PY'-GARG.   An animal of the *goat* kind.

Q.

Q *before* U.

QUAILS.   The *Quails* mentioned in facred writ, which fell around the camp of the *Ifraelites* in the wildernefs, are fuppofed by *fome* to be *locufts,* which are in great flights to this day, and are ufed as food; and, by fome, thought to be delicious food—by *others* they are thought to be a
bird

bird which travels in vaſt flights to this day; ſome think, of the *blackbird* kind—perhaps they might be of that kind which are now called *wild-pigeons*; for in *New Mexico,* and almoſt in all *North America,* thoſe pigeons were, not long ſince, ſo numerous, that they ſometimes concealed the ſun in their flight: and it is too well known to be denied, that a flight of them hath continued as it were in a ſtring for a long time, for the length of *twenty* miles and more—the expreſſion of *feathered fowl* made uſe of by the *Pſalmiſt,* ſeems to favour the opinion of their being *birds,* as *locuſts* have no feathers.

QUAR'-TUS, [Κύαρτ℗, i. e, *the fourth.*] A diſciple of the apoſtles: the Greeks ſay, he was one of the *ſeventy* diſciples, and biſhop of *Berythus.*

QUA-TER'-NI-ON, [Τετραδίον.] A file of *four* ſoldiers, among the romans.

QUIN'-TUS MEM'-MI-US, [Κοίντ℗ Μέμμι℗, i. e. *the fifth defiled.*] The name of a *roman* ambaſſador, in the *ſecond* book of *Maccabees.*

R.

R *before* A.

RA-AM'-AH, [Ραμμὰ. 'Ρεγμὰ, i. e. *a breaking.*] The *fourth* ſon of *Cuſh,* who peopled part of *Arabia.*

RA-AM-I'-AH, [Ρεεμαὶ, i. e. *thunder of the Lord, evil from the Lord, ſhepherd of the Lord.*] One who returned from the babyloniſh captivity.

RA-AM'-

RA-AM'-SES, [Ραμεσση.] See RAMESES.

RAB'-BAH or RAB'-BATH, ['Ραββα, i. e. *much*; *a chiding*; *great*; *fighting against*.] A city mentioned by *Joshua*: the metropolis of *Syria*, in the tribe of *Judah*.

RAB'-BAH or RAB'-BAT AM'-MON, [''Αμβα. 'Ραββα, i. e. *great*; *or chiding*.] A chief city of the *Ammonites*, to the *east* of *Jordan*; it was afterwards named *Philadelphia*, after Ptolomy *Philadelphus*.

RAB'-BI or RAB-BO'-NI, ['Ραββι. 'Ραββωνι, i. e. *master*.] A title of dignity among the *Jews*.

RAB'-BITH, ['Ραββιθ.] One of the border towns of the tribe of *Issachar* in *Palestine*.

RAB-BO'-NI, See RABBI.

RAB'-MAG, [Νασερραβαμαθ, i. e. *dissolving the multitude, melting*.] The name of a babylonish prince.

RAB'-SA-CES, [Ραψακης.] The same with *Rab-shakeh*.

RAB'-SA-RIS, ['Ραβσαριν. 'Ραφις, i. e. *master, set over eunuchs*.] A prince of *Babylon* chief of the eunuchs of king *Sennacherib*.

RAB'-SHA-KEH, ['Ραψακης, i. e. *master, set over the drinkers*.] The chief butler or cupbearer of *Sennacherib* king of *Assyria*, and sent to summon king *Hezekiah* to surrender to him.

RA'-CA or RA'-CHA, ['Ρακα, i. e. *vain*; *empty*.] A *Syriac* word, signifying, *a strong idea of contempt*: which whoever uttered to another was subject to punishment by the civil magistrate, as well as to the vengeance of heaven.

RA'-CHAB, ['Ραχαβ.] The wife of *Salmon* and mother of *Boaz*.

RA'-CHAL, ['Ραχαλ, i. e. *to whisper, an apothecary, a factor*.] A city in the land of *Palestine*, in the tribe of *Judah*.

RA'-CHEL, ['Ραχηλ, i. e. *a sheep*.] The daughter of *Laban*, sister to *Leah*, wife of the patriarch *Jacob*, and mother of *Joseph* and *Benjamin*.

RAD'-

RAD'-DA-I, ['Παδδαὶ, i. e. *ruling, coming down.*] The *fifth* son of *Jesse*, and brother of king *David.*

RA'-GAU, [Ραγαῦ, i. e. *a companion, his shepherd, breaking afunder.*] One who is mentioned by St. *Luke* in his genealogy of *Joseph* — also a place fuppofed to be in *Media.*

RA'-GES, ['Ράγοις.] A city of *Media* upon the mountains of *Ecbatana.*

RA'-GU-A, ['Ραγαῦ, i. e. *a friend.*] One of the anceftors of *Joseph* the hufband of the virgin *Mary,* mentioned by St. *Luke.*

RA-GU'-EL, ['Ραγνὴλ i. e. *the shepherd of God, a friend of God, the breaking afunder of God.*] Father of *Sarah,* and father in law of young *Tobias,* in the *Apocrypha* — also another name for *Jethro* the father in law of *Mofes.*

RA'-HAB or RA'-CHAB, ['Ραὰβ, i. e. *proud, strong, broad, a street.*] An harlot, or rather an * innkeeper, in *Jericho,* who entertained the fpies which *Joshua* fent to fearch out the land of *Canaan*—lower *Egypt* is alfo fo called by the *Pfalmift,* and by the prophet *Ifaiah.*

RA'-HAM, ['Ραὲμ, i. e. *mercy, compaffion, a friend.*] A fon of *Shema,* of the pofterity of the patriarch *Judah.*

RAK'-EM, [Ροκόμ, i. e. *void; pictures.*] One of the pofterity of the patriarch *Manaffeh.*

RAK'-KATH, ['Ρακκὰθ, i. e. *emptinefs, spittle, time.*] A city of *Palestine,* in the tribe of *Naphtali.*

RAK-KON, ['Ηρακκᾶν, i. e. *void, vain, divers pictures.*] A city of *Palestine,* in the tribe of *Dan.*

RAM, ['Ραμ, i. e. *high, casting away.*] A defcendant from *Judah;* he was the fon of *Hezron.*

---

* The original word *zonah* as frequently fignifies an *Inn-keeper* as an *Harlot;* and the moft learned *Jews* paraphrafe the word, by a feller of provifions.

RA'-MA

RA'-MA or RA'-MAH, ['Ραμᾶ, i. e. *high, caſt a-way.*] A city of *Paleſtine*, in the tribe of *Benjamin*, about *ſix* miles diſtant from *Jeruſalem* to the north—the prophet *Samuel* was born here—alſo a city in the tribe of *Naphtali*, on the frontiers of *Aſher*.

RA'-MATH, ['Ραμὰ. Βαμὲθ, i. e. *the ſame as Ramah.*] A city of *Paleſtine*, in the tribe of *Simeon*.

RA-MATH-A'-IM ZO'-PHIM, [Αρμαϑαίμ. Σιφὰ.] A city of *Paleſtine*, on the road from *Joppa* to *Jeruſalem*, in the tribe of *Ephraim*.

RA'-MA-THEM, ['Ραμαθὲμ, i. e. *high; caſt away.*] A government of *Samaria* added to *Judæa*.

RA'-MATH-ITE, [i. e. *exalted, lofty, caſt away.*] One who was an inhabitant of *Ramath*.

RA'-MATH LE'-HI, [i. e. *elevation of the jaw bone.*] A city of the *Philiſtines*.

RA'-MATH MIS'-PEH, [Μασσκφὰ.] A city of *Paleſtine*, in the tribe of *Gad*.

RA-MES'-ĒS, ['Ραμεσσῆ, i. e. *thunder, blotting out evil, broken in ſunder of a moth.*] A city of lower *Ægypt*, to the eaſt of the river *Nile*: *Goſhen* was the land of *Rameſes*: it was the *firſt* encampment of the *Iſraelites*.

RA'-MI-AH, ['Ραμία, i. e. *exaltation of the Lord.*] One who returned from the babyloniſh captivity.

RA'-MOTH, ['Ραμὼθ, i. e. *ſeeing or beholding death, eminences, high places.*] A city of refuge in *Paleſtine*, in the tribe of *Gad*, *eaſt* of the river *Jordan*, in the mountains of *Gilead*: ſometimes called *Ramoth-Gilead*—alſo one who returned from the babyloniſh captivity.

RA'-MOTH GIL'-E-AD, ['Ραβὼϑ Γαλααδ.] See RAMOTH.

RA'-PHA. ['Ραφὰ, i. e. *releaſe, medicine, a recreating, a giant.*] A deſcendant from the patriarch *Benjamin*.

RA-PHA'-EL, ['Ραφυὴλ Ραφαὴλ, i. e. *the phyſic of God.*] One of the *ſeven* archangels.

RA'-PHAH,

RA'-PHAH, ['Ραφὰ, i.e. *the same as Rapha*.] The
    fifth son of the patriarch *Benjamin*.
RA'-PHA-IM, ['Ραφαεὶν.] An ancestor of *Judith*,
    in the *Apocrypha*.
RA'-PHON, ['Ραφὼν.] A place in the land of *Gilead*.
RA'-PHU. See RAPHA.
RAS'-SIS, ['Ρασσὶς.] A place in *Arabia*.
RA-THU'-MUS, ['Ράθυμ☉.] One of king *Artaxerxes's*
    court, and an historian.
RA'-ZIS, ['Ραζὶς, i.e. *the secret or mystery of the Lord*.]
    An elder of *Jerusalem* after the babylonish cap-
    tivity.

R *before* E.

RE-A-I'-AH, ['Ραῒα. 'Ρεῒὰ, i.e. *the vision of the Lord*.]
    The son of *Shobal*, and grandson of the patriarch
    Judah—also others.
REB'-A, ['Ροβὸκ, i.e. *the fourth*; *lying by*.] A king
    of *Midian*, slain in the time of *Moses*
REB-EK'-AH or REB-EC'-CA, ['Ρεβέκκα, i. e. *fed*;
    blunt contention; *or contention hindered*.] The
    daughter of *Bethuel*, wife of the patriarch *Isaac*,
    and mother of *Esau* and *Jacob*.
RE'-CHAB, ['Ρηχάβ, i. e. *a rider*; *riding*; *a cart
    drawn with four horses*.] The father of *Jonadab*,
    who was the founder of the order of the *Recha-
    bites*; one of king *Saul's* captains.
RE'-CHAB-ITES. An order of people who engaged
    to drink no wine, to build no houses, to sow no
    grain, to plant no vineyards, to have no lands,
    and to dwell in tents all their lives.
RE'-CHAH, ['Ρηχά.] A city mentioned in *Chro-
    nicles* only, but uncertain where.
RED SEA. The sea between *Ægypt* in *Africa*, to
    the east: and west of *Arabia* in *Asia*: so called
    from *Edom*, which signifies red: it is also called
    the sea of Edom; the north part of it was where
    the *Israelites* passed through it in their flight
    from *Ægypt*: they also encamped there.

RE-EL-

RE-EL-AI'-AH, ['Ρεελίας, i. e. *a shepherd to the Lord, a companion to the Lord himself.*] One, of the race of priests, who returned to *Jerusalem* with *Zerubbabel.*

RE-EL-I'-AS. See REELAIAH.

REE-SAI'-AS, ['Ρησαιος.] One who returned from the babylonish captivity.

REF'-UGE CITIES. There were *six* cities of refuge in *Palestine*, to which, he who slew another in the heat of passion (which is termed in the english law, *man-slaughter*) might fly from the avenger: there were *three* of them on the *east* side of the river *Jordan*, viz. *Bezer, Golan*, and *Ramoth-Gilead:* the other *three* were on the *west* side of *Jordan*, viz. *Kedesh* of *Naphtali, Hebron*, and *Shechem.* These cities were to have good roads and bridges to them, and direction posts on the cross roads: the man-slayer was to continue there until he could be tried at law: if it turned out to be *murder*, he was to be put to death; if only *man-slaughter*, he was to reside in the city to which he had fled until the death of the *high-priest*; and if found out of its bounds before that time, the avenger of blood might kill him.

RE'-GEM, ['Ραγὲμ, i. e. *stoning, stoned, purple.*] A son of *Jahdai*, of the posterity of *Judah.*

RE'-GEM MEL'-ECH [Θερεγμαμελὲχ, i. e. *stoning of the king, a counsellor of the king.*] A man of note among the *Jews*, in the time of *Darius* king of *Persia.*

RE'-GOM, ['Ραγὲμ.] See REGEM.

RE-HAB-I'-AH, ['Ρααβιά, i. e. *the breadth of the Lord, the street of the Lord.*] The eldest son of *Eleazar* and grandson of *Moses.*

RE'-HOB, ['Ροὸβ, i. e. *breadth; dilating; a street.*] A city of *Palestine* in the tribe of *Asher*, given to the *Levites*—also the name of a *Levite*—also a king of *Zobah.*

RE-HOB-O-AM, ['Ροβοὰμ, i. e. *dilating the people, the breadth of the people.*] The son and successor of king *Solomon*; in his reign the *ten tribes* revolted

volted under *Jeroboam* the fon of *Nebat*; he reigned feventeen years, and died A. M. 3046.

RE-HO'-BŌTH, ['Ροωϭωθ, i. e. *breadth; largenefs; ftreets.*] A city of *Affyria* built by *Afher*—alfo a river of *Idumæa* or *Edom*.

RE'-HU. See REU.

RE'-HŪM, ['Ρεημ, i. e. *pitiful; pitied; godly; a friend.*] One who returned from the babylonifh captivity.

RE'-I, ['Ρησὶ, i. e. *my fhepherd; companion; friend; my evil.*] One of note who adhered to king *David* againſt *Adonijah*.

REK'-EM, ['Ρεκὸμ, i. e. *void; vain; divers pictures.*] The fon of *Hebron* of the pofterity of *Judah*—alfo a city of *Paleftine* in the tribe of *Benjamin*—alfo a king of *Midian*.

REM-AL-I'-AH, ['Ρομελιος, i. e. *the greatnefs of the Lord; caft away from the Lord.*] The father of *Pekah* king of *Ifrael*.

REM'-ETH, ['Ρεμμὰς, i. e. *highly; caft away.*] A city of *Paleftine* in the tribe of *Iffachar*.

REM'-MŌN, ['Ερεμμὼν, i. e. *a pomegranate; high.*] A city of *Paleftine* in the tribe of *Simeon*.

REM'-MŌN METH'-O-AR, ['Ρεμμωνὰμ Μαθαρὶμ.] A city of *Paleftine* bordering on the tribe of *Zebulun*, to the *eaft* of that tribe.

REM'-PHAN, ['Ρεφὰν. 'Ρεμφὰν, i. e. *prepared; fet in array.*] An idol: the *Syrians* called the planet *Saturn, Remphan*.

RE'-PHA-ĒL, ['Ραφαὴλ., i. e. *the medicine of God.*] One of the porters or guards of the temple of *Jerufalem*.

RE'-PHAH, ['Ραφὴ, i. e. *the releafing of the fnare.*] One of the pofterity of the patriarch *Ephraim*.

RE-PHA-I'-AH, ['Ραφαἱα, i. e. *the medicine of the Lord; the recreating of the Lord.*] The fon of *Tola*, and grandfon of the patriarch *Iffachar*.

RE'-PHA-IM, ['Ραφαὶν, i. e. *giant; preferver.*] A place of *Paleftine*, in whofe valley *Saul* encamped againſt *David*.

RE'-PHA-

RE'-PHA-IMS, ['Ραφαείν, i. e. *giants ; physicians ; reservers ; released.*] The giants of the land of *Canaan ;* supposed by some to be descended from one *Rapha.*

RE'-PHI-DIM, ['Ραφιδείν, i. e. *bending things ; litter ; slacked hands.*] The *eleventh* encampment of the *Israelites,* where water gushed out of the rock.

RE'-SEN, [Δασὴ, i. e. *a bridle.*] A city of *Assyria* built by *Asher.*

RE'-SHEPH, ['Ρασὴφ.] One of the posterity of the patriarch *Ephraim.*

RE'-U, ['Ραγάυ, i. e. *his shepherd ; a companion ; friend ; evil ; a breaking asunder.*] One of the posterity of the patriarch *Shem,* who lived 239 years and died A. M. 2026.

REU'-BEN, ['Ρυβήν, i. e. *the vision of his son ; the son of vision.*] The eldest son of *Jacob* and *Leah,* born A. M. 2246.

REU'-BEN-ITES. The posterity of the patriarch *Reuben.*

RE-U'-EL, ['Ραγυήλ, i. e. *a shepherd of God ; the friend of God ; the breaking asunder of God.*] The father in law of *Moses*—also a son of *Esau,* by *Bashemath* the daughter of *Ishmael*—also a descendant from the patriarch *Gad.*

REV-E-LA'-TION, ['Αποκάλυψις.] The last canonical book of the *New Testament* so named ; it being a series of the revelations of *John* the apostle, and beloved disciple of our *Saviour.*

REU'-MAH, ['Ρεῦμα, i. e. *high ; elevated.*] A concubine or second hand wife to *Nahor* the brother of *Abraham.*

RE'-ZEPH, ['Ραφὶς, 'Ραφὲθ, i. e. *a pavement ; stretching out ; a burning coal ; a fiery stone.*] A place mentioned in *Scripture,* supposed to be in *Assyria.*

RE'-ZI-A, ['Ρασιά, i. e. *a messenger.*] One of the posterity of the patriarch *Asher.*

RE'-ZIN, ['Ρασὼν, i. e. *affection ; a runner ; a post messenger.*] The last king of *Syria,* who invaded *Ahaz* king of *Judah :* but *Ahaz* afterwards defeated and put him to death.

S   RE'-ZON,

RE'-ZON, ['Ραζὼν, i. e. *small; lean; secret; a secretary; a prince.*] One who is supposed to have been an *Arabian* captain or robber, the son of *Eliada.*

R *before* H.

RHE'-GI-UM, ['Ρήγιον, i. e. *a breaking.*] A city of *Italy,* in the kingdom of *Naples:* now *Reggio.*

RHE'-SA, ['Ρησὰ, i. e. *affection; a meeting; an head.*] One mentioned by St. *Luke* in his genealogy of *Joseph* the husband of the virgin *Mary.*

RHOD'-A, ['Ροδή, i. e. *a rose.*] A damsel convert to christianity, mentioned in the book of *Acts.*

RHODES, ['Ρόδ☉, i. e. *a rose.*] A large island *south* of the province of *Caria* in *lesser Asia*; famous for the statue of the *Colossus* of the sun, one of the seven wonders of the world.

RHOD'-OC-US, ['Ρόδοκ☉, i. e. *a chariot of a rose colour.*] One who was a traitor in the army of *Judas Maccabæus.*

R *before* I.

RI'-BAI, ['Ρηβαὶ. 'Ριβὰ, i. e. *strife, chiding, multiplying.*] One whose son *Ittai* was one of king *David*'s worthies.

RIB'-LAH, ['Ραβλαὰμ, i. e. *greatness to him, a chiding confirmed.*] A city of *Syria,* one of the *east* boundaries of the land of *Canaan.*

RIM'-MON, ['Ρεμμὼν, i. e. *a pomegranate apple, exalted.*] A god of the *Syrians,* supposed to be the *sun*—also a village of *Palestine,* in the tribe of *Simeon,* given to the *Levites*—also the father of *Baanah* and *Rechab,* two of *Saul*'s captains.

RIM'-MON PA'-REZ, ['Ρεμμὼν Φαρές.] The *sixteenth* encampment of the *Israelites.*

RIN'-NAH, ['Ρενὰ, i. e. *a song, rejoicing.*] A descendant from the patriarch *Judah.*

RI'-PHATH, ['Ριφὰθ, i. e. *medicine, release.*] The second son of *Gomer* and grandson of *Japhet.*

RIS'-

RIS'-SAH, ['Ρεσσά, i. e. *a sprinkling upon, the dropping of an house.*]   The *eighteenth* encampment of
the *Israelites.*

RITH'-MAH, ['Ραθαμᾶ, i. e. *a juniper tree, a sound
or noise.*]   The *fifteenth* encampment of the
Israelites.

RIV'-ER OF Æ'-GYPT.   Now, the river *Nile*; as
taking this name from *Nilus*, one of the antient
kings of *Ægypt*—it is. called in sacred writ, *the
river of Ægypt*, as the river *Euphrates* is there
called the *great river.*

   The river *Nile* is much noted in antient history—it was first called *Oceanus*; then *Aetus* or
Aquila; afterwards *Ægyptus* and generally so by
Homer; and afterwards *Triton*, from the three
former names: at last, the *Nile.*

   This river rises in *Abyssinia* from two small
springs about a stone's throw from each other,
the. larger being about two feet diameter; but
being joined by many rivers emptying into it,
it runs meandring many hundred miles, until it
empties into the *mediterranean sea.*—The fertility
of *Ægypt* is owing to the overflowings of this
river — there are what they call *Nilometers*, to
measure the rising of the river; it is said that
the present *Nilometer* is a large square reservoir
surrounded by a gallery for the observers of. the
rise of the river to walk on—in the midst of this
reservoir or bason is an octagonal pillar of marble, divided into parts and marked — a canal is
cut from the river to this reservoir, by which is
seen daily the rise of the river—some say, if it
rises only about *eighteen* or *twenty feet* a famine
ensues, but if it exceeds *twenty-four* or *twenty-five
feet* it doth great damage: though others make
the lowness and the height of the waters mate-
rially different.   The river begins to rise about
midsummer, and ceases to rise in *August*, and falls
in *September.*

S 2   The

The *Sphinxes* were deſtined to ſhew at what time of the year the waters began to riſe—they were a ſymbolic figure, with the head of a *woman* and the body of a *lion*, ſignifying that the *Nile* began to ſwell in the months of *July* and *Auguſt*, when the ſun paſſes through the ſigns of *Leo* and *Virgo*—ſeveral of theſe *Sphinxes* are ſtill to be ſeen: one of which, ſays *Thevenot* the traveller, is 26 feet high, and 15 feet from the ear to the chin; but *Pliny* ſays, the head was 102 feet about, and 62 feet above the belly; that the body was 143 feet long, and was thought to be the ſepulchre of king *Amaſis*.

RIZ'-PAH, ['Ρεσφὰ, i. e. *ſtretched out.*] A concubine, or wife of the ſecond order, to king *Saul*; a daughter of *Aiah*.

R before O.

RO-GEL'-IM, ['Ρωγελλὶμ, i. e. *a foot or footman, ſearching out, an accuſer, cuſtom.*] A place in the country of *Gilead* in the tribe of *Gad*, beyond *Jordan*, where lived *Barzillai* the friend of *David*.

ROH'-GAH, ['Ραυγὰ, i. e. *filled*; *drunk with talk*; *filled with ſeparation.*] One of the deſcendants from the patriarch *Aſher*.

RO-I'-MUS, ['Ροΐμ☉.] One who returned from the babyloniſh captivity.

RO'-MANS, ['Ρομαῖοι.] The people of the *roman* government: alſo the *ſixth* canonical book of the *New Teſtament* ſo named.

RO-MAN-TI-EZ'-ER, ['Ρομεμθιὲζερ, i. e. *exalting; aid; I have exalted my palace.*] One of the ſingers of the temple of *Jeruſalem*.

ROME, ['Ρώων, i. e. *prevailing; mighty; ſtrong; exalted; high.*] The capital city of *Italy*, founded 748 years before the chriſtian Æra, in the reign of *Hezekiah* king of *Judah*.

ROSH, ['Ρὼς, i. e. *an head; top; the beginning.*] One of the deſcendants from the patriarch *Benjamin*.

R before

R *before* U.

RU'-BY. A beautiful gem of a *red* colour mixed
with *purple*; some call it a *Sardius*.

RU'-FUS, [Ρυφος, i. e. *red*.] A *Cyrenean*, mentioned by St. *Mark* with distinction.

RU'-HA'-MAH. A word signifying, *having obtained*
mercy.

RU'-MAH, [Ρυμά, i. e. *high; exalted; cast away*.]
A place from whence king *Jehoiakim*'s mother
came.

RŪTH, ['Ρϑ, i. e. *watered; filled; made drunken*.]
A *Moabitish* woman who married *Boaz* the great
grandfather of king *David*: the *eighth* canonical
book of the *Old Testament* is called after her
name, it being the sequel of the book of *Judges*.

S.

S *before* A.

SA-BAC-THA'-NI, [Σαβαχθανί.] An *hebrew* word
signifying, *thou hast forsaken me*.

SAB'-A-ŌTH, [Σαβαωθ. Σαββαωθ, L. *Sab'aoth*.] The
greek word signifying, *the Lord of Hosts, or the God*
of armies.

SA'-BAT, [Σαφὰτ.] One of the servants of *Solomon*.

SAB'-A-TUS, [Σαβαθος.] A porter or guard of the
temple after the babylonish captivity.

SAB'-BAN, [Σαβαννος.] One who returned from
the babylonish captivity.

SAB-

SAB-BA-THE'-US, [Σαββαῖος.] One whofe family returned from the babylonifh captivity.

SAB-BE'-US, [Σαββαῖος.] One who returned from the babylonifh captivity.

SAB-DE'-US, [Ζαβδαῖος.] A prieft who returned from the babylonifh captivity.

SAB'-DI, [Ζαβδὶ, i. e. *dowry, flowing with abundance.*] One who had the care of king *David's* vineyards and wine cellars.

SA-BE'-ANS, [Σαβαεὶμ, i. e. *leading into captivity, going about, drunken men, old men.*] The pofterity of *Seba,* in *Africa.*

SA'-BI, [Σαβιη.] A fervant of *Solomon.*

SAB'-TAH [Σαβαθὰ, i. e. *a going about, compafs, old age.*] One of the fons of *Cufh,* and grandfon to *Ham.*

SAB'-TE-CHA, [Σεβεθακά, i. e. *the caufe of fmiting, the fmiting of old age.*] The *fifth* fon of *Cufh,* who was the father of *Nimrod.*

SA'-CAR, [Σαχάρ, i. e. *wares, a prince, drunkennefs.*] The *fourth* fon of *Obed-Edom.*

SACK'-BUT. A mufical ftringed inftrument, of a fhrill found, having generally but *four* ftrings: in ufe in *Chaldæa.*

SA-DA-MI'-AS. An anceftor of *Efdras* in the *Apocrypha.*

SA'-DAS. One who returned from the babylonifh captivity with his family.

SAD-DE'-US, [Λοδδαῖον.] A jewifh captain in the treafury office, who returned from the babylonifh captivity.

SAD'-DUC, [Σαδδὺκ.] An anceftor of *Efdras,* in the *Apocrypha.*

SAD-DU'-CEES, [Σαδδυκαῖοι, i. e. *juft men, juftified, cut, fchifms.*] A *jewifh* fect, whofe founder was *Sadoc:* they difbelieved a refurrection, a future ftate, angels, and fpirits.

SA'-DOC, [Σαδὼκ, i. e. *juft, juftified.*] The founder of the fect of *Sadducees:* he lived about thirty years before the chriftian Æra, and was, in his opinions,

opinions, fucceffor to *Antigonus Soccbæus,* who fucceeded *Simon the juft* in the high priefthood.

SA-HA-DU'-THA, JE'-GAR, [i. e. *the heap of witnefs.*] See JEGAR SAHADUTHA.

SA'-LA, [Σαλὰ, i, e. *fending;* *fpoiling.*] One mentioned by St. *Luke,* in his genealogy of *Jofeph* the hufband of the virgin *Mary.*

SA'-LAH, [Σαλὰ, i. e. *miffion;* *branches;* *dart;* *that fpoils or is fpoiled.*] He is alfo called *Shelah;* which fee; he died A. M. 2126, Æt. 433.

SAL'-A-MIS, [Σαλαμὶς, i. e. *fhaken;* *toft;* *beaten.*] A city of the ifle of *Cyprus* in the *mediterranean* fea.

SAL-A-SA'-DA-I, [Σαλασαδαί.] An anceftor of *Judith* in the *Apocrypha.*

SA-LA'-THI-EL, [Σαλαθιὴλ, i. e. *afked;* *lent of God.*] A grandfon of king *Jofiah.*

SAL'-CAH or SAL'-CHAH, [Σελχά, i. e. *thy bafket;* *thy lifting up.*] A city of *Bafhan;* afterwards in the tribe of *Gad.*

SA'-LEM, [Σαλὴμ, i. e. *peace.*] The city of *Jerufalem* fo called. It is fuppofed to have been built by *Melchifedeck,* who is called king of peace or of *Salem.*

SA'-LIM, [Σαλεὶμ, i. e. *foxes, fifts, pathways.*] A city of *Paleftine,* in the tribe of *Ephraim.*

SAL'-LA-I, [Σαλαὶ, i. e. *an exaltation, treading underfoot, a bafket.*] The name of one who returned from the babylonifh captivity.

SAL'-LU, [Σαλὰ. Σηλὼ, i. e. *the fame as Sallai.*] The fon of *Mefhullam,* of the tribe of *Benjamin.*

SAL'-LUM, [Σαλὰμ, i. e. *peaceable.*] The *fourth* fon of king *Jofiah.*

SAL-LU'-MUS, [Σαλὰμ©.] One who returned from the babylonifh captivity, a porter or guard of the temple.

SAL'-MA or SAL'-MAH, [Σαλμά, i. e. *peace, perfection, retribution, a garment.*] The fon of *Nahfhon,* of the pofterity of *Judah* — alfo a fon of *Caleb.*

SAL'-MŌN, [Σαλμὼν, i. e. *a peace maker, perfect, giving again.*] The father of *Boaz*—alfo a moun-tain. See *Zalmon.*

SAL-MO'-NE, [Σαλμώνη, i. e. *a flowing, commotion, a breaking in pieces.*] A fea-port city on the ifle of *Crete* or *Candy.*

SA'-LŌM, [Σαλὰμ, i. e. *peace.*] Grandfather of *Joachim,* the high prieft of the *jews*—the father of *Chelcias,* in the *Apocrypha.*

SA-LO'-ME, [Σαλώμη, i. e. *the fame as Salmon.*] The wife of *Zebedee,* and mother of *James* the greater, and of *John* the evangelift—alfo a queen of the *Jews,* called by the greeks *Alexandra,* B.C. 78.

SA'-LU, [Σαλώ, i. e. *exaltation; treading under foot; a bafket.*] The father of *Zimri,* of the pofterity of *Simeon.*

SA'-LŪM, [Σαλὰμ.] A porter or guard of the tem-ple after the babylonifh captivity.

SAM'-A-ĒL, [Σαμαὴλ.] An anceftor of *Judith,* in the *Apocrypha.*

SAM-AI'-AS, [Σαμαίας, i. e. *hearing or obeying the Lord.*] One who returned from the babylonifh captivity.

SA-MA-RI'-A, [Σαμαρεία, i. e. *a keeping; an adamant ftone; a bryar; a thorn.*] A city of the province of *Syria,* and capital of the ten tribes: it was built by *Omri* king of *Ifrael,* and derived its name from *Shemer,* of whom *Omri* purchafed the hill on which it was built, for about 350l. fterling: now *Sebafte.*

SA-MAR'-I-TANS, [Σαμαρεῖται, i. e. *keepers; thorny places; dregs.*] The people of *Samaria.*

SAM'-A-TUS, [Σαμαῖος.] One whofe family returned from the babylonifh captivity.

SAM-EI'-US, [Σαμαῖος.] One who returned from the babylonifh captivity.

SAM'-GAR NE'-BO, [Σαμαγὼθ; i. e. *pepper of a ftranger prophecying, or of a ftriver fpeaking.*] A prince of *Babylon.*

SA'-MI,

SA'-MI, [Σαϐεὶ.] One whose sons were porters or guards of the temple.

SAM'-IS, [Σαμις. Σομεις.] One who returned from the babylonish captivity.

SAM'-LAH, [Σαμλὰ, i. e. *raiment*; *his left hand*; *his name*; *his astonishment*.] The name of a king of *Edom*.

SAM'-MŪS, [Σαμμὺς.] One who returned from the babylonish captivity.

SA'-MOS, [Σάμ©, i. e. *full of gravel*.] An island of the *Archipelago* or *Ægean sea*, on the coast of the lesser *Asia:* now *Susan*.

SA-MO-THRA'-CI-A, [Σαμοθράκη, i.e. *full of gravel, or rough*.] An island of the *Ægean sea*; so called, as peopled by *Samians* and *Thracians*.

SAM'-PSA-MĒS, [Σαμψάμης.] A place mentioned in the *first* book of *Maccabees*.

SAM'-SŌN, [Σαμψὼν, i. e. *his son, his ministry, there the second time*.] The *fifteenth* judge of *Israel*; the son of *Manoah*; he was remarkable for his strength, and destroying numbers of the *Philistines*; he died A. M. 2869.

SAM-U'-EL, [Σαμυὴλ. L. *Sam'uel*, i. e. *heard of God, asked of God*.] A prophet and the *seventeenth* judge of *Israel*; the son of *Elkanah* and *Hannah*, of the tribe of *Levi:* he died two years before king *Saul*, A. M. 2947, Æt. 98: two of the canonical books of the *Old Testament* are called after his name.

SAN-A-BAS'-SA-RUS, [Σαναϐασσαρός.] A ruler among the *jews* after the babylonish captivity.

SAN'-A-SIB, [Σανασιϐ.] One whose family returned from the babylonish captivity.

SAN-BAL'-LAT, [Σαναϐαλλὰτ, i. e. *a bramble or an enemy hid in secret*.] The chief of the *Samaritans* who opposed *Nehemiah* the governor in building the walls of *Jerusalem*.

SAND'-ALS, [Σανδολιαί.] At first were only *soles* tied to the feet with strings: afterwards, *shoes* were called *sandals*.

SAN'-

SAN'-HE-DRIM. The great council of the *jewish* nation, confifting of *feventy* fenators.

SAN-SAN'-NAH, [Σεθεννὰκ. Σαέννα, i. e. *a bough, a bramble of the enemy.*] A city of *Paleftine*, in the tribe of *Judah*.

SAPH, [Σὲφ, i. e. *a bafon to wafh the feet in ; a cup of gold ; a threfhold ; a poft ; a bulrufh ; the fea.*] A giant flain by *Sibbechai* the *Hufhathite*.

SAPH-AT, [Σαφὰτ.] One whofe fons returned from the babylonifh captivity.

SAPH-AT-I'-AS, [Σὰφατιάς.] One who returned from the babylonifh captivity.

SAPH'-IR, [Σενναὰρ. Σαινάν, i. e. *delightful.*] *Samaria* is fuppofed to be meant.

SAPH'-ETH, [Σαφυΐ.] One who was a fervant of *Solomon*.

SAP-PHI'-RA, [Σαπφεῖρα, i. e. *declaring ; numbering ; fear ; handfome.*] The wife of *Ananias*, who was ftruck dead with him, for attempting to deceive the Holy Ghoft.

SAP'-PHIRE, [Σαπφειρ℗.] A precious gem of a deep *blue* colour ; the *fecond* ftone in the *fecond* row upon the jewifh high prieft's breaft plate.

SA-RA-BI'-AS, [Σαραβίας.] One whofe family returned from the babylonifh captivity.

SA'-RAH or SA'-RAI, [Σάρα. Σάῤῥα, i. e. *a lady ; dame ; princefs.*] The wife of the patriarch *Abraham*, and mother of *Ifaac*—alfo the wife of *Tobias* and daughter of *Raguel* in the *Apocrypha*—alfo a daughter of *Afher*.

SA-RA-I'-AH, [Σαραΐα, i. e. *my prince of the Lord, or the fong of the Lord.*] One of the pofterity of the patriarch *Judah*.

SA-RAI'-AS, [Σαραίας, i. e. *my prince of the Lord ; or the fong of the Lord.*] A prieft who returned from the babylonifh captivity ; the father of *Jofedec* and of *Efdras*.

SA-RA-MA'-EL or SA'-RA-MEL, [Σαραμὲλ.] A place mentioned in the *firft* book of *Maccabees*, which fome fuppofe to be *Millo* ; others *Jerufalem*.

SA'-RAPH,

SA'-RAPH, [Σαράφ.] One of the posterity of the patriarch *Judah*.

SAR-CHED'-ON-US, [Σαχερδονός.] A king of *Assyria*, grandson to *Enemessar*; called also *Eserhaddon*.

SAR-DE'-US, [Ζεραλίας. Ζαρλαίας.] One who returned from the babylonish captivity.

SAR'-DIS, [Σάρδεις, i. e. *the prince or song of joy, that which remains, a pot or kettle*.] A city of *Asia Minor:* the capital city of *Cræsus* king of *Lydia*.

SAR'-DITES, [i. e. *the taking away of dissension; a dyer's vat*.] The descendants from *Sered*.

SAR'-DI-US or **SAR'-DINE STONE,** [Σάρδι◉, i. e. *redness*.] A precious gem of a *red* flaming colour, which some translate *ruby*, or *cornelian:* it was the *first* stone in the *first* row of the jewish high priest's breast plate.

SAR'-DON-YX, [Σαρδόνυξ.] A stone of a *paleish red* colour mentioned in the book of *Revelation*.

SA'-RE-A. A *scribe* mentioned in the second book of *Esdras*.

SA-REP'-TA, [Σαρεπτὰ, i. e. *perplexity of bread; a goldsmith's shop*.] See ZAREPHATH.

SAR'-GON, [Σάργων, i. e. *taking away a defence; a garden; a net*.] The name of a king of *Assyria*.

SA'-RID, [Σαρείδ, i. e. *remaining; the hand of a prince; the song of the hand*.] A border of the inheritance of *Zebulun*, in the land of *Palestine*.

SA'-RON, [Σαρώνα, i. e. *his plain field; his song*.] A fertile region of *Palestine*, stretching from *Cæsarea* to *Joppa*.

SA-RO'-THIE, [Σαρωθὶ.] One whose family returned from the babylonish captivity.

SAR-SE'-CHIM, [Ναζυσάχαρ, i. e. *a setting before of coverings*.] One of the chief of the babylonian army.

SA'-RUCH, [Σαρὰχ, i. e. *a branch; palm trees; a twig cut off from a tree*.] One who is mentioned by St. *Luke* in his genealogy of *Joseph* the husband of the virgin *Mary*.

SA'-TAN,

SA'-TAN, [Σατὰν. Σατανᾶς, i. e. *contrary*, *an adver-
sary*, *an enemy*, *an accuser*.] A name generally
given to the *Devil*.

SATH-RA-BAZ'-NES, [Σαθραβηζάνης.] A ruler in
Syria, mentioned in the *first* book of *Esdras*.

SATH-RA-BOU-ZA'-NES. See SATHRABAZ-
NES.

SA'-TYRS. Some translators call them *wild bucks*,
which inhabit defart places—fome call them *apes*,
and *wild goats*.

SA'-VA-RAN, [Σαυαρὰν.] The furname of *Eleazar*,
the brother of *Judas Maccabæus*.

SA-VI'-AS, [Σαυία.] An anceſtor of *Esdras*, in the
Apocrypha.

SAUL, [Σαῦλ⊙·, i. e. *lent*; *ditch*; *fepulchre*; *death*;
hell.] A *Benjamite*, the fon of *Kiſh*, and *firſt*
king of *Iſrael*, he died A. M. 2949 or B. C.
1055, after a reign of *nine* years—alfo a king of
Edom—alfo the name of St. *Paul* before his converfion.

S *before* C.

SCEV'-A, [Σκευᾶς, i. e. *fet in order*; *prepared*.] The
name of a *Jew*, who was chief of the fynagogue
at *Ephefus* in St. *Paul*'s time.

SCHE'-CHEM, [Σηκίμων.] See SHECHEM.

SCRIBES, [i. e. *writers*.] Doctors of the *jewiſh* law.

SCYTH'-I-ANS, [Σκύθαι, i. e. *tanners*; *leather dreſ-
fers*.] Inhabitants of *Scythia*.

SCY-THOP'-OL-IS, [Σκυθᾶν Πόλις, i. e. *a city
of tanners or leather dreſſers*.] A city between
feventy and *eighty* miles from *Jerufalem*: called
alfo *Bethſhean*.

SCY-THOP-OL'-I-TANS, [Σκυθοπολίται.] The inhabitants of *Scythopolis*.

S *before* E.

SE'-BA, [Σαβὰ, i. e. *captivity*; *compaſſing about*; *an
old man*.] One of the fons of *Cuſh* and grandfon
to *Ham* the patriarch.

SE'-BAT,

SE'-BAT, [Σαϐὰτ, i. e. *a sceptre; rod; a tribe.*] The *Chaldee* name for the jewish *eleventh* month.

SE'-CA-CAH, ['Αιοχιοζὰ, i. e. *a little shadow; a cover-ing; a defence; anointing; beholding.*] A city of *Palestine*, in the tribe of *Judah*, in the wilder-nefs.

SECH-EN-I'-AS, [Σεχενίας.] One who returned from the babylonish captivity.

SE'-CHU, [Σηχύ, i. e. *a defence; a bough; saying no-thing.*] A place of *Palestine*, where *Saul* enquired for *Samuel* and *David*.

SEC-UN'-DUS, [Σεχοῦνδ☉, i. e. *the second.*] A dif-ciple of St. *Paul*, who followed him out of *Greece* into *Asia*, A. D. 58.

SED-EC-I'-AS, [Σεδεκίας.] The fame as *Zedekiah* the fon of *Josiah* king of *Judah*.

SEERS. See PROPHETS.

SEG'-UB, [Σεγὺϐ, i. e. *made strong; exalted.*] A fon of *Hezron*, a descendant from the patriarch *Judah*, by the daughter of *Machir*.

SE'-IR, [Σηεὶϱ, i. e. *bristled; hairy; a kid, a devil: a tempest.*] A country of *Idumæa* or *Edom*, to the east and south of the *dead sea*; in which were the famous mountains of *Seir*: taken by *Esau* from the *Horites*.

SE'-IR-ATH, [Σετειϱωθὰ, i. e. *the same as Seir.*] A place in the land of *Moab*.

SE'-LA, [i. e. *a rock.*] A place in the wildernefs, through which the *Ifraelites* paffed in their way to *Canaan*.

SE'-LA HAM'-MAH-LE'-KOTH, [i. e. *the rock of divifions.*] A place in the land of *Palestine*.

SE'-LAH, [Διάψαλμα, i. e. *a rock.*] A note of mu-fick, or of praife, frequently ufed in the book of *Pfalms*, anfwering to our *Amen*.

SE'-LED, [Σαλὰδ, i. e. *affliction; a warning.*] The fon of *Nadab*, of the tribe of *Judah*.

SEL-EM-I'-AS, [Σελεμίας.] One who returned from the babylonish captivity.

SEL-EU-CI'-A, [Σελεύκεία, i. e. *troubled; broken in pieces; flowing over.*] A city of *Seleucis*, built by

Seleucus Nicanor—alfo a city of *Cilicia:* both in
Syr.

SEL-EU'-CUS, [Σελεύκ☉, i. e. *the fame as Seleucia.*]
An *Afiatick* king of *Syria*, died 280 years before
the chriftian Æra, Æt. 78, he reigned 32 years.

SĒM, [Σἠμ.] See SHEM.

SEM-A-CHI'-AH, [Σαμαχία, i. e. *cleaving or joined
to the Lord.*] One who was a *Levite*, and a porter or guard of the *jewiſh* temple.

SEM-A-I'-AH or SEM-A-I'-AS, [Σαμαϊα, i. e. *hearing or obeying the Lord.*] The *firſt* born ſon of
Obed-Edom.

SEM'-E-I, [Σεμεῖ, i. e. *hearing or obeying.*] One
mentioned by St. *Luke* in his genealogy of
Joſeph the reputed father of our *Saviour.*

SE-MEL'-LI-US, [Σαμέλλι☉.] Secretary to king
Artaxerxes.

SEM'-IS, [Σεμεῖς.] A *Levite* who returned from the
babyloniſh captivity.

SEN'-A-AH, [Σενναὰ, i. e. *a bramble; an enemy.*] A
city of *Paleſtine.*

SEN'-EH, [Σεννά, i. e. *a bramble; an enemy.*] The
name of a *rock* by which *Jonathan*, the ſon of
Saul, paſſed, to go over to the *Philiſtines.*

SE'-NIR, [Σανὶρ, i. e. *a ſleeping candle; proſpering of a
teacher; a changing.*] A part of *Canaan*, in the
half tribe of *Manaſſeh.*

SEN-NACH-E'-RIB, [Σενναχηρίμ. ΣενναχηρὶϚ, i. e.
*the bramble of deſtruction; the ſword or the deſtruction
of the enemy.*] A king of *Aſſyria*, in the reign of
Hezekiah king of *Judah:* he was ſlain in the temple of his god *Niſroch*, about A. M. 3294.

SEN'-U-AH, ['Ασανὰ, i. e. *a bramble; an enemy.*]
One who returned from the babyloniſh captivity.

SE-O'-RIM, [Σεωρίμ, i. e. *gates; hairs of the head,
tempeſts; devils; goats.*] One who belonged to
the family which was the *fourth* in order of the
facerdotal family.

SEPH'AR, [Σαφηρὰ, i. e. *a book; a ſcribe; a number;
a haven.*] A mountain to the eaſt of *Paleſtine.*

SEPH'-

SEPH'-AR-AD, ['Αφαραδ, i. e. *a book descending, the end of a rule ruling.*] The word signifying, *the borders of the south of Judæa, or Palestine.*

SEPH-AR-VA'-IM, [Σεπφαρυαιμ, i. e. *books; scribes; numbers; a haven of the sea.*] A country of *As-syria.*

SEPH'-AR-VITES. The people of *Sepharvaim,* who offered their children in sacrifice to idols.

SEPH-E'LA, [Σεφηλα.] The southern part of the plain of *Jezreel.*

SERAH, [Σαρα, i. e. *mistress of favour; the song of favour.*] A daughter of the patriarch *Asher.*

SE'-RAI'-A, [Σαραιας, i. e. *my prince of the Lord; the song of the Lord.*] One who was secretary to king *David*—also others of that name.

SER-A-I'-AH, [Σαραια.] A son of *Kenaz,* of the po-sterity of *Judah.*

SER'-APH-IM *, [Σεραφειμ, i. e. *burning; fiery.*] Angels of the first order in the *jewish* œconomy.

SER'-ED, [Σερεδ, i. e. *a dyer's vat.*] One of the poste-rity of the patriarch *Zebulun.*

SER'-GI-US PAUL'-US, [Σεργι◦ Παυλ◦, i. e. *a net.*] A proconsul or governor of *Cyprus* Isle, converted to christianity by St. *Paul,* about A. C. 44.

SE'-RON, [Σηρων.] A general of the army of *An-tiochus Epiphanes,* defeated by *Judas Maccabæus.*

SER'-UG, [Σερȣχ, i. e. *a bough; a plant.*] A descen-dant from the patriarch *Shem,* died A. M. 2049, Æt. 230.

SES'-IS, [Σεσις.] One who returned from the baby-lonish captivity.

SES'-THEL, [Σεθηλ.] One who returned from the babylonish captivity.

SETH, [Σηθ, i. e. *set; put.*] A son of *Adam* and *Eve,* born A. M. 130, died A. M. 1042, Æt. 912.

---

* It ought to have been translated *Seraphim,* but in the two places of our version where they are mentioned, it is *Seraphims.*

SETH-

SETH'-AR or SETH'-ĒR, [Σαθὴς, i. e. *hid*; *deſtroy-*
ing.] One whom *Moſes* ſent to ſearch out the
land of *Canaan.*

S *before* H.

SHA'-AL-AB'-BIN, [Σααλαβὶν, i. e. *the underſtanding
or ſon of a fox.*] A city of *Paleſtine*, in the tribe
of *Dan.*

SHA-AL'-BIM, [Σαλαβὶν, i. e. *looking back on the
hearts; a fox in the ſea.*] A place in *Paleſtine*, the
ſame as *Silbon* beyond *Jordan.*

SHA-AL-BO'-NITE, [ὁ Σαλαβωνίτης, i. e. *the building of a fox; or the path of underſtanding.*] *Eliahab*,
one of king *David's* worthies, was a *Shaalbonite*,
or a citizen of *Shaalbon* in *Judea.*

SHA'-APH, [Σαάφ, i. e. *fleeing; thinking.*] A ſon
of *Jahdai*, of the poſterity of *Judah*—alſo others
of that name.

SHA-A-RA'-IM, [Σαρεὶμ, i. e. *gates; eſtimations;
tempeſts; hairy; goats.*] A ſon of *Uzzah*, who
was put to death for touching *the ark of* GOD—
alſo a city in the tribe of *Simeon*, afterwards
yielded to the tribe of *Judah*, and called *Sha-
raim.*

SHA'-ASH-GAZ, [Σασαγὰ Γαὶ, i. e. *regarding; paſſing over; preſſing a fleece of wool.*] A chamberlain
of king *Ahaſuerus.*

SHAB-BE-THA'-I, [Σαββαθαὶ, i. e. *my reſt.*] The
name of one of the *Levites.*

SHACH'-I-A, [Σεχιά, i. e. *the protection of the Lord.*]
One of the poſterity of the patriarch *Benjamin.*

SHAD'-RACH, [Σεδράχ, i. e. *a fine field; thy ſending.*]
One of the three friends of the prophet *Daniel*,
whom *Nebuchadnezzar*, by *Daniel's* deſire, appointed over the affairs of his kingdom: his name
was *Hananiah*, and changed to *Shadrach.*

SHA'-GE, [Σαγή, i. e. *ignorant; comprehending; touching ſoftly; much multiplying.*] The father of *Jonathan*, and one of king *David's* worthies.

SHA.

SHA-HAZ-I'-MATH, [Σασειμὰθ. Σασιμὰ.] A city which was one of the boundaries of the tribe of *Iſſachar*.

SHAL'-LE-CHETH. The name of one of the gates of the city of *Jeruſalem*.

SHA'-LEM, [Σαλημ, i. e. *peace.*] A city of *Shechem*, in the land of *Paleſtine*.

SHA'-LIM, [Σααλειμ, i. e. *foxes; fiſts; path ways.*]. A city of *Paleſtine*.

SHAL-I'-SHA, [Σαλισά, i. e. *three; principal.*] A city of *Paleſtine*.

SHAL'-LUM, [Σελλὲμ, i. e. *peaceable; perfect; giving again.*] The *fourth* ſon of *Joſiah* king of *Judah*, who ſucceeded his father by the name of *Jehoahaz*; and was carried priſoner into *Ægypt*—alſo others of that name.

SHAL'-MAI, [Σελμεῖ. Σελαμὶ, i. e. *my garment.*] One whoſe children were of the order of *Nethinims*.

SHAL'-MAN, [Σαλμάν, i. e. *peaceable.*] He is ſuppoſed to be *Shalmaneſer* king of *Aſſyria*.

SHAL-MA-NES'-ER, [Σαλαμανασσὰρ, i. e. *peace bound; retribution; taken away.*] A king of *Aſſyria*, who beſieged *Samaria*, took the city, and alſo *Hoſhea* king of *Iſrael*, whom he carried away captive: he began to reign A. M. 3276, and died A. M. 3290.

SHAM'-A, [Σαμμά, i. e. *hearing or obeying.*] One of king *David*'s valiant men.

SHAM-AR-I'-AH, [Σαμορία, i. e. *the keeping; hardneſs or throne of the Lord.*] One of king *Rehoboam*'s ſons.

SHAM'-ED, [Σάμηδ, i. e. *deſtroying; wearing out.*] One of the poſterity of the patriarch *Benjamin*.

SHAM'-ER, [Σεμμήρ, i. e. *a keeper; hardneſs; a thorn; dregs.*] One of the poſterity of the patriarch *Levi*.

SHAM'-GAR, [Σαμεγὰρ, i. e. *deſolation of the ſtranger; named a ſtranger; a ſtriving; conſidering with a man's ſelf of a name.*] The ſon of *Anath*: he was the

fourth

fourth judge of *Ifrael:* he flew 600 *Philiftines* with an ox-goad; he died A. M. 2690.

SHAM' HŪTH, [Σαμαώθ, i. e. *defolation; perdition.*] A captain of the courfe of waiting in the *fifth* month in king *David's* reign.

SHA'-MIR, [Σαμιρ, i. e. *prifon; bufh; lees; thorn.*] A city of *Paleftine,* in the tribe of *Judah,* in the mountains.

SHAM'-MA, [Σαμα, i. e. *defolation; perdition; deftruction; aftonifhment there.*] One who was of the tribe of *Afher.*

SHAM'-MAH, [Σομε. Σαμά, i. e. *the fame with Shamma.*] An *Hararite,* one of king *David's* worthies and his brother—alfo a grandfon of *Efau.*

SHAM'-MA-I, [Σαμαῖ, i. e. *my name; my defolations or perditions; the heavens.*] A fon of *Anam,* of the tribe of *Judah*—alfo others of that name.

SHAM'-MŌTH, [Σαμαώθ, i. e. *names; defolations; perditions.*] An *Hararite,* one of king *David's* worthies.

SHAM-MU'-A, [Σαμμέ. Σαμαά, i. e. *hearing; obeying.*] The fon of *Zaccur,* of the tribe of *Reuben,* who was fent to fpy out the land of *Canaan*— alfo a fon of king *David.*

SHAM-MU'-AH, [Σαμμῆς.] The fame with *Shammua.*

SHAM-SHE-RA'-I, [Σαμσαρία, i. e. *the name of a conqueror; there a finger or conqueror.*] One of the pofterity of the patriarch *Benjamin.*

SHAPH'-AM, [Σαφάμ, i. e. *a coney; one hid; a lip; laid up; the banks or breaking of things.*] One of the pofterity of the patriarch *Gad.*

SHAPH'-AN, [Σαπφαν. Σεφφὰν, i. e. *the fame as Shapham.*] One of the fcribes in the reign of king *Jofiah.*

SHAPH'-AT, [Σαφάτ, i. e. *a judge; judging.*] One of the pofterity of king *David*—alfo one fent by *Mofes* to fpy out the land of *Canaan*—alfo *Elifha's* father.

SHAPH'-ER, [Σαφὰρ, i. e. *beauty, a cornet.*] The *Twentieth* encampment of the *Ifraelites.*

SHAR'-

SHAR'-A-I, [Σαρὶ, i. e. *my lord*; *my prince*; *my song*.]
One who returned from the babylonifh captivity.

SHAR'-A-IM, [Σαχαρὶμ, i. e. *a song*.] A city of
Palefline, in the tribe of *Judah* in the valley.

SHAR'-AR, [Σαράρ, i. e. *the navel*; *thought*; *finging*;
the Lord.] The father of *Ahiam*, one of king
David's worthies.

SHAR'-E-ZER, [Σαρασὰρ, i. e. *a treafurer*; *he that
feeth the narrow fireight*; *the treafure of one finging*.]
The *fecond* fon of *Sennacherib* king of *Affyria*,
who flew his father in the temple of his god
Nifroch.

SHA'-RŌN, [Σαρών, i. e. *a plain field*; *his fong*.]
Three cantons in the land of *Palefline*, known by
this name: this place was proverbial, to denote
a place of extraordinary beauty and fruitfulnefs,
as *the rofe of Sharon*.

SHA'-RŌN-ITE. An inhabitant of *Sharon*.

SHA-RU'-HEN. A city of *Palefline*, in the tribe of
Simeon.

SHASH'-A-I, [Σεσεἰ, i. e. *rejoicing*; *mercy*; *filk*; *flax*;
linen.] One who returned from the babylonifh
captivity.

SHA'-SHAK, [Σωσὴκ, i. e. *a fack of flax*; *the kifs*; *the
cup of joy*.] One of the pofterity of the patriarch
Benjamin.

SHA'-VEH KIR-JATH-A'-IM, [Σαυᾶ Καριαθαὶμ,
i. e. *the plain of Kirjathaim*.] A place where
dwelt the *Enims*, an antient people beyond the
river *Jordan*.

SHA'-VETH, [Σαβύ.] A valley which was near to
Sodom.

SHA'-ŪL, [Σαὴλ, i. e. *afked*; *lent*; *a grave*; *hell*.]
One of the pofterity of the patriarch *Levi*—alfo
a fon of the patriarch *Simeon*.

SHA-ŪL'-ITES, [Σαηλοῖ.] The pofterity of *Shaul*.

SHAU'-SHA, [Σεσὰ.] A fcribe in the reign of king
David.

SHE'-AL, [Σααλ, i. e. *the fame as Shaul*.] One who
returned from the babylonifh captivity.

SHE-AL'-TI-EL; [Σαλαθιὴλ, i. e. *afked*; *lent of God.*] The father of *Zerubbabel.*

SHE-AR-I'-AH, [Σααρία, i. e. *the gate of the Lord*; *the tempeft of the Lord.*] One of the defcendants from king *Saul.*

SHE-AR-JA'-SHŪB, [i. e. *the remnant fhall return.*] It was the name given to the prophet *Ifaiah's* fon.

SHE'-BA or SHE'-BAH, [Σαβα. Σαβεὲ, i. e. *captivity; compaffing about; an old man.*] The fon of *Raamah*; fuppofed to have peopled *Arabia felix*, or *happy Arabia*—alfo a place fuppofed to be in *Arabia*, from whence their queen came to vifit king *Solomon*—alfo a city of *Palestine* in the tribe of *Simeon*—alfo a fon of *Joktan.*

SHEB'-AM, [Σεβαμὰ, i. e. *compaffing about, old men.*] A country of *Palestine*, proper for cattle, in the tribe of *Reuben.*

SHEB-AN-I'-AH, [Σωβενία, i. e. *the Lord turning; taking captive; the underftanding or building of the Lord.*] One who was a prieft in the reign of king *David.*

SHEB'-AR-IM, [Σεβαρεὶμ, i. e. *breakings; hopes; lookings for.*] A place of *Palestine*, near to the city *Ai.*

SHEB'-AT, [i. e. *a fcepter, a rod.*] A *jewifh* month, being the *fifth* of the civil, and *eleventh* of the facred year, anfwering to part of our *January* and *February.*

SHEB'-ER, [Σαβὲρ, i. e. *a breaking; hope.*] A fon of *Caleb*, of the pofterity of the patriarch *Judah.*

SHEB'-NA, [Σοβνάς, i. e. *fit down now; knit together now; taking captive now; building; he which underftandeth.*] One who was a *fcribe* in the reign of king *Hezekiah.*

SHE-BU'-EL, [Σηβαὴλ, i. e. *the turning, the captivity or the feat of God.*] The eldeft fon of *Gerfhom*, and grandfon to *Mofes.*

SHEC-AN-I'-AH, [Σεχενία, i. e. *the habitation of the Lord.*] The name of feveral men mentioned in *Scripture.*

SHE'-

SHE'-CHEM, [Συχέμ, i. e. *a part; portion; shoulder.*]
The son of *Hamor* and prince of the *Shechemites*
—also a city of *Samaria*, 40 miles from *Jerusalem* and *ten* miles from *Shiloh:* a city of refuge,
called also *Sychar.*

SHE'-CHEM-ITES, [Συχίμοι.] The people of *Shechem.*

SHED'-E-ŪR, [Σεδιὴρ, i. e. *a field of light or fire;
the light of the Almighty.*] The name of one who
was of the tribe of *Reuben.*

SHE-HAR-I'-AH, [Σααρίας, i. e. *the mourning of the
Lord, or the blackness of the Lord.*] One of the
posterity of the patriarch *Benjamin.*

SHEK'-EL, [Σίκλος.] A *jewish* piece of money, not
coined, but by weight; amounting to about *two
shillings and four-pence* sterling.

SHE'-LAH, [Σαλὰ. Σηλώμ, i. e. *sending; spoiling.*]
The son of *Arphaxad,* and grandson of the patriarch *Shem*—also a son of the patriarch *Judah.*

SHE'-LAN-ITES, [i. e. *dissolving.*] The family of
Shelah.

SHEL-EM-I'-AH, [Σελεμία, i. e. *the peace, perfection
or retribution of the Lord.*] One of the porters or
guards of the temple of *Jerusalem.*

SHE'-LEPH, [Σαλέφ, i. e. *drawing out.*] One of the
posterity of the patriarch *Shem.*

SHEL'-ESH, [Σελλῆς, i. e. *a captain, a prince.*] One
of the posterity of the patriarch *Asher.*

SHEL'-OM-I, [Σελεμί, i. e. *peaceable; perfect; giving
again.*] One who belonged to the tribe of *Asher.*

SHEL-O'-MITH, [Σαλωμίθ, i. e. *the same as Shelomi.*]
A daughter of *Zerubbabel,* a prince of *Judah.*

SHEL-O'-MOTH, [Σαλωμώθ, i. e. *peaceable.*] One
of the priests at the close of king *David's* life.

SHEL-U'-MI-EL, [Σαλαμιήλ, i. e. *the same as Shelemiah.*] A son of *Zurishaddai,* prince of the tribe
of *Simeon.*

SHEM, [Σὴμ, i. e. *a name; renowned; report; put.*]
A son of *Noah* the patriarch, born A. M. 1559,
died A. M. 2158, Æt. 600: some suppose him
to be *Melchisedeck:* others that *Pluto* is *Shem; Ham,*

                Jupiter;

Jupiter; and *Japhet*, *Neptune*, in the heathen mythology.

SHEM'-A, [Σαμμαί. Σαμὰ, i. e. *hearing*; *obeying*.] A city of *Palestine*, in the tribe of *Judah*—also one of the sons of *Hebron*, of the posterity of *Judah*—and others of that name.

SHEM'-A-AH, [Σαμαά, i. e. *hearing*; *obeying*.] The father of *Joash*, of the kindred of king *Saul*, of the tribe of *Benjamin*.

SHEM-A-I'-AH, [Σαμαία, i. e. *hearing or obeying the Lord*.] One of the posterity of the patriarch *Simeon*.

SHEM-A-RI'-AH, [Σαμαραία, i. e. *the keeping of the Lord*.] One who resorted to king *David* at *Ziklag*.

SHEM'-EB-ER, [Συμοϐὸϱ, i. e. *the name*; *report of a strong man*; *the name of a bird*; *destroying strength*.] A king of *Zeboim*, who, with the four other confederate princes, was defeated by *Chederlaomer*.

SHEM'-ĒR, [Σεμηϱ, i. e. *a keeper*.] A man of whom *Asa* king of *Judah* bought an hill in *Samaria*, where he built the city *Shemer*.

SHEM-I'-DA, [Σαμεῖδα, i. e. *a name of knowledge*; *the knowledge of the heavens*.] A son of *Gilead*, of the tribe of *Manasseh*, and head of the *Shemidaites*.

SHEM-I'-DA-ITES. People of the family of *Shemida*.

SHEM'-IN-ITH, ['Αμασενιθ, i. e. *the eighth*.] A word in the title of some of the *Psalms*: it is supposed to mean *an harp with eight strings*.

SHEM-IR'-A-MŌTH, [Σεμιραμωθ, i. e. *the heights of the heavens*; *the height of a name*.] A *Levite*, and porter or guard of the temple of *Jerusalem*.

SHEM-U'-ĒL, [Σαμηήλ, i. e. *appointed or established of God*.] The son of *Tola*, and grandson to the patriarch *Issachar*.

HEN, [i. e. *tooth*; *ivory*; *change*; *he that sleeps*.] A city in the land of *Palestine*.

SHEN-AZ'-AR, [Σανασὰρ, i. e *the treafurer of a tooth, or of one fleeping; an enemy of tribulation.*] The name of one of king *David's* pofterity.

SHEN'-IR, [Σανὶρ, i. e. *a fleeping candle; the profpering of a candle or of the teacher.*] Mount *Hermon* was fo called by the *Amorites.*

SHEP'-HAM, [Σεπφαμὰρ, i. e. *judging.*] One of the eaftern boundaries of *Palefline.*

SHEPH-AT-I'-AH, [Σαφαἶία, i. e. *the Lord judgeth; the judgment of the Lord.*] A fon of king *David* by *Abital*—alfo others of that name.

SHE'-PHI, [Σωφὶ, i. e. *a beholder; a honeycomb; a garment; a looking for.*] A defcendant from the patriarch *Efau.*

SHE'-PHO, [Σωφὰρ, i. e. *a defart; a bank; a breaking afunder.*] A defcendant from the patriarch *Efau.*

SHEPH-U'-PHAN, [Συφηφὰμ, i. e. *a ferpent.*] A fon of *Bela,* and grandfon of the patriarch *Benjamin.*

SHER'-AH, [Σαραά, i. e. *flefh; confanguinity; leaven; remaining.*] A defcendant from the patriarch *Ephraim.*

SHER-E-BI'-AH, [Σαραβία, i. e. *the drought of or prevailing with the Lord; finging with the Lord.*] A *Levite* who fealed the covenant with *Nehemiah* the governor.

SHE'-RESH, [Σῆρϑ.] One of the pofterity of the patriarch *Manaffeh.*

SHE-REZ'-ER, [Σαρασὰρ.] A man of note among the *Jews.*

SHESH'-ACK, [i. e. *thy flax; thy joy.*] A name given to *Babylon* by the prophet *Jeremiah: Shefhack* was fuppofed to be a babylonifh idol.

SHE'-SHAI, [Συσὶ. Σεσεὶ, i. e. *fix; rejoicing; mercy; flax.*] The name of a *giant,* one of the fons of *Anak.*

SHE'-SHAN, [Σωσὰν, i. e. *a lily; a rofe; joyfulnefs; flax.*] A fon of *Ifhi,* of the tribe of *Judah.*

SHESH-BAZ'-ZAR, [Σασαβασὰρ, i. e. *joy in tribulation; an affirming of joy; joy of gathering grapes.*]

T 4

A prince

A prince of the tribe of *Judah*, who had the care of the facred veffels of the temple when *Cyrus* reftored them to the *Jews*: he is fuppofed to be *Zerubbabel*.

SHĒTH, [Σήθ.] See SETH.

SHE'-THAR, [Σηθὰρ, i. e. *fearching out*; *a remnant*; *hid*; *putrified*.] The name of one who was a prince of *Media* and *Perfia*.

SHE'-THAR BOZ'-NA-I, [Σαθαρ Βῳζαναὶ, i. e. *defpifing me*; *he that fearcheth out my defpifers*.] A governor under *Darius* king of *Perfia*.

SHE'-VA, [Σϐὶ. Σὰϰ, i. e. *vanity*; *a lifting up*; *tumult*.] One who was a *fcribe* in the reign of king *David*.

SHEW BREAD. So called becaufe expofed to public view before the *ark*.

SHIB-BO'-LETH, [i. e. *an ear of corn*.] It was the word which the *Gileadites* ufed as the teft of an *Ephraimite*; for the *Ephraimites* could not, from difufe, pronounce the hebrew letter *Schin*; therefore they faid *Sibboleth* inftead of *Shibboleth*.

SHIB'-MAH, [Σεϐαμὰ, i. e. *overmuch captivity*; *much fitting*.] The name of a city of the *Amorites*.

SHICH'-RŌN, [Σοχὼθ. Σαϰχαρῶνα, i. e. *drunkennefs*; *a price*; *his wares*.] One of the boundaries of the tribe of *Judah*, in *Paleftine*.

SHIG-GAI'-ON, ['Αγνόημα, i. e. *the reproof of falfehood*.] The title of the *feventh Pfalm*: fome fuppofe it to be an inftrument of mufick; others, that it was an air or tune to which this *Pfalm* was fung: the learned *Calmet* thinks it ought to be tranflated, *a fong of trouble*, *or a fong of confolation of David*.

SHI'-HŌN, [Σιωνὰ, i. e. *a found*; *a noife*; *the wall of ftrength*; *grief*.] A city of *Paleftine*, in the tribe of *Iffachar*.

SHI'-HOR, [Σειὼρ, i. e. *black*; *troublous*; *mourning*.] One of the fouthern boundaries of the land of *Canaan*.

SHI'-HOR LIB'-NATH, [Σειὼρ Λαϐανάθ.] One of the boundaries of the tribe of *Afher*, in *Paleftine*.

SHI-

SHI-I'-HIM, [Σελλεῖμ, i. e. *the same as Shilhi.*] A boundary city of the tribe of *Judah*, toward the coast of *Edom*, south.

SHIL'-HI, [Σαλαὶ, i. e. *a sending*; *a bough*; *a weapon*; *armour*; *spoiled.*] The father of *Azubah* the mother of king *Jehosaphat.*

SHIL'-HIM, [Σελλεῖμ.] See SHIIHIM.

SHIL'-LEM, [Σολλήμ, i. e. *peace*; *perfectness*; *retribution.*] The name of one of the sons of the patriarch *Naphtali.*

SHIL'-LĒM-ITES. The descendants from *Shillem.*

SHI'-LŌH or SHI'-LO, [Σηλὼ, i. e. *dissolving*; *putting off one's shoes*; *mocked*; *deceiving*; *sent.*] A famous city of *Palestine*, in the tribe of *Ephraim*—also the word used by the patriarch *Jacob* to foretel the coming of the *Messiah*, and is generally applied to *Jesus Christ* by the antient *Jews*, and always by the *Christians.*

SHI-LO'-AH, [Σιλωὰ, i. e. *the same meaning as Shilhi.*] A small river running through *Jerusalem*, at the foot of mount *Zion.* See *Siloam.*

SHI-LO'-NI, [Σηλωνί, i. e. *tarrying*; *a peace maker*; *abounding*; *mocking*; *deceiving.*] The name of a man of the tribe of *Judah.*

SHI-LO'-NITES, [Σηλωνῖται.] The descendants from *Shiloni.*

SHIL'-SHAH, [Σελσά, i. e. *three*; *the chief*; *a captain.*] One of the posterity of the patriarch *Asher.*

SHIM'-E-A, [Σαμαὰ, i. e. *hearing, obeying.*] One of the sons of king *David*, by *Bathsheba.*

SHIM'-E-AH, [Σαμαὰ, i. e. *named*; *put to*; *perdition*; *desolation.*] A prince of the family of *Benjamin*, the son of *Mikloth*—also king *David*'s brother.

SHIM'-E-AM, [Σαμαὰ.] The same person as *Shimeah.*

SHIM'-E-ATH, [Σεμααθ.] An *Ammonitish* woman, the mother of *Zabad.*

SHIM'-E-ATH-ITES. The descendants from *Shimeath*; a family of *scribes*, skilled in prophecies.

SHIM'-E-I, [Σεμεεί, i. e. *hearing, obeying*; *the name of an heap, or destroying the heap.*] The son of *Gera,*

Gera, a kinfman of king *Saul*, who curfed and infulted king *David*, and was put to death by king *Solomon*—alfo others of that name.

SHIM'-E-ŌN, [Σεμεὼν, i. e. *hearing*; *obedient.*] One who returned from the babylonifh captivity.

SHIM'-HI, [Σαμαϊθ, i. e. *that hears or obeys.*] One of the pofterity of the patriarch *Benjamin*.

SHIM'-I, [Σεμεεί.] One of the fons of *Gerfhom*.

SHIM'-ITES, [Σεμωῖται.] The defcendants from *Shimi*.

SHIM'-MA, [Σαμαὲ, i. e. *hearing*; *obeying.*] The third fon of *Jeffe*, and brother to king *David*.

SHIM'-ŌN, [Σεμὼν, i. e. *putting*; *put*; *a gift of providing*; *fatnefs*; *oil.*] A defcendant from the patriarch *Judah*.

SHIM'-RATH, [Σαμαράθ, i. e. *hearing*; *obedient.*] One of the pofterity of the patriarch *Benjamin*; the fon of *Shimhi*—alfo an *ammonitifh* woman the mother of *Zabad*.

SHIM'-RI, [Σεμρὶ, i. e. *keeping*; *a thorn*; *dregs.*] One of the *Levites*, the fon of *Elizaphan*.

SHIM'-RITH, [Σαμαρίθ, i. e. *the fame as Shimri.*] A *moabitifh* woman, the mother of *Jehozabad*.

SHIM'-RŌN, [Σαμρὰμ, i. e. *keeping*; *a thorn*; *dregs of them.*] The fourth fon of the patriarch *Iffachar*—alfo a city of *Palefline*, in the tribe of *Zebulun*.

SHIM'-RŌN-ITES. The inhabitants of *Shimron*.

SHIM'-RŌN ME'-RŌN, [Συμρὼν, i. e. *a keeper of bitternefs*; *firong myrrh.*] A city of *Palefline*, on the *weft* fide of the river *Jordan*.

SHIM'-SHAI, [Σαμψαι, i. e. *my fon.*] The name of a *fcribe* in the time of *Ezra*.

SHIN'-AB, [Σενναὰρ, i. e. *the tooth of the father*; *the father of changing*; *the fleeping of the father.*] A king of *Admah*, one of the cities of *Pentapolis*.

SHIN'-AR, [Σενναὰρ, i. e. *the watchings of one fleeping*; *the making bare of a tooth*; *the changing of a city.*] A province of *Babylon* in *Afia*, where the tower of *Babel* was begun.

SHIPH'-I,

SHIPH'-I, [Σαφαΐ, i. e. *a multitude.*] A prince of the tribe of *Simeon.*

SHIPH'-MITE. One who was of the posterity of *Shiphi.*

SHIPH'-RAH or SHIPH'-RATH, [Σεπφώρα, i. e. *fair; a pipe; doing well; goodness.*] The name of one of the *egyptian* midwives who saved the *hebrew* children.

SHIPH'-TAN, [Σαβαθᾶν, i. e. *a judge; judging.*] One of the posterity of the patriarch *Ephraim.*

SHI'-SHA, [Σίισὰ, i. e. *six; of marble; pleasant; the lifting up of a gift.*] The father of two of the scribes of king *Solomon.*

SHI'-SHAK, [Σηπὰκ, i. e. *thy flax; thy joy; present of the bag.*] A king of *Egypt* in the reign of *Rehoboam* king of *Judah,* who carried away the treasures of the temple and of the king's palace.

SHIT'-RA-I, [Σατραΐ, i. e. *a binding; drawn together.*] An inhabitant of *Sharon,* who had the care of king *David*'s herds of cattle.

SHIT'-TAH TREE, [Πύξ◌, i. e. *a thorn.*] A tree mentioned in *Isaiah,* chap. xli, ver. 19, the word *puxos* (Πύξ◌) which our translators have rendered *Shittah-tree,* is the *greek* word for the *box-tree.*

SHIT'-TIM, [Σατίειν, i. e. *spreadings out; turnings aside; whips; thorns.*] A place where the *Israelites* encamped, supposed to have derived its name from the *Shittim* trees which grew there: the *Shittim* wood is supposed to be the finest kind of *cedar* wood, which is said to be hard, tough, beautiful, and durable—afterwards it was in the tribe of *Reuben.*

SHIT'-TIM WOOD. A wood which some suppose to be the finest kind of *Cedar wood.*

SHI'-ZA, [Σιζά. Σαιζὰ, i. e. *this gift; sprinkling on a gift.*] The father of *Adina,* one of king *David*'s worthies.

SHO'-A or SHO'-AH, [Σηὲ, i. e. *tyrants.*] Supposed to be a title or degree of honour among the *Babylonians.*

SHO'-

SHO'BAB, [Σωβὰβ, i. e. *returned*; *a spark.*] One of the fons of king *David* by *Bathfheba*—alfo a fon of *Caleb.*

SHO'-BACH, [Σωβὰχ, i. e. *a net*; *a lattice*; *thy captivity*; *thy converfion*; *a dove-houfe.*] A general of *Hadadezer* king of *Syria*, whom king *David* defeated and wounded.

SHO'-BA-I, [Σωβαΐ, i. e. *a turning captivity*; *fitting.*] One whofe children were of the order of *Nethinims.*

SHO'-BAL, [Σωβὰλ, i. e. *a path*; *an ear of corn*; *the thigh.*] The fon of *Caleb*, of the pofterity of *Judah*—alfo the fon of *Seir* the *Horite.*

SHO'-BEK, [Σωβήκ, i. e. *made equal to vanity*; *put to emptinefs*; *forfaken.*] One of the chiefs of the people in the time of *Nehemiah.*

SHO'-BI, ['Ουεσβὶ, i. e. *the fame with Shobai.*] One who affifted king *David* in his difficulties.

SHO'-CHO, [Σωχῶ. Σοκχὼθ, i. e. *a defence*; *a hough*; *flacknefs.*] A city of *Palefine*, in the tribe of *Judah.*

SHOCH'-OH, [Σοκχὼθ.] Probably the fame with *Shocho.*

SHO'-HAM, ['Ισοὰμ, i. e. *a precious ftone called* onyx; *a keeping back*; *the delay of them.*] One of the pofterity of the patriarch *Levi.*

SHO'-MER, [Σωμὴρ, i. e. *a keeper*; *an adamant ftone*; *a thorn*; *dregs.*] One of the pofterity of the patriarch *Afher.*

SHO'-PHACH, [Σωφὰχ, i. e. *pouring*; *poured forth*; *a vain vial.*] Captain of the hoft of *Hadadezer* king of *Syria.*

SHOPH'-AN, [Σοφὰρ. Σοφὰν, i. e. *a rabbit*; *hid*; *laid up*; *wearing*; *a breaking.*] A city of the *Amorites*, built by the patriarch *Gad.*

SHO-SHAN'-NIM, [i. e. *thofe that fhall be changed*; *a fong of rejoicing.*] In the title of fome of the *Pfalms*, this word is fuppofed to mean an inftrument of mufick of *fix* ftrings.

SHO-SHAN'-NIM E'-DUTH. Suppofed to be an inftrument of mufick of *ten* ftrings.

SHU'-A,

SHU'-A, [Σωλὰ, i. e. *crying*; *saving*.]   A grand-
daughter of the patriarch *Asher* by *Heber*—also a
canaanitish woman, wife to the patriarch *Judah*,
and mother of *Er*, *Onan* and *Shelah*.

SHU'-AH, [Σαυὰ, i. e. *speaking*; *praying*; *intreating*;
humiliation; *a ditch*; *a swimming*.] A son of *Abraham* by *Keturah*—also a concubine of *Judah*.

SHU'-AL, [Σηὰλ, i. e. *a fox*; *a path way*; *a little fist*.]
One of the posterity of the patriarch *Asher*—also
a country mentioned in the first book of *Samuel*;
but uncertain where.

SHU'-BA-EL, [Σωβαὴλ, i. e. *the returning captivity*;
seat of God.]   One of the posterity of the patriarch *Levi*.

SHU'-HAM, [Σαμὲ. Σαμεῖ, i. e. *a talking or thinking
or humiliation or budding forth, of those things*.] One
of the posterity of the patriarch *Dan*.

SHU'-HAM-ITES.   The descendants from *Shuham*.

SHU'-HITES, [Σαυχέοι.]   A people to the west of
Uz and south of the *Sabeans*; descended probably from *Shuah*, the son of *Abraham*.

SHU'-LAM-ITE, [Συλαμίτις. Συναμίτις, i. e. *peaceable perfect*.]   A name given to the spouse in
the song of *Solomon*, in allusion to the name of
Solomon.

SHU'-MATH-ITES, [i. e. *renowned*; *comfortless*; *a-
stonished*.]   A family mentioned in the *first* book
of *Chronicles*; but whence the term, is uncertain.

SHU'-NAM-ITE, [Σωμανίτι®.]   An inhabitant of
Shunem, as was *Abishag* whom king *David* chose
for a bed-fellow in his old age.

SHU'-NEM, [Σηνὰμ, i. e. *the sleeping of them*; *a changing*; *their second*.]   A city of *Palestine*, in the
tribe of *Issachar*.

SHU'-NI, [Συνὶ, i. e. *changed*; *sleeping*.]   One of the
sons of the patriarch *Gad*.

SHU'-NITES.   The posterity of *Shuni*.

SHU'-PHAM, [Σωφὰν, i. e. *wearing out those*; *the
beard or lip of those*; *the bank or shore of them*.] One
of the posterity of the patriarch *Benjamin*.

SHU'-PHAM-ITES. The descendants from *Shupham*.

SHUP'-

SHUP'-PIM, [Σατφὶν, i. e. *the same as Shupham.*] One of the posterity of the patriarch *Benjamin.*

SHŪR, [Σὴρ, i. e. *a wall; an ox; beholding.*] A city of *Arabia Petræa,* which gave name to the wilderness of *Shur.*

SHU'-SHAN, [Συσὰν, i. e. *a lily; a rose; joyfulness.*] The capital city of *Susiana* in *Persia.*

SHU'-SHAN E'-DUTH. An instrument of musick of *six* strings used in the jewish temple worship.

SHU'-THE-LAH, [Σηθαλὰ, i. e. *a plant of greenness; moist drink; putting moistness.*] One of the sons of the patriarch *Ephraim.*

SHU'-THAL-I'TES, [Σηθαλοῖ.] The descendants from *Shuthelah.*

S *before* I.

SI'-A, [Σιαὰ Ασυῖα, i. e. *a moving; help.*] The name of one who returned from the babylonish captivity.

SI'-A-KA, [Σιαὰ, i. e. *moving.*] One whose children were of the order of *Nethinims.*

SI'-BA. See SEBA.

SIB'-BACH-AI, [Σεβοχὰ. Σοβοχαὶ, i. e. *a bough; of springs; a cottage.*] An *Hushathite,* one of king *David*'s valiant men.

SIB-BO'-LETH. See SHIBBOLETH.

SIB'-MAH, [Σεβαμὰ, i. e. *overmuch captivity; much hoarseness; sitting.*] One of the boundary cities of the tribe of *Reuben,* situated on the mount, supposed to be *Abarim,* which overlooked the valley or great plain.

SIB'-RA-IM, [Σαβαρὶμ.] A place in *Syria.*

SI'-CHEM, [Συχὲμ. Σίκιμα, i. e. *a part; portion; shoulder.*] A city of *Palestine,* in the tribe of *Ephraim:* now *Naplosa.*

SIC'-Y-ŌN, [Σικυῶν.] A city of *Peloponnesus* in *Greece:* it was so called, and the whole *Peninsula* of *Peloponnesus* was called *Sicyonia,* from *Sicyon* its

nineteenth

nineteenth king: originally it was called *Ægialia,* from *Ægialus* its firſt monarch.

SID'-DIM, [i. e. *the laboured field.*] A vale, which is now the *ſalt or dead ſea,* or lake *Aſphaltites.*

SI'-DE, [Σιδη.] A maritime city of *Pamphylia* in *Aſia.*

SI'-DON, [Σιδων, i. e. *a hunter; hunting; the ſhip of judgment.*] The *eldeſt* ſon of the patriarch *Canaan*—alſo a city on the ſea coaſt of *Phœnice* founded by *Zidon:* now *Sayd.*

SI-DO'-NI-ANS, [Σιδώνιοι.] The inhabitants of *Sidon* city.

SI-GI'-O-NOTH, [i. e. *according to variable ſongs or tunes.*] It is ſaid to be a particular tune, or notes in muſick.

SI'-HA. See SIA.

SI'-HON, [Σηων, i. e. *a plucking up by the roots; a concluſion.*] A king of the *Amorites,* who, refuſing a paſſage through his country to the *Iſraelites,* was ſlain in battle.

SI'-HOR, [Σειωρ, i. e. *black; trouble; early in the morning.*] The river *Nile* in *Ægypt,* ſo called by *Joſhua* and *Iſaiah.*

SI'-LAS, [Σιλας, i. e. *conſidering; marking.*] He was ſuppoſed to be one of the *ſeventy* diſciples of our *Saviour.*

SIL'-LA, [Σελα, i. e. *an exalting; a treading under foot.*] A place mentioned to be near the houſe of *Millo* in *Jeruſalem.*

SI-LO'-A. See SHILOAH.

SI-LO'-AH or SI-LO'-AM, [Σιλωα. Σιλωαμ, i. e. *ſent; ſending; a bough; a weapon; armours.*] A famous fountain or pool under the walls of *Jeruſalem,* toward the *eaſt,* between the city and the brook *Kidron.*

SI-LO'-E, [Σιλωαμ, i. e. *the ſame as Siloam.*] The name of a tower of the city of *Jeruſalem.*

SIL-VA'-NUS, [Σιλuανος, i. e. *of the wood.*] Suppoſed to be the ſame perſon with *Silas,* who ſome ſay ſuffered martyrdom in *Macedonia.*

SI-MAL-CU'-E, [Σιμαλχue, i. e. *the king God; the kingdom of God: the meſſenger of God.*] A noted
arabian

arabian in the *firſt* book of *Maccabees*, who educated *Antiochus* the ſon of *Alexander*.

SIM'-E-ŌN, [Συμεὼν. Σιμεὼν, i. e. *hearing*; *obedient*.] The ſon of the patriarch *Jacob* by *Leah:* the tribe of *Simeon* in *Pal ſtine* lay to the *weſt* and *ſouth* of the lot of *Judah*; the tribe of *Dan* and the *Philiſtines* were to the *north*, the *mediterranean ſea* to the *weſt*, and *Arabia Petræa* to the *ſouth*— alſo the name of an holy man at *Jeruſalem*, who expected the coming of *Chriſt*, and lived to ſee him.

SIM'-E-ŌN-ITES. Thoſe who belonged to the tribe of *Simeon*.

SI'-MŌN, [Σίμων, i. e. *hearing*; *obeying*.] The name of ſeveral men in ſacred writ, as *Simon Peter* the apoſtle—alſo *Simon* the *Cyrenean*, or of *Cyrene*, who bore our *Saviour*'s croſs, in part, to the crucifixion—alſo *Simon* the *Canaanite* called *Zelotes*—alſo *Simon Magus* the impoſtor, of *Samaria*, in St. *Paul*'s time—alſo *Simon Maccabæus* ſurnamed *Theſſi*, a *jewiſh* high prieſt, and a warrior, about A. M. 3860—alſo *Simon* the tanner mentioned in *Acts*.

SIM'-RI, [i. e. *an adamant ſtone*; *a thorn*.] A porter or guard of the temple of *Jeruſalem*.

SIN, [Σὶν, i. e. *a dart*; *armour*; *coldneſs*.] The *eighth* encampment of the *Iſraelites*, lying between *Elim* and mount *Sinai:* it is called the wilderneſs of *Sin*.

SIN'-A-I, [Σινᾶ. L. *Sin'-a-i*, i. e. *a bramble*; *enmity*.] A mountain of *Arabia Petræa* in *Aſia*, on which the law was delivered to *Moſes:* the *twelfth* encampment of the *Iſraelites* was in *its* wilderneſs.

SI'-NIM, [i. e. *the ſouth country*.] The name of *Peluſium*, a city in *Ægypt*.

SIN'-ITES, ['Ασευναῖοι, i. e. *borders*.] The deſcendants from *Canaan* the patriarch.

SI'-ŌN, [Σιὼν, i. e. *an heap*; *a tomb*; *looking glaſſes*; *drought*.] A mountain of *Jeruſalem*, where the city of *David* was built, and where the temple is ſaid to be built, although ſtrictly it was built

on

on mount *Moriah*, which is part of mount *Zion*.
Zion is also one of the names of mount *Hermon*.

SIPH'-MOTH, [Σαφθ] A place in the land of
Palestine.

SIP'-PAI, [Σιππαι, i. e. *a threshold; a water pot; a
silver cup; an end.*] One who was of the race of
the *giants* or *Anakims*.

SI'-RACH, [Σειράχ, i. e. *an hissing; a song of the brother; an empty gift.*] The father of *Jesus* in the
Apocrypha.

SI'-RAH, [Σειρᾶ.] A place near to *Jerusalem*, noted
for a *well*.

SIR'-I-ON, [Σειριω, i. e. *a breast plate; deliverance;
song of the dove.*] The name given to mount
Hermon by the *Sidonians*.

SIS-AM-A'-I, [Σοσομαι, i. e. *an house; swallow of waters; blindness.*] One of the posterity of *Judah*.

SIS'-ER-A, [Σισάρα, i. e. *seeing a swallow, an horse or
a moth.*] General of the army of *Jabin* king of
Canaan, who was slain by *Jael* the wife of *Heber*
—also others of that name.

SI-SIN'-NES, [Σισιννης.] A governor of *Cæle Syria*
or *hollow Syria*.

SIT'-NAH, [i. e. *hatred.*] The name of a *well*, dug
by the patriarch *Isaac* in *Gerar*.

SI'-VAN, [Σιιαν, i. e. *bush or thorn.*] The babylonish
name of the *third* jewish month, answering to
a part of our *May* and *June*.

S before M.

SMYR'-NA, [Σμύρνα, i. e. *myrrh.*] A city of *Asia*
minor in the *Archipelago*: now *Ismyn*.

S before O.

SO, [Σηγωρ, i. e. *a measure; a veil.*] A king of
Ægypt, supposed to be *Sabacon*.

SO'-CHOH, [Σωχω, i. e. *a covering; a bough.*] A city
of *Palestine* in the tribe of *Judah*, in the valley.

U SO-COH,

SO'-COH, [Σωχὰ, i. e. *tabernacles.*] One of the posterity of the patriarch *Judah*—also a city of *Judah.*

SO'-DI, [Σὑδὸς, i. e. *my secret.*] One whose son *Moses* sent to spy out the land of *Canaan*; the father of *Gaddiel.*

SOD'-OM, [Σοδόμα, i. e. *their secret; a heel; their morter.*] The capital city of *Pentapolis* in *Afia*, which, with *Gomorrah, Admah* and *Zeboim*, were destroyed by fire, or lightning: they stood upon a fruitful plain, where now is the *dead sea*, or lake of *Sodom*, called also lake *Asphaltites*, because of the *asphaltus* or *bitumen* with which it formerly abounded.

SOD'-OM-A, [Σοδόμα.] *Sodom* so called.

SOD'-OM-ITES. The inhabitants of *Sodom.*

SOL'-OM-ŌN, [Σολωμὼν. Σολομών. L. *Sol'omon*, i. e. *peaceable.*] The son of king *David* by *Bathsheba*, and who succeeded his father in the kingdom: he was born A. M. 2971, reigned about 40 years, and died A. M. 3029 or 975 years before the christian Æra, aged 58.

SONG OF THE THREE CHILDREN. The name of an *Apocryphal* book.

SONG OF SOL'-OM-ŌN. The *twenty-second* canonical book of the *Old Testament.*

SO'-PA-TER, [Σώπατρ⊙, i. e. *keeping his father without danger; the health of the father.*] One whom St. *Paul* salutes as his kinsman—also one mentioned in the *second* book of the *Maccabees.*

SOPH-E'-RETH, [Σεφηρὰ, i. e. *a scribe shewing or numbering.*] The name of one of king *Solomon's* servants.

SO'-REK, ['Αλσωρήχ, i. e. *a vine; a vineyard; hissing.*] A valley of *Philistia*, where *Delilah* lived who betrayed *Samson*; it was in the tribe of *Judah.*

SO-SIP'-A-TER, [Σωσίπατρ⊙.] See *Sopater.*

SŌS'-THEN-ĒS, [Σωσθένης, i. e. *a mighty or strong saviour.*] A chief of the *Jewish* synagogue at *Corinth* in St. *Paul's* time, who was seized on and beaten, when *Gallio* refused to hear the accusation against St. *Paul.*

SO'-STRA-

SO'-STRA-TUS, [Σωςρᾶτ&, i. e. *keeping his army from danger; the health of the army.*] A commander of the fortrefs of *Jerufalem* under *Antiochus Epiphanes.*

SO'-TA-I, [Σωταὶ, i. e. *a conclufion in pleading; a bending.*] The name of one of king *Solomon's* fervants.

S *before* P.

SPAIN, [Σπανία, i. e. *rare; precious.*] A large kingdom of *Europe*, furrounded by *Italy*, *France*, the *mediterranean fea*, *Portugal*, the *atlantick ocean*, and the bay of *Bifcay.*

SPAN. A meafure of about *nine inches.*

SPAR'-TA, [Σπάρτα, i. e. *fowed; fowing.*] A city of *Greece*, fometimes called *Lacedæmon.*

SPIKE'-NARD. It is the *nardus* or *nard* brought from the *Eaft Indies*, and from *Alexandria* in *Ægypt*—it is an aromatic plant of a moft fragrant perfume.

S *before* T.

STA'-CHYS, [Στάχυς, i. e. *an ear of corn.*] A convert to chriftianity, mentioned by the apoftle *Paul* in his epiftle to the *Romans.*

STAC'-TE, [Στακτή.] A *gum* that diftils from the *myrrh-tree.*

STEPH'-A-NAS, [Στεφανᾶς, i. e. *a crown; crowned.*] A man of note at *Corinth*, converted by St. *Paul.*

STEPH'-EN, [Στέφαν&, i. e. *a crown; crowned.*] The *firft* chriftian martyr; he was ftoned to death: he was chief of the *feven* deacons of the church, chofen A. D. 53.

STO'-ICKS, [Στωϊκοι, i. e. *a porch.*] A fect of *greek* philofophers at *Athens*, followers of *Zeno*, who taught in a common porch in that city: they held that a wife man ought to be free from all paffions, not to be moved with joy or grief, efteeming all things to be ordered by neceffity or fate.

STONE or WHITE STONE. It was an antient cuftom of delivering a *white ftone* to fuch who

were

were acquitted in judgment; or to such as conquered in the games.

STO'-RAX. It is a dry, solid *resin*, of a reddish colour and fragrant smell—it is produced from a tree
which grows in *Syria* and in the *East Indies*.

STORK. A bird of the size of a *crane*, or about 3
feet high—its colour is white and brown—the
nails of its feet resemble a man's nails—its bill is
long and jagged—it has long and red legs—it
feeds on serpents, frogs, &c. in marshy places—
it lays but four eggs and sits upon them thirty
days—it is remarkable for its *filial piety*. One of
the seven wise men of *Greece* being asked by
Cræsus king of *Lydia*, which was the most happy
animal? answered, *the stork, because it performs
what is just and right by nature, without any compul-
sive law.*

S *before* U.

SU'-AH, [Σ𝜐ὲ, i. e. *rooting up; treading under foot.*]
One of the posterity of the patriarch *Asher*.

SU'-BA, [Σ𝜐ϛὰ.] One of the servants of *Solomon*.

SU'-BA-I, [Σ𝜐ϛαὶ.] One whose sons were servants
of the temple.

SUC'-COTH, [Σοϰχὼθ, i. e. *tabernacles; tents; booths.*]
The *second* encampment of the *Israelites*—also a
city in the land of *Canaan*, in the tribe of *Gad*,
in the valley.

SUC'-COTH BEN'-OTH, [Σωχὼθ Βενὶθ, i. e. *the
tabernacles of daughters; the anointing of daughters.*]
A place set up in *Samaria* by the men of *Babylon*,
where young women prostituted themselves in
honor of the goddess *Myletta* or *Venus*.

SUCH'-ATH-ITES. Were *Kenites* descended from
Hamath the father of the *Rechabites*.

SUD, [Σ𝜐δ. Σ𝜐δὰ, i. e. *my secret.*] A *river* mentioned
in the book of *Baruch*—also one whose sons were
servants of the temple.

SU'-DI-AS, [Σ𝜐δίος.] A *Levite* who returned from
the babylonish captivity.

SUK'-

SUK'-KI-IMS, [i. e. *anointing*; *anointed*; *covered*; *sha-dowed*.] A people of *Africa*, suppofed to be the *Troglodytes* who lived near the *Red Sea*.

SUR, [Συδά, i. e. *a giving back*; *rebellion*.] The *eaft* gate of the temple of *Solomon* was fo called.

SU'-SA, [Συσⓢ, i. e. *an horfe*; *a fwallow*; *a moth*.] The metropolis of *Perfia* in *Afia*.

SU'-SAN-CHITES, [Σωσαναχαῖοι, i. e. *lilies*; *rofes*.] A people of *Affyria*, or *Perfia*.

SU-SA'N-NAH, [Σωσάννα, i. e. *a lily*; *a rofe*; *a joy-fulnefs*.] The daughter of *Chelias* and wife of *Jo-achim*, of the tribe of *Judah*; one of the *Apocry-phal* books is entitled *the hiftory of Sufannah*.

SU'-SI, [Σωσί, i. e. *an horfe*; *a fwallow*; *a moth*.] One whofe fon *Mofes* fent to fpy out the land of *Canaan*.

S before Y.

SYC'-A-MINE or SYC'-A-MORE, [Συκάμινⓢ. Συ-κόμορⓢ.] A tree called the *ægyptian fig-tree*, which bears a fruit nearly like to a *fig*.

SY-CE'-NE. A city of *Ethiopia* in *Africa*, between *Thebes* and the cataracts of the river *Nile*.

SY'-CHAR, [Συχὰρ, i. e. *a conclufion*; *finifhing*.] A city of *Samaria*, 40 miles from *Jerufalem* and 10 miles from *Shiloh*: a city of refuge.

SY-E'-LUS, [Συῆλⓢ.] A governor of the temple of *Jerufalem* in king *Jofiah*'s reign.

SY-E'-NE, [Σύηνη, i. e. *bufh*; *enmity*.] The border of *Ægypt* towards *Ethiopia*.

SYN'-A-GOGUE, [Συναγωγή.] *Synagogues* were buildings for public worfhip among the *jews*—it is faid, that there were no fynagogues erected, until after their return from the babylonifh cap-tivity—but it feems to be probable, that thofe, who lived at a diftance from *Jerufalem*, where the temple worfhip was held, muft have had fome other place to worfhip in than in the open air.

U 3

SYN'-TY-CHE, [Συντυχὴ, i. e. *coming*; *telling a tale*.] A virtuous woman of note, mentioned by St. *Paul*.

SY'-RA-CUSE, [Συράκυσαι, i. e. *drawing violently*.] A famous city on the *east* side of the island of *Sicily* in *Italy*.

SYR'-I-A, [Συρία, i. e. *high defcending*; *the flander of them*.] In *hebrew* it is called *Aram*, from the patriarch *Aram* who first peopled it: it is a country bounded by the river *Euphrates* on the *east*; by the *mediterranean fea* on the *west*; by *Cilicia* on the *north*; and by *Phœnicia*, *Judæa* and *Arabia deferta* on the *fouth*.

SYR'-I-A DA-MAS'-CUS, [Συρία Δαμασκὸς.] The capital of *Syria*.

SYR'-I-A MA'-AC-AH, [Συρία Μααχὰ.] A place in *Syria*.

SYR'-I-ANS, [Σύροι.] The people of *Syria*.

SYR'-I-ŌN, [Σιριὼν.] See SIRION.

SY'-RO-PHE-NI'-CI-A, [Συροφοιναϑα, i. e. *rednefs*; *purple*; *drawing into it*.] A country of *Afia*: *Phœnicia* is properly called fo; *Sidon* is its capital.

SY'-RO-PHE-NI'-CI-AN, [Συροφοινίσσα.] An inhabitant of *Syrophænicia*; the *Canaanitifh* woman is fo called by St. *Mark*, being of *Phœnicia*.

T.

T *before* A.

TA'-AN-ACH, [Θαναχ, i. e. *breaking afunder;
humbling thee; anfwering to thee.*] A city of *Paleftine*, in the half tribe of *Manaffeh.*

TA'-AN-ACH SHI'-LO, [Θηναcὰ Σέλλϰϛ, i. e. *diffolving; breaking a fig tree; a little fig tree of
abundance or peace.*] One of the borders of the
tribe of *Ephraim*, in *Paleftine.*

TAB'-BA-ŌTH, [Taϭaὼθ, i. e. *rings; circles; drown-
ed; good time; a good hour.*] One whofe children
were of the order of *Nethinims.*

TAB'-BATH, [Taϭáθ, i. e. *good; goodnefs.*] A city
in the land of *Paleftine.*

TA'-BE-AL, [Taϭєὴλ, i. e. *good God.*] One mentioned by the prophet *Ifaiah*, but uncertain who
he was; but probably one who had efpoufed the
caufe of the enemies of *Judah.*

TA'-BE-ĒL, [Taϭєὴλ, i. e. *good God.*] One who
joined in writing a letter to *Artaxerxes* king of
Perfia, againft building the city of *Jerufalem.*

TA-BEL'-LI-US, [Taϭέλλιϴ.] One of king *Artaxerxes's* court.

TAB'-E-RAH, [i. e. *a burning.*] The name given
to a place where the children of *Ifrael* complained
in the wildernefs.

TAB'-ER-NA-CLE. A building in form of a tent,
fet up for the performance of religious worfhip
by the *Ifraelites* in the wildernefs, and continued
 until

until the building of the temple of *Jerusalem* by king *Solomon*. The feast of *Tabernacles* was a solemn festival of the *Jews*, observed after harvest on the *fifteenth* day of their month *Tisri*, or part of our *September* and *October*, in commemoration of the divine goodness which protected them in the wilderness, and caused them to dwell in *booths* or *tents*.

TAB'-I-THA, [Ταβιθὰ, i. e. *a roe buck*.] A christian widow of *Joppa*, ~~whom St.~~ *Peter* restored to life.

TA'-BŌR, [Θαβὼρ, i. e. *choosing; purity; contrition; breaking asunder*.] A remarkable mountain and city in *Judæa*, in the tribe of *Zebulun*, from whence was our *Saviour's* transfiguration.

TA'-BRET. An instrument of musick like a small *drum*, beaten upon by the fingers in chorus.

TAB'-RIM-ŌN, [Ταβρεμὼν, i. e. *a good pomegranate apple; high goodness; the navel; the middle; prepared*.] The father of *Benhadad* king of *Syria*.

TACH'-ES. The *taches* of the *tabernacle* were hooks, buckles, or clasps used for its curtains.

TACH'-MO-NITE. See HACHMONITE.

TAD'-MŌR, [Θαδμὼρ, i. e. *confession; praise of bitterness; myrrh of confession; the praise of a master or Lord*.] A city built by king *Solomon* in a wilderness of *Syria*, on the borders of *Arabia deserta*: it was also called *Palmyra* by the *Greeks*: *Tadmor* was the *Syriac* name: it was *two hundred* and *three* miles east from the head of the *mediterranean* sea.

TA'-HAN, [Θαὲν, i. e. *beseeching; merciful; full of grace; pitching tents*.] One of the posterity of the patriarch *Ephraim*.

TA'-HAN-ITES. The descendants from *Tahan*.

TA-HAP'-EN-ES, [Ταφνης, i. e. *the cover of confidence; hidden confidence*.] A city of *Egypt* in *Africa*, sixteen miles south of *Pelusium*.

TA'-HATH, [Θααθ, i. e. *fear; under; a going down*.] The *twenty-third* encampment of the *Israelites*; in the

the wildernefs—alfo one of the pofterity of *Levi,*
and of *Ephraim* alfo.

TAH'-PEN-ĒS, [Θεκεφενῆς, i. e. *hidden temptation;
flight; a covered banner.*] The name of a queen
of *Ægypt,* wife to one of the *Pharaohs.*

TAH'-RE-A, [Θαράχ, i. e. *anger; wicked contention;
contention of the fhepherd.*] One of the pofterity of
Saul king of *Ifrael.*

TAH'-TIM HOD'-SHI, [Θαβασών Αδασαι.] A place
of *Palestine,* probably near to *Gilead,* but uncertain where: it is mentioned in 2d *Sam.* xxiv. 6.

TAL'-ENT, [Τάλαντον.] A talent of gold is worth
about 5250l. fterling.

TAL'-I-THA CU'-MI, [Ταλιθὰ Κῦμι.] The *Syriac*
word, for, *my daughter, arife!*

TAL'-MAI, [Θολμὶ, i. e. *a furrow; delaying waters;
the affembling of waters.*] The father of *Maacah*
the wife of king *David,* and mother of *Abfalom*
and *Tamar*—alfo a fon of *Anak.*

TAL'-MŌN, [Τελμὰν, i. e. *dew prepared or numbered;
the gift of the dew.*] One who returned from the
babylonifh captivity.

TAL'-SAS, [Ταλσάς.] A *prieft* who returned from
the babylonifh captivity.

TAL-MAH, [Θημὰ, i. e. *blotting out; wiping away;
fhaving; fmiting.*] One whofe children were of
the order of *Nethinims.*

TA'-MAR, [Θάμαρ, i. e. *a palm tree.*] A daughter
in law of the patriarch *Judah,* wife to *Er* and
Onan, and mother of *Pharez* and *Zarah*—alfo the
daughter of king *David* by *Maacah*—alfo one of
the borders of the land of *Judæa.*

TAM'-MŪZ, [Θαμμὕζ, i. e. *confumed; a fire.*] The
name of a pagan deity, whom fome fuppofe to be
Adonis; others *Ofiris,* an idol of the *Ægyptians.*

TA'-NACH, [Τανὰχ, i. e. *breaking afunder; humbling
thee; anfwering to thee.*] A city of *Palestine,* in
the half tribe of *Manaffeh,* given to the *Levites.*

TAN'-HU-METH, [Θαναμὰθ, i. e. *confolation.*] One
whofe fon remained with *Gedaliah* the governor,

in *Jerusalem*, when it was taken by *Nebuchadnez-zar*.

TA'-NIS, [Τάνεως, i. e. *a motion*; *moving or moved*.] A city of *Ægypt*.

TAPH'-ATH, [Τεφὰθ, i. e. *a distilling from the head*; *a drop*; *a little one*.] The name of one of king *Solomon*'s daughters.

TAPH'-NĒS, [Ταφνὴς, i. e. *hidden temptation*; *sleight*; *a covered banner*.] The name of a city of *Ægypt* mentioned in the book of *Judith*. See TAHA-PENES.

TAPH'-ŌN, [Τεφών.] A city of *Palestine*.

TAP-PU'-AH, [Θαπφὺς. Ταφὺτ, i. e. *an apple*; *a swelling in the body*; *a tying*.] A city of *Palestine*, in the tribe of *Judah*, in the valley—also a son of *Hebron*.

TA'-RAH, [Ταρὰθ, i. e. *an hair*; *a wretch*; *a banished man*.] The place of the *twenty-fourth* encampment of the *Israelites*; in the wildernefs.

TAR-A'-LAH, [Θαρελὰ, i. e. *the searching out of slander or of strength*.] A city of *Palestine*, in the tribe of *Benjamin*.

TA'-RE-A, [Θαραὰ, i. e. *howling*; *doing evil*; *the chamber of guiseful evil or of a companion*; *chance*; *earthly*; *lesser*.] The son of *Micah* and grandson of *Jonathan* the son of king *Saul*.

TAR'-PEL-ITES, [Ταρφαλαῖοι, i. e. *ravishers*; *wearied*; *the hill of wonder*; *the keeper of decay*.] A people who lived beyond the river *Euphrates* in *Asia*.

TAR'-SHIS, [Θάρσεις, i. e. *contemplation*; *examination*; *of the joy*; *of the marble*; *precious stone*.] One of the sons of *Javan*.

TAR'-SHISH, [Θαρσὶς, i. e. *the same as Tarshis*.] A place with which *Tyre* carried on a great trade; some take it to be *Spain*.

TAR-SHI'-SI. A prince of *Media* and *Persia*.

TAR'-SUS, [Ταρσός, i. e. *winged*.] The capital of *Cilicia* in *Asia*, and native place of St. *Paul*.

TAR'-TAK, [Θαρθὰκ, i. e. *chained*; *bound*; *shut up*.] A deity of the *Avites*.

TAR'-TAN, [Θαρβὰν, i. e. *searching out*; *beholding a gift*; *the gift of the turtle bird*; *the law of them*.] A general of the army of *Sennacherib* king of *Aſſyria*, whom he ſent againſt *Jeruſalem*.

TAT'-NA-I, [Θανθαναῖ, i. e. *rewarding*; *a rewarder*.] A governor of *Samaria*, who oppoſed the rebuilding of the temple at *Jeruſalem*.

TAV'-ERNS (*three*.) The three taverns, where St. *Paul*'s friends met him, was an *Inn* not far from *Rome*. Some ſay, that *Tres Tabernæ*, or as it is tranſlated, the *Three Taverns*, was a city 33 miles from *Rome*; others, not ſo far.

T before E.

TEB'-AH, [Ταβὲη, i. e. *murder*; *butchery: a guarding of the body*; *a cook*.] One of *Nahor*'s ſons by his concubine *Reumah*.

TEB-A-LI'-AH, [Ταβλαὶ, i. e. *the baptiſm of the Lord*; *goodneſs to the Lord himſelf*.] One of the porters or guards of the temple of *Jeruſalem*.

TE'-BĒTH, [Τηβὴθ, i. e. *good*; *goodneſs*.] The *babyloniſh* name of the *tenth* month of the *Hebrews*, anſwering partly to our *December* and partly to *January*.

TE-HAPH'-NE-HĒS, [Τάϕνης, i. e. *moved*.] The ſame with *Tahapanes*.

TE-HIN'-NAH, [Θεενά, i. e. *a beſeeching*; *mereiful*; *prayer*; *very thankful*; *a favour*.] The name of one of the tribe of *Judah*.

TEK'-EL, [Θεκὲλ, i. e. *weight*.] The word ſignifies, *thou art weighed in the balances and art found wanting*.

TEK-O'-A or TEK-O'-AH, [Θεκωὲ. Θεκηὲ, i. e. *a pipe*; *noiſe*; *faſtened*.] A city of *Paleſtine*, in the tribe of *Judah*, about *twelve* miles ſouth of *Jeruſalem*—alſo the name of one of the tribe of *Judah*.

TEK-O'-ITES, [Θεκωῖται.] The inhabitants of *Tekoah*.

TEL-

TEL-A'-BIB, [i. e. *an heap of new grain.*] A city
by the river *Chebar*, where the *Jews* were kept
prisoners.

TEL'-AH, [Φαλεές, i. e. *a moistening; greenness; making green.*] One of the posterity of the patriarch
Ephraim.

TEL'-A-IM. A city of *Palestine.*

TEL-AS'-SAR, [i. e. *taking away; an heaping up.*] A
country of *Mesopotamia* in *Asia.*

TEL'-EM, [Τελμὼν, i. e. *a lamb; the dew of them; the
shadow of them.*] A city of *Palestine,* in the tribe
of *Judah*—also, one who returned from the babylonish captivity.

TEL-HAR-E'-SHA or TEL-HAR'-SA, [Θελαρησὰ,
i. e. *an heaping up of deafness; hanging up of the
plough; the word of doubtfulness.*] A city of the
babylonian empire.

TEL'-MEL-A or TEL'-MEL-AH, [Θελμελὲχ, i. e.
an heap of salt; the doubtfulness of salt.] A city of
the *babylonian* empire.

TE'-MA, [Θαιμὰν, i. e. *a marvelling at perfection; the
south wind.*] A son of *Ishmael*—also a country
of *Arabia,* inhabited by the descendants from
Tema.

TE'-MAN, [Θαιμὰν, i. e. *south; perfect; there.*] A
son of *Eliphaz,* and grandson of *Esau;* his
country was the eastern province of *Idumæa* or
Edom.

TE'-MAN-I, [Θαιμανών, i. e. *moist; perfect; the
south; ordained.*] A country of *Idumæa* or *Edom.*

TE'-MAN-ITES, [Θαιμανόι.] The posterity of
Teman.

TE'-MEN-I, [Θαιμὰν, i. e. *moist; perfect; the south;
ordained.*] One of the posterity of the patriarch
Judah.

TENTH DEAL. A *jewish* measure containing between three and four quarts *english* measure.

TEPH'-O, [i. e. *a place.*] A fort rebuilt by *Bac-
chides.*

TER'-AH, [Οάῤῥα, i. e. *smelling; breathing; driving
away.*] The father of the patriarch *Abraham,*
and

and the fon of *Nahor*; he died A. M. 2083, Æt.
205.

TER'-A-PHIMS, [Θεραφίν, i. e. *images*; *forms.*]
Images or fuperftitious figures kept in the houfes
of the antients; not improbably, their houfhold
gods.

TE'-RESH, [Θαρὰς, i. e. *fmelling*; *breathing*; *driving
away.*] One who confpired to murder king
Ahafuerus.

TER'-TI-US, [Τέρτιℴ, i. e. *the third.*] The ama-
nuenfis of St. *Paul* when he wrote his epiftle to
the *Romans.*

TER-TUL'-LUS, [Τερτύλλℴ, i. e. *declaring falfe
things*; *a liar*; *wondrous.*] An advocate who
pleaded againft St. *Paul*, before *Felix.*

TE'-TA, [Τηλὰ. 'Ατηλὰ.] One who returned from
the babylonifh captivity.

TET'-RARCH, [Τετράρχης.] The title of a fove-
reign prince over the *fourth* part of a province or
kingdom.

.T *before* H.

THAD-DE'-US, [Θαδδαῖος, i. e. *praifing*; *confeffing.*]
The furname of *Lebbeus*, one of the twelve difciples of our *Saviour.*

THA'-HASH, [Ταὰμ. Τοχὸς, i. e. *hafting.*] One
of *Nahor's* fons by his concubine *Reumah.*

THAM'-AH, [Θημὰ, i. e. *blotting out*; *wiping away*;
fmiting.] One whofe children were of the order
of *Nethinims.*

THAM'-NA-THA, [Θαμναθὰ.] A city of *Paleftine.*
See *Thimnathath.*

THA'-RA, [Θάρα, i. e. *a good, fmall.*] One mentioned in St. *Luke's* genealogical lift.

THAR'-RA, [Θάρρα.] An eunuch of *Artaxerxes*
king of *Perfia.*

THAR'-SHISH, [Θαρςὶς.] A defcendant from the
patriarch *Benjamin.*

THAS'-SI, [Θασσὶ, i. e. *forgetful*; *a debtor.*] The
furname of *Simon* the fon of *Mattathias*, in the
Apocrypha.

THE-

THE'-BEZ, [Θηϐης, i. e. *an egg*; *a filken garment*; *flax*.] A city of the *Canaanites*; in the half tribe of *Manaffeh*.

THEC-O'-E, [Θεκωὲ, i. e. *hope*; *alive*; *congregation*.] A wildernefs near to the *dead fea* or *lake* of *Sodom*.

THEL-AS'-SAR, [Θαλασσὰρ, i. e. *taking away*; *heaping up*.] A place fuppofed to be in *Affyria*.

THEL-ER'-SAS, [Θελερσὰς, i. e. *an heaping up of deafnefs*; *the wood of dolefulnefs*.] A place in the babylonian empire.

THE-O'-CA-NUS, [Θεωκανὸς.] One whofe family returned from the babylonifh captivity.

THE-OD'-OT-US, [Θεόδοτ⊙, i. e. *given to God*.] A *Syrian* commiffioner fent to treat of peace with *Judas Maccabæus*.

THE-OPH'-I-LUS, [Θεόφιλ⊙, i. e. *a friend or lover of God*; *devout*; *beloved of God*.] The perfon to whom St. *Luke* addreffes his gofpel and the *Acts* of the apoftles: fome fuppofe him to have been a magiftrate of *Achaia*; others, that it is a common name for any good man.

THER'-AS, [Θερὰς.] A river mentioned in the *Apocrypha*.

THER'-MEL-ETH, [Θερμελὲθ.] One whofe family returned from the babylonifh captivity.

THES-SA-LON'-I-ANS, [Θεσσαλονίκεες.] The people of *Theffalonica*—alfo the title of *two* canonical books of the *New Teftament*.

THES-SA-LON-I'-CA, [Θεσσαλονίκη, i. e. *the other victory of God*; *the putting of the other victory*.] A city of *Macedonia*, of great note, called fo by *Philip* of *Macedon*, in memory of his victory over the *Theffalians*: now *Salonichi*, in *Turkey* in *Europe*.

THEU'-DAS, [Θευδᾶς, i. e. *flowing with water*.] A falfe apoftle mentioned in the book of *Acts*.

THIM'-NA-THATH, [Θαμναθὰ.] A city of *Paleftine* in the tribe of *Dan*. See *Thimnathah*.

THIS'-BE, [Θισϐὴς.] A city of *Galilee* in the land of *Canaan*.

THO'-

THO'-MAS, [Θωμᾶς, i. e. *a twin; deepneſs without bottom.*] An apoſtle of *Jeſus Chriſt:* he was called *Didymus,* as being a twin: he is ſuppoſed to have been martyred in *Eaſt India.*

THOM'-O-I, [Θομοὶ.] One whoſe ſons were ſervants to the temple.

THRA'-CI-A, [Θράκη, i. e. *a ſpark; ſtony.*] The country of *Thrace* in *Europe.*

THRA-SE'-AS, [Θρασαιῶ. L. *Thra'ſeas,* i. e. *the ſame as Tarſhiſh.*] The father of *Apollonius* in the ſecond book of *Maccabees.*

THUM'-MIM, ['Αληθεία.] See URIM.

THY-A-TI'-RA, [Θυατείρα, i. e. *a ſweet ſavour of labour; ſacrifice of contrition.*] A city of *leſſer Aſia,* on the frontiers of *Myſia* and *Lydia:* now *Akiſhar.*

T before I.

TI-BER'-I-AS, [Τιϐεριάς, i. e. *a good viſion; a navel; breaking aſunder.*] A famous city of *Paleſtine,* on the ſouthern extremity of *Galilee,* on the weſt ſhore of the lake of *Genneſareth* or ſea of *Tiberias;* built by *Herod Agrippa,* in honour of *Tiberius* emperor of *Rome.*

TI-BER'-I-US CÆ'-SAR, [Τιϐεριῶ Καίσαρ, i. e. *the ſame as Tiberias.*] The ſecond emperor of *Rome,* who began to reign A. D. 2; reigned *twenty-two* years and an *half,* and died A. D. 37, Æt. 78.

TIB'-BATH, [Ταϐάθ. Τιϐχάθ, i. e. *a killing; a cook.*] A city of *Syria.*

TIB'-NI, [Θαμνὶ, i. e. *chaff; hay.*] One who was ſet up for king of *Iſrael* in the civil wars of that kingdom.

TI'-DAL, [Θαργὰλ, i. e. *breaking the yoke; the knowledge of lifting up.*] A king who is ſtiled *king of nations;* whoſe dominion was part of that valley where *Sodom* ſtood, and is now the *dead ſea.*

TIG'-LATH PIL-ES'-ER, [Θαγλαθ Φαλλασὰρ, i. e. *he hath taken away or forbidden a marvellous captivity; forbidding ſnow falling.*] A king of *Aſſyria* in
the

the time of *Ahaz* king of *Judah*; he began to reign in *Babylon*, A. M. 3258.

TI'-GRIS, [Τίγρις, i. e. *the sharpness of swiftness*; *a sharp sound*; *a voice*.] A famous river of *Affyria* in *Afia*, near to which stood the city of *Nineveh*.

TIK'-VAH or TIK'-VATH, [Θεκυέ, i. e. *hope*; *a little line*; *congregation*.] The father of *Shallum* who was hufband to *Huldah* the prophetefs.

TI'-LON, [Θιλὼν, i. e. *murmuring*.] One of the pofterity of the patriarch *Judah*.

TIM'-BREL. An inftrument of mufick much ufed among the *jews*, of the *drum* kind, to be beat upon to caufe a found.

TI-ME'-US, [Τιμαῖος, i. e. *perfect*; *honourable*; *admirable*.] The father of blind *Bartimeus*.

TIM'-NA, [Θεμνὰ. Θαμνά, i. e. *a forbidding or a perfect perturbation*.] One who was a concubine of *Eliphaz* the fon of the patriarch *Efau*—alfo a fifter to *Lotan*.

TIM'-NAH, [Θαμνὰ, i. e. *the fame as Timna*.] A city of *Palefine*, in the tribe of *Judah*, in the mountains—alfo the name of a *Duke* a defcendant from *Efau*—alfo a city in the tribe of *Dan*.

TIM'-NATH, [Θαμνὰ, i. e. *image*; *figure*; *enumeration*.] A city of the *Philifines*, the birth-place of *Samfon's* wife; in the tribe of *Judah*.

TIM'-NA-THAH, [Θαμναθὰ.] A city of *Palefine*, in the tribe of *Dan*. See *Thimnathath*.

TIM'-NATH HE'-RES or TIM'-NATH SE'-RAH, [Θαμνασαρὰχ. Θαμνασαρὶς, i. e. *the image of the fun*; *a figure enlarged*; *an ordained flench*; *a numbering the reft*.] A city of *Palefine*, in mount *Ephraim*, where that great general, *Jofhua*, was buried.

TIM'-NITE. An inhabitant of *Timnath*.

TI'-MON, [Τιμων, i. e. *honourable*; *precious*.] One of the *feven* deacons of the *firft* chriftian church.

TIMOTH'-E-US, [Τιμόθεος, i. e. *the honour of God*; *honouring of God*; *precious to God*.] The name of two generals of the army of *Antiochus Epiphanes*, who

who were defeated by *Judas Maccabæus*—alfo a difciple in the book of *Acts.*

TIM'-OTH-Y, [Τιμοθέ©, i. e. *the fame with Timotheus.*] A difciple of St. *Paul* whom he calls his fon, and from whom are named the *two* canonical epiftles of St. *Paul* to *Timothy*, in the *New Teftament: Timothy* fuffered martyrdom at *Ephefus,* of the church of which he was bifhop.

TIPH'-SAH, [Θάψα, i.e. *a paffing over; an halting; the paffover.*] A place on the *weft* fide of the river *Jordan.*

TI'-RAS, [Θίρας, i. e. *a deftroyer.*] The feventh fon of *Japhet* and grandfon to *Noah.*

TI'-RATH-ITES, [i. e. *fingers; porters.*] A family who defcended from *Hemath,* head of the family of the *Rechabites.*

TIR'-HA-KAH, [Θαραχὰ, i. e. *a dull fearcher out; a beholder; an hindrance of the law.*] An *æthiopian* king, who affifted king *Hezekiah* againft *Sennacherib* king of *Affyria.*

TIR'-HA-NAH, [Θαραμά, i. e. *a fearcher of mercy; the turtle bird of mercy.*] A fon of *Caleb,* of the pofterity of *Judah.*

TI'-RI-A, [Θιριὰ, i. e. *a fearch; fearching out; beholding.*] One of the pofterity of the patriarch *Judah.*

TIR'-SHA-THA, ['Αθερσαθὰ, i. e. *that overturns the foundation; beholding the year or time; him who hath authority over us.*] A title of *governor;* as *Nehemiah* was *Tirfhatha.*

TIR'-ZAH, [Θερσά, i.e. *pleafing well; willing; pleafant; running.*] A daughter of *Zelophebad*—alfo a city of *Paleftine,* in the tribe of *Ephraim.*

TISH'-BITE, [Θεσβίτης, i. e. *taking captive; turning; fitting; dwelling.*] The furname of the prophet *Elijah,* from *Thefbon* a city of the tribe of *Manaffeh,* on the *eaft* fide of the river *Jordan,* near to mount *Gilead.*

TI'-TUS, [Τίτ©, i. e. *honourable.*] A difciple of St. *Paul,* from whom is derived the title of one of

the

the canonical books of the *New Teſtament:* he was biſhop of *Crete* iſle, and was buried there, Æt. 94.

TI'-TUS MAN'-LI-US. An ambaſſador from the *Romans* to the *Jews.*

TI'-VAN. See SI'VAN.

TI'-ZITĒ, [Θωσαί, i. e. *a ſcattering; ſcattered; going out.*] An inhabitant of *Tiza.*

T *before* O.

TO'-AH, [Θοὺ, i. e. *a weapon, a dart.*] One of the poſterity of the patriarch *Levi.*

TŌB, [Τώϐ, i. e. *good; goodneſs.*] A place where *Jephthah* dwelt; but the ſituation uncertain.

TŌB AD-O'-NI-JAH, [Τωϐαδωνίας, i. e. *a good governor or Lord; a good foot of the pillar of the Lord.*] A *Levite* in the reign of king *Je-hoſhaphat,* ſent by him to inſtruct the cities of *Judah,* in the principles and duties of religion.

TO'-BI-AH, [Τωϐίας, i. e. *a good lord; the goodneſs of the Lord.*] An *Ammonite* who oppoſed the rebuilding of the temple at *Jeruſalem.*

TO'-BI-AS, [Τωϐίας, L. *To'bias,* i. e. *the ſame as Tobiah.*] The ſon of *Tobit*—alſo the father of *Hircanus.*

TO'-BI-E, [Τωϐίας, i. e. *a meaſured well; a good meaſure; good wine.*] A place in the land of *Paleſtine,* in the tribe of *Gad.*

TO'-BI-EL, [Τωϐιὴλ.] The father of *Tobit.*

TO'-BI-JAH, [Τωϐίας, i. e. *a good lord; the goodneſs of the Lord.*] A *Levite* in king *Jehoſhaphat's* reign, ſent by him to inſtruct the cities of *Judah.*

TO'-BIT, [Τωϐὶτ, i. e. *the ſame as Tobiah.*] The ſon of *Tobiel,* of the tribe of *Naphtali:* after whom was named the apocryphal book *Tobit.*

TOCH'-

TOCH'-EN, [Θοχχὰν, i. e. *the middle; between the middle; prepared.*]   A city of *Palestine*, in the tribe of *Simeon.*

TOG-AR'-MAH, [Θογαρμά, i. e. *strong; bony; overmuch inhabited; a stranger; fearing greatly.*]   The *third* son of *Gomer*, and grandson of *Japhet.*

TO'-HU, [Θοῦ, i. e. *living.*]   An ancestor of the prophet *Samuel.*

TO'-I, [Θοὲ. Θαεί, i. e. *erring.*]   A king of *Hamath* in *Syria.*

TO'-LA, [Θωλὰ, i. e. *a worm.*]   The *ninth* judge of *Israel*, who died A. M. 2796, B. C. about 1208 years; having ruled 23 years—also a son of *Issachar.*

TO'-LAD, [Θωλὰδ, i. e. *a nativity; generation.*]   A city of *Palestine*, in the tribe of *Simeon.*

TO-LA'-ITES, [Θωλαιοῖ, i. e. *little worms.*]   The descendants from *Tola.*

TOL'-BA-NĒS, [Τολϐάνης.]   One who returned from the babylonish captivity, a porter or guard of the temple.

TO'-PAZ, [Τωπάζον.]   A precious stone, being the *second* in the *first* row of the *jewish* high priest's breast plate: it is of a beautiful *yellow* colour: it is also called a *chrysolite.*

TOPH'-EL, [Τοφὸλ, i. e. *decay; foolishness.*]   A place supposed to be in the country of *Moab.*

TOPH'-ET, [Ταφὲθ, i. e. *a timbrel; tabret; a leading aside; an enlarging.*]   A place in the valley of *Hinnom*, where sacrifices were offered to the god *Moloch*, and a drum beat to drown the cries of their children who passed through the fire in sacrifice, and were perhaps burnt there; as the expression of, *the high places of Tophet*, may mean their altars.

TO'-U. [Θωῦ.]   The same with TOI.

T *before* R.

TRA-CHO-NI'-TIS, [Τραχωνῖτις, i. e. *ftony; cruel.*]
A province between the land of *Paleftine,* and
Cœle-Syria.

TRI'-BUNES. In the book of *Maccabees,* are meant
the captains of the armies.

TRI'-POL-IS, [Τρίπολις, i. e. *of three cities.*] A city
of *Phœnicia,* in *Afia,* lying on the mediterranean fea:
now *Koenikoi.*

TRO'-AS, [Τρωὰς, i. e. *bored through.*] A city of
Phrygia or *Myfia* in *Afia,* fouth of old *Troy:* old
Troy was built about the time of *Mofes.*

TRO-GYL'-LI-UM, [Τρωγυλλίον, i. e. *a pantry.*] A
city of the ifle of *Samos* in the *Archipelago,* on the
coaft of *Afia-minor.*

TROPH'-I-MUS, [Τρόφιμ☉, i. e. *nourifhed; brought
up.*] A difciple of St. *Paul,* and faid to have
been martyred in the reign of *Nero* the *roman*
emperor.

TRY-PHE'-NA, [Τρύφαινα, i. e. *delicious; delicate.*]
A chriftian woman mentioned by St. *Paul* in his
epiftle to the *Romans.*

TRY'-PHON, [Τρύφων, i. e. *the fame as Tryphena.*]
A perfon mentioned in the firft book of *Maccabees,*
who was an adherent of the party of king *Alexander* the fon of *Antiochus Epiphanes.*

TRY-PHO'-SA, [Τρυφῶσα, i. e. *the fame as Tryphena.*] A chriftian woman mentioned by St.
Paul in his epiftle to the *Romans.*

T *before* U.

TUB'-AL, [Θοβὲλ, i. e. *born; brought; worldly; confufion; flander.*] The *fifth* fon of *Japhet,* and
grandfon of *Noah.*

TUB'-AL CA'-IN, [Θοβελχαὶν, i. e. *worldly poffeffion;
poffeffing confufion; imitating flander.*] The fon of
the patriarch *Lamech* by *Zillah,* and the inventor
of brafs and iron inftruments: he is fuppofed to
be the *Vulcan* of the heathens.

TU-BI-

TU-BI-EN'-I, [Τϐιένοι, i. e. *ſtraw*; *anſwering well.*] Certain *Jews* ſo called, in the 2d book of *Maccabees*, from their living in the land of *Tob* or *Tubin*, which lay on the northern ſide of *Manaſſeh's* lot, on the other ſide of the river *Jordan*.

T before Y.

TY'-CHI-CUS, [Τύχικὸς, i. e. *caſual*; *happening*.] A diſciple and fellow labourer of St. *Paul*.

TY-RAN'-NUS. [Τυράννℴ, i. e. *ruling*; *a prince*.] Suppoſed to be a converted *Gentile* at *Epheſus*; in whoſe ſchool St. *Paul* preached.

TYRE, [Τύρℴ, i. e. *a breaking with a flail*; *a ſiege*; *binding*; *a ſinging*; *ſtrength*; *a rock*.] A city of *Phenice* in *Aſia*, about *ſixty* miles ſouth weſt of *Damaſcus*, on the *mediterranean ſea*; it is called the daughter of *Zidon*, as being colonized by the *Zidonians*: the old city *Tyre* ſtood on the continent, and was taken by *Nebuchadnezzar* after *thirteen* years' ſiege, about 563 years B. C. new *Tyre* was built on an iſland, about *half a mile* from the continent, and was taken and deſtroyed by *Alexander* the great, after a *ſeven* months' ſiege.

TYR'-I-ANS. The inhabitants of *Tyre*.

TY'-RUS. See TYRE.

V an

V and U.

V *before* A.

VA-JE'-ZA-THA, [Ζαβωγαθά, i. e. *sprinkling the chamber.*] One of *Haman's* ten fons, whom the *Jews* put to death.

VA-NI'-AH, ['Ουβανία, i. e. *nourifhment of the Lord*; *the weapons of the Lord.*] The name of one who returned from the babylonifh captivity.

VASH'-NI, [Σανì, i. e. *fecond*; *changed*; *a tooth*; *my year.*] The eldeft fon of the prophet *Samuel.*

VASH'-TI, ['Aşì, i. e. *drinking*; *doubling*; *putting*; *hemp.*] A *Jewefs,* the queen of king *Ahafuerus.*

U *before* C.

U'-CAL, [i. e. *power*; *prevalence.*] One mentioned in the book of *Proverbs,* but uncertain who.

U *before* E.

U'-EL, [Ουήλ, i. e. *defiring God.*] One who return-ed from the babylonifh captivity.

V *before* I.

VI'-OL. A ftringed inftrument of mufick, among the *jews,* to be played upon with a bow, as a violin is.

U before

U *before* L.

U'-LA-I, ['Ουλαι, i. e. *strength*; *a fool, senseless*.] A river which divides the province of *Susiana* in *Persia* from *Elam*.

U'-LAM, ['Ουλὰμ, i. e. *a porch*; *a gallery*; *strength*; *foolishness of them*.] One of the posterity of *Manasseh* the patriarch—also a descendant from king *Saul*.

UL'-LA, ['Ολὰ, i. e. *a lifting up*; *a sacrifice killed on the altar*; *an infant*; *a little one*.] One of the posterity of the patriarch *Asher*.

U *before* M.

UM'-MAH, ['Αμμὰ, i. e. *darkened*; *covered*; *his people*; *with him*.] A city, one of the borders of the tribe of *Asher*, in *Palestine*.

U *before* N.

UNCLEAN AND CLEAN ANIMALS.

Under the *mosaick* constitution various kinds of animals were *prohibited*, and other kinds *allowed*, for food. The reasons for which were *moral, political, and natural*—the two former in order to preserve the *jews*, as a distinct people, from the idolatrous nations, in the worship of *one God* only, as hath been already hinted in the case of *unleavened bread*.

The *natural* reason for the prohibition might be, that the prohibited animals were of an alkalescent nature, and so, productive of various diseases in the hot climate of *Judæa*, agreeably to the remarks of a noted english physician—more especially the *swine*, which feeds upon all manner of filth, and, as divers writers of note have observed, is apt to breed the *leprosy* in warm cli-

X 4

mate

mates, and other *scrofulous* diforders; the word *scrofula*, being derived from the latin word *scrofa*, a *sow:* the *swine* being fubject to the *leprofy* and the *meafles*, proceeding from its bad feeding.

The mofaick rule was, *among beafts*, that what-ever *parted the hoof, was cloven footed and chewed the cud*, was allowed to be eaten: thofe that were *prohibited* are thus claffed in the 11th chapter of *Leviticus*, viz.

The *Camel.*
Coney which is fuppofed to be a fpecies of rat, be-tween a coney and rat, common in *Ægypt* and *Paleftine.*
Hare.
Swine.

Prohibited Fifh

Were thofe, which have not *fins*, nor *fcales*,

Prohibited Fowls.

The *Bat*	The *Kite*
Cormorant	*Lapwing*
Cuckow	*Night-hawk*
Eagle.	*Ofpray*
Fowls that creep, going on all fours, as *Bats* and all kinds of *Flies.*	*Offifrage*
	Owl
	Great and little Owl
	Pelican
The *Gier Eagle*	*Raven*
Hawks	*Stork*
Heron	*Swan* and *Vulture.*

Thofe which go on their paws, on *all* fours, were prohibited, viz.

The *Chamelion*	The *Moufe*
Ferret	*Snail*
Lizard	*Tortoife*
Mole	*Weafel*

The

The following were accounted *clean*, viz.

All flying creeping things which go upon *all* fours,
and have legs about their feet to leap with, as

The *Bald-Locust*
    Beetle, suppofed to be another fort of *Locuft*
    Grafshopper
    Locuft.

U'-NI-CORN. It is an animal having but *one* horn,
and mentioned in feveral places in *facred writ.*
It is by many fuppofed to be fictitious; as there
is no land animal, now known, of that kind:
although there is a fifh, called a *fea unicorn*, as
having an horn projecting from its nofe, paral-
lel with its body. That mentioned in the book
of *Job*, is thought, by fome, to be meant the
wild bull of *Arabia*, as the hebrew name of it is
Reem, which is mentioned in feveral places of
facred writ as of the *beeve* kind—but, father *Lobo*,
the portuguefe jefuit, fays, that when he was
in *Abyffinia*, towards the beginning of the laft
century, he faw an *unicorn*, but could not come
near to him—he defcribes it, as having the fhape
of a beautiful *horfe*, exact and nicely proportioned,
of a bay colour, with a black tail, which, he fays,
in fome provinces is long, in others fhort: fome
have long manes hanging to the ground—they are
timorous, and never feed but when they are furrounded with other animals to defend them—it is
alfo faid, that the *elephant* feeds with other animals
around him which *he* defends.

UN'-NI, ['Avi, i. e. *an anfwer or a fong; afflicted;
    poor.*] A *Levite* and porter of the temple of *Je-
    rufalem.*

V *before*

V *before* O.

VOPH'-SI, [Βαφσί, i. e. *a thing broken; parched; a portion; diminished.*] One, whose son *Moses* sent to spy out the land of *Canaan.*

U *before* P.

U'-PHAZ, [Μωφὰζ, i. e. *pure gold.*] A place which is supposed to be the same with *Ophir.*

U-PHAR'-SIN, [Φαρές.] The word signifies, *and they divide it.*

U *before* R.

UR, [Χώρ, i. e. *fire; light.*] A city of *Chaldæa,* in *Asia*—also the father of *Eliphal.*

UR-BA'-NE *, [Ουρβανός, i. e. *civil; courteous; gentle in speech.*] One who is mentioned by St. *Paul* in his epistle to the *Romans,* and his fellow helper.

U'-RI, ['Ουρὶ, i. e. *my light or fire.*] A descendant from the patriarch *Judah,* and a grandson of *Caleb*—also others.

U-RI'-AH, ['Ουριάς, i. e. *the fire or the light of the Lord.*] The unfortunate husband of *Bathsheba*; a brave warrior, and one of king *David*'s worthies —also the name of a *jewish* priest.

U-RI'-AS, ['Ουρίας.] A principal man among the *jews,* after the babylonish captivity.

U'-RI-EL, [Ουριὴλ, i. e. *light or fire of God.*] The father of *Michaiah* the wife of king *Rehoboam* and mother of king *Abijah.*

U-RI'-JAH, ['Ουρίας, i. e. *the fire or the light of the Lord.*] A prophet, the son of *Shemaiah,* who

---

* It might have been more properly translated *Urbanus*; as many other names in the same chapter are, in the nominative case, *as Narcissus, Rufus,* &c.

                    prophesied

prophesied against *Jerusalem*, and was slain by order of *Jehoiakim*, king of *Judah*—also an high priest in the reign of *Ahaz* king of *Judah*.

U'-RIM and THUM'-MIM, [Δήλωσις και 'Αλήθεια, i. c. *Urim signifies light, and Thummim, perfection or truth.*] The *jewish* oracle, during the *Theocracy*; supposed to difcover the will of Heaven by the fplendor of the ftones in the breaft-plate which the high prieft wore, when it was confulted by a *king, the prefident of the fanhedrim* or a *general of an army*, or upon public important occafions; but not upon private: in cafe of a war, fome fuppofe, that upon confulting this oracle, the uncommon fplendor of thofe ftones, which were marked with the names of each tribe, pointed out which of the tribes were to enter the lifts againft the enemy.

After the directions for finifhing the high prieft's breaft-plate, *Mofes* was ordered to put into it the *Urim* and *Thummim*; but what was meant by the *Urim* and *Thummim*, the fentiments of the learned are fo various, that it feems impoffible, at this day, to fettle the meaning: it is fuppofed to have continued until *Solomon* had built his temple; and that after that time the will of Heaven was confulted by *prophets*; and that after the rebuilding of the temple upon the return from the babylonifh captivity, the will of Heaven was difcovered by the *Bath-col* or *daughter of the voice*, by which is meant a voice from Heaven, as at the baptifm of our *Saviour*.

The breaft-plate worn by the *jewifh* high prieft was about *ten inches* fquare, and was fet with *twelve* precious ftones, on each of which was engraven the name of one of the twelve tribes of *Ifrael*. They were fet in *four* rows, *three* in each row, and divided from each other by the little golden fquares or partitions in which they were fet. The upper or firft row was fet with a *fardius*, a *topaz* and a *carbuncle*—in the *fecond* row, were an *emerald*, a *fapphire* and a *diamond*—in the

third

third row were a *ligure*, an *agate* and an *amethyst*
—and in the *fourth* row were a *beryl*, an *onyx* and
a *jasper*. It was called the *breast-plate of judgment*,
as having the divine oracle of *Urim* and *Thum-*
mim annexed to it.

For the colours of the stones, see under the
article of each stone.

U *before* T.

U'-TA, ['Ουτὰ.] One whose sons were servants of
the temple.

U'-THA-I, ['Ουθαὶ, i. e. *mine iniquity*; *time*; *forward-*
ness; *an hour*.] The son of *Ammihud*, of the tribe
of *Judah*.

U'-THI, [Ουθι.] One who returned from the babylonish captivity.

U *before* Z.

UZ, ['Ουζ, i. e. *counsel*; *words*; *fastened*.] The
eldest son of *Aram*, and grandson to the patriarch *Shem*—also the son of *Dishan*, a duke of
Edom—also a country supposed to be in *Arabia*,
where *Job* lived.

U'-ZA-I, ['Ευζαὶ, i. e. *then or he*.] One who assisted
in repairing the walls of *Jerusalem*.

U'-ZAL or U'-SAL, ['Αιζὴλ, i. e. *wandering*; *sail-*
ing; *distilling from the head*.] One of the posterity of the patriarch *Shem*.

UZ'-ZA, ['Οζα. 'Αζά, i. e. *strength*; *a goat*.] One of
the posterity of the patriarch *Benjamin*, whose
children were of the order of *Nethinims*.

UZ'-ZAH, ['Οζᾶ, i. e. *the same as Uzza*.] The son of
Abinadab; he was instantly struck dead for touching the ark with unhallowed hands.

UZ'-ZEN SHE'-RAH, [Οζαν Σεηρὰ, i. e. *an ear-lap*
of flesh; *an ear-lap remaining*.] A city of *Pa-*
lestine, in the tribe of *Ephraim*, built by *Sherah*
the daughter of *Beriah*.

UZ'ZI,

UZ'-ZI, ['Oζι, i. e. *strong*; *my strength*; *my goat*.] The *sixth* high priest of the jews—also others of that name.

UZ-ZI'-AH or AZ-A-RI'-AH, ['Oζια. 'Aζαρια, i. e. *the strength of the Lord*.] A king of *Judah*, died A. M. 3246—also *Uz'-zi-a*, one of king *David*'s worthies—also others.

UZ-ZI'-EL. ['Oζιηλ, i. e. *the strength of God*; *the buck goat of God*.] The son of *Kohath*, a *Levite*, and chief of the family of the *Uzzielites*, and uncle to *Aaron*.

UZ-ZI'-EL-ITES. Those of the family of *Uzziel* the *Levite*.

W.

W *before* A.

WATCH. The *first* watch was from sun set to the *third* hour of the night. The *second*, or middle watch, from the *third* hour to the *sixth*, or midnight. The *third* watch, or cock crowing, from midnight to *three* o'clock, or the *ninth* hour. The *fourth* watch from the *ninth* hour to sun rise.

WAVE OF'-FER-ING. See OFFERINGS.

W *before* E.

WEEKS. There were three sorts of *weeks* among the Jews, viz. 1. The weeks of *days*, which were reckoned from one Sabbath to another. 2. Weeks

2. Weeks of *years*, i. e. from one fabbatical year to another, confifting of *feven* years. 3. Weeks of *feven* times *feven* years, or 49 years, reckoned from one Jubilee to another.

W before I.

WILD'-ER-NESS. The *Hebrews* gave this name to places not cultivated, on which trees grew wild, and which were chiefly deftined to feeding cattle.

WIS'-DOM. The name of one of the books of the *Apocrypha*.

WITCH. One, who by juggling deludes the fenfes with falfe appearances of things—or one that doth mifchief to man or beaft by evil arts—or a foothfayer. The word in the original is of the feminine gender, becaufe women are fuppofed to be addicted to this crime: but there are men-witches, who are commonly called *wizards*.

WIZ'-ARD. A wizard was one who pretended to confult familiar fpirits, and foretel future events by practifing evil arts.

X.

X before A.

XAN'-THI-CUS, [Ξανθικός.] A *macedonian* month, anfwering to part of our *February* and part of our *March*.

Y before

Y.

Y *before* E.

YEAR. The *jewish* year was divided into *sacred* and *civil:* the *sacred* year was for the performance of their religious rites and ceremonies: the *civil* year for the ordering of their political affairs.

The *months* stand thus in the *sacred* year,

1.	NI'-SAN		*March* and *April*
2.	JI'-AR		*April* and *May*
3.	SI'-VAN		*May* and *June*
4.	THAM'-MUZ		*June* and *July*
5.	AB		*July* and *August*
6.	E'-LUL	answering to part of our	*August* and *September*
7.	TIS'-RI		*September* and *October*
8.	MAR'-SCHE-VAN		*October* and *November*
9.	CHIS'-LEU		*November* and *December*
10.	THE'-BET		*December* and *January*
11.	SE'-BAT		*January* and *February*
12.	A'-DAR		*February* and *March*

The *civil* year began with *Tisri* or *September,* and ended with *Elul* or *August.* At first, the *Hebrews* measured their months according to the sun, and then each month consisted of *thirty* days;

days; but after their departure from *Ægypt,*
their months were *lunar,* the *firſt* month contained *thirty* days, the next *twenty-nine* days and
ſo on alternately: the new moon was always
the beginning of the month.   When it is ſaid
that the *Hebrew* months anſwer to ours, it is
to be underſtood with ſome latitude, for the
lunar months can never anſwer to *ſolar* months:
the vernal Equinox falls in the month of *March*
according to the *ſolar* year, but in the *lunar* year
the new moon will fall in the month of *March*
and the full moon in the month of *April*; ſo that
the *Hebrew* months will commonly partake of two
of our months.   The *Jews* in every three years
intercalated a *thirteenth* month to make the *ſolar*
and *lunar* year equal: this month they called
Veadar, or the ſecond *Adar.*   After the babyloniſh
captivity the *Hebrews* took the names of their
months from the *Chaldæans* and *Perſians,* among
whom they had lived: *four* of the original names
of their months are mentioned in Sacred Writ,
as *Abib, Niſan, Zif, Ethanim*; which *ſee.*

Z.

Z before A.

ZA-AN-A'-IM. A city of *Palestine*, in the tribe of *Naphtali*.

ZA'-AN-AN, [Σεννααρ, i. e. *a going forth.*] A name supposed to signify the city of *Jerusalem*.

ZA-AN-AN'-NIM, [Βεσενανιμ, i. e. *movings; one sleeping.*] A boundary of the tribe of *Naphtali*, in *Palestine*.

ZA'-A-VAN, [Ζωκαμ, i. e. *trembling.*] One of the posterity of the patriarch *Esau*.

ZAB'-AD, [Ζαβαδ, i. e. *dowry; endowed.*] A grandson of *Jarha*, who married *Sheshan*'s daughter—also the name of one of king *David*'s valiant men—also others of that name.

ZAB-AD-Æ'-ANS, [Ζαβαδαιοι.] *Arabians*, who dwelt to the *east* of the mountains of *Gilead*.

ZAB-AD-AI'-AS, [Ζαβαδαιας.] One who returned from the babylonish captivity.

ZAB'-BAI, [Ζαβη, i. e. *flowing.*] One who returned from the babylonish captivity.

ZAB'-BUD, [Ζαβυδ, i. e. *a dowry; endowed.*] One of the sons of *Bigvai*, who returned from the babylonish captivity.

ZAB-DE'-US, [Ζαβδαιος.] See SABDEUS.

ZAB'-DI, [Ζαβδι, i. e. *a dowry; endowed.*] One of the posterity of the patriarch *Benjamin*.

ZAB'-DI-EL, [Ζαβδιηλ, i. e. *the dowry of God; endowed of God.*] A king of *Arabia*, in *Asia*—also others.

ZAB-IN'-A, [Ζεβεννας.] See ZEBINA.

Y

ZAB'-

ZAB'-ŪD, [Zaßůð, i. e. *a dowry; endowed.*]   A fon of *Nathan* a principal officer of king *Solomon.*

ZAC'-CA-I, [Zακχαï. Zαxχός, i. e. *pure meat; juft; made juft.*]   One who returned from the babylonifh captivity.

ZAC'-CŪR, [Zακχȑg, i. e. *mindful; of the male kind.*]   A *Levite* who fealed the covenant with *Nehemiah* the governor—alfo the fon of *Mifhma.*

ZACH-A-RI'-AH, [Zαχαρίας, L. *Zachd'rias*, i. e. *mindful of the Lord; man of the Lord.*]   A king of *Ifrael* who reigned fix months and was murdered by *Shallum* who fucceeded him—alfo the *eleventh* of the twelve lefler prophets, after whom the canonical book *Zechariah* in the *Old Teftament* was named—alfo the father of *John* the *Baptift,* a prieft of the family of *Abiah*—alfo the fon of *Jehoiada* the high prieft; he was put to death by order of *Joafh,* A. M. 3164.

ZACH'-ĒR, [Zακχȑg, i. e. *the fame as Zaccur.*]   One of the pofterity of the patriarch *Benjamin.*

ZAC-CHE'-US, [Zακχαῖος, i. e. *pure meat; juft; made juft.*]   A farmer of the revenues in our *Saviour's* time, at whofe houfe our *Saviour* lodged.

ZA'-DŌK, [Σαδὼκ, i. e. *juftified; juft.*]   An high prieft of the *Jews,* in the reign of king *Saul;* the fon of *Ahitub,* of the race of *Eleazar* and pofterity of *Levi*—alfo others of that name.

ZA'-HAM, [Σαάμ, i. e. *detefting; unclean.*]   One of the fons of king *Rehoboam.*

ZA'-IR, [Σιάϱ, i. e. *little; a broken flail.*]   A city near to *Edom.*

ZAL'-APH, [Σελὲφ, i. e. *a fhadow; ringing; fhaking.*]   One whofe fon *Hanum* affifted in repairing the walls of *Jerufalem.*

ZAL'-MŌN, [Σαλμών, i. e. *darknefs; his image; the fhadow of a gift.*]   A mountain in the neighbourhood of *Shechem*—alfo the name of one of king *David's* worthies.

ZAL-MO'-NAH, [Σελμωνά, i. e. *a gift of the fhadow; our image*]   The *thirty-fifth* encampment of the *Ifraelites;* in the wildernefs.

ZAL-

ZAL-MUN'-NAH, [Σαλμανὰ. Σελμωνὰ, i. e. *a shadow or image of perturbation.*] The name of a king of the *Midianites.*

ZAM'-BIS, [Ζαμϐὶς.] One who returned from the babylonish captivity.

ZAM'-BRI, [Ζαμϐρὶ, i. e. *singing; a vine; a thinking.*] A son of *Salom,* mentioned in the *first* book of *Maccabees.*

ZAM'-ŌTH, [Ζαμώθ.] One who returned from the babylonish captivity.

ZAM-ZUM'-MIMS, [i. e. *thinking wickedness; wickedness of wicked men.*] A people of a giant race who dwelt to the *east* of the river *Jordan,* in the country afterwards possessed by the *Ammonites.*

ZAN-O'-AH, [Ζανώ. Ζανόε, i. e. *forgetfulness; casting form; that rest; that comfort.*] A city of *Palestine,* in the tribe of *Judah,* in the mountains—also one of the patriarch *Judah's* posterity.

ZAPH'-NATH-PA-A-NE'-AH, [i. e. *a man to whom secrets are revealed; a saviour of the world.*] The ægyptian name, given to the patriarch *Joseph* by *Pharaoh* king of *Ægypt.*

ZA'-PHON, [Σαφὰν, i. e. *the north east wind; hid; a beholder.*] A city which was one of the boundaries of the tribe of *Gad,* in *Palestine.*

ZA'-RA, [Ζαρὰ, i. e. *rising; clearness.*] One who is mentioned in St. *Matthew's* genealogical list.

ZA'-RA-CES, [Ζαρὰκης.] Brother to king *Joachim.*

ZA'-RAH, [Ζαρὲ, i. e. *rising; clearness.*] A city of *Palestine,* in the tribe of *Judah.*

ZA-RA-I'-AS, [Ζαραίας, i. e. *the Lord rising.*] An ancestor of *Esdras,* in the *Apocrypha.*

ZA'-RE-AH, [Σαρὰ, i. e. *leprosy; an hornet.*] A village of *Palestine,* in the tribe of *Judah.*

ZA'-RE-ATH-ITES. The inhabitants of *Zareah.*

ZAR'-ED, [Ζαρεδ, i. e. *a strange going down; power spread abroad.*] A valley in the wilderness, where the *Israelites* pitched their tents.

ZA-REPH'-ATH, [Σαρεπτὰ, i. e. *the perplexity of bread; the persuasion of perplexity.*] A city of *Phænicia,* on the *mediterranean* sea, between *Tyre* and *Sidon*, where the prophet *Elijah* dwelt in the poor widow's houfe during a famine; and where he wrought the miracles of the *oil* and *meal*, and raifing the widow's fon from death: it is called *Sarepta* in the *New Teftament*.

ZAR'-E-TAN, [i. e. *tribulation*; *perplexity*; *a binding*.]. A place near to the city *Adam*, not far from the river *Jordan*.

ZAR'-ETH SHA'-HAR, [Σεϱαδὰ, i. e. *of the mourning*; *bringing together*; *the form of blacknefs*.] A city of *Paleftine*, in the tribe of *Reuben*, to the *eaft* of the river *Jordan*, fituate in the mount of a rich valley.

ZAR'-HITES, [Ζαραῶι, i. e. *clear*.] The defcendants from two families, viz. one from *Zerah*, the fon of the patriarch *Simeon*; the other from *Zerah*, the fon of the patriarch *Judah*.

ZAR'-TAN-AH, [Σεσαθὰν. Σαϱθὰν, i. e. *the fame with Zaretan*.] A place of *Paleftine*, near to the city of *Jezreel*.

ZAR'-THAN, [Σαϱθὰν, i. e. *the fame with Zaretan*.] A place near to the river *Jordan*; perhaps *Zaretan*.

ZATH'-O-E, [Ζαθόη.] See ZATTHU.

ZATH-U'-I, [Ζατθύι.] See ZATTHU.

ZAT'-THU, [Ζατθύϊα, i. e. *an olive tree*.] One of the chiefs of the people who fealed the covenant with *Nehemiah* the governor.

ZAT'-TU, [Ζατθύὰ, i. e. *the fame meaning as Zatthu*.] Probably the fame man as *Zatthu*.

ZA'-VAN, [Ζηκάμ. Ζαὰν.] One of the pofterity of the patriarch *Efau*.

ZAZ'-A, [Ζαζὰ, i. e. *belonging to all*; *a wild beaft*; *fhining bright*; *going back*.] A fon of *Jonathan* the fon of *Jada*, of the pofterity of the patriarch *Judah*.

Z *before* E.

ZEB-AD-I'-AH, [Ζαβαδία, i. e. *the dowry of the Lord*.] One of the pofterity of the patriarch *Benjamin*—alfo one who reforted to king *David* at *Ziklag*.

ZEB'-

ZEB'-AH, [Ζεϐεὰ, i. e. *sacrifice*; *a beaſt killed in ſacri-*
fice for victory; *a beheading*; *a killing.*]   A prince
of *Midian*, ſlain by *Jonathan* the ſon of king *Saul.*

ZEB-A'-IM, ['Ασεϐωειμ.]   A place, mentioned *Ezra*
ii. 57.

ZEB'-ED-EE, [Ζεϐεδαίος, i. e. *a dowry*; *endowed.*]
The father of *James* and *John* the diſciples of
our *Saviour.*

ZEB-IN'-A, [Ζεϐεννὰς, i. e. *a flowing*; *flowing now*;
a ſelling or buying.]   One who returned from the
babyloniſh captivity.

ZEB-O'-IM, [Σεϐωΐν. Σεϐοείμ, i. e. *little does*; *goats*;
fair or chief; *willing.*]   One of the *four cities* of
Pentapolis which were deſtroyed by fire from
Heaven.

ZEB-U'-DAH, [Ζαϐϵδὰ, i. e. *endowed*; *an endowing.*]
The mother of *Jehoiakim* king of *Judah.*

ZEB'-UL, [Ζεϐἡλ, i. e. *a dwelling or dwelling place*;
abiding.]   An officer of *Jerubbaal* or *Gideon.*

ZEB-U'-LON-ITES, [Ζαϐηλωνῖτοι.] The deſcendants
from the patriarch *Zebulun.*

ZEB-U'-LUN, [Ζαϐυλών, L. *Zabu'-lon*, i. e. *the ſame
meaning as Zebul.*]   The *ſixth* ſon of the patriarch
Jacob, by *Leah.*

ZECH-A-RI'-AH, [Ζαχαρίας.] See ZACHARIAH.

ZE'-DAD, [Σηδαδα, i. e. *his ſide*; *his hunting*; *his traps.*]
A city of *Paleſtine*, one of its northern boundaries.

ZED-EK-I'-AH, [Σεδεκίας, i. e. *the juſtice of the Lord*;
the juſt of the Lord.]   The laſt king of *Judah* before the babyloniſh captivity, the ſon of king
Joſiah; he reigned about 590 years B. C.—alſo
two falſe prophets in the time of king *Abab*, and
of *Jeremiah.*

ZEEB, [Ζηϐ, i. e. *a wolf.*]   A princeſs of the *Midianites*, who was ſlain by the children of *Ephraim.*

ZEL'-AH, [Ζελαλόφ, i. e. *a rib*; *a ſide*; *an halting.*]
A city of *Paleſtine*, in the tribe of *Benjamin*, where
king *Saul* was buried.

ZEL'-EK, [Σελλήκ, i. e. *the ſhadow or the ringing of
one ſmiting.*]   An *Ammonite*, who was one of king
David's worthies.

Y 3   ZEL-

ZEL-OPH'-E-HAD, [Σαλφααδ, i. e. *the shadow of fear; the ringing of fear.* The son of *Hephar,* of the tribe of *Manasseh.*

ZE-LO'-TES, [Ζηλωτὴς, i. e. *jealous; full of zeal.*] SIMON (*not Peter*) One of the twelve apostles of our *Saviour;* called *Zelotes,* probably for his being a person of great zeal.

ZEL'-ZAH, [Σελσὰχ, i. e. *noon tide.*] A village on the border of the tribe of *Benjamin.*

ZEM-A-RA'-IM, [Σομώρων, i. e. *wool; pith of trees.*] A city of *Palestine,* in the tribe of *Benjamin,* near to *Bethel*—also a mountain in mount *Ephraim.*

ZEM'-AR-ITE, [Ζαμαραῖος.] The descendants from the patriarch *Canaan.*

ZEM-I'-RA, [Ζεμιρὰ, i. e. *a song; a vine; a palm; a thinking.*] One of the posterity of the patriarch *Benjamin.*

ZEN'-AN, [Σεννὰ, i. e. *coldness; a target; weapons.*] A city of *Palestine,* in the tribe of *Judah;* in the valley.

ZE'-NAS, [Ζηνας, i. e. *living.*] A *jewish* doctor of the law, and a disciple of St. *Paul.*

ZE-O'-RIM, [Σεωρὶμ, i. e. *gates; tempests.*] The name of a *jewish* priest. See SEORIM.

ZEPH-AN-I'-AH, [Σοφονίας. Σαφανία, i. e. *the hiding or secret of the Lord; the beholder of the Lord.*] A son of *Maaseiah;* the *second* priest or deputy of *Shemaiah* the high priest—also the *ninth* lesser prophet, the son of *Cushi,* of the tribe of *Simeon,* in the reign of king *Josiah;* after whom the canonical book *Zephaniah,* of the *Old Testament,* was named—also others of that name.

ZEPH'-ATH, [Σεφὲθ, i. e. *looking glasses; a covering; a looking for; an honey comb.*] A city of *Palestine,* called afterwards *Hormah,* in the tribe of *Simeon.*

ZEPH'-ATH-AH. A valley of *Palestine,* near *Mareshah.*

ZE'-PHI or ZE'-PHO, [Σωφὰρ, i. e. *the north east wind; hid; a beholder.*] The son of *Eliphaz* and grandson of *Esau* the patriarch.

ZEPH'-

ZEPH'-ŌN, [Σαφὼν, i. e. *the same meaning as Zepho.*] One of the posterity of the patriarch *Gad.*

ZEPH-ŌN'-ITES. The descendants from *Zephon.*

ZER, [i. e. *perplexity; a bond; a bringing together of strength; a rock.*] A city of *Palestine,* in the tribe of *Naphtali.*

ZE'-RAH, [Ζαρὰ, i. e. *rising; clearness.*] A king of *Æthiopia,* who was defeated by *Asa* king of *Judah* —also a son of the patriarch *Simeon,* and another of the patriarch *Judah*—also a son of *Reuel.*

ZE-RA-HI'-AH or ZE-RA-I'-A, [Ζαραΐα, i. e. *the Lord rising; the clearness of the Lord.*] The son of *Uzzi* of the posterity of *Levi.*

ZE'-RAU, [Ζαρά.] The father of *Achan.*

ZER'-ED. [Ζαρέτ, i. e. *the same meaning as Zared.*] A brook in the land of *Moab.*

ZER'-E-DA, [Ζαριδὰ, i. e. *perplexity.*] A city of *Palestine,* in the tribe of *Ephraim,* the native place of *Jeroboam* the son of *Nebat.*

ZER-E'-DA-THAH, [Ζαριδαθὰ, i. e. *perplexity.*] A city of *Palestine,* in the tribe of *Ephraim;* called also *Zathan.*

ZER'-ER-ATH, [Ταγαραγαθὰ, i. e. *perplexity.*] A Country of *Canaan.*

ZE'-RESH, [Ζωσάρα, i. e. *scattering heritage.*] The wife of *Haman* the prime minister of king *Ahasuerus.*

ZE-R'ETH, [Σερέθ, i. e. *tribulation; a bond; a bringing together of strength; a rock.*] One of the posterity of the patriarch *Judah.*

ZE'-RI, [Σερὶ, i. e. *a bond; a bringing together; resin; a rock; strong.*] A singer at the temple of *Jerusalem,* the son of *Jeduthun.*

ZER'-ŌR, [Σερώρ, i. e. *a bond; abiding; a little stone.*] Grandfather to *Kish,* king *Saul's* father.

ZER-U'-AH, [Ζαρυὰ, i. e. *full of leprosy; an hornet.*] The mother of *Jeroboam* the son of *Nebat.*

ZER-UB'-BA-BEL, [Ζοροβάβελ, i. e. *banished; a stranger to confusion or to Babel.*] The son of *Judah,* of the race of king *David*—also others.

ZER-U-I'-AH or ZER-VI'-AH, [Σαρϰίας, i. e. *pcrplexity*; *tribulation of the Lord*; *a bringing together.*] The fifter of king *David*, and mother of *Joab*, *Abifhai*, and *Afahel*.

ZE'-THAM, [Ζηθὰν, i. e. *their olive*; *a place where olive trees grow.*] One who was over the treafures of the temple.

ZE'-THAN, [Ζαιθὰν. Ζηθὰν, i. e. *the fame as Zetham.*] A great warrior, defcended from the patriarch *Benjamin*.

ZE'-THAR, [Ζηθὰρ, i. e. *fearching out diligently*; *the olive tree of beholding*; *the turtle bird.*] A chamberlain to king *Ahafuerus*.

<h3 style="text-align:center">Z before I.</h3>

ZI'-A, [Ζιά. Ζυὲ, i. e. *fweat or fwelling.*] One of the pofterity of the patriarch *Gad*.

ZI'-BA, [Σιβà, i. e. *an army*; *ftrength*; *a fhip coming.*] A fervant of king *Saul*, who betrayed *Mephibofheth* the fon of *Jonathan*, and got half of his eftate from him.

ZIB'-E-ŌN. See ZIBION.

ZIB'-I-A, [Σεβιà, i. e. *a little doe or goat*; *chief*; *the Lord ftanding*; *willing.*] One of the pofterity of the patriarch *Benjamin*.

ZIB'-I-AH, [Σαβιà, i. e. *the fame with Zibia.*] The mother of king *Joafh*.

ZIB'-I-ŌN, [Ζεβεγὼν, i. e. *iniquity ftanding*; *dipped*; *dipping in.*] An *Hivite*, the grandfather in law of *Efau* the patriarch — alfo a fon of *Seir* the *Horite* — alfo a wife of *Efau*.

ZICH'-RI, [Ζεχρεί, i. e. *a remembering*; *mankind.*] Several of the pofterity of *Benjamin* of that name; alfo one of *Levi*.

ZID'-DIM, ['Αοσνδεὶμ, i. e. *huntings*; *treafons*; *deftructions.*] A city of *Palefline*, in the tribe of *Naphtali*.

ZID-KI'-JAH, [Σεδεκίας, i. e. *the juftice of the Lord*; *the juft of the Lord.*] One who fealed the covenant with *Nehemiah* the governor.

ZI'-DŌN

ZI'-DON or SI'-DON, [Σιδῶν, i. e. *a hunter; hunting; the ship of judgment.*] The *eldest* son of the patriarch *Canaan.* See SIDON.

ZI-DON'-I-ANS, [Σιδωνιοι.] The people of *Zidon* or *Sidon.*

ZIF, [i. e. *splendor; beauty; comeliness.*] The *Jews* second month of the *sacred* year, which was its name when they left *Ægypt*; but it was afterwards changed to *Jiar,* answering to part of our *April* and part of *May.*

ZI'-HA, [Σιαά, i. e. *brightness; whiteness; drought.*] One whose sons were of the order of *Nethinims.*

ZIK'-LAG, [Σικελὰγ, i. e. *the pouring out of water of a measure; making narrow a measure.*] A city of *Palestine,* in the tribe of *Simeon.*

ZIL'-LAH, [Σελλά, i. e. *a shadow; a roasting; a roaring; talk.*] One of the wives of *Lamech* the patriarch.

ZIL'-PAH, [Ζελφὰ, i. e. *a distilling from the head or mouth; contempt of the mouth.*] *Maid* to *Leah* the wife of *Jacob,* by whom he had the patriarchs *Gad* and *Asher.*

ZIL'-THAI, [Σαλαθὶ, i. e. *my shadow; my ringing; my talk.*] One of the posterity of the patriarch *Benjamin.*

ZIM'-MAH, [Σεμμά, i. e. *thought; wickedness; dishonesty.*] One of the posterity of the patriarch *Levi.*

ZIM'-RAM or ZIM'-RAN, [Ζομβρᾶν, i. e. *a song; singing; a vine; thinking.*] The son of the patriarch *Abraham* by *Keturah.*

ZIM'-RI, [Ζαμβρὶ, i. e. *the same as Zimran.*] A prince of the tribe of the patriarch *Simeon*; whom *Phineas* stabbed in his lewd embraces with *Cozbi* a *Midianitish* woman — also a general of the cavalry of *Elah* king of *Israel*—also the father of *Moza.*

ZIN, [Σὶν, i. e. *weapons; target; coldness.*] Another name for *Kadesh,* in the wilderness, towards the *Red Sea.*

ZI'-NA,

ZI'-NA, [Ζιξὰ, i. e. *all manner of ways; a wild beaſt; a ſhining bright; going back.*] Tne ſon of *Shimei,* a deſcendant from *Levi.*

ZI'-ŌN or SI'-ŌN, [Σιών, i. e. *an heap; a tomb; looking glaſſes; drought.*] A mountain of *Jeruſalem,* on which the temple built by king *Solomon* and the city of *David* ſtood.

ZI'-ŌR, [Σιὼρ, i. e. *little; the ſhip of one watching.*] A city of *Paleſtine,* in the tribe of *Judah,* in the mountains.

ZIPH, [Ζιφ, i. e. *that mouth; that cheek; falſe; falſhood.*] A city of *Paleſtine,* in the tribe of *Judah* in the mountains—alſo a wilderneſs in the tribe of *Judah*—alſo ſeveral men of that name.

ZIPH'-AH, [Ζεφα; i. e. *the ſame with Ziph.*] One of the poſterity of *Caleb,* of the tribe of *Judah.*

ZIPH'-I-ŌN, [Σαφὼν.] See ZEPHON.

ZIPH'-ITES, [Ζιφαῖοι.] The inhabitants of *Ziph,* and deſcendants from *Ziph.*

ZIPH'-RŌN, [Ζεφρωνὰ, i. e. *the falſhood of a ſong; rejoicing.*] A city bounding the land of *Canaan* on the north.

ZIP'-PŌR, [Σεφὼρ, i. e. *a bird; a ſparrow; a crown; a deſart; a kid; early.*] The father of *Balak* king of *Moab.*

ZIP-PO'-RAH, [Σεπφώρα, i. e. *a mourning; beauty; a trumpet.*] The daughter of *Jethro,* the wife of *Moſes,* and mother of *Eliezar* and *Gerſhom.*

ZITH'-RI, [Σεγρεί, i. e. *my ſecret; my refuge; hid; tumbling wide.*] One who deſcended from the patriarch *Levi.*

ZIZ, [Ασσεῖς, i. e. *a flower; a young ſpring; a buſh of hair curled; fight; a wing.*] A mountain or cliff mentioned in the ſecond book of *Chronicles.*

ZI'-ZA or ZI'-ZAH or ZI'-NA, [Ζιζὰ, i. e. *all manner of ways; a wild beaſt; ſhining bright; a going back.*] A prince of the tribe of *Simeon.*

Z *before* O.

ZO'-AN, [i. e. *moving*; *moved*.] The capital of lower *Ægypt* in the time of *Moses*; afterwards *Tanis*.

ZO'-AR, [Σηΐῶρ. Σαάρ, i. e. *little.*] One of the *five* cities of *Pentapolis*, to which *Lot* was to flee for refuge; the other four, viz. *Sodom, Gomorrah, Admah,* and *Zeboim,* were deſtroyed by lightning.

ZO'-BA or ZO'-BAH, [Σωβᾶ, i. e. *an army; warring; a commandment in that; a ſwelling.*] A city of *Syria,* in *Aſia.*

ZO-BE'-BAH, [Ζωβηβά, i. e. *an army; warfare in that; ſwelling in that.*] One of the poſterity of the patriarch *Judah.*

ZO'HAR, [Σαάρ, i. e. *white; bright.*] The father of *Ephron,* who ſold to the patriarch *Abraham* the burying ground for his wife *Sarah*—alſo a ſon of the patriarch *Simeon.*

ZO'-HEL-ETH, [Σωελέθ, i. e. *creeping much; drawing.*] The name of a *ſtone,* juſt under the walls of *Jeruſalem,* near to the fountain *Rogel.*

ZO'-HETH, [Ζωχάθ, i. e. *a ſeparation; amazing; that broken aſunder; that going down.*] One of the poſterity of the patriarch *Judah.*

ZO'-PHAH or ZO'-PHAI, [Σηφί, i. e. *a viol; binding a commandment; a beholder; an honey comb.*] Two of that name, one a deſcendant from *Levi,* and the other from *Aſher.*

ZO'-PHAR, [Σωφὰρ, i. e. *the morning time; a crown; a ſparrow; a kid.*] One of *Job's* friends, who is called a *Naamathite,* and ſuppoſed to be from ſome part of *Arabia.*

ZO'-PHIM, [Σωφίμ, i. e. *a field where men may ſee far off.*] A plain near mount *Piſgah,* called *the field* of *Zophim;* probably *Ramathaim Zophim.*

ZOR'-AH, [Σαρὰθ. Σαραὰ, i. e. *leproſy; an hornet.*] A town of *Paleſtine,* in the tribe of *Dan.*

ZOR'-ATH-ITES, [Σαραθοί.] The inhabitants of
  Zorah.
ZOR'-E-AH, [Σαραὰ.] A city of *Palestine*, in the
  tribe of *Judah*, in the valley.
ZOR'-ITES, [Σαραοί.] The people of *Zorah*.
ZOR-OB'-A-BEL, [Ζοροϐάϐελ, i. e. *the same with
  Zerubbabel*.] One mentioned by St. *Luke* in his
  genealogical list.

Z before U.

ZU'-AR, [Σωγάρ, i. e. *little*; *the commandment of the
  city*.] One who was of the tribe of *Issachar*.
ZUPH, [Σὺφ, i. e. *a watch*; *covering*; *an honey comb*;
  swimming; *looking for*.] An ancestor of *Elkanah*
  the father of *Samuel*—also a place called *the land
  of Zuph*.
ZUR, [Σὺρ, i. e. *a rock*; *strong*; *plan*; *form*; *binding*.]
  A part of *Midian*—also a king of *Midian*.
ZU'-RI-EL, [Συριὴλ, i. e. *the rock of God*; *the strength*;
  the forming or binding of God.] The name of one
  of the *Levites*.
ZU-RI-SHAD'-DAI, [Συρισαδαί, i. e. *the rock,
  strength, fashion of the Almighty*; *splendor*; *beauty*;
  revolters.] The father of *Shelumiel*, chief of the
  tribe of *Simeon* at the departure of the *Hebrews*
  from *Ægypt*.
ZU'-ZIMS, [i. e. *posts*; *lintels over a door*; *shining*;
  departing; *money*; *strong*.] *Giants* who dwelt beyond the river *Jordan*, and who were conquered
  by *Chederlaomer* and his allies.

A Table

A Table of the Jewish Coins, with the value of each in English Money.

				£.	S.	D.
Gerah				0	0	$1\frac{59}{160}$
10	Bekah			0	1	$1\frac{11}{16}$
20	2	Shekel		0	2	$3\frac{3}{8}$
1000	100	50	Maneh or Mina hebraica	5	14	$0\frac{2}{4}$
60,000	6000	3000	60	Talent	342	3	9

	£.	S.	D.
Solidus Aureus or Sextula worth	0	12	$0\frac{1}{2}$
Siclus Aureus worth	1	16	6
A Talent of Gold worth	5475	0	0

A Table of the Jewish Measures of Capacity for things *liquid*.

						Gal.	pts.	sol. in.	decs.
Caph.							$\frac{5}{8}$	0	177
$1\frac{1}{3}$	Log						$\frac{5}{6}$	0	211
$5\frac{1}{3}$	4	Cab					$3\frac{1}{3}$	0	844
16	12	3	Hin			1	2	2	533
32	24	6	2	Seah		2	4	5	67
96	72	18	6	3	Bath Epha	7	4	15	2
960	720	180	60	30	10	Coron or Chomer } 75	5	7	625

A Table of the Jewish Measures of Capacity for things *dry*.

							Pecks	G.	pints	—	sol. in.	dec.
Gachal							0	0	$1\frac{7}{120}$	— 0		31
20	Cab						0	0	$2\frac{5}{6}$	— 0		73
36	$1\frac{4}{5}$	Gomer					0	0	$5\frac{1}{16}$	— 1		211
120	6	$3\frac{5}{3}$	Seah				1	0	1	— 4		036
366	18	10	3	Epha			3	0	3	— 12		107
1800	90	50	15	5	Letech		16	0	0	— 26		500
3600	180	100	30	10	2	Chomer or Coron	32	0	1	— 18		969

(Column headings: Eng. corn mea. sol. in. dec. — Pecks G. pints.)

Scripture Measures of Length, reduced to English Measure.

							English feet	in.	dec.
Digit							0	0	912
4	Palm						0	3	648
12	3	Span					0	10	944
24	6	2	Cubit				1	9	888
96	24	8	4	Fathom			7	3	552
144	36	12	6	$1\frac{1}{2}$	Ezekiel's reed		10	11	328
192	48	16	8	2	$1\frac{1}{3}$	Arabian pole	14	7	104
1920	480	160	80	20	$13\frac{1}{3}$	10	Scheenus mea- sured line	145	11	4

The

The longer Scripture Measures.

N. B. The east used another Span equal to $\frac{1}{3}$ of a cubit.

						Eng. miles	paces	feet	decs.
Cubit						0	0	1	824
400	Stadium					0	145	4	.6
2000	5	Sabbath day's journey				0	729	3	
4000	10	2	Eastern mile			1	403	1	
12000	30	6	3	Parasang		4	153	3	
96000	240	48	24	8	a day's journey	33	172	4	

Jewish Weights reduced to English Troy Weight.

		Pounds	oz.	dwts.	grains
Shekel		0	0	9	$2\frac{4}{7}$
60	Maneh	2	3	6	$10\frac{2}{7}$
3000	50	Talent	113	10	1	$10\frac{2}{7}$

N. B. In reckoning Money, 50 Shekels made a Maneh; but, in Weight, 60 Shekels.

In the Tables of Money, Silver is reckoned at five Shillings the ounce, and Gold at four Pounds the ounce.

The

The names and order of the Books in the BIBLE,
with the number of *Chapters* in each Book.

In the OLD TESTAMENT.

Chapters.		Chapters.		Chapters.	
Genesis	50	2d Chronicles	36	Daniel	12
Exodus	40	Ezra	10	Hosea	14
Leviticus	27	Nehemiah	13	Joel	3
Numbers	36	Esther	10	Amos	9
Deuteronomy	34	Job	42	Obadiah	1
Joshua	24	Psalms	150	Jonah	4
Judges	21	Proverbs	31	Micah	7
Ruth	4	Ecclesiastes	12	Nahum	3
1st Samuel	31	Solomon's Song	8	Habakkuk	3
2d Samuel	24	Isaiah	65	Zephaniah	3
1st Kings	22	Jeremiah	52	Haggai	2
2d Kings	25	Lamentations	5	Zechariah	14
1st Chronicles	29	Ezekiel	48	Malachi	4

The APOCRYPHA.

1st Esdras	9	Book of Wisd.	19	Hist. Susannah	1
2d Esdras	16	Ecclesiasticus	51	Hist. Bel & Dragon	1
Tobit	14	Baruch with Jeremiah	6	Prayer of Manass.	
Judith	16			1st Book Mac.	16
The rest of Esther	6	Song of 3 Children	1	2d Book Mac.	15

The NEW TESTAMENT.

Matthew	28	Philippians	4	James	5
Mark	16	Colossians	4	1st Peter	5
Luke	24	1st Thessalons.	5	2d Peter	3
John	21	2d Thessalons.	3	1st John	5
The Acts	28	1st Timothy	6	2d John	1
Romans	16	2d Timothy	4	3d John	1
1st Corinthians	16	Titus	3	Jude	1
2d Corinthians	13	Philemon	1	Revelation	22
Galatians	6	Epistle to the Hebrews	13		
Ephesians	6				

FINIS.